TO CARL,

Thank you for helping
preserve Hurley's History.
Thank you twice for being
a part of that history.

Gardiner J. deMarche

MORE THAN A GAME

Gardner LaMarche

Published by Gardner LaMarche

228 Robin Hood Lane • Circle Pines, MN 55014

gardielamarche@gmail.com

Designed by JS Print Group, Inc.

Printed by JS Print Group, Inc.

10 9 8 7 6 5 4 3 2 1 0 First Edition

ISBN-13: 978-0-578-54205-8

ACKNOWLEDGEMENTS

———————

This book was started in 1997, although I did not know it at the time. It was just a local area history paper prepared for a history class called "The Craft of Historical Writing," taught by Dr. Ronald Mershart on the campus of UW – Superior. The title I gave it was "United They Stand" and it was about the Hurley High School class of 1949. It totaled about forty pages. My wife Terri told me then that I should write a book about that era in Hurley. I didn't take her advice then. I'm a little slow on the uptake at times.

In 2014, there was some excitement in Hurley about the possibility that Hurley's 1949 state basketball championship would be featured in a documentary. The producer of that documentary was a man named Carter Kuehn. I dug out the only copy of "United They Stand" and the cassette tapes of the interviews conducted in 1997 and made copies for Carter. The funding for the documentary fell through. The project was shelved. Let me be clear that Carter did all he could humanly do to convince the decision makers that the project was worthy. He was deeply hurt by the decision because he like so many others found the people of Hurley and the area to be so genuine and the story compelling.

When I contacted Carter in March of 2018 he willingly gave me all the research he had on hand. While most of it was in the form of pictures (he was doing a documentary, not a book) he had uncovered some nuggets that helped shape the direction this book would take. I soon discovered that a story of the 1949 championship would be incomplete without the readers knowing the rest of the story. The book grew in size and scope. The story of the championship in 1949 is the culmination of 26 years of not just Hurley history, but of the Gogebic Range and Ashland as well.

In October of 1997 I interviewed the following people in Hurley; Ted Erspamer, Pete "Pupsy" Savant, Anna Kangas Gertz, Ellen Kivi Skoveria, Doris Valle Soine, George Romanowski, Joanne Kopacz Sullivan, Doris Morello Thompson, and Helen Misuraco Kasper. Ted, Pupsy, Doris Morello Thompson, and Helen are still with us as of this writing. Ted, Ellen, George, Helen, and both Doris' were parents of some of my friends and classmates. Those interviews are still on tape and have also been digitized. They are very funny, touching, and sometimes very emotional. I found out that Carl Vergamini lived about four blocks from me in Superior at that time. He invited me to his house and there I was given an interview by the coach himself. By the time it was done, there was no doubt in my mind that he was a leader. It was also very clear that he understood what makes a young athlete tick. Every time I listened to the interviews when putting together this story, I was transported back to the kitchen tables and living rooms of these wonderful people. I still get goose bumps from some of those recordings.

Beginning in April of 2018 and through June of 2019 more interviews were conducted with people who were students in the 1940's. Eino Martino, Carl Kaffine, Tony Brunello, Bill Cattoi, Len Bartolutti, Wayland Baron, Clayton Corrigan, Gloria Stremski Fillion, and Ted Erspamer again were all more than generous with their time.

All the interviews help give the story its humanity. It would have been easy to just report the news as it happened and leave it at that, but the news is just news. History is about human beings.

Meeting with Sy Castagna, retired Hurley teacher and Saxon High School basketball coach in 1949 was a double blessing. At 97 years old his memory was vivid and his sense of humor as keen as ever. Sy passed away this past winter. He taught in five decades. His students have many a happy memory of Sy working his magic tricks before starting class.

I am grateful to the sons of Carl Vergamini for their time and their recollections of their dad. Jerry, Phil, and Greg consider themselves fortunate to have been raised by Carl and Ruth Vergamini. I hope they know that there is a generation of Hurley athletes who trusted, respected and loved their father too. Leaving Hurley was difficult for the Vergamini family. They became part of the fabric of the town. Ruth was especially connected. Only Ruth loved Hurley more than Carl and that is saying a lot.

Roy Wolff is a man who loves basketball above all other sports, and it's not even close. Roy comes from Wauwatosa, Wisconsin where he was a proud Red Raider. He is a high school basketball expert who can tell you about the basketball fever that gripped the Midwest in the 1940's onward. Having a cup of coffee with Roy is a treat to be savored. His love for the game inspired me to get back to work. How much does Roy love basketball? He is writing a series of letters to his grandchildren about life and basketball. They will be treasured by them.

Bud Grant, NFL Hall of Fame coach and Superior native gave great insights to me on high school sports during his 1942 – 1945 high school career, which brought him and his Superior Central teams into three basketball games and one football game versus Hurley. As an added bonus he shed a great deal of light on town baseball as it was in those days. Coach Grant's dad was from Odanah and actually played for a time in Hurley for the town team. He later became the Fire Chief in Superior.

Thank you to all who have supported me in this endeavor. My big sisters Mary Jo and Christy gave me encouragement and believed that their snot nosed little brother could get this thing done. Many friends also encouraged me along the way. Pete Lewinski, now the head basketball coach of the Ironwood Red Devils encouraged me to write this for years. My daughter April and her husband Colin stood behind me when I was just talking about it. April simply said, "Why don't you just do it?" There was no good answer to that question so I got started.

Finally, after fifteen months of research and writing, I thank my wife Terri and son Chris who has been so supportive and so patient with me. "Are you done yet?" was Chris's question nearly every day. Now I can say, "YES!"

All pictures are from the Hurley High School Yearbooks.

TABLE OF CONTENTS

_____

TABLE OF CONTENTS

———————

March 1946

Phil studied the branches of the trees across the street. Winter was letting go earlier than usual in Northern Wisconsin. The sky was displaying a smattering of puffy white clouds against a Columbia Blue backdrop. In the northern sky the depth of that blue seemed to reach into the heart of the universe. From his seat on the stump he witnessed a red squirrel chattering its displeasure at the sparrows who invaded its privacy 20 feet above the ground. Amused, the boy broke into a broad smile as he watched the sparrows fly off in search of peace and quiet. The squirrel returned to its search for nesting materials. Phil's mind returned to the task at hand. He was waiting.

The lad rose from the stump and slowly walked around it, studying it as if it held a great secret. Exasperated by his endless waiting, he kicked at the stump. Growing bored and ever more impatient, he kicked the stump again, this time sending a chip of bark across the front lawn. The game was on! Phil kicked again and again. The bark held tight to the stump, but the boy was persistent. Soon he had cleared a small swath of bark exposing the wood it once protected. Pleased with his handiwork, Phil sat back down with a deep sigh and stared at his now scuffed Buster Brown shoes.

To Phil time had stood still that sunny spring morning. At three years old, no one would blame him for being impatient, and today, this precocious boy was even more impatient than ever. He had been waiting for this day to arrive for nearly his entire lifetime. His hopes that it would be the best day in history were fueled by his brother

Jerry, who repeatedly told him how great it would be. Jerry was a "big kid," who at age seven knew what he was talking about. Jerry told him how things used to be, before the war. His mother, Ruth, kept Jerry's memories alive for the past two and a half years. Phil was too young to share those memories, but he was a believer.

Phil's mind began to wander as the vigil continued. He was distracted by a passing car, a 1936 Studebaker in pristine condition. The driver, Sam, waved. Phil waved back half-heartedly. He was at the end of his rope. He sat back down on the stump with an abruptness that would send shockwaves through the spine of an adult. He stared down; his head resting in his hands, his elbows on his knees. Suddenly, he felt a presence and looked up. A big bear of a man in uniform was rapidly walking toward him. Phil just knew. He shot to his feet and ran right at the big man who was now down on one knee. With a shout of "Daaaaaddyyy!" and a leap that would do an Olympic long jumper proud, he flew into the arms of his father. Carl Vergamini's strong arms engulfed little Phil as the big man sighed with contentment. Rising to his feet while cradling Phil in his arms, Carl walked through the front door of the family's apartment on Cooper Street and into the arms of Jerry and Ruth. Phil and Jerry Vergamini would never forget that day and that embrace. After two and a half years of waiting, it really was the best day ever.

Seven months after World War II ended, their life could return to normal. Lieutenant (Junior Grade) Carl Vergamini, United States Navy Reserve, was home and once again he became just Dad. The Vergamini family was reunited and the town of Hurley, Wisconsin reclaimed its high school coach and Physical Education teacher. For the Hurley area and its populace, things were about to get very exciting. The Vergamini boys' "best day ever" would usher in the little mining town's halcyon days.

CHAPTER ONE

Genesis

Hurley, Wisconsin exists because it sits on top of huge deposits of iron ore. Prior to the discovery of iron ore in 1879, few people had ever set foot in those Northeastern Wisconsin hills just south of Lake Superior. Subtract the ore deposits and there would be no town. It was not a place that welcomed human existence. Winters near the shores of the Big Lake are long, cold, snowy, and very unforgiving. The rocky ground and short summers were not conducive to farming. Still the speculators, bankers, investors, adventurers, and finally, families would fuel the birth of settlements on both sides of the East Branch of the Montreal River, the Michigan-Wisconsin border.

Besides iron ore the area was rich with virgin white pine forests. Beginning in the 1870's, just ahead of the iron ore boom, those majestic trees, reaching an average height of about 80 feet, with some reaching skyward 150 feet or more were logged until depleted around 1900. Logging continued as the lumber barons harvested the hardwoods left in the area. By 1930 they too were gone. Logging thereafter would be a relatively small enterprise.

The logging industry did bring some settlers to the area, but the loggers were mostly single men or men who left their families behind in more civil surroundings. Loggers tended to be men who were looking for work, more so than the opportunity to settle down. The industry was highly transient, and they moved from one logging camp to another, leaving hundreds of square miles of stumps in their wake.

Hurley was established in 1884, named for Michael Angelo "Glen" Hurley, a prominent Wausau attorney who was a partner in the Northern Chief Mining Company. The first mining machinery arrived at the Germania Mine that same year. The "Iron Ore Boom" started with barely a whimper. In 1885 a Mr. Swanson described Hurley as "a snake trail boasting only four buildings along its entire length." It would not remain a snake trail for long. The mining boom brought so many speculators to Hurley that "the solitary wilderness was turned into a beehive of activity."

Towns and hamlets grew up around Hurley, wherever there were mines, lumber, or an opportunity to farm. Carey, Oma, Upson, Saxon, Iron Belt, Pence, Gile, Montreal, and Kimball all supported their townspeople with grocery stores, train depots, saloons, and community centers. Mines with such names as Germania, Little Colby, Minnewawa, Nimikon, Bessemer, Montreal, Moore, Pence, Old Nakomis, Vaughn and Daisy were among the forty-two that existed in the county in 1887.

From its humble beginnings, Hurley grew into the hub of all the mining and logging activity on the Wisconsin side of the East Branch of the Montreal River. Soon trains, hundreds of cars long would pass through town carrying loads of iron ore westward to the docks of Ashland, Wisconsin and points south. Passenger trains linked the area with the rest of the country and the world. The town grew with the mining industry and soon Silver Street became home to general stores, boarding houses, barber and butcher shops. Tailors, shoe makers, lawyers, bankers and those in other services found a place to set up shop as well.

The logging industry with its labor intensive jobs required thousands of workers to harvest the trees in the majestic forests of Northern Wisconsin and the Upper Peninsula of Michigan. The forests for hundreds of miles in any direction of Hurley were alive with these lumberjacks. They worked long days, lived in logging camps under Spartan conditions, and were generally a tough breed of men. Most were young and single. Unlike most miners, they were not looking to put down "roots", but looking to make some money and move on. The two things they wanted most when given time off were booze and the company of women. Saloons and taverns sprung up along Silver Street and other locations in town. This did much to satisfy the desire for booze for both logger and miner. The desire for women gave birth to Hurley's notorious "Lower Block" stretching from the Montreal River west to 1st Avenue and on the south side of the street to 2nd Avenue. Entrepreneurs with far less scruples than the mainstream merchants and bar keepers built their saloons along that stretch. Most were, in fact, brothels doubling as saloons. They were designed to entertain lonely loggers and miners and of course, separate them from their hard earned wages.

And so the two faces of Hurley developed along with the two largest enterprises in the area. On the one hand, thousands of loggers and many a single miner poured into town on weekends to spend their money. Hotels, cafés, bars, and brothels were filled. On the other hand, married miners and some of the loggers who stayed on found a home for their families. As the logging industry died and the lumberjacks moved on, Hurley's "lower block" became a destination for people from all walks of life looking for the type of entertainment they could not find in their own communities.

Hurley's reputation as a Wild West frontier town was well earned. To this day, the town's image to the rest of the world is a snapshot of what became this neon lighted block, a place people flocked to let their hair down. Hurley's Silver Street became famous for reasons that would make most parents in any community cringe and worry.

CHAPTER TWO

For Posterity

As mining operations grew and more and more people arrived, Hurley kept pace. Houses were built one after another. Families made them into homes. In May of 1886 Hurley's first school was established by Professor C.H. Carna. With two teachers and 100 students of all ages, Hurley began its rich tradition of providing its children with a quality education. The earliest settlers in town wasted no time in making their priorities crystal clear. Their children would have an education and a better life then they had. By 1893 the first graduates of the Hurley Free High School, six girls, received their diplomas. The class motto, "Perseverance Wins Success," let their parents know they received that message, loud and clear.

It should come as no surprise that the girls would choose such a motto. Perseverance was a visible character trait of Hurley's citizenry throughout their childhood. Following the establishment of the town and the outlying areas, fires became public enemy number one. Most buildings were wooden structures, heated by stoves burning wood or coal. Commercial buildings and family homes required a great deal of fuel to stave off the winter cold. The Montreal River Miner, the area's first newspaper, spent much time, ink, and space reporting these disasters. Many fires destroyed multiple buildings, and some businesses were consumed multiple times. Each time, the people rebuilt their homes and businesses.

Hurley, like most towns of the day, had many hazards. Safety standards were virtually non-existent in mining, railroading, and construction. Many workers perished in mining accidents ranging from fires, cave-ins, falling rocks, heavy equipment accidents, and the like. Railroad workers were killed or maimed as were many folks caught unaware while crossing tracks. Workers without safety harnesses fell from roofs, scaffolding, and ladders. Lumberjacks, sawmill workers, and farm workers were not exempt. Danger was a workman's constant companion.

Mothers and fathers knew the dangers, but also saw the opportunity for a better future, not only for themselves, but especially for their children. They correctly saw education as not just important, but essential for the success of their kids.

In addition to Hurley, every hamlet sprouted a school. Attendance eventually became compulsory until age 14. Only a few went on to attend high school as most boys and many girls went to work on farms, in the mines, sawmills, and shops. Hurley was very much a frontier town with an insatiable appetite for manual laborers. It would take changes to child labor laws, a continuing influx of immigrant workers who valued education, and the arrival of one educator who would win the trust and respect of the entire community to make a high school education not just a dream, but a reality for Hurley's youth.

In 1904 J.E. Murphy arrived in Hurley as the newly hired principal of the Hurley High School. In the previous two decades, the town had become a bustling center for mining and industry on the Wisconsin side. By 1907 J.E. Murphy became the Superintendent of the Hurley school district. Mr. Murphy became an institution in Hurley, serving until 1955. Under his leadership, and fueled by his vision of what constituted a complete high school education, Hurley quickly gained a reputation as one of the state's finest school districts. His belief that the children of Hurley would find success was founded in his observations of Hurley's hard working citizens. He said:

> What constitutes a town? Its industries? To some extent yes. Its business? Again to some extent, yes. Its wealth and resources? To some extent, yes. But far more important than all of these, the very raw material from which all industries, business, wealth, and resources spring, the real wealth, the real resources of a city lie in the character and equality of its people. In this most priceless of all resources, Hurley has been and will always be rich.

By 1916, there was a clear need for Hurley to build a high school. The site selected was between 3rd and 4th Avenues on Poplar Street. Building began in 1917. Although the building was not in the exact geographic center of town, it quickly became the heart of most activities for Hurley's youth and their watchful parents. With new facilities and superb teachers, enrollment continued to grow as more and more parents insisted that their children complete all twelve years of the available public education. Hurley began to retain most of them in school until graduation. Graduates went on to work on the Gogebic Range and beyond. Hurley graduates became more sought after by employers and colleges with each passing year.

With the new high school now built, keeping these students engaged in healthy activities during and after school hours started to become a priority. J.E. Murphy and his high school principal, Harold Connors, saw the need to have a full time, dedicated physical education teacher and coach for its fledgling athletic teams. In the summer of 1923 they found the person they wanted to guide the program.

CHAPTER THREE

Roy Melvin Comes To Hurley

The first two decades of the Twentieth Century saw an exponential growth in the popularity of spectator sports. Baseball became the national pastime and football became the primary collegiate sport. Baseball had been played professionally since the 1860's and was the sport of choice for participants and spectators alike. The first college football game was played in 1869 between Rutgers and New Jersey (now Princeton). Professional football began in 1892 and teams sprouted in towns and cities across the nation. The game evolved and by 1920, the National Football League was formed. It would be decades before the NFL would become as widely watched as the college game.

Baseball, boxing, and football, in that order, became the focal point of the participants and fans. By the early 1920's people attended professional and college games in increasingly larger numbers. Baseball had its mega star in Babe Ruth, who hit the ball further than any ball player ever had before. It was not just the incredible distance he hit his home runs, but also the frequency in which they were hit. In short order, "The Babe" rewrote the record books. He did not just break records, he absolutely shattered them. Every boy in America who played ball wanted to be like Babe Ruth.

College football captured sports fans attention every autumn. The 1920's had perhaps the most iconic football coach of all time in Notre Dame's Knute Rockne. The University of Illinois boasted the incomparable, Harold "Red" Grange, their record setting running back. The National Football League was just beginning to catch on with tough guy coaches like George Halas of the Bears and Curley Lambeau of the Packers.

Boxing matches became increasingly popular with larger and larger purses for the more famous participants. Boxing in fact was the second most popular sport in the country and would remain so until the 1950's when it would be eclipsed by football. Jack Dempsey was immensely popular as the reigning heavyweight champion from 1919 – 1926. When he was defeated by Gene Tunney in September of 1926 boxing fans were stunned. When Tunney defeated Dempsey again 364 days later, it was the talk of the sports world. The sporting world was now big business and boasted a huge following. Newspapers, large and small, all had pages dedicated to sports news. The hungry public could not get enough.

The impact of an ever-rising interest in sports was immediate on youth athletics, particularly in high school. With more and more students staying in school until graduation and with child labor laws firmly in place, children in the country began to emulate their heroes and fill their time with sports. High school sports that had started in the 1890's for just a few became available in most every school in the land. It was in this new reality that Hurley's Lincoln School found itself when J.E. Murphy made his decision to put the school on the sports map.

When a superb athlete named Roy Melvin left the campus of the University of Wisconsin in the spring of 1923, he had just been offered a contract to play professional baseball with the Cincinnati Reds. Instead of traveling south, he chose to travel north to Hurley, where he would spend the summer playing baseball for that professional team.

Baseball was the king of sports throughout the United States. Almost every town fielded a team to compete against their neighbors. Some employers fielded company teams, and many churches also had teams. It did not take long for these friendly games to become very serious business. Towns and companies began to recruit players to represent their city or brand. These players were paid a tidy sum of money for the times. In 1923 Roy was offered $50 per game for three games a week, for twelve weeks, for a total of $1800.00. Coming to Hurley to play ball was strictly a business decision for Roy as he likely was not offered more than that to play in the Reds' minor league system.

After striking out three times and not getting a hit in his first game for the Hurley Nine, Roy went on a tear, hitting two long home runs in the next two games. The 26 year old quickly became a fan favorite. He also had quite a resume. He began his college education at the University of Wisconsin only to have his senior year stopped cold by World War I. He enlisted in the Navy as a radio operator and rear seat gunner in Navy aircraft. After his discharge Roy was coaxed by one of his former Madison teammates who was now the baseball coach at the River Falls Normal School (now known as UW-River Falls) to join him there. Roy did, and he played baseball, football and basketball for the college. He earned his teaching certification in physical education while at River Falls. He then returned to Madison where he earned his Bachelor of Arts degree in History from the University of Wisconsin.

As an accomplished ball player, Navy veteran, certified physical education teacher, and a history major, it didn't take long before he caught the eye and came under the scrutiny of Mr. J.E. Murphy. Satisfied that he found his man, Mr. Murphy offered Roy the position of teacher and coach at Hurley High School. Roy, a native of tiny Fish Creek, Wisconsin, accepted the position and returned to small town life. What started out as a summer of baseball, became a long and successful career. Hurley and Roy Melvin found each other at just the right time.

CHAPTER FOUR

Coach Melvin Gets
The Ball Rolling

As the popularity of sports continued to grow, high school athletics became increasingly popular as well. Schools began playing for fun and bragging rights around the turn of the twentieth century. Later schools banded together in competitive conferences and started keeping score and naming champions. School and town pride began to show through the choice of colors that adorned the uniforms of their teenaged athletes. Hurley's colors were orange and black.

In 1923 Hurley High School fielded athletic teams in football and basketball including a girl's basketball team. Most boys also played baseball, and it was by far their sport of choice, but in general high schools did not even attempt to field a baseball team. The boys ended up playing for town teams throughout America. Town teams ruled the local baseball scene until the 1950's. Hurley and the rest of the Gogebic Range were no different. They played baseball from May until September. Many played for multiple teams in different leagues. These ball games drew big crowds and sometimes huge crowds. When a player would hit a game winning home run or pitched an exceptional game, the spectators would often pass a hat around the stands and folks would drop in some money. In the 1920's a young player could receive an appreciative gift of $5.00 and up, which was not small change in those days. After high school, Tom "The Runt" Hunt, a member of Roy Melvin's first football and basketball teams at Hurley once had a game winning home run for the Hurley team as they defeated a barnstorming team loaded with well-known stars.

The hat was passed and little Tom had more money than he had ever had at one time. Over $25.00, mostly in change, was handed to him.

Roy Melvin wasn't the only well known player to make a tidy sum for playing town ball. Many a talented player would play ball well into their 40's and found it a good way to supplement their incomes. Talented players were in demand. After college in 1949, Bud Grant, a former star athlete at Superior Central High School and the University of Minnesota played "town ball" for Gordon, Wisconsin among other teams in the summer while playing professional basketball for the Minneapolis Lakers in the winter. "I made more money playing town baseball in the summer than I ever did playing for the Lakers." Of course as a coveted clean-up hitter and a pitcher with a 60 – 2 won – loss record, he commanded a nice contract. It would take the Philadelphia Eagles and an NFL football contract to finally lure Grant away from town ball.

Given the circumstances, one can see why Roy Melvin did not field a baseball team for Hurley High School. It would have met with indifference from most boys who dreamed of playing for the town teams, and probably would have incurred the furor of the townspeople in the area as they all had at least one team they cheered for on which the boys played. There also was one other small detail. Who would they have played? No other schools fielded baseball teams either. The simple truth is that baseball was just too popular to have teenage boys confined to playing for only a school. It would not be until the late 1940's that high school baseball would be played in Hurley and most of Wisconsin. Even then most players chose to play for one of the town teams.

It wasn't as if Hurley didn't field athletic teams prior to the arrival of Coach Melvin. Hurley played football against local schools since at least 1902 if not sooner. Basketball soon followed. Records are sketchy and not all games were reported to or recorded by the local newspapers. The games were popular with the students but were not big spectator sports like baseball was. The Michigan teams from Wakefield, Bessemer, and Ironwood faced off regularly with the Wisconsin teams from Ashland and Hurley. With the rivalries came ever larger crowds of spectators.

In the fall of 1923, Hurley's new coach welcomed 24 boys to the high school football team. As Coach Melvin handed out leather helmets, pads, and the uniforms, he noticed that most of the boys were not very big. Most football players of the day were tiny compared to today's standards. He must have been pleased with their toughness and effort when the first practice ended. No coach ever forgets their first team. They became special as they progressed through the season, taking on the attitude and attributes of their coach. Roy Melvin himself was not a big man. He was the runt of his family and an undersized athlete throughout his high school and college career. Through mental toughness and self discipline he became a success on and off the field. He would expect nothing less from his players.

The 1923 Hurley football team was led by their senior quarterback, Tom "The Runt" Hunt. The team leader lived up to his name, standing about 5'4" tall. Still there were others smaller than him on that team. A speedy and agile freshman halfback by the name of Mario Giannunzio provided the team with a spark as he became a threat to score every time he touched the ball. The other boys were proving day in and day out that they were dependable and tough as nails. Just as Coach Melvin started feeling good about his team's chances for a successful season, he discovered that things would be very difficult indeed.

For the most part, in the previous two decades the Michigan teams dominated Hurley and Ashland, especially in football. It wasn't that the Wisconsin teams were terrible. They just had a huge disadvantage.

In those days, most states did not have an age limit for people to remain in high school in pursuit of a diploma. In largely rural states, it was essential for high school students to help on the farm in the late summer and springs. Planting and harvesting were labor intensive endeavors that required many hands. Also many students took jobs to assist their families. They missed large chunks of school and were allowed re-enroll yearly until enough credits could be earned for graduation. It was not uncommon for some to be well over age 21 before earning a diploma. Most states continued to allow students to be in high school into their twenties, but in 1930 36 states agreed that the age of 20 would be the cut-off for high school athletic eligibility. The rest varied between 19 and 21. Michigan adopted age 21 and Wisconsin adopted 19. By the late 1930's Michigan reduced the age limit to 20. Wisconsin rules stated that if a player turned 19 before a season began, that player was ineligible. So if a basketball season began on November 15, a player who turned 19 on November 16 could play, but a player who turned 19 on November 14 could not.

So the new coach faced a new reality. The Michigan teams could suit up grown men against his already smallish boys. The Michigan teams, especially Bessemer and Ironwood, would have been good without that advantage as they produced strong teams and superb athletes. With the added age advantage they proved to be nearly unbeatable for Hurley and Ashland.

Hurley would finish the 1923 football season with a record of 3 wins, 3 loses and a tie in seven games. The tie occurred when boys sent shockwaves through the area as they battled the powerful

Bessemer squad to a 0 – 0 final score. Missing from the schedule was Ironwood. It was decided after the game in 1920 that the schools should not compete in sports against one another. Hurley had a 6 – 0 lead late in that game when a sideline brawl broke out. It threatened to get out of hand with spectators from both sides looking to get involved. When order was restored, Coach Moss of Ironwood decided it was better to forfeit the game than continue. It would be four years before the arch rivals would play each other again.

In November of 1923 Coach Melvin collected the football uniforms and issued basketball uniforms to eight boys. The sport had been gaining in popularity among players and spectators, with high school games showing a marked increase in attendance.

Basketball was the brainchild of Dr. James Naismith. He wanted to maintain athletes' conditioning during the cold winter months in Springfield, Massachusetts. The first game was played in 1891 at the Springfield YMCA with the players using a soccer ball and a peach basket hung ten feet off the floor. It was an excruciatingly slow moving sport compared to the game as we now know it. But it was something new to do during the long, cold winter months. In less than two years the game spread to high schools, again as a way to combat the "dead time" in winter when football and baseball could not be played. In 1896 the game spread to colleges, and basketball began its slow transformation into the fast-paced game we know today.

Basketball rules in 1923 included the "center jump" to start the game just like today. Unlike today the center jump occurred after each made basket. Players were allowed 3 fouls instead of 5 before being disqualified from the game. There was no uniformity in the size of basketball courts because many schools had small gymnasiums. In larger venues the ball would often have to be retrieved from the stands when it was thrown or knocked out of bounds. Many of these venues erected a chain link or chicken wire fence around the playing surface to prevent that from happening. Some schools used netting. The result was the game did not have to be stopped to retrieve the ball and basketball players became known in the news as "cagers". Games were often referred to as "cage matches". With these rules and conditions in place games were usually very low scoring. In 1922, Fond du Lac defeated New Richmond in the Wisconsin State Championship game 22 – 19. That was a very typical score. Many games did not reach 30 points total by both teams combined.

Also contributing to the low scoring games was that many high school gyms in those days were built without basketball in mind. Because many gyms had low ceilings, players learned to shoot the ball without an arch. Players adjusted instead by using two hands to push the ball on a flat "line drive" trajectory toward the basket. Backboards and their size were also different from gym to gym. All were made of wood, but the density, thickness and type of wood was not standard, causing each gym to have its own peculiar bounces. Some gyms were too narrow for a regulation size court, some were perfect squares rather than rectangular. Other gyms had overhangs, a low beam, or balconies which hindered both passing and shooting the ball. This gave the home team a tremendous advantage as they knew best how to manipulate the dimensions in their favor. Player substitution rules allowed a player to re-enter a game only once after being removed. By 1934 the rule was changed to allow a player to re-enter the game twice. The rule was reasonable as player fatigue was not much of a factor given that the game moved rather slowly in those times.

Roy Melvin would see his Hurley basketball teams through a host of rule changes that began to modernize the game. Through it all he could count on two things. The Hurley boys would be tough, and with only a few exceptions, they would always be the smaller team. The 1923 – 24 basketball season saw Hurley compile of record of 7 wins and 6 losses, including two wins over Bessemer. The people of Bessemer were used to seeing their boys soundly defeat Hurley on a regular basis, but they knew a good thing when they saw it and were true sportsmen. This is from the Bessemer Herald, as quoted by Stuart Melvin in his book, "A Coach for All Seasons, the Roy Melvin Story".

> Coach Roy Melvin has made a good record since
> he took up the athletic reins at Hurley High last
> fall. His football and basketball teams have been
> among the best in the history of Hurley athletics. His
> football eleven tied Bessemer High last fall and his
> basketball outfit has won two games from the locals
> - performances which are rare indeed in Bessemer –
> Hurley contests. Fans also have had an opportunity
> to see Melvin display his prowess in baseball and
> basketball since he came to Hurley. That town sure
> gained in athletic prestige since Melvin got there.

That is certainly high praise from the town that in 1920 saw their school defeat Hurley twice in football by an aggregate score of 120 – 0.

By any measure, Roy Melvin's first year of coaching was a huge success. The people of Hurley began to believe that their teams not only could beat other teams from Wisconsin, but proved they could compete with the Michigan teams as well. The coach would soon introduce track and tennis to the school's competitive sports teams.

The kids from Hurley were given the opportunities envisioned by J. E. Murphy and Harold Conners when they hired Coach Melvin. What must have been especially rewarding for those two men was that Roy Melvin was more than a coach. He skillfully used athletics as a means to hone his player's work ethic and character. He insisted on hard work, discipline, and teamwork. He also insisted his players display sportsmanship and self control. He believed he was helping prepare his players and students for life. He also believed it was time for Hurley to work things out with the folks at Ironwood High School and start playing ball again.

CHAPTER FIVE

Red Devils And Midgets

People who have been raised in Hurley have heard variations of the story of how Hurley High School became known as the Midgets. One story that has been told is that the nickname was first heard in the 1920's either during or right after a football game with the Red Devils. The story goes like this: Hurley was ahead in a game being played on Ironwood's Longyear Field. Every time it looked like the physically superior Ironwood team would score they were thwarted by the small kids from the other side of the border. An exasperated Ironwood reporter/official/fan/coach or possibly the public address announcer loudly exclaimed, "I can't believe we're losing to this bunch of midgets!"

If this story is indeed true we can eliminate the years of 1921, 1922, 1923, 1926, 1927, and 1928 as the teams did not play each other in football those six years. That leaves us with 1920, 1924, 1925 and 1929 as the years that this story could have happened. Given the historical facts it is even possible that the year could have been 1919.

In 1919 Hurley defeated Ironwood in football 13 – 6 in Ironwood. In the 1920 game Hurley held a 6 – 0 lead late in the game, threatening to win "The Game" two years in a row for the first time. Then "The Brawl" broke out. That game was played in Hurley. In 1924 Ironwood defeated Hurley 53 – 0. In 1925 they beat Hurley again, in Hurley 47 – 0! In 1929 they defeated Hurley 7 – 0 with the game being played in Ironwood.

Thus, if this story were true, the game had to be played in Ironwood, and at some point during the game, Ironwood would have to have been on the short end of the score. Eliminate 1924, 1925, and 1929 as the year Hurley received their nickname, as they never lead during those games. Eliminate the 1920 brawl game as it was played on Hurley's field and that leaves us with 1919.

Also, forget about the 1930's being the time frame in which the Red Devils named Hurley the Midgets. From 1930 through 1934 Ironwood defeated Hurley each year. Hurley never led at any point during those 5 games. You can't have a lead if you do not score. Ironwood shut out Hurley in each game and over the course of those five years outscored them 80 – 0. In 1935 Hurley battled the Red Devils to a 0 – 0 tie. Again, they never led in the game. In 1936 and 1937 Hurley scored. Ironwood won the '36 game 25 – 7 and the '37 game 19 – 6. It is possible that Hurley could have held a lead in either of those games but by this time the nickname had already stuck to the school for at least 13 years

Did the 1919 game give Hurley High School its nickname? Possibly. The only other win versus Ironwood in the '20's or '30's came the next year in the forfeited "Brawl Game". It may have been that the person who shouted, "I can't believe we're losing to a bunch of Midgets!" was watching the game in Hurley in 1920. It is possible, but less likely, as many people have told the story and stated it was the Ironwood public address announcer or another in Ironwood who made the remark. In either case, if the story is true (and it's a big if) it seems like 1919 or 1920 was the likely time the Red Devils of Ironwood gave Hurley High School their nickname. There's just one thing; there is no mention of Hurley "Midgets" in the Ironwood Daily Globe, the Bessemer Herald, or the Iron County Miner (Montreal River Miner) until 1924 and then only in the Globe.

The second story isn't as folksy, but this one is known for a fact. In the autumn of 1924, the Ironwood Daily Globe began to refer to the Hurley football team as "Melvin's Midgets". The first time was on Monday, October 24, 1924. Hurley had battled Wakefield to a 20 – 20 tie after losing to the Cardinals three weeks previously by a score of 39 – 7. On November 3 the term, "Melvin's Midgets" appeared for the second time in an article which described Hurley's 55 – 6 triumph over Park Falls. On Friday, November 7, 1924, it appeared for the third time and twice in a five day period referencing the upcoming football game between Hurley and the powerful Bessemer Speed Boys the next day. Bessemer edged Hurley 17 – 14. It seems that this attempt at clever alliteration is the first time the nickname "Midgets" appears in print and as such is a permanent record. Stories and tales are fun, but facts are facts. Were the Hurley athletic teams referred to as "Midgets" prior to 1924? It is possible, but it can't be verified anywhere in the public record. We do know they definitely were from October 24, 1924 onward. As is often the case in sports, a sports writer comes up with the nicknames. This version of how Hurley became the "Hurley Midgets" is indeed factual and that makes it 99.99 percent the most likely scenario. As the Montreal River Miner printed on March 5, 1944, "The Midgets didn't get their name for the same reason you call a 250 pound man 'Tiny.' No, they got it in a more logical way – because they were small."

It is also a fact that of the Gogebic Range's five largest communities, Hurley was the smallest in population. One can surmise that people living in the area during those days might have thought that the nickname was fitting. In 1920 the population of Ironwood, Michigan was 15,739. Wakefield, Michigan had 4,151 inhabitants. Bessemer, Michigan sported 5,482 people within its city limits and Ashland, Wisconsin had 11,334 people. Hurley's population was the smallest at 3,188. The fact that Hurley thought of Ironwood as their arch rivals must have been somewhat amusing to Red Devil fans given the football dominance they exerted over their little neighbors. It was as if Hurley was the little brother who always tried to best his bigger and stronger older brother. The older brother would just keep pushing the pesky little brother to the side, never letting the little guy get a clean shot at him. Of course Ironwood could not let Hurley beat them and give their neighbors bragging rights. It truly would have been humiliating. As amused as they may have been over the thought that Hurley believed they actually belonged on the same field with their beloved Red Devils, they feared losing to them. And that healthy fear was what kept it a true rivalry.

So how did the other area schools get their nicknames? Wakefield became the Cardinals in the most democratic way, by popular vote of the students. H. O. "Sonny" Sonnesyn, a Duluth sports writer, is credited with coining the names of at least two Gogebic Range teams. He called Bessemer the "Speed Boys" because of Tony Gotta and his swift teammates in the early 1930's. Saint Ambrose became the "Ramblers" because they did not have a gym of their own and traveled to all their games. Ashland was initially called the "Ore Dockers," because that was the largest industry in town. They then became the "Purgolders" because of their colors. In the late 1940's it was changed back to "Ore Dockers." Last, but not least, Ironwood became the "Red Devils" by "popular decree of alumni and friends of the school." Red because of the color of their uniforms and, "the word 'devil' when applied in a familiar way, means a person with super abundant energy, a fighting spirit, good sportsmanship, and excellent skill." "Devil" in the vernacular of the day could also mean "devil of a good fellow." Other interesting nicknames of local teams were the Washburn "Castle Guards," the Mellen "Granite Diggers," the Watersmeet "Nimrods," and the Drummond "Fire Brigade" who are now known as the "Lumberjacks and Lumberjills."

And so Hurley High School became known as the Midgets. The one thing the people of Hurley knew for sure was they used that nickname to openly display the strength of character of their community and small team. Hurley High School proudly showed the area that their small community and small kids were as strong as the steel made from the iron ore their people mined from the earth. Playing the other teams on "The Range" in each season, the Hurley athletes found that Bessemer, Wakefield, Ashland, and especially Ironwood would enter each contest mentally and physically ready to play. Games were a test of will, strength, power, agility, mental and physical toughness, and most importantly, strength of character. As both wins and losses occurred between all the teams, they learned about sportsmanship, making a supreme effort, teamwork, and the importance of commitment and preparation. The Range teams were a reflection of each other. Each proudly represented their mining community, or in the case of Ashland, the town that shipped all that ore. United by their common labor, immigrant backgrounds, frontier mentality, and devotion to their youth, they formed a deep, albeit, grudging respect for one another. Iron sharpens iron. The growth process of the Hurley athletic program had begun.

CHAPTER SIX

Coach Melvin:
The Early Years 1923 - 1931

The story of a coach's success is most often measured by the number of wins and losses their teams earn. This is a fair and accurate measure at the professional level to be sure, as winning is the reason a coach is hired. At the college level, especially smaller colleges, that measure is also accompanied by the coach's ability to teach and help develop young athletes into adults of character and integrity. At the high school level, coaching is indeed a whole new ballgame.

High school coaches, especially in small communities and at public schools do not choose their players from a pool of talent larger than their school enrollment. Coaches normally are also teachers at the school they coach for. If they are a physical education teacher, they have the advantage of working with students to develop their physical skills, and thus they can encourage those students to join the teams. Small town coaches were also neighbors and friends to many in town. Like most other teachers, they established strong bonds within their communities. They knew their players when they were just little kids. They were trusted and respected. In the first 75 years of the last century that was normally the case in most high schools.

Coach Roy Melvin not only coached Hurley's football and basketball teams, he also began a track team and then a tennis team. He worked diligently to provide his students with opportunities to develop as athletes and as people. In the area, and in the state of Wisconsin, his reputation as a coach grew with each passing year, and in Hurley his reputation was sterling silver. His students respected him; his players trusted and revered him. In short he was everything J.E. Murphy and Harold Conners had hoped for when they hired him. He built his teams with toughness, an emphasis on fair play, sportsmanship, and integrity. Coach expected and received all that from his players. They represented Hurley High School and the community with grace and dignity. "Melvin's Midgets" earned respect from the loaded Michigan teams and became feared opponents in Northern Wisconsin. And they did it despite compiling a losing record.

From 1923 through the 1930 – 31 school year Coach Melvin's football teams compiled a record of 19 wins, 26 loses, and 3 ties. In basketball the record was 54 wins and 70 losses. As mentioned earlier, the Michigan teams had the advantage as they could suit up players well over the age of 21. The fact that Hurley was competitive in such an environment was a credit to the coach and his players. Faced with adversity in each contest, especially football, they persevered and grew stronger for it.

Just how big was the disadvantage created by the age rules in Michigan? Hurley played Ironwood five times from 1924 – 1931 losing each time. In those five games they were outscored 154 - 0. It should be noted that in 1929 the Midgets battled the Red Devils in a titanic struggle before losing 7 – 0. Their record against Wakefield from 1923 – 1931 was 2 wins, 5 losses and 2 ties. Versus Bessemer it was 1 win, 9 losses, and 2 ties. In his first nine years as Hurley's head football coach, Roy Melvin's record against Michigan teams (including Saint Ambrose and Iron River) was 4 wins, 20 losses, and 5 ties. Against Wisconsin competition during that time his record was 15 wins, 6 losses, 0 ties. The difference is that Hurley won over

70 percent of their games against Wisconsin competition and only 20 percent against teams from Michigan.

The question is did Hurley gain anything by playing the Michigan teams during that era? It is true they lost a lot of games, especially in football, where an age advantage is a size and strength advantage. In basketball the advantage was somewhat negated by the fact many football players in their twenties dropped out of school after football season to go back to work. Some stayed on to play basketball, but Hurley seemed to always have a fighting chance on the hardwood. On the gridiron the men, more often than not, simply ran over the boys.

If Hurley did not schedule the three Michigan teams from The Range, they would have to schedule 3 more Wisconsin teams. Ashland was the closest, 36 miles to the west, and they were already on each other's schedule. They already played Park Falls which was over 50 miles away. In 1923 they even played Northland College, which was located in Ashland. That illustrates another problem of that time. Many smaller towns in the area did not field a football team because so many of their boys spent their after school hours working on family farms. Couple that with the highway system being in its infancy, and you have less than ideal travel conditions. A 50 mile trip today is normally less than a one hour drive. In the 1920's it could take more than two hours or more, depending on weather conditions. There simply were no other teams Hurley could schedule.

Why would a high school even consider playing a college team in football? The simple answer is that the players loved to play the game. Also what harm could there be in playing a college team when you already played three or more games a year against high school teams with college age players? The players loved football and they wanted to play. So yes, Hurley did gain the opportunity to simply have a full football schedule. They also gained the opportunity for Coach Melvin to become Teacher Melvin, as he used those often blistering defeats to teach his players about the unfairness of life and the value of standing tall in the face of adversity. His players would become better and stronger people because of their love for a sport.

One can surmise that Roy Melvin was indeed a clever and innovative football coach who had to work extra hard to prepare his teams for games in which they were overwhelming underdogs. He became known as a defensive mastermind especially later in his career. That genius started in his early years at Hurley. Coaching his first two football games against the powerful Red Devils of Ironwood must have been disheartening. In 1924 Ironwood won 53 – 0. In 1925, it was 47 – 0. In 1924 Wakefield defeated Hurley 39 – 7. Bessemer beat Hurley twice in 1924, 13 – 0 and 17 – 14. That was after Hurley tied the Speed Boys in Melvin's first year 0 – 0.   What Roy Melvin learned was that if his teams were to ever beat the Michigan squads they needed to play stouter on defense and they needed to be tougher than their larger, older opponents. With each passing year, the gap closed with some memorable wins and hard fought ties.

Because of the disadvantages facing Coach Melvin throughout his early years in Hurley, he impressed upon his players they would not make excuses, they would work as hard as humanly possible to overcome all obstacles, and they would never, ever quit. His players believed in him and emulated his work ethic. Hurley's athletes built a tradition of having a special toughness that left the opposition battered and exhausted, regardless of the score. After those precious victories and many a lopsided defeat, Hurley's kids walked off the fields and courts with their heads held high. Was playing physically bigger and stronger teams worth the pain of defeat? Yes, iron sharpens iron.

By the end of the 1931 school year, Michigan teams could no longer suit up players over the age of 21. The maximum age difference was now less than two years. By the late 1930's that age discrepancy almost disappeared, putting teams from both states on equal footing with no players over the age of 19 allowed to compete. The difference then became that Wisconsin teams could not have a player on the team who was over 19 when the season began. Michigan teams were allowed to play boys until their 20th birthday.

1931 would prove to be a banner year for Roy Melvin. In addition to his Hurley athletic teams now being able to play on a more equal basis with the Michigan teams, his personal life took the best turn of all. The coach was smitten by a Hurley fourth grade teacher who hailed from Ashland. In August of 1931 he married Lucille (Lou) Fitzgerald. Together they started a family which would include two boys and a girl. Stuart, Tom, and Maggie became known as the "Melvin kids" in town. Hurley's coach became a family man. 1931 was a watershed year for Roy Melvin and Hurley Athletics.

CHAPTER SEVEN

Turning The Corner: 1931 – 1940

In 1931 - 32 Hurley posted its' best record ever in basketball with a 12 – 5 season. In football they broke through with a record of 3 wins, 2 losses, and 2 ties. They clearly had skills and heart. They also had a very special athlete who began his 10th grade year in 1931. Some tremendous athletes had worn the Orange and Black for Hurley prior to 1931, including Ed Sybeldon, Tom "Runt" Hunt, Mario Gianunzio, Gil Trier, and Tom "Five Yard" Kirby, but no one in town had seen the likes of tiny Ted Gentile before. Standing just 5'1" and weighing in at about 110 pounds, he proved to be the mightiest of all the Midgets. Coach Melvin, who played and coached for over 60 years, called him "pound for pound and inch for inch, the greatest athlete I have ever seen!" After high school Ted would go on to star at Superior State Teacher's College (Now known as the University of Wisconsin – Superior).

Hurley's fortunes on the athletic fields had taken a turn for the better as far as wins and losses were concerned. Remarkably, the tenacious attitude of her athletes remained in high gear. It was a good thing too. As the Michigan teams began to adjust to life without their older players, they too found that rock solid competition caused them to dig deeper than ever before. The Range teams took special pride in that fact that they would beat up on each other and that outsiders could not beat any of them with regularity. By 1937 they officially formed the Michigan – Wisconsin Conference, or as people in the area called it, "The MW". Prior to making it official, the Range teams and towns did keep track and did claim championships. Hurley and

Ashland began to sport better records and the rivalries grew to a fever pitch.

In December of 1933 a catastrophe occurred in the Melvin household. Returning from a Christmas visit to Lucille's parents in Ashland, the Melvin's came home to cold house. Roy went to the basement to relight the fire in the coal burning furnace. As he struck a match, there was an explosion. Soot and cinders blew forcefully into Roy Melvin's' face and eyes. He was blinded!

The doctor believed that Roy would regain his vision, but the question of when became paramount. In a genuine display of respect, remarkable for its sincerity, Coach Mark Almli came to Hurley to direct their holiday practice sessions in basketball. What is most remarkable is that Mark Almli was also the coach for the Ironwood Red Devils. Familiarity does not have to breed contempt. Arch rivals and respected friends those Red Devils were. Coach Almli was a "devil" of a good fellow.

With bandaged eyes, the Coach was back on the Hurley bench in a few weeks. The Ironwood Daily Globe gave this account of the game:

> The Hurley team was directed from the bench by
> Coach Roy Melvin, who sat on the bench with his
> eyes bandaged and listened to the account of the
> game. After the game you would have sworn that
> Melvin saw the contest, for he knew all of the details
> even to the point of how many shots each player
> took and the mistakes they made. Melvin, more
> than ever, demonstrated that he has a wonderful
> basketball mind.

How does a person coach a basketball team he can't see perform? The answer is he had Teddy Gentile. His most polished athlete became his eyes on the court and Teddy relayed all that was happening on the court, allowing the Coach to make adjustments. Later in life the coach declared that, in that year while coaching blind, he became a complete coach because "I could not see, so I learned to think." This incident also cemented his relationship with Teddy Gentile. They became and remained lifelong friends.

As the playing field between Michigan and Wisconsin teams was leveled by the late 1930's the Michigan teams, sensing the rise in Hurley's fortunes, refused to go down. They wanted to prove that the previous years were not a fluke due to any advantage in age, but rather than an advantage in skills. The scores tightened up in football and lopsided wins by Michigan teams disappeared, but still they won most of the time.

In 1932 Ironwood beat Hurley 12 – 0. In 1933 it was 13 – 0. The gap appeared to close, but still not enough to defeat or even score on the Red Devils. By 1935, the unthinkable happened. Hurley tied Ironwood 0 – 0 and then defeated Bessemer 7 – 6. A first ever area championship could have been had except for Wakefield's banner year and the 13 – 0 defeat they handed to Hurley. So close, yet so far. In 1936 Hurley scored against Ironwood for the first time since 1920 but lost 25 – 7. The Michigan teams' margin of victory had shrunk, but they still held on to the football bragging rights.

By the late 1930's Hurley's hard work and Michigan's age rules began to show in even closer scores on the football field. Still the Michigan teams from the Range stubbornly refused to yield. By 1940 Ironwood had not known defeat at the hands of a Hurley football team in 20 years. From 1931 – 1940 the football Midgets record against

Ironwood was 0 wins, 8 losses, and 2 ties.   In that same time their record against Wakefield was 3 wins, 5 losses, and 2 ties. Versus Bessemer it was 2 wins, 6 losses, and 2 ties. The difference in the scores from the 1923 – 1930 era and the 1931 – 1940 era showed vast improvement as the lopsided, even inhumane defeats suffered in the 1920's were proven to be a thing of the past.

In basketball Hurley fared better than in football. From 1931 – 1940 the Midgets compiled a strong record of 91 wins and 75 losses. They would have won the conference title twice, had there been an official conference. In 1938, they finished the regular season with a record of 6 wins and 9 losses. No one gave that team much of a chance in the Wisconsin State Tournament, but the Midgets, after drawing an opening round bye, caught fire and defeated the heavily favored Park Falls Cardinals in the first game of the Class B District tournament. That gave the Hurley boys the opportunity to Play Superior East in the District Championship game. They stunned East 21 – 14. That win propelled the Midgets into the District Tournament Championship game to play the big, physical Cumberland Beavers for the right to play in the State Class B Tournament in Madison.

Basketball has always been an unpredictable game, especially at the high school level. Roy Melvin's best basketball team to this point was the 1935 – 1936 team that boasted sterling 14 – 5 record. That team could not win the District Title and went home before qualifying for the State Finals, subsequently breaking the hearts of the Midget faithful. Now in 1938, basketball fans in Wisconsin were shocked by Hurley's two wins in the District, defeating the two favored teams rather handily.

Hurley versus Cumberland was a mismatch of huge proportions. Cumberland was heavily favored and had to only make a short 14 mile trip to Rice Lake High School, which hosted the district meet. Hurley traveled 130 miles for the game. It was in this game that the disparity in gym sizes and layouts was clearly pronounced. Rice Lake had a small gym. Actually, it was more than just small; it was tiny even by the standards in those days. That negated Hurley's speed advantage and gave Cumberland's big players the advantage of getting back on defense rather quickly as they didn't have far to run on that short court. That crowded court worked to Cumberland's advantage as they had only to run a little and rebound. They did and they defeated Hurley in a close game 26 – 22. The Beavers were in fact as big as advertised with all 5 starters standing at least 6 feet tall and their center at 6'4". They would go on to finish 3rd in the state in Class B.

Throughout the Melvin years, the boys loved playing football, even if it meant getting bulldozed. They played baseball all summer long in one or more leagues, and for most of them, it was the sport they loved above all others. Basketball, which was the least of the three sports in the minds of many, was where they began to excel. In the next decade, Hurley not only would become synonymous with basketball excellence, but they would come to epitomize the power of small town basketball in the 1940's and 1950's throughout the Midwest.

CHAPTER EIGHT

Giving The Devils Their Due!

Hurley and Ironwood. History tells us that they almost became one town. It seems that there was some confusion about the east and west branches of the Montreal River and which of them formed the Michigan – Wisconsin border. Of course Michigan wanted to have the border at the west branch giving their state more land and more importantly, more iron ore! When the courts ruled in favor of Wisconsin, Hurley and Ironwood developed as separate cities in two separate states. The border became the east branch of the Montreal River and as rivers go, it's not very wide or deep. Many a kid has stood on one side or the other and thrown rocks to the other state. In the long, cold winters epic snowball fights would break out along the river with the kids from both sides raining down hundreds of snowballs on the other state. The only thing on the line was the most important thing: bragging rights.

History and geography has conspired to create this rivalry. Geography put the two towns, located in two states, shoulder to shoulder, like siblings sharing the same bed. Not the same, but not very different. Yet it sometimes seemed to the youth of each town that they were worlds apart.

One world, Ironwood, seemed to the Hurley kids like a big city, with bigger buildings, exciting dime stores, a store dedicated just to music, another just to paint, one just for men's clothing, another just for women's clothing, a Sears, a JC Penney's, and a Montgomery Wards. Best of all was the beautiful, iconic Ironwood Theatre, where kids from all over the Range could watch a Saturday Matinee for just a dime. Ironwood had a daily newspaper. To a kid from Hurley Ironwood was sophisticated, big, and bold. It also had a superb education system and Ironwood High was second to none.

The other world, Hurley, had the lower block of Silver Street. When meeting people from other places, many from Hurley have experienced the shock of hearing how horrible it must have been to grow up there. What did these folks think Hurley kids did for fun? For a Hurley kid, and most of the folks in town, Silver Street's lower block was just "there". It wasn't paid much mind for the most part because it was not their center of attention. No, Hurley was not as sophisticated as Ironwood. It was in fact a place people went to be "naughty". But for the vast majority of the townspeople, their focus was on raising their family, their work, the mines, and church. Just like their brethren across the Range.

Hurley had fine grocery stores, a hardware store, butcher shops, a cobbler shop, a dry cleaner, gas stations and everything else any other town had. Hurley had Italian restaurants that were local favorites. But Hurley's best feature was that they also had an education system as good as could be found anywhere. Hurley High was held in the highest esteem by colleges and employers throughout Michigan and Wisconsin. J.E. Murphy and Harold Conners were respected and honored throughout the state. And yet, so many people not from Hurley, especially many who had never been there, thought of the town only as a den of iniquity.

If Ironwood High grew into the role of the big brother in this rivalry, it was because they were indeed bigger. They had a bigger town, a more populous state, and bigger and more athletes. Hurley was truly the kid brother. It was a much smaller town, with fewer and smaller athletes. The big brother was tall, strong and good looking. The little brother wanted to be like him but was short and scrawny. The big brother brushed aside the little brother whenever the little guy threatened him and often times administered a good old fashioned butt whipping. The little brother grew up with a chip on his shoulder!

So by 1941 this rivalry was kept alive in football only by the memory of 1919 and 1920. That was last time the little brother was able to bushwhack the big guy. Since then Hurley could not buy a win. The composite score of those 14 games played in those years was 287 – 26. The Red Devils won twelve of the games with Hurley's moral victories not being victories at all. All they could manage was the 0-0 tie in 1935 and a 6-6 tie in 1940, a game that was made even more painful because the Midgets held the lead until a fluke play allowed Ironwood to tie the game in the waning seconds.

With basketball it was a different story; Hurley could compete and win. Thus the rivalry lived on. What enabled the little brother to compete on even footing with the big brother in basketball?

Football requires eleven players from each team to be on the field at all times. It was not uncommon in those days for Ironwood to suit up 70 – 100 players for a game. In basketball it is five on five. Rosters were restricted to ten or twelve players for the game. The number of players required for basketball versus football shrinks the advantage of a school having more athletes. If a town has a smaller pool of athletes to begin with, it is at a disadvantage playing a sport that requires more players. Small towns found it easier to compete in basketball because most could often find five players to match up with the top five from a larger school. The big difference was usually found in the skills of the bench players, with the bigger schools normally having the advantage. Also a basketball team, unlike most other sports teams, can create a more competitive team with one extremely talented player who can dominate a game supported by 4 average to below average players.

One of the biggest rule changes in basketball history occurred in the late 30's with the "center jump" being eliminated after each score. Instead the ball was inbounded by the team who had just been scored upon. This did much to even the playing field for small schools that most often lacked a tall player who could control the center jump. The result was that teams with taller players had to spend much more time playing defense. Smaller teams soon figured out that they could speed up the game by pushing the ball up court quickly to catch the bigger team unaware and also to exhaust them. The pace of the game increased immediately. Athletes who could run hard, pass the ball, and move with lateral quickness became coveted basketball players. Tall players have always been important to any team, but now talented small players could impact the game as well.

In high school, football teams usually play each other once per year. In basketball most teams sharing the same conference play twice a season. Games are indoors and in the earlier days they were played in small gyms where the spectators were literally close enough to reach out and touch a player. Five hundred people at a football game can raise a huge cheer. Squeeze those same five hundred people shoulder to shoulder inside a small gym and you have a noise level that rivals that of 100,000 at an outdoor football game. It becomes so loud that players can't hear their teammate calling out plays from five feet away. For the players it becomes a surreal atmosphere in which you literally see lips moving, but can't hear a single word. The crowd noise generated in those crackerjack box sized gyms gave a small school playing on its home court a huge emotional lift. Close games, played twice a year, with each team hosting the other, capacity crowds shoehorned into close confines, the rabidity of the fans, town pride, and an iron clad determination by both teams to defeat the other fueled rivalries like no other sport.

So basketball largely kept the Ironwood – Hurley rivalry alive throughout the 1920's and 1930's. Through it all the teams approached each game with an edge that bordered on contempt, yet respect. The games were heated, hard fought, and contentious. The crowds filled the gyms to capacity and beyond. Like the two towns, the spectators stood shoulder to shoulder, packed in like sardines, raising the temperature to sweltering proportions. By the games' end they, like the players, would be physically drained and emotionally spent.

Those Red Devils dominated the Midgets in football and early on in basketball. They also brought out the best in the Hurley athletes despite many lopsided scores. To be sure, so did the Bessemer Speed Boys, the Wakefield Cardinals, and the Purgolders from Ashland. They were arch rivals, brothers sharing the same bedroom, but Ironwood was the Super Arch Rival, the brother who shared the same bed, shoulder to shoulder. The little brother just needed to beat the big brother. The little brother wanted to prove that he could be all that the big brother was. Little brothers grow up and brothers respect each other more and more as time goes by. They are not the same, but they are not very different.   When brothers become adults they understand they are all on equal footing. Ironwood and the rest of the Range was about to see the Hurley athletic program reach adulthood. The rivalries would intensify and even more legends would be born.

CHAPTER NINE

Hard Times, Changes And Teenagers

One would think that the people of Hurley and the rest of the Range would have been hit extra hard by the Great Depression. It is hard to determine how hard-hit the area was. It is true that there was a down turn in iron ore production and many people did lose jobs. The Depression did bring about harder times, but life for iron miners, cold climate farmers, rail workers, dock workers, small business owners, tradesmen and others scratching out a living on the Range was never easy to begin with. When speaking to those who lived through those years, it seems as if they were just used to hard times. Because they never had much in the way of luxury, there was not a big change in the standard of living for most people in the area. Great Depression poor or just plain poor-- to many people of the Range, there was not much difference!

There was just enough work available to maintain a fairly steady population on the Range steady between 1930 – 1940, with Bessemer, Hurley and Ashland showing very slight growth, and Wakefield's population declining slightly. Ironwood was not so fortunate. The Range's largest town lost 6.5% of its population from 1930 – 1940, going from 14,299 to 13,369 inhabitants.

The Depression brought about many changes in America. Prohibition ended in 1933. Franklin D. Roosevelt was elected president and brought about sweeping social changes, including the New Deal. The Dust Bowl did unprecedented damage to agriculture and the ecology of the Great Plains, causing a mass migration to California and other places. Work projects and new laws designed to get workers with families back on the job rolled out of Washington, DC with regularity. Lesser known, but perhaps the most far reaching change, was the growth of high school enrollment, graduation, and the rise of a new sub culture in the country – teenagers!

Beginning around 1900, child labor laws were enacted to protect young people from the deprivations of adult work. Some children, as young as 10 years old, were employed not just on the family farm, but in the textile industry, mines, factories, as domestics, and in the trades. Of course the toll on life and limb was extraordinary. The laws had the desired effect as fewer and fewer young children worked. As a result school enrollment increased. As more and better laws were passed, more kids went to school. Enrollment did not just increase in the elementary grades, but it became even more pronounced in high schools.

In the 1910's factories especially became more efficient and even fewer young people were hired. As this trend continued many boys did not begin seeking employment until they turned 16. More states also continued to pass laws requiring mandatory education to 14 years old. Then came the Great Depression and sweeping changes would inadvertently bring about the birth of what we know today as the teenager.

When FDR took office, laws and public policy changed dramatically. Employers would be fined if they did not release young people not supporting a family and hire men who were trying to support a family. As a result, large numbers of teens became unemployed. High school enrollment which had steadily increased since being at 14% of

13 – 18 year olds in 1900 now ballooned to 71% by 1940. Graduation rates also increased from about 30% in 1930 to over 50% in 1940.

Prior to the Depression, high school attendance was seen as a luxury by many people in the working class. That, coupled with the fact that a good many jobs required skills that could be learned quickly at work, ensured many boys and girls would be lured into the work place before they would graduate. Therefore high school graduation was seen as an endeavor for middle class and above. Now with so many 14 – 18 year olds in one place a metamorphosis was underway. High school aged youth began to see themselves as part of a unique group. Their new friendships cut across socioeconomic lines. Not only was there an expectation that most would enroll in high school, but there was also an expectation that they would graduate.

Hurley had a bit of a head start on the national trend. The immigrant families placed a premium on education and insisted their children not only attend school, but that they also study hard and achieve. Although many did not complete high school, the numbers were always quite high. By the time the Great Depression hit the country, Hurley High School had a solid gold reputation of excellence, with a very high number of graduates going on to college. Still, the events and circumstances of the Depression ensured even more young people would enroll in and graduate from high school. It was one of the good things to come out of the Great Depression!

As the 1940's approached and the Great Depression ebbed, America's and Hurley's high school aged kids would become known as "teenagers". They saw themselves as being apart from the children still in elementary grades, and also saw themselves as being different than adults. They began to coin their own phrases, listen to their style of music, dance new dances, wear different clothes, and generally live a more carefree life than their predecessors.

The high school was now more than ever the gathering place for teens. As before they brought an abundance of energy to the hallways, classrooms, and gymnasiums. Now they brought it in unprecedented numbers. J.E. Murphy, Harold Conners, Roy Melvin, and other town leaders knew exactly what was needed to meet the needs of these teenaged dynamos.

CHAPTER TEN

Youth Is Served

In 1937, the superintendent of mines in Montreal asked Roy Melvin to plan out a summer youth sports program for boys and girls 5 – 15 years of age to include those living in Hurley, Cary, Gile, Pence, and Montreal. The plan was approved and budgeted. The Coach supervised activities at each of the five school grounds, with the center of activity being in Montreal. The obvious benefits for the kids were immediately noticeable as they had a healthy outlet for all their energy and the activities were free, which was no small thing during The Depression.

The other benefit was that the Coach had an opportunity to get to know the youngsters before they started high school. He also could ensure that in each activity they were taught proper technique and fundamentals. Activities such as baseball, archery, horse shoes, darts, jump rope, folk dancing, volleyball, and others were made safe and fun. Tennis and basketball were also activities provided. The Coach soon realized that having a head start on coaching and teaching youngsters would only help them develop as athletes. Athletes he would be coaching in just a few years in high school.

Roy Melvin supervised so many kids in so many sporting activities during the summer, but in the winter basketball took full control of the sports scene. Many schools in the area competed in downhill skiing, but it was basketball by far that had captured the hearts and imaginations of so many youngsters. All you need to play basketball is a ball and a hoop. Hoops could be found a hanging from garages in the alleys of each Range town. School yards had them and some were nailed to telephone poles.

Kids would gather at their favorite hoop during winter and begin the process of preparing the court. A recent snow would be met with shovels and often with the feet of the neighborhood kids. A little snow meant "panking down" the snow   underfoot until it was hard packed. The panking process was well thought out as kids stepped side by side up and down and over again until they would get a true bounce of the ball on the surface. A group of highly motivated ball players could have the half court sized area panked in a few minutes. So adept were these youngsters that the term "panked" is still used in the area around Hurley.

Kids would alternate playing with mittens and then without, alternating as their hands needed to be warmed. Closer to the basket, where most of the action took place, the packed down snow would become slick, even icy from the constant motion of feet. As the game became more treacherous underneath the hoop, the players would begin to launch shots from ever increasing distances in order to get better footing. By playing in these conditions, many area players became deadly outside shooters. It was another circumstance that helped the game change over the years. Outstanding outside shooters who played prior to the three point shot being implemented in high school basketball in 1987 can only look back and wonder what might have been.

Kids' time was less regimented in those days, and prompted by their parents to "go outside and play" they did. They honed their basketball skills by taking acrobatic shots, trying new ways to get open and generally forgetting to enforce any rules. They had fun. There was no adult watching to ensure that their creativity was stifled.

Coaching would come when they joined a team. For now they were growing and learning to use their often uncoordinated bodies in a coordinated way. It was where they learned to love the game. It was where they developed lifelong friendships. It was where they learned to respect each other and the game itself. And later on most of them learned to apply the lessons of basketball to life. Coaches would help guide them.

Ironwood started a Junior High Tournament and League as early as 1934. Wakefield, Bessemer, and Ramsey Junior Highs followed and they competed against each other with each town crowning a champion.

Ashland also had youth basketball as early as 1936 and they played a game versus Gurney and Cedar, whose youngsters would attend Saxon High School when they reached 9th grade.

There is no mention in the Ironwood Daily Globe, Montreal River Miner, or Iron County News of a grade school or Junior High School basketball league or tournament until 1942. It was then that the inaugural Iron County Junior High Basketball Tournament was held. It was sponsored by the Iron County Superintendent of Schools with assistance from Coach Roy Melvin and his assistant coach, Ted Gentile. There were eight teams entered. Mercer, Saxon, Iron Belt, Montreal, Cary, Pence, Saint Mary's, and Lincoln (Hurley) were the eight schools represented, which were all that were in the county. The winner was Montreal and they received the Montreal River Miner trophy for their efforts. The tournament was the culmination of a season of play. It was a time when those Junior High games were not covered by the local news outlets, probably because no one reported the scores as the Ironwood, Bessemer, Ashland and Wakefield teams did.

Paul Santini, the former Hurley football and basketball great and now the County Superintendent of Schools, was the driving force behind the Iron County League and Tournament. His efforts brought forth a highly successful and productive competition that lasted until the late 1970's. The tournament, which was always held the week after the Wisconsin State Tournament concluded, gave the basketball hungry fans another weekend of competition to savor. The tournament's success was evident in the number of spectators who watched. The crowds were not packed into the new gym as tightly as they were for high school games, but they routinely drew over 1,000 spectators for the games.

One tradition that started with the league and tournament was that high school basketball team members often coached or assisted in coaching the Junior High teams. They also were selected to referee the games. It served the purpose of those high school players becoming even more aware of the rules and nuances of the game. Sportsmanship and respect for the game and its players was the inevitable result.

In 1942 a new generation of basketball players watched and played in the tournament. They were in grades 5, 6, 7, and 8. They received their baptism into the rabidity of Hurley basketball. They caught the fever. They would grow up play the game like no others in the history of the school.

CHAPTER ELEVEN

The 1941 Football Season And The Game That Changed Everything

Excitement was running high among the Hurley boys as Roy Melvin handed out football uniforms to his team in August of 1941. From the opening conditioning drills and then into practice, the atmosphere was charged with the belief that this year would be special.

The optimism of the boys and the Hurley fans was founded in the belief that they did indeed have a group of athletes that would prove to be the equal of any team in the M-W conference in both basketball and football. Two juniors in particular would lead them. Dom Moselle, a quick, slippery, and tough fullback was thought to be the best football player Hurley had ever put in uniform. That was saying a lot, and "Smiling Dom," as he was often referred to by the Iron County Miner and Ironwood Daily Globe sports writers, must have blushed at such talk. He knew he was following in the footsteps of some superb players including the incomparable Ted Gentile and Len Calligaro, a 1939 graduate who was now starring for the Badgers at the University of Wisconsin. In basketball Don Dick had made his mark, and likewise many thought him to be the best player Hurley ever put on the hardwood. Along with Dom Moselle and Glenn Stenman the three sophomores were the core of the 1940 – 41 basketball team that finished third in the M-W conference and fashioned a record of 9 wins and 7 losses. A fourth sophomore, Ted Thomas, also saw significant playing time.

With Roy Melvin entering his 19th year at the helm, his players' belief in him had never been higher. In football the previous season Hurley came so very close to turning the tables on their arch rivals from across the river, scrapping with the Ironwood Red Devils to a 6 – 6 tie in Hurley. It was a game in which people on both sides thought the undersized Hurley boys outplayed the big Red Devil squad. Now at the beginning of the 1941 – 42 school year all the Midgets could think of was finishing the job and having the best season in the school's history.

As many thought they would, Hurley started the 1941 football season red hot. They took down two M-W foes to start, defeating Ashland 21 – 6 and shutting out Wakefield 25 – 0. With the boys playing fast and loose, the little team shocked their opponents with their speed, quickness, and Melvin's own version of the Wing T offense from which the Hurley team was unafraid to pass the ball. Not a lot of passing was done in those days and a team running a Wing T almost always ran the ball. The Midgets liked to pass, making it a double rarity. Park Falls became their third victim as they suffered a 31 – 6 loss to the surprising Midgets. It was official; they had special toughness like no other Hurley team had possessed before. They were going to need it, as their next opponent would outweigh them by an average of 40 pounds per man. That opponent was their personal boogeyman, the Ironwood Red Devils. Before the start of the season this 1941 version of the Red Devils was thought by the pundits to be the best team in the Red Devils' storied history.

The Ironwood Daily Globe sports page headline on Thursday, October 9, 1941 captured the anticipation of this matchup in big, bold letters. "Red Devils vs. Midgets Friday Night. 'Nuff said!" The article went on to say, "It'll be size and sheer power against a swift and tricky offense." The game was scheduled for Ironwood High School's Longyear Field, which was among the first in the Upper Peninsula of Michigan to have lights. By 1941 only Bessemer and Hurley still played their home games on Saturday afternoons using what light Mother Nature provided. The Red Devils seemed to have it all: size, power, tradition, and a lighted field to boot. They were determined to ensure Longyear Field would remain Hurley's personal pit of misery.

Despite Ironwood's two decades of football dominance, the consensus among students, fans and sports writers on both sides of the river seemed to be that this game, like last year's, was going to be a nail-biter. The two teams could not be more different in their style of play. Hurley's hopes were further buoyed by the fact that the powerful Red Devils were defeated earlier in the season by the Bessemer Speed Boys 7 – 6. Living up to their nickname, the Bessemer eleven used their speed and quickness to keep the massive Ironwood squad off balance during the entirety of that contest. People on The Range had a feeling that this year would be like no other in the history of the M-W Conference as these three teams began to distinguish themselves as dominant. Ironwood could ill afford to lose another conference game as two losses would not be good enough to be the champion. They were more motivated than ever to defeat Hurley. By doing so they could hope for one of the other teams, possibly Hurley, to knock off Bessemer and at least gain a share of the title.

Throughout the week leading up to the game, and especially on Friday, the atmosphere in the two towns was becoming super charged. Both schools had loud and spirited pep rallies with the bands and cheerleaders exhorting their peers to make more noise than ever before. People talked football in the dime stores, at the market, the butcher shops, barber shops and at work in the mines. Friday, October 10, 1941 was going to be memorable.

As the 7:30 PM kickoff approached fans began pouring into Longyear Field, filling the stands and then the roped off area on either side of the stands and behind the end zones. Hurley fans had become known as willing travelers over the past decade as they would go and cheer their teams on whether playing near or far. For this game many simply caught the trolley or walked across one of the two bridges connecting the towns. About half the fans present that night were from Hurley or the outlying area on the Wisconsin side. The place was packed with 3000 charged up fans who brought an electric, emotional intensity no one would ever forget.

During the pregame warm ups, Hurley fans looked on in anticipation as they noticed the most apparent discrepancy between the two teams. The Red Devils were as massive as advertised. Would Hurley's undersized linemen be able to block the Devils' behemoths well enough to create an opening for their speedy backs to get through? Would the big kids from Ironwood wear them down and score late to ruin another game for the underdog Midgets? Highlighting the size discrepancy was one of Hurley's starting lineman; Bill Secor weighed in at just 122 pounds. Some say for him to have weighed that much he had to have had rocks in his pockets. After watching their team buzz through the first three opponents on the schedule, they now were faced with the same reality every Hurley fan for the previous two decades understood; their neighbors once again fielded an imposing and intimidating team.

With history telling Hurley fans that things could go wrong in a hurry when taking on the Devils, Hurley kicked off. Ironwood could not move the ball for a first down and punted. With Dom Moselle plunging into the heart of the mighty Ironwood defensive line and using options, feints, misdirection plays, and pitches to super speedster Joe Tomasin and the little scat back, Bill Zell, the Midgets kept the Devils in a state of confusion. When Hurley quarterback Dick Guenther rushed for 13 yards to the Ironwood 22 yard line, he was hit out of bounds, which drew the yellow referees' flag. That gave Hurley a first down at the eleven yard line on the penalty. They pushed the ball to the 1 yard line. With everyone at Longyear Field expecting Hurley's strongman fullback Moselle to get the ball and crash into the huge Devil line one more time, Guenther instead faked it to Smiling Dom and pitched it to Tomasin who sped to the end zone untouched around the right side. The extra point attempt failed. Just like in 1940, Hurley took a quick 6 – 0 lead. The fans on the visitors' side of Longyear were delirious with joy.

Ironwood took the ensuing kickoff and again they could get nothing going against the swarming Hurley defense and had to punt. Tomasin fielded it at his 40 and raced 25 yards to the Ironwood 35 yard line and the Midget offense went back to work. Moselle lost five yards back to the 40 when he had to jump on his own fumble. Tomasin then bolted 18 yards on another pitch to the 22. Hurley managed to pick up another first down and then Guenther missed on a pass. Doing the unexpected once more, Guenther passed again and this time Zell made the twisting catch and crossed the goal line. Sensing the Ironwood team's frustration and confusion, Coach Melvin dug deeper into his bag of tricks faking the kick for the extra point and passing again. This time Tomasin made the reception all alone in the end zone for the point. Hurley 13, Ironwood 0! The visitors' side of the field was now a mad house of noise, hugs, and emotion. Scoring once on an Ironwood football team was rare for the Midgets. Scoring twice in one game was something that had not happened in 22 years. Scoring twice in one quarter on the Devils had never happened – ever!

In 1919 Hurley defeated Ironwood 13 – 6. Since then they never scored more than 7 points in any game versus the Devils attaining that score twice. They also scored six points in a game three times in the period. They were shutout in every other contest. The disputed 1920 game ended up in the books as a Hurley win by the score of 1 – 0 on the forfeit. Hurley did actually lead that game 6 – 0 when it was called. Ironwood was truly a nightmare for Hurley on the football field.

As the first quarter belonged to Hurley, so the second quarter belonged to Ironwood. After Hurley's next drive stalled at the Ironwood 27 yard line, the Devils methodically marched down the field as their big 243 pound fullback, Matt Ulasich, bludgeoned the small Hurley line into submission. From Hurley's eleven yard line, Ironwood pulled out a surprise of their own with quarterback Pavlovich connecting on a pass to Ulasich who made a superb catch on the high throw for the score. Ironwood converted the extra point and the lead was cut to 13 – 7.

In football, conventional wisdom dictates that bigger teams wear out smaller teams. It was certainly the case in 1940 as the unflappable Devils came from behind to tie the Midgets in Hurley. Now at the end of the first half of play in 1941 the Devils shoved Hurley around the field on their long sustained drive to the end zone. The Hurley team looked exhausted. They needed a spark in the worst way and would get it from a most unexpected source.

The Hurley band took the field at halftime as it was traditional in those days for each teams' band to have the opportunity to perform.

When a school has a marching band that receives accolades for their performance on the sports page after a game, you know they put on one heck of a show. Jim Rasmusen of the Ironwood Daily Globe heaped praise on the Band for their "pepped up" version of the song "Daddy." It seems the Midget musicians were swinging and strutting to the point the fans could not sit still. The energy the Hurley fans and players needed was thus provided by band leader Oscar Swee and his remarkable and energetic team of musicians. What a high octane power source they were. The fires were re-lighted.

Hurley received the opening kick-off of the second half with Bill Zell returning the ball 25 yards to the Hurley 32 yard line. The re-energized Midgets moved the ball deep into Ironwood territory reaching the Devils four yard line when a penalty and several ill-fated plays stalled the Midgets. Ironwood took over and began to march the other way. The third quarter ended with Ironwood 52 yards away from the Hurley end zone and once again moving the ball in their typical battering ram style. But they were to open the fourth quarter with a fourth down.

On the first play of the final quarter, Ironwood dropped into punt formation. The Hurley fans were breathing easier now as the drive was finished and they would get the ball back. Then the unthinkable happened. Instead of punting, big Matt Ulasich took off and pounded his way forward to the Hurley 46 yard line, gaining 6 yards and the first down. The size and strength of the Devils was again grinding Hurley into dust. The Ironwood faithful were now anticipating the inevitable score and victory. The Hurley cheerleaders, band, and fans rose and exhorted their little team to stand and fight. On first down Ironwood was thrown back for a 1 yard loss. The cheers from the Hurley side began to crescendo again even louder than before.

Ironwood attempted a pass but the small, agile, and speedy Hurley defensive front stormed the Ironwood wall and buried the quarterback for a 12 yard loss. Again the visitor's side of the field erupted in a cacophony of sound that bordered on insanity. It was now third down and 23 yards to go for a first down. Ironwood again attempted to pass. Under siege the Ironwood quarterback Pavlovich could not find an open receiver and his heave thudded harmlessly to the turf.

Now forced to punt and with the Hurley defense ready for a fake, the Devils kicked away. To the delight of the Hurley fans and the horror of the Ironwood sideline the kick covered all of 15 yards. Hurley had its long awaited break, twenty-one years in the making. This time they wouldn't crack.

Two decades of total and complete domination by their most bitter foe was not on their minds. This was not revenge. It was a desire to play the game and make the next play. These Hurley Midgets were different! They did not dwell on the negative and they were not afraid to lose. They only wanted to win. On first down Moselle slammed into the rugged Red Devil line for two yards. Then Zell darted for eight more. Hurley had a first down on the Ironwood 44 yard line. Coach Melvin called for the play Ironwood had the most trouble stopping throughout the game. With a quick snap the handoff went to lightning quick Joe Tomasin on a quick opener. Before the defense could even react to the snap he was through the hole for a 39 yard gain to the Ironwood 5 yard line. Moselle again pounded forward into the heart of the defense for two yards on the next play and then Zell took it to the end zone. Moselle kicked the extra point and Hurley led 20 – 7.

Sensing that their season was on the brink, Ironwood gamely fought back but their drive stalled. With the opportunity to put the game away, Hurley fumbled the ball and Ironwood was back in business. The Hurley fans were beside themselves. Their beloved boys could not give life to this Red Devil team yet again. So they rose up and instead of groaning they refused to give in to 21 years of tortured football history. They expended all their energy urging the Midgets to hold. On the next play Hurley intercepted the ball! The Midgets then dug deep, determined to end the game once and for all. They drove the ball to the Ironwood ten yard line as the final seconds ticked off the clock. And then it was over.

The scene was sheer bedlam as the fans rushed the field. The Ironwood Daily Globe wrote that the "Hurley players were in as much danger of getting hurt by the fans as they were during the contest." Roy Melvin was hoisted on the shoulders of the fans and paraded around the field.

Goal posts were almost always constructed of wood in those days. Ironwood did not lose often and even less often on their own field. That season, for the first time ever, they lost to both Bessemer and Hurley on their own turf. After the Bessemer game, the Speed Boys fans tore down the wooden posts on the south end of the field in celebration. It was not considered to be poor sportsmanship, but was often expected in fierce rivalry games. That was one reason they were rather flimsy to start with.

Ironwood then put in a steel goal post and sunk it into the ground with concrete. The following week they replaced the north end wooden post with another steel one, also sunk in concrete. The exuberant Hurley fans were not deterred by steel. Hell, they probably mined the ore that made it! They also had made big plans.

In a stroke of devious genius, an Iron County Highway Department truck, equipped with acetylene torches, was parked outside of

Longyear Field. The persistent fans worked for 20 minutes at their task. Finally down came the north end post. This goal post was going for a 1.6 mile ride. The fans carried it out of Longyear Field and down the street to Ironwood's main street, Aurora Street. Still on the shoulders of the fans, Roy Melvin and his assistant coach, Teddy Gentile, reluctantly went for the same ride. From there they and the post were carried straight into Hurley, up Silver Street, and on to the high school via Fourth Avenue. They were met there by the man most people in Hurley respected above all others, J.E. Murphy. The ecstatic crowd fell silent, expecting to be chastised by the stoic man. Instead the smiling Murphy said," I just want to go under the goal post like the Hurley players did tonight."

On Monday, thinking that all the fun that needed to be had, was indeed had, Principal Harold Conners called the Iron County Highway Commissioner to ask him to get his men to return the post to Ironwood. As it turned out, the Hurley fans had been cutting the post into souvenir pieces throughout the weekend and there was not enough of it left to put back. The folks in Ironwood understood and just replaced the post.

How important was the Hurley victory? Those who lived in Hurley in those days never, ever forgot it. For one sophomore on that Hurley team the memory was still as vivid in 2018 as it was in 1941. To Eino "Lefty" Martino, that win was the highlight of his high school career. The sheer and spontaneous release of joy it gave the players, the fans, and the town can't be understated. It validated the fact that the Hurley Midgets now belonged among the very best in Northern Wisconsin and the U.P. of Michigan. They were all aware of the long, uphill journey it had been. Eino would go on to play on championship teams in football and basketball, and be elected to the Hurley High

School Athletic Hall of Fame. He was elected to the Wisconsin Track Coaches Association Hall of Fame after 52 years as the track coach at Cornell High School in Wisconsin. To him nothing compared to ending Ironwood's 20 year reign of football terror over his beloved Hurley Midgets.

Riding the intoxicating effects of their biggest win in history, the boys from Hurley were primed to continue their winning ways against the Bessemer Speed Boys at Massie field in Bessemer. On Saturday, October 18, 1941 the two undefeated teams collided. Hurley received the opening kick-off and fumbled the ball away to the Speed Boys. The Bessemer squad lived up to their name and scored on the next play from 20 yards out. The two teams battled to a standstill the rest of the way and the game ended 7 – 0 in favor of the Speed Boys.

Hurley rebounded by winning their remaining games of the season, crushing two Wisconsin teams, the Phillips Loggers 32 – 0, and the Washburn Castle Guards 53 – 0. They completed the greatest football season Hurley had ever known to that point with a sterling record of six wins and one loss. The lightning quick squad produced on both offense and defense. In seven games, they outscored their opponents 172 – 26 including four defensive shutouts. They came so very close to their first conference championship. Only one of the finest Bessemer teams in their own storied history blocked that feat as the Speed Boys completed an undefeated season and were declared as the best team in Michigan's Upper Peninsula. Despite all the accomplishments of the 1941 Midget team, it seemed as if the only thing anyone wanted to talk about was that the "streak" was over. With that monkey off their backs, came a new confidence. A new day was dawning for Hurley Athletics.

CHAPTER TWELVE

A Basketball Happy Town
Catches Basketball Fever!

On The Range Roy Melvin was considered to be an outstanding basketball coach. His teams were typically undersized but tough as nails. The Ironwood Daily Globe had this to say in the December 4, 1937 sports page, "Any basketball team that plays the Hurley Midgets is assured of a hard battle......Last night the Ironwood Red Devils got more than a battle, they got a 17 – 13 drubbing at the hands of Coach Roy Melvin's alert little cagers." Year after year he always seemed to get the most out of his boys. His overall record from 1923 – 1940 was 145 wins and 145 losses. In four of those seasons they won ten or more games including a 14 – 5 record in the 1935 – 1936 season. Hurley's best basketball season ever to that date had its stellar season ended by Superior East in the Rice Lake Regional on March 21, 1936 by a score of 22 – 19. Especially painful was that the Midgets held the lead 16 – 14 at the end of the third quarter. The loss put Superior East into the 16 team State Tournament in Wisconsin Rapids while the Hurley squad went home.

As the Hurley football players turned in their uniforms following their stellar 1941 season, Coach Melvin was doing double duty by handing out uniforms and gear to his basketball players. Many on the team played football that fall. One who did not was junior Don Dick. He played basketball. Period! And what a player he was! He was a smooth shooter and strong rebounder finishing second in shooting during the M-W Conference the year before. No one kept rebounding records back then, but a search of the Ironwood Daily Globe reveals that the Hurley boy also controlled the boards in most games. But he was actually a triple threat as he typically guarded the opponents' best scorer or their biggest player. Add in his versatility (he could play center, guard and forward) and it is easy to see why he was already thought to be the best basketball player Hurley ever had.

Dom Moselle, the fearless football fullback, Glen Stenman, and Ted Thomas, all juniors became starters for the Hurley five. Dick Guenther, the football quarterback, transferred from Crystal Falls, Michigan. There he was a stellar player, helping lead that team to the Michigan Upper Peninsula Class "C" Title the previous year. He was the only senior starter. Joe Tomasin, Bill Zell, Tooci, Bill Kirby and Don Trembath rounded out the reserves. Hurley did not have a noticeably big team, but for one of the few times since 1923, they did not have a small team either.

The game had changed over the years, especially in the mid to late 1930's. With the center jump after each score eliminated, the pace picked up. As teams adjusted to the new rules it became clear that a player being disqualified after just three fouls was no longer a good idea. The pace of the game had increased and players had to run the floor like never before. Now players would not foul out of a game until they were whistled for a fourth foul. These changes brought about a new wave of strategies employed by coaches. With the increased pace some saw advantages to "slowing" the game down. They insisted their team pass the ball for long periods of time before shooting, thus taking a quick, fast opponent out of rhythm. Watching video from those times of teams who employed that style, you can see the endless weaving and screens that kept the ball moving. They froze the ball, but it was only a well disciplined team that could make it happen. Other coaches with faster teams tried to push the offensive pace of the game to wear out the opponents and seize a quick and large lead. Many games became a test of wills as the coaching philosophies collided head on. Scoring increased in most contests, but when two "slow down' teams played the scores could be even lower than before the rule changes.

Another change that was slow to come was the way players shot the ball. In an age where so many gyms had low ceilings, players took "set shots" keeping both feet planted on the floor and shooting the ball on a low trajectory. Often these shots were taken with two hands as the shooter would try to "bank" the ball off the backboard into the hoop. As older schools with tiny gyms began to replace them with state of the art facilities built with basketball in mind, the set shot began to fade away and be replaced by the jump shot. With a higher ceiling players could put more arch and also more spin on a shot which allowed for truer bounces. In the early 1950's the jump shot became the norm. The set shot remained a part of the game finally fading into oblivion in the 1960's. The closest thing to a set shot today now is when a player shoots a free throw.

Hurley fans had a history of supporting their teams both at home games and on the road. The small gym that was constructed as part of the new high school in 1917 was easily packed. It could not hold everyone who wished to see a game, especially if that game was against another M-W team. With the expectations for the 1941 – 42 edition of Midget basketball running sky high it was apparent that a larger venue was in order. Hurley would make do for one more season before unveiling their new state of the art gymnasium in time for the 1942 – 1943 school year. There would be one more year of playing in the jam packed crackerjack box, and with a superb team the tight confines would bring out the "fanatic" in those fans. Excitement for basketball was now equal to that for football among the citizenry.

On November 11, 1941 Hurley traveled 13 miles west to play their Iron County brethren, the Saxon Knights. Saxon was a tiny town and as such played what was referred to as "district" basketball. Hurley was considered by people to be a small school, and it was, but tiny Saxon was exponentially smaller. Both teams scheduled this season-opening, non-conference game, as coaches often do, to see where their teams were in regard to talent and skill. Saxon was usually the best of the three Iron County high schools that played "district" ball, having good success versus Mercer and Iron Belt, schools equal in size to them. The boys from Saxon had a habit of playing good ball, but this year they were no match for Hurley.

With Don Dick scoring 17 points in just two quarters Hurley dominated the Knights and won easily 38 – 8. Roy Melvin knew that despite the score, he needed to work on a few things to get his team running smoothly. He would have 15 days to prepare for the next opponent who would be bigger and equally fast as his boys. That opponent would be the Ironwood Red Devils, and they had revenge on their minds! On November 27, 1941, Hurley returned to Ironwood's Luther L. Wright High School, this time to play indoors. Ironwood opened the game playing tough defense and the first period ended tied at 5 - 5. The Midgets got untracked in the second stanza and opened a 13 – 7 halftime lead. They continued to play stellar defense in the second half as Don Dick showed he "had a knack for smothering the ball on defense" and was cited for his clever passes as well. The game ended with Hurley winning in convincing fashion 29 – 16. As Dick, Guenther, and Stenman enjoyed solid games in the scoring column, Dom Moselle, the second leading scorer for the team the previous season ended the game without a point for the second straight game of the season. This concerned the Ironwood Daily Globe sports writer only in that he wrote that once the strong football fullback overcame the aches and pains of the football season, he would be another hard man to stop for the Hurley five. As a sign that they were no longer anyone's underdog, the Globes' opening sentence in the write up started out with, "The Hurley Midgets lived up to expectations last night….." It had been a long time in the making, but now as December 1941 approached, this team and these athletes were expected to win and to win often.

The first day of December found the Ashland Purgolders hosting Hurley. Ashland's Dodd Gymnasium was the envy of every school in the area. It was spacious, well lit, and beautiful. It was also the model used by the people of Hurley when planning their new gym. It held about 2000 fans and the fans packed this modern marvel to the rafters in anticipation of beating their Wisconsin rival from the east.

Once again Don Dick displayed his skills in scoring 10 points, controlling the boards, playing sticky defense, and rallying his cohorts. Hurley won 26 – 22 to spoil the Purgolders night. Ashland rallied late after being behind 24 – 14. Dom Moselle broke into the scoring column with five points and Bill Zell provided a big spark for the Midgets coming off the bench for 4 points.

The game illustrated another one of the changes taking shape in high school basketball at the time. With their new gym the Purgolders sported the new, state of the art backboards. They were not rectangular or square as found in most gyms. Instead they were shaped like a fan and painted white to give players a good view of the orange hoop. The new design had much less surface space than the old design did. The rounded and smooth corners were designed to help cut down on injuries that occurred when a player, trying to block a shot underneath the basket would hit their hand on the corner of the old backboards. Hurley seemed bothered by this new design, missing several open shots that would have blown the game wide open. Eventually they, along with everyone else, would get used to the new design. Within a few years every gym would have it.

On Friday, December 5, Hurley made the trip to Wakefield. They were heavy favorites to defeat the Cardinals and stay undefeated. While Roy Melvin was not exactly turning his basketball team into a track team, they still played a much more up-tempo game than the Cardinals, who were a very methodical and deliberate team on offense. In other words, on offense they played "keep away" from their opponents and they did it well. This was going to be a classic test of old style basketball versus the new.

Under Coach Fred Trewyn's shrewd direction, the Wakefield five ganged up on Don Dick, denying him the ball and causing many errant passes. When on offense they were deliberate as they hung on to the ball until they got the shot they wanted. They did not want many. Frustrated by the excruciatingly slow pace, and the inability to get Dick the ball, the Hurley boys played "ragged, listless ball most of the way". The frustration was especially felt by Dom Moselle as for the third time in four games, he was held scoreless. Wakefield led at the half 7 – 5! They had the Midgets playing their game. Late in the game, leading 20 – 13, the Cards finally cracked and Hurley scored 6 straight points. Armand Cirilli, writer for the Montreal River Miner wrote, "But for the exception of the closing moments when Hurley came out of the 'trance' the game was as dull as an octogenarian chess game." Hurley fouled with ten seconds left and the Wakefield fans watched as their team stalled away the final seconds to upset the favored Hurley team. Hurley's fast start to the season was slowed to a grinding halt in Wakefield. The Cardinals were now in first place in the M-W conference. Melvin's boys would not be thinking of the loss for long as the most cataclysmic event of the century was coming to America's doorstep.

CHAPTER THIRTEEN

A Stunned And Angry Nation Rolls Up Its Sleeves

In 1941 Sundays were truly a day of rest for most Americans. Stores were closed, workers had the day off, and a Sunday drive was the favorite pastime for many. Sunday dinner was a big event, and for most the dinner came in the early to mid afternoon. Television was in its infancy, unreliable, and not commercially available, so when families and friends gathered they provided their own entertainment. People played cards, games, and made music and sang. Some just chewed the fat, relishing conversations with those around them.

1941 was also in the middle of the golden age of radio, and by now most families owned one. The radio was displayed in a prominent place in the home. Families and friends would gather around to listen to their favorite shows. Radio producers were resourceful and downright ingenious as they captured the imaginations of their listeners with stories of detectives, cowboys, star crossed lovers and all of Hollywood's other genres, which had been produced in the movies. The sounds of storms, creaking doors, farm animals, bells, cars, trains, planes, paper being ripped apart, and a host of others filled the airways during these productions. Variety shows featuring contemporary musicians and comedians were wildly popular. Americans loved radio.

On Sunday, December 7, 1941, people all across the nation were enjoying their day of rest. In Hurley as well as across the Range, people were in church, coming home from church, preparing Sunday dinner, relaxing with families and listening to the radio. It was a scene played out on farms, in towns, and cities in all 48 states. At 11:48 AM local time on the range, 353 planes launched from six aircraft carriers of the Japanese Imperial Fleet swept down on the United States Pacific Fleet in Pearl Harbor, Hawaii.

A series of miscalculations, miscommunications, and the refusal to believe that any one nation would launch an attack on another nation without first formally declaring war led to the Japanese achieving total surprise. The Army Air Corps Base at Hickam Air Field was hit at the same time as the Pacific Fleet, losing 188 aircraft on the ground and leaving the Hawaiian Islands without air support. By the time the second wave of attackers turned back to their carriers, eight of the Navy's battleships were hit. Four were sunk into the mud at the bottom of the shallow harbor while four others were so severely damaged it would be nearly two years before they would be back in action. Three cruisers, three destroyers, and several auxiliary vessels were also damaged and out of action. Most appalling and devastating was the death toll. 2,403 sailors, marines, soldiers and airmen were dead and another 1,100 were wounded. The bulk of the Pacific Fleet's firepower was gone. The only good news to come out of the attack was that the three aircraft carriers were not at Pearl Harbor that fateful day. For the next six months they were all that stood between the rampaging Japanese military and total capitulation. It is shocking to historians that the Japanese did not launch a third wave of attacks which would have destroyed the huge fuel depot and the machine and repair shops at Pearl Harbor. Had they done so it is doubtful that what was left of the fleet could have been sustained. They would have had to withdraw to the West Coast, a move that would have been a disaster, either extending the war by years, or with the U.S. having to accept a peace treaty which would have left

Japan in control of the Hawaiian Islands and the ability to control all of Asia and Australia. A completely unprepared America was at war. History would prove it was a war that was closer to being lost than most people ever thought possible.

Within an hour after the start of the attack, people in America were beginning to hear the news. They were stunned, shocked, confused, and afraid. In short order all those feelings would turn to outrage. Now they would unite as the nation had never united before. At the time of the attack America was bitterly divided on whether or not the country should be involved in another foreign war. Germany, Italy and their allies had been waging war in Europe since the Germans invaded Poland in September of 1939. Europe was now under the heel of the Nazis with only Britain holding out. In Asia, Japan invaded the Manchurian region of China in 1933, and then moved on to Korea and then China proper. As the sad, gut wrenching pictures and stories made their way to American news outlets, the nation was torn between isolationists and those who wanted to intervene. It was a giant rift, but in the space of just a few hours it was gone.

The debate on whether or not America should declare war on Germany (in addition to Japan) ended on December 12, 1941 as Adolph Hitler declared war on the United States in a long winded speech at the Reichstag in Berlin. America was now in a two front war with nations who had massive and well-equipped militaries. In order to catch up, America needed to mobilize men and build a fighting force. It also needed to produce steel, steel, and more steel. That was going to require more iron ore. Almost all of it would come from the Minnesota Iron Range and the Gogebic Range of the Western Upper Peninsula of Michigan and the northeast corner of Wisconsin.

Hurley became a hotbed of iron ore production. The previously busy railroad tracks just north of Silver Street began to see the ore trains run without ceasing. More miners were hired and more miners worked overtime and on weekends. Although the life blood of the Range was iron ore production and people were back to work and unemployment was nonexistent, the constant stress of the war and the uncertainty of the outcome took a toll on people. The reality that beloved family members were in the service and apt to be in harm's way compelled people to do more. As more and more of Hurley's young men (and often young women) entered the service, community members worked even harder. This was very personal indeed!

CHAPTER FOURTEEN

Keep Calm And Carry On!

When Britain went to war against Germany in 1939, the government printed posters by the tens of thousands with the simple phrase "Keep Calm and Carry On." As the war took one bad turn after another and Germany began bombing British cities, the citizenry there did indeed carry on in the face of tragedy and overwhelming odds. As strange as it sounds, the British leadership under Winston Churchill understood that doing the simple and familiar things that made up British life before the war would contribute to higher morale in the populace. They sought normalcy at a time when many thought nothing could be normal. It was a good idea and it worked!

At the onset of America's reluctant entry into the war, President Franklin D. Roosevelt was determined to maintain the morale of the American people. He refused to allow for the cancellation of popular radio shows, concerts, plays, shows, and sporting events. He deemed such things as critical to maintain the health of the war effort. Instead he used such events to further the war effort as War Bonds were sold and patriotism was displayed. The NFL and college football completed their seasons. At the high school level, it was the same. Changes in the way seasons were conducted due to transportation restrictions were to come, but the shows and the games would go on. On the Range this meant that they would continue to pack the football stands and gyms to watch their beloved teams play.

With the ever present reality of war lurking in the background, the nation did all it could to return to life as usual. With only a few exceptions, on the home front the show did in fact go on. People continued to attend church, movies, plays, shows, and sporting events. They not only attended, but they did so in even greater numbers. In uncertain times people like to be around other people. There is comfort in doing so.

So when Hurley resumed their season with their first home game of the year on December 12, 1941, the tiny gym was packed with fans. The Phillips Loggers were the opponents. Those worried about how the boys would react to their first loss of the season didn't need to concern themselves. Jumping on the Loggers early and scoring often, the team built a comfortable 31 – 8 halftime lead and coasted to a 52 – 23 win. Five days later they defeated Glidden 52 – 28 to end the 1941 portion of the season with a record of 5 – 1. After a three-week layoff for the holidays, the Midgets resumed action versus the Washburn Castle Guards. Again it was no contest as they ran off a 55 – 12 victory. The easy part of the schedule was done. It was now time to prepare for the M-W Conference-leading Wakefield Cardinals, who were bringing their grinding, slow paced game to the Hurley gym.

Playing on Hurley's home court did not phase the Cardinals one iota. They stuck doggedly to their game plan, frustrating the Hurley squad with their keep away tactics. Defensively they again dogged the Midgets, contesting every pass and every shot. At the end of the first quarter they led by the paltry score of 3 – 1. Finally the Midgets decided that if you can't beat them, join them. With Don Dick leading the charge, they caught fire on the defensive side of the ball. Now it was the Wakefield boys feeling the pressure defense that they were so willing to dish out. The Cardinals could not buy a basket except from the free throw line. Hurley took a 9 – 7 halftime lead and continued their determined defensive play into the second half. The Cards could manage to get only four shots to fall from the field the entire game, one of them as time expired. They did rack up 9 free throws. Hurley, led by Dick's defense and senior Bill Kirby's inspired play off the bench, ground out a tough, hard fought 24 – 17 win. Hurley now was 7 – 1 for the season, their best start ever. With the loss Wakefield dropped into a tie for second place with Hurley in the M-W Conference. Hurley would take on Bessemer in their next conference bout, but first they had another match with Glidden. The result was another lopsided win over the Glidden five, 55 – 17.

With basketball fever on the Range ratcheted up a few more notches than usual, Hurley traveled to Bessemer on the evening of Friday, January 30th. With Ironwood making the trip to Wakefield, the conference standings could be in for some changes. It was Ironwood, finally playing some consistent ball, who handed the scrappy Cards their third straight defeat by a score of 29 - 20. Those two teams were now tied for third place, smack dab in the middle of the conference standings. In Bessemer the Midgets and Speed Boys were locked in a classic struggle for superiority. Bessemer led 12 – 10 after one period. Hurley, clamping down on defense, evened the score at 18 – 18 at halftime. Both teams continuously worked the ball low for shots in the lane and along the baseline. At the end of three periods the score remained tied at 26 all. It was then that the Hurley Five found the offense that enabled them to crush their Wisconsin opponents. Don Dick exploded, finishing the game with 23 points. Seniors Joe Tomasin and Dick Guenther hit for 8 and 7 respectively. When the dust settled, Hurley outscored Bessemer 17 – 6 in the final stanza for a convincing 43 – 32 win. The loss dropped the Speed Boys to 3 – 1 in the conference and they now trailed Hurley who sat atop the league with a record of 4 – 1. Hurley's faithful fans began drooling as their beloved team was cooking up their first ever conference championship.

CHAPTER FIFTEEN

The M-W Conference:
A Tough Neighborhood to Play In

The Range teams of Wakefield, Bessemer, Ironwood, Hurley and Ashland had been playing each other since the beginning of the century in high school sports. Starting around 1920 the outcomes of those games were beginning to be reported by the area newspapers, at least in football. Basketball was just starting to catch on. Overall records were tracked closely, but there was no official championship to be had. When a season ended, people would agree or disagree on which school boasted the best team. There was a lot of bragging, arguing, and disagreement, but no trophy and no officially recognized championship team. That all changed in 1937.

The schools, their administrators, and their coaches agreed to form a conference. In deference to the geography the new conference would be called the Michigan - Wisconsin Conference. The Wisconsin Interscholastic Athletic Association (WIAA) and the Michigan High School Athletic Association (MHSAA) had no objections to a cross state league. It seems as though in those days they were more concerned about students having the opportunity to play, more so than dictating which side of the border their opponents should be from.

This new conference made perfect sense. Geographically the schools were close to one another. They were all very competitive and growing more so by the year. They would have to travel long distances to play other schools that were their size or larger, saddling the schools with expenses other schools in other conferences would not have. And finally those other schools of approximate size did not want to travel those long distances either. The M-W schools were in fact quite isolated when considering the long bus trips on two lane highways and roads. Still the roads were constantly improving, and competition from farther away did come, but it would not be a big factor in scheduling until after World War II.

In the next 36 years of its existence, the M-W would be regarded as a tough affiliation of teams. In 1960 Northwestern of Maple came into the conference and remained until the conference disbanded in 1973. In 1961 Superior East entered and the conference had 7 members. At the end of the 1964 - 1965 school year Superior East and Superior Central combined into Superior Senior High School. With Superior East now defunct, Superior Cathedral joined the Loop. After winning the M-W crown in basketball in 1969 and boasting one of the top ranked teams in the state of Wisconsin, they dropped out of the conference as their high school also closed its doors. Their students enrolled at the mega-school, Superior Senior High.

While the M-W Conference had a long and storied history, there can be no doubt that its reputation was forged in the 1940's. During that time, they would distinguish themselves as one of the premier basketball conferences in two states. In any given game any conference school proved capable of defeating any other regardless of records. The quest for dominance was fraught with the possibility of being trampled by what was thought to be an inferior team. There was no rest; there were no breaks, no easy wins, or one second of time off when playing a conference foe. As a result by the mid-1940's the Range schools were scheduling the toughest non-conference opponents they could find to help them prepare mentally and physically for the conference grind. The M-W Conference teams could count on entering their state regional playoffs with the experience of playing some of the toughest schedules of any teams in their states.

CHAPTER SIXTEEN

The M-W Conference:
A Tough Neighborhood To Win In

On the morning of Saturday, January 31, 1941, the Hurley Midgets found themselves alone at the top of the Michigan – Wisconsin Conference Basketball Standings with a record of 4 – 1. They had been playing stellar ball on offense and defense. With their five straight victories over Wisconsin opponents, they had won 9 of their first 10 games.

Hurley's next game was for fun and did not count towards their record. On Thursday, February 5, they played an exhibition game versus their alumni to benefit the National Foundation for Infantile Paralysis. The proceeds went to pay for an iron lung for the Foundation. The game became known locally as "The Iron Lung Game." Both Roy Melvin and J.E. Murphy were involved in the committee to set up the game. Several other civic minded people shared in the spotlight as the proceeds were turned over to the Iron County chapter of the foundation. This was the only game the Midgets would play between January 30 and February 10 when they again defeated the outgunned Saxon Knights 40 – 15.

Hurley felt as if they had a score to settle with Bessemer. The heartbreaking 7- 0 loss to the Speed Boys in football cost the Midgets their first ever Conference championship and an undefeated season. Instead the Bessemer boys ruled the league and the entire Upper Peninsula of Michigan with their undefeated football team. The Speed Boys were now looking to accomplish the amazing feat of winning the conference championship in both sports. To do so they had to defeat Hurley on their home court and avenge the 11 point loss they suffered two weeks earlier in Bessemer.

This Bessemer team had lost twice to Iron River, Michigan and their superb 6' 6" center, Edward Zyskowski, who torched Bessemer for 50 points in the two games. If it were any consolation to the Speed Boys, Iron River also blew out Ironwood 50 – 36 with, "Zys" scoring 18 points. The Big Man was having his way with every team on Iron River's schedule. It would take the Wakefield Cardinals to reclaim the honor of the M-W and defeat Iron River. Playing their methodical "grind it out" game, the Cards did what nobody had ever done before or after; they held Edward Zyskowski without a point in their 26 – 23 victory! Probably the most stunning win by an M-W team versus a non-conference opponent that season was Ironwood's 30 – 24 win versus Crystal Falls, Michigan and their legendary coach, Eddie Chambers. Crystal Falls was in the middle of winning six straight Michigan Upper Peninsula Tournament Class C Championships from 1938 – 1944. In 1943 there was no tournament in Michigan as they opted to play only local regional championships due to World War II gas rationing and the difficulty of travel.

With Hurley trying to win a conference title for the first time in any sport, and Bessemer itching to prove that their four losses were an aberration, the two teams collided in Hurley. Bessemer's well rounded team was led by big Bill Lucas, their high scoring center. Everyone on the Range was buzzing about him and Don Dick going head-to-head in the pivot. Both teams had speed and quickness. Both played strong defense and both had players, besides their centers, who could score. Conventional wisdom held that Hurley with the home court advantage was favored to win and all but sew up the title. In the M-W

Conference nothing was conventional, especially in this topsy-turvy season. The Speed Boys, losers of two straight conference games, had their backs to the wall. Hurley, riding the crest of a seven game winning streak, was poised to get the job done.

The game started fast with Bessemer jumping ahead 11 – 5 after one quarter. Hurley battled back and closed the lead to 20 – 17 at the half. The game was decided in the third quarter. Lucas exploded, tossing in hook shots from every angle, despite being closely guarded by Dick. As Dick had dominated in the first meeting between the teams, Bill Lucas now dominated this rematch. The Speed Boys outscored the Midgets 13 – 5 in the period to take a 33 – 22 lead en route to a 39 – 28 win. The two teams were now tied atop the conference standings with records of 4 – 2. Ironwood and Wakefield were right behind at 4-3. Ashland remained winless at 0 – 6 despite several close games.

Hurley had two games left on the conference schedule. Next up was Ironwood followed by Ashland, teams they defeated earlier in the year. Bessemer had to play the ever tough Wakefield Cardinals and Ashland. Both Bessemer and Hurley figured to beat the downtrodden Purgolders. Hurley knew Ironwood wanted revenge and Bessemer knew they had their hands full with Wakefield.

As always seemed the case, Ironwood was standing in Hurley's path. The Red Devils never went away. Even in this, their inconsistent season, they caught fire at the end and were now a formidable foe. Oddly, if the Red Devils could beat Hurley and Wakefield could upend Bessemer, there could be a four way tie for the conference title, providing that Ashland would cooperate and lose to Hurley and Bessemer. That four of the five teams had a chance claim a piece of the championship with one week to go only proved that the M-W was indeed one tough basketball league.

On Wednesday night, February 18, The Devils made the short trip to the Hurley gym. They had indeed improved since that early season loss to the Midgets in Ironwood. Hurley jumped out to an early lead and finished the first quarter with an 11 – 6 lead. Ironwood was not fazed and closed the gap to 17 – 16 at the half. The second half was nothing but a titanic struggle as each team clamped down defensively. The game became a pressure cooker and both teams felt it with both only able to score four points each in the third quarter. Hurley's little gym was crowded to the rafters and hot as the Amazon rainforest. The fourth quarter was more of the same. Hurley's defense continued to smother the Red Devils' offense. For the game Ironwood could hit only 9 shots from the field. Giving what Hurley gave them, they dropped in 10 of 11 free throws in regulation time to tie the Midgets at 28 – 28 at the end of the fourth quarter. When Dick Guenther left the game after fouling out with his fourth transgression, the Hurley attack became disorganized. The senior guard's poise and confidence was sorely missed. In the overtime period neither team could score until Doug Langdon of Ironwood tossed in the Devils' eleventh free throw of the game with 26 seconds remaining. That was the difference. The Devils hit 11 of 12 free throws while Hurley could mange on 4 of 7 charity shots. Once again the Red Devils thwarted the Midgets and spoiled their bid for their first conference championship. Now it would take Wakefield to upend Bessemer on Friday night and force a four way tie for the title.

Wakefield, in their typical fashion, slowed the game with the Speed Boys to a crawl. It was the Cards leading at the half by the pedestrian score of 11 – 10. In the third and decisive quarter, Bessemer showed it was having none of the drama of a tie for the conference championship. One can only imagine the scene in the Speed Boy locker room at half time. The first year coach, Al Butherus, was about to be inducted into the Army and was leaving for Tulsa, Oklahoma right after the game for training. Inspired to send their mentor off with a win, the Speed Boys shifted into high gear and motored to a 25 – 16 lead at the third quarter mark. They then held off the pesky Wakefield Five for the 32 – 24 win. That same night Hurley got back on the winning track after suffering two consecutive gut-wrenching defeats to their Michigan rivals by beating Park Falls 48 – 28 in a non conference match. Only a miracle could help Ironwood and Hurley gain a piece of the conference title now. Ashland had to pull off an upset of epic proportions against the Speed Boys. With the Purgolders mired in a season-long basketball funk, the Speed Boys dispatched them 48 – 32 to clinch the M – W title with a record of 6 – 2.. Ashland then yielded to the Midgets in the last regular season game 30 – 21.

The Midgets completed the regular season with an overall record of 12 – 3 and were 5 – 3 in the conference, good for a second place tie with Ironwood. Wakefield's late season fade left them in fourth place at 4 – 4 and the hapless Ashland Five could not muster a single win in conference play going 0 – 8. The shining moment to their season was two upset wins over the big school Superior Central Vikings. It was a rough year for the Purgolders. Although no one knew it yet, the town on the Chequamegon Bay was about to see a sudden reversal in its fortunes beginning in the next year.

CHAPTER SEVENTEEN

The Tournament: Where Dreams Go to Die

In high school basketball the end to the regular season is the beginning of tournament time. A fresh start was awaiting every team. All across the country, every high school basketball player begins to dream about the ultimate in their sport; a state championship. Every kid with a basketball hoop in their yard, hanging on the garage or barn, or playing in a school yard has imagined hitting the shot that wins the tournament and brings their school and their town a championship.

The Wisconsin State Basketball tournament began in 1916 with Fond du Lac defeating Wisconsin Rapids 22-7. Lawrence College hosted the tournament that year and through 1920 when it was moved to the University of Wisconsin Field House in Madison. It has been held there every year since except for 1936, when it was conducted in Wisconsin Rapids. In 1998 the Kohl Center became the venue as the old field house was replaced. In the beginning there was only one class and one championship, and all schools competed for it, regardless of size. In 1934 the tournament had two classes. In 1936 it became three classes until 1940 when it reverted back to a single class tournament. It remained a one class tournament until 1972. The number of teams qualifying for the State Tournament in Madison has changed several times. There have been 4, 8, and 16 teams at the tournament when it was a single class. In 1934 and 1935 there were 8 Class A teams and 16 Class B teams competing for the two championships making it in those two years, the most crowded tournaments of all.

In 1942 16 teams would qualify to play in Madison. Hurley was placed in the Superior Regional Tournament, one of 16 regional tournaments in the state. The winners would all advance to play in the state tournament. Hurley was bringing a record of 12 Wins and 3 losses to the four day basketball extravaganza. Ashland won only four games in the year, but two of them were against Superior Central. Other teams included Park Falls, Phillips, Superior Central, and the favorite, Superior East. Prentice and Drummond, winners of their Class C district meets, qualified to round out the slate.

Play opened up on March 4 with Superior East upping its perfect record to 15 – 0 as they easily handled the Ashland Purgolders 40 – 12. Superior Central had a rough time with the Drummond Fire Brigade before subduing the tough little school 26 – 19. On March 5 Phillips shocked favored Park Falls 23 – 15 in the first upset in the regional schedule. Hurley, as expected, had an easy time with Prentice as 9 of the 10 Midgets scored on the way to a 42 – 16 route. Ashland won in the consolation round as they defeated Drummond 28 – 20. With the first round of games completed, Superior East looked like the cream of the crop with Hurley looking like the team they would play for the region Championship.

Hurley had no trouble defeating the Phillips Loggers 44 – 20 in the semi finals. The Midgets cruised throughout the game and were never threatened. The game between the two Superior teams was a different story. Superior East had made the trip to Madison the previous year and reached the final four of the sixteen team state tournament. Standing undefeated on the current season and winning games handily all year, they were easily thought to be the best of the northern schools and were highly regarded throughout the entire state. Superior Central had an up and down year, losing twice to

East, and surprisingly, twice to Ashland. It seemed to basketball fans throughout the area that East was destined to make a return trip to Madison. Coach Harry Conley of Central had other plans. Coach Conley had won two state titles in 1935 and 1936 and took third place in 1937. He was itching to get back to the big dance. Strangely, in both '35 and '36, Superior East also played as one of the eight teams in the Class A State Tournament in Madison, an anomaly of the scheduling of the regional tournaments in those years. History was on the side of the Superior teams who were clearly the cream of the crop in Northern Wisconsin basketball.

To negate their arch rival's height, speed, rebounding, and defensive advantages, Central took a page from the Wakefield Cardinals and slowed the game to a snail's pace. They were patient, methodical, and stubborn. They were also victorious as they defeated East 24 – 21. On that team was a rangy freshman forward by the name of Harry Peter "Bud" Grant. The kid could play. Grant would go on to graduate from Superior Central in 1945. After serving in the Navy, Grant went on to star at the University of Minnesota in football, basketball, and baseball. In 1950 he was selected as the 14th overall pick in the NFL draft by the Philadelphia Eagles. He was also selected in the 4th round of the NBA draft by the Minneapolis Lakers. He signed with the Lakers and played for them for two years before turning to the Eagles and the NFL. After playing in the NFL and the Canadian Football League he would coach in the CFL and then become the most successful coach in the history of the Minnesota Vikings leading them to four Super Bowl appearances. He thus ended his athletic career as he started it, as a Viking. He and his Superior Central Vikings basketball team were now set to take on Hurley and their future NFL player.

The chances of two basketball teams meeting in a tournament game for the right to go to the State tournament each having a future NFL football player on their roster must be pretty small. On Saturday, March 7, 1942 that was the scenario in the Superior State Teachers College gym. Hurley's "Smiling" Dom Moselle would play for the Cleveland Browns, the Green Bay Packers, the Philadelphia Eagles, and also in the CFL. After serving in the Army during World War II, he played football at Superior State Teachers College where he set the school's career rushing record and records for most touchdowns in a season and a career. He later earned his Master's Degree in Education and taught for three years at Wabash College before moving back to Superior State (now University of Wisconsin – Superior), where he was a teacher and a coach until he retired in 1986.

Hurley took the early lead in the game at 7 – 6 after one period. At the halftime it was 14 – 13 in favor of Central. It was then that the Midgets, led by the cool ball handling, scoring and passing of Dick Guenther and Don Dick's scoring and rebounding, that the Hurley boys forged a lead of 24 – 17. The Midgets were in complete control now and they looked to knock out the Vikings and earn their first trip to the State Tournament. It was early in the fourth quarter that disaster struck the Midgets yet again. Dick Guenther picked up his fourth foul and was banished to the bench. Guenther had always been unfazed by pressure. Hurley had lost their best and coolest ball handler. They then lost their composure. Central rallied with their methodical passing game and harassed the Midget backcourt into turnovers. Central shot into the lead at 31 – 27 with two minutes left in the game. Bill Kirby gave Hurley life as he drilled a long range shot to cut the lead to two points. Central held the ball until Bud Grant, the unflappable freshman, fired one in from the corner giving the Vikings the lead at 33 – 29. The Midgets were out of miracles and Central pulled one off earning the right to play in Madison. The final score stood at 33 – 29. Once again the Hurley Midgets were runner ups. Once again the wheels fell off the cart at just the perfect time for someone else to best them.

Superior Central would go on to win their first two games of the State Tournament reaching the final four. They lost to Marinette in the semi-finals but ended up as one of the top four teams in Wisconsin. Hurley had completed their most successful season in history finishing with a record of 14 wins and just 4 losses. They had much to be proud of, and the town was beaming with pride. Still, they were left to wonder what might have been. If only dreams did come true! If only...

CHAPTER EIGHTEEN

The End Of An Era

As spring arrived in Hurley in 1942, Roy Melvin began working his track athletes. Most boys who played ball started practicing with the many town teams. Montreal, Cary, Gile, Upson, Kimball, Saxon, Mercer, Hurley, and all the other hamlets and towns on The Range seemed to have a team. No sport in the area or in the country had more participants. America was baseball happy. There was nothing different about the summer of 1942 if you were a kid. The adults worried and fretted about The War, but on the surface life seemed normal. Coach Melvin again headed his summer program in Montreal, boys and men played ball, people attended games and followed their teams religiously. America was remaining calm and carrying on, but in ways big and small, the war was beginning to permeate every phase of life in America and around the globe.

On August 15 Bessemer High School announced the arrival of their new athletic director and head coach. Gordon Pashka, the former star lineman for the Minnesota Gophers was their man. Pashka took over for Al Butherus who had to leave the team before the end of the basketball season in March to enter the Army. That looked to be the only change in the M-W conference from the year before, and everyone expected the announcement to be made. It was good news for Bessemer, but then came the bombshell!

Lyn Hovland, the Ashland coach accepted an offer to coach at Rice Lake, Wisconsin, leaving the door to the Ashland job open. That was big news for Ashland, but the rest of The Range only looked on wondering who would take Hovland's old position. Certainly no one in Hurley could imagine what was happening behind the scenes. On August 20 The Ironwood Daily Globe sports page headline relayed the shocking news in big bold letters.

"Melvin Resigns Hurley Post After 19 years to Take Similar Position at Ashland High School"

The people of Hurley read the story in disbelief. Roy Melvin leaving Hurley! It seemed like nonsense. The Coach was a part of Hurley's fabric. He was respected, trusted, and looked up to. Roy Melvin was one of them! Surely he would change his mind. Why would he leave and why would he leave for Ashland?

In his book, "A Coach for All Seasons", Stuart Melvin admitted he did not understand his father's decision then or when he wrote the book over 60 years later. The Melvin's had just bought a house in Hurley the autumn before. Support for Coach Melvin and the athletic program was superior in every way; the administration, the fans, the faculty, the students and his players were 100% behind him. The new gym, which would become the envy of every school who ever played in it, was ready for the new school year. He thought the world of his assistant coach, Teddy Gentile. Yet the decision was made to depart for Ashland. Melvin was quoted in the Ironwood Daily Globe on August 20 as saying, "No one will know how much I wanted to stay in Hurley this year, but the offer and opportunities at Ashland are much too good to turn down."

The offer surely offered better pay, maybe even much better pay. It would have to be in order to give up a house you owned for less than a year. It is understandable how a husband and father of three would want to provide better for his family. Add the fact that Lou Melvin grew up in Ashland and the attraction became stronger. Who could blame him for taking a better deal for his family? But just what were the opportunities that awaited Coach Melvin in Ashland? He gives us a glimpse in the farewell letter he wrote that was published in the Montreal River Miner on August 28, 1942. He wrote, "If the Ashland boys like football and basketball as well as the Hurley lads, and if they are a little bigger, I should do well at the Bay City." He went on to praise his small Hurley players, listing eleven who all weighed less than 130 pounds and four who weighed less than 115 pounds. All had stellar high school careers, and many went on to play in college.

So there you have it. Size does matter, and one would think that a coach as astute as Roy Melvin knew that. In Ashland he saw a town that was over three times larger than Hurley. His teams played Ashland for 19 years and he could see the difference. He had to wonder about the untapped potential of those big kids on the bay. Jim Rasmusen, the Ironwood Daily Globe writer had these thoughts. "Frankly speaking, Ashland High School has had more talent…. and less results in past years than any other school in the conference. We've seen good players lose their poise rather than improve. It has been the same in football and in basketball. We'll wager that in one, two, or three years, things will be different." Rasmusen would prove to be right. Ashland's athletic fortunes were going to rise exponentially.

It turned out that Roy Melvin was a hot commodity. Rhinelander High School in Wisconsin, about 80 miles south of Hurley also wanted his services. Russell Leskell, who led the Hodags with their phenomenal star, Johnny Kotz, to the 1939 State Basketball Championship with a perfect record of 20 – 0, was entering the service. The catch was that Rhinelander was granting him a leave of absence and wanted him back after the war. To Melvin it must have been a flattering offer, but Ashland wanted him for the long haul, and he did not want to be a stopgap coach.

In normal times, under normal conditions, Hurley would have had a coach waiting in the wings. Ted Gentile, Melvin's former star player and now one of his closest friends, would in all likelihood have been selected as Hurley's next coach. He was a known commodity and an able assistant coach who was ready for the job. World War II was now disrupting every aspect of life. Ted Gentile was also about to enter the Army and was awaiting his assignment. Jim Rasmusen wrote in the Ironwood Daily Globe about this. "Lots of fellows are being deprived of opportunities by the war and it would not be fitting to dwell too much on any one. But Ted Gentile undoubtedly would have made the big step into Melvin's shoes if he were not subject to call very soon."

Against the backdrop of World War II these were minor issues indeed. All around the country men were entering the services in unprecedented numbers. By the end of the war, over 16 million men and 350,000 women served their country in the Armed Services. All were deprived of opportunities. For those on the home front the worry for loved ones never ended. Hurley and America were not done feeling the effects of the war. In fact they were just beginning.

CHAPTER NINETEEN

The Decision

The Hurley School Board convened on the night of August 19, 1942 to consider Roy Melvin's resignation. Of course they approved it, as nobody wanted to stand in the way of someone seeking opportunities elsewhere. The real discussion came in how they would find a new coach. The job was thought to have been offered to former Hurley football and basketball standout, and former successful coach at Saxon, Paul Santini. The big problem with that was Paul Santini was the current Superintendent of Iron County Schools which included Iron Belt, Saxon, and Mercer. If in fact it was offered, he turned it down, probably because it was a step down from his current position.

The War was causing schools everywhere to scramble as young coaches, especially unmarried men and then married men without children, were about to be drafted. Most of these coaches, all with college degrees, did not wait to be drafted. Instead they volunteered as they found that by doing so they were given a commission as an officer and often had a choice of specialties. They were sought after as pilots, supply officers, administrators, and as platoon commanders in combat units.

There was a trickledown effect as coaches in smaller schools started looking at the opportunities for better pay and better facilities at larger schools which had just lost a coach. Saxon and Mercer were without a basketball coach at the beginning of the 1942 – 1943 school year. As tiny schools they would have the most difficulty finding a coach. To fill the void many teachers with limited or no experience as a coach, and often not as a player, took these openings so the kids could field a team.

The Hurley school board was now looking at 15 candidates who applied for the position. Among them was Lyn Hovland who started the entire episode when he resigned from the Ashland post to take the job in Rice Lake. He then reneged on that deal to take position at a small college in Illinois. Suffice it to say, Hurley did not seriously consider that application. That left about 12 others from all over the Midwest to be considered. Travel and face-to-face interviews were rare due to gas rationing during the war. The board had to rely upon the resumes and the references provided by the candidates. One stood out more than others. The candidate was a 1940 graduate from the University of Iowa. He was the captain of the Hawkeye wrestling team and an offensive lineman for their football team. That team was led by Niles Kinnick who won the Heisman trophy as the most outstanding college football player in the country. That Hawkeye team became legendary and they earned the name of "Iron Men". It was one of those "Iron Men" who was tabbed to become the next coach at Hurley High School. His name was Carl Vergamini.

When the 25-year-old from Council Bluffs, Iowa, received the call from Hurley he was already considering at least 3 other offers. Two were in the local areas of Western Iowa and Eastern Nebraska. One was from a Chicago school. Hurley became the fourth offer. Carl and his wife Ruth, proud parents of 3 year old Jerry Vergamini, had to make a decision. Ruth grew up in the tiny town of West Branch, Iowa. It's only claim to fame was as the birthplace of Herbert Hoover, the thirty-first President of the United States. Like Herbert Hoover, she was born and raised as a Quaker. Upon marrying Carl she converted to Catholicism and was known as a very devout member of the church.   Together they decided to choose Hurley. As a small town it satisfied Ruth. As a great place to hunt and fish, it satisfied Carl. The little family was moving from the southwest corner of Iowa to the northeast corner of Wisconsin. The journey was uneventful, but upon arrival in Hurley, they were about to embark on the ride of their lives.

CHAPTER TWENTY

Into The Cauldron

The one thing Carl Vergamini did not have in his transition to Hurley was time. On Monday morning, August 31, Ted Gentile handed out the football uniforms and gear to about 50 hopeful players. Roy Melvin made the drive from Ashland to assist him and say his goodbyes to his former players. Practice started on Tuesday, September 1. Carl and his family were not expected for another 5 days or so.

The school board wisely decided to lure Ted Gentile on as Vergamini's assistant until his induction into the Army. That decision would pay dividends for the new coach and the team. The Michigan teams had already begun practice two weeks earlier and were preparing for their first games that week. Time was of the essence and Ted Gentile expertly filled the gap. When the new coach did arrive he found his new team already working and eager to impress him.

The pressure of his first full time head coaching position did not faze Carl Vergamini. He had played Big Ten college football and was a captain of the highly successful Iowa wrestling team. Huge crowds and big games were a part of his life. He was nonplussed by crowd noise, expectations, rabid fans, or close games. As a physical education teacher and part time coach in Omaha, Nebraska and Council Bluffs, he saw some of what coaches had to deal with at the high school level. What he could not have envisioned as a young first year head coach was the scrutiny a small town could put him under. It started before he even set a foot in the school, or in town for that matter. Jim Rasmusen of the Ironwood Daily Globe was quick to give advice to the new coach, before he even knew who that coach would be. He wrote, "Whoever the Hurley board does hire should be content to let this years' team ride along in the direction Melvin has them pointed. If he does, the Midgets may be championship caliber." Also appearing in the Ironwood Globe was this, "If Vergamini chooses to teach a new system to the team the outcome can only be told by the results." On September 12, one week before the Hurley - Ashland game, the first of the season for both teams, he said, "Any radical departure from the modification of the intricate "T" formation Hurley introduced last year, which worked wonders for Melvin and should give good results this year.........would probably have drastic results."

Armand Cirilli writing for the Montreal River Miner provided the microscopic scrutiny the new coach and team was under. On September 18, previewing the Hurley – Ashland game scheduled for that night (the game was postponed until Monday, September 21 due to poor field conditions in Ashland) he wrote, "The Hurley fans too have nothing to yell about. The team has looked very poor to date. With few instances the line has failed to jell and the backfield has been mutilating the plays." He also went on to praise some aspects of the team and also praised the coaching of Gentile and Vergamini as they were insistent on the players mastering the basic fundamentals, especially blocking. Earlier, he hit the nail on the head when he wrote on September 11, "It is our opinion that Vergamini and Gentile are much tougher taskmasters than Roy Melvin." No Hurley player would have ever argued that point.

Upon arrival in Hurley, Coach Vergamini went immediately to work. With so little time before the first game, he and Ted Gentile were up against it. Compounding the situation was that the first game would be in Ashland against Roy Melvin's Purgolders. In Ashland their team was "sounding the battle cry "Beat Hurley."" Since Melvin's arrival there was resurgence in interest in football by the boys of that city. The Ashland fans, tired of being also-rans in the M-W Conference, were excited to see a new era dawning for their teams. Excitement was running high in both towns and the game promised to be a hard fought affair.

Armand Cirilli predicted "a general exodus" from Hurley to Ashland for the game. Just when the two towns could not be more focused on the event, the rains came to the area and flooded the Ashland field. The game was postponed until Monday.

On Monday evening the teams were ready to play and get their belated seasons underway. It rained up until game time and then a beautiful moonlit night emerged from the clouds. Still, the field was in poor condition. Hurley kicked off and Ashland went to work. The Midgets held and forced the Purgolders to punt. A bad snap and poor kick gave Hurley the ball deep in Ashland territory. In short order Dom Moselle showed why he was considered among the best players in the area as he took off for a 20 yard touchdown to put Hurley up 6 – 0. It was not the start Roy Melvin wanted for his new team, but for Carl Vergamini it was just what he had wished for. The Ashland 11 was not dismayed. With a new determination they started to dominate the game with terrific line play on both sides of the ball. They finally scored and went into halftime tied with Hurley 6 – 6. Hurley regrouped at the half and came out playing better as they scratched out two more scores for the 18 – 6 victory.

It was a tough and physical game played on a rain soaked field. The poor footing hampered both teams. Neither coach was impressed by what they saw of their own teams. Vergamini simply stated, "Hurley was lucky to win."   Armand Cirilli of the "Miner" was adamant that Hurley had looked terrible in practice leading up to the game. As he chided the players for "fumblitis" in practice and sloppy play in general, he did concede that the field conditions contributed to the slow start by the Hurley squad. The general consensus was that Ashland outplayed Hurley and was indeed going to be a team to be reckoned with. Hurley, it was predicted, would also get better as the season progressed. Again iron sharpened iron.

In fact, Ashland was done being a pushover in conference play. The five team Michigan – Wisconsin league was now populated by teams who could and would beat any of the others, and do it even when they were having a "bad" season. Hurley and Ashland, the two Wisconsin teams in the loop were no longer looked down upon by their bigger more successful Michigan foes. Ashland especially would now match any team from Michigan in size.   The Ashland athletes were invigorated and as more and more of them started to believe in their new coach, more of them joined the Ashland teams. With Roy Melvin in Ashland, the two Wisconsin towns were losing the kinship they shared as the "whipping boys" of the Michigan teams. From here on out they were out to demolish each other, just like they always wanted to do to the guys from the other side of the river. As this football season would soon prove, the future of the M-W Conference in both football and basketball was going to be full of surprises.

CHAPTER TWENTY ONE

If At First You Do Succeed, It Was Probably Too Easy

The 1942 M-W conference was a collection of tough teams. Three of the five members had new coaches. Bessemer seemed to find yet another gem in Gordon Pashka. Ashland was reaping the benefits of the coach they snatched from under the noses of the Hurley School Board, and a young, unproven Carl Vergamini was now the Hurley mentor. Jack Kraemer was still at Ironwood and was as skilled and clever as ever. Wakefield had Glen Hunter running the football program once again.

In Hurley, Carl Vergamini was working overtime trying to catch up with the rest of the league. After just over two weeks on the job, he was still learning the names of his players, students, and co-workers. He continued to stress fundamentals in blocking and tackling. He expected improvement and he was a hard driving instructor. Practices entailed more than running plays. Practice was the laboratory he used to hone very specific skills, using very specific drills. Perfect technique became more important than strength, size, speed, and agility. There were no excuses tolerated and none given. The players began to see the improvement day by day. They began to believe in their new coach, but dang, he was tough!

On September 26 Hurley went to Wakefield for a Saturday afternoon contest with the Cardinals. They were still stung by their less than stellar performance against Ashland, with Armand Cirilli writing in the Montreal River Miner the day before that the Ashland game "proved that the Midgets are average players with possibilities." With that reminder, they took the field, which was a "sea of mud" that obliterated the players' jerseys and made them unrecognizable within the first few minutes of the game.

This time a better prepared Hurley squad did not let the field conditions hamper their performance. With three weeks of Coach Vergamini's drills under their belts, the Midgets displayed "vicious tackling and blocking" throughout the game. Their defense allowed only two first downs to the Cardinals until the second string defense took over in late in the fourth quarter. Dom Moselle "ran wild" over the Wakefield defense for two touchdowns, and Ted Thomas scored on a perfectly executed end around for the third score, earning the pair the moniker of "Touchdown Twins" in the Ironwood Daily Globe's sports page.

Their second straight conference win put the Midgets in familiar territory as they were once again tied with Bessemer. The Speed Boys defeated Ironwood in a classic battle in Bessemer the same afternoon Hurley handled Wakefield. For the second consecutive season the Bessemer 11 could manage only one touchdown against the Red Devils but again made it stand up for the 7 – 0 win. Albin Pertile of the Speed Boys provided the score on a 75 yard interception return in the third quarter. That game saw a snow squall to go with the same sloppy conditions present in Wakefield. And so ended another typical weekend of M-W football.

The next weekend of play saw Ashland score its first conference football win since 1940 with a 12 – 6 win over Wakefield. Ironwood defeated Hibbing, Minnesota, 20 – 6, Bessemer lost to Calumet, Michigan and their all – world running back, Joe Sossi 13 – 6. The talk in the UP and Northern Wisconsin centered on who the better back was, Sossi or Moselle. Armand Cirilli paid compliments to Sossi saying, "We may not see another player like him this year." He also pointed out that Sossi was about to turn 20 years of age and was playing his last high school game versus Bessemer due to the new eligibility rules. Dom Moselle was only 17.

Hurley defeated Park Falls 27 – 13 with Moselle running for 187 yards and scoring two touchdowns yet again. It was the first home game of the year for Hurley and they finally played on a dry field. Next up for Hurley was "The Game" with Ironwood and their battering ram backfield led by Matt Ulasich.

With the sting of losing to Hurley on their home field the year before still fresh in their minds, the Red Devils came to Hurley on October 10 looking to repay the Midgets and to carry off a Hurley goalpost. It was a hard hitting and vicious battle. Like the year before Hurley scored first with Moselle hitting Ted Thomas with a bullet for a 24 yard score in the second period. Ironwood scored in the third period. On second down and 20 from their own 10 yard line, Ironwood scored with a lightning strike! Johnson, the Devils' QB stepped into a throw that was caught on the run by Pollard who raced down the field for the 90 yard score. The point after put the Red Devils in their customary position, leading Hurley by a score of 7 – 6.

The stunned Hurley squad battled back in the fourth quarter, pushing the ball downfield to the Ironwood 22 yard line. Sensing that the game hung in the balance, Ironwood unleashed its huge defensive line to stifle the Midgets, forcing a fumble and gaining possession at the 16 yard line. With the lead and control of the ball, it looked like Hurley was going to have to replace a goal post. The Red Devils rocked the Hurley defensive front with Ulasich and Pollard gaining yards in steady chunks. Then, Pollard fumbled! A huge gasp rose from the crowd. The referees worked frantically to untangle the pile of bodies. When they finally reached the bottom of this sea of bodies it was revealed that somehow, some way, Pollard had recovered his own drop! Ironwood retained possession with the clock winding down. The Red Devil faithful breathed a collective sigh of relief.

After 21 years of humiliation and bad breaks, Hurley accomplished the unthinkable in 1941 by defeating the Red Devils. They did not want to wait 21 more years to gain another victory over their arch rivals. The defense, with every player finding just one more ounce of energy suddenly stopped the Devil rushing attack cold. They then forced an incomplete pass. Ironwood had to punt. History repeated itself! The Ironwood punter shanked it! Hurley miraculously had the ball on the 34 yard line. The Midgets had time and field position. Dom Moselle took the snap and the big fullback flipped a quick pass to ultra speedy Steve Mrdjenovich who raced 33 yards to the one yard line before being knocked out of bounds. On the next play, with everyone expecting Moselle to carry the ball, he did just that, leveling two defenders on his way to the end zone for the score. Again the extra point was no good but Hurley led 12 – 7.

Ironwood still had one more chance to take the win. With a furious effort the Devils mixed runs and passes to drive the ball to the Hurley 28. With time ticking off the clock, they threw four straight passes. All four were incomplete as the Hurley defense was not about to be scorched by the pass twice in one game. The game was over and Hurley had defeated Ironwood twice in a row!

The joyous celebration that ensued did not compare to one in 1941. This win was expected by the Hurley fans. It was considered a mild upset by the Ironwood Daily Globe as they thought the Ironwood size advantage would wear out the smaller Hurley defense.

Carl Vergamini, who had spent entire practices insisting on proper technique in blocking and tackling, saw those efforts pay off.   Still this win was sweet to the boys from Hurley. They heard the word on the street that they were not as good as last year's team. That may very well have been true, but they were every bit as tough as evidenced by Steve Mrdjenovich. When Steve suffered a separated shoulder the doctor popped it back in place and he returned to the game. With that kind of toughness they again defeated a team that was more than a match for them. They also had a very special athlete in Dom Moselle. He was one of a kind as a football player and was clearly the team leader. As they made their way from the field that afternoon they were battered, bruised, and aching from the constant pounding dished out by Ironwoods' big team. Meanwhile Bessemer had the weekend off and watched from the stands. The well rested Speed Boys again stood between Hurley and the coveted M-W Conference title.

CHAPTER TWENTY TWO

———————

Melvin Makes Good On His Promise

The Bessemer Speed Boys were the scourge of the Upper Peninsula of Michigan. They were the only undefeated football team in the UP in 1941 and were off to another superb start. Prior to their 13 – 6 loss to Calumet and Joe Sossi, they suffered the loss of their outstanding quarterback and defensive back, Albin Pertile. The hero of the Ironwood game broke his leg in practice and was out for the rest of the season. Despite that, the Speed Boys outplayed Calumet in every phase of the game except the final score. They sorely missed their firebrand leader.

Hurley, coming off their tough win versus Ironwood was feeling pretty good about their chances against the Speed Boys. They had always played Bessemer well and blowouts were rare between the teams. Fans on both sides of the river expected another rough and tumble ballgame in Hurley. For the second year in a row it would most likely decide the conference championship. Hurley was undefeated at 3 wins and 0 losses while Bessemer was 2 – 0 in the M-W with Ashland remaining to be played in conference after the Hurley game. A Hurley win would clinch the Midgets' first ever conference title. A Bessemer win against Hurley and then versus Ashland would win it up for the Speed Boys.

On Saturday afternoon on October 17, the Speed Boys and Midgets stepped onto the Hurley field. The game started slowly with neither team scoring in the first quarter. Then the Speed Boys struck and did so decisively, scoring twice in the second quarter and once each in the third and fourth quarters. They controlled the tempo of the game with their offensive and defensive lines doing all the dirty work necessary to throttle the Hurley eleven. Bessemer played their best game in two years and Hurley played their worst. The final score of 24 – 6 left the home team bewildered. It was a bitter pill to swallow for young Carl Vergamini and one of the worst losses his football team would ever be handed in his career. He would learn his lesson well. He understood the task ahead. Winning in the M-W would not be easy, but he would see to it that the Hurley Midgets would get there, and do so sooner rather than later.

Bessemer now had a stranglehold on the conference championship. They needed only to beat Ashland, something they had done with great regularity over the past two decades. Ashland lost on Friday Night to Ironwood 19 - 6. The prognosticators saw only a "slim" chance of Bessemer losing to the Purgolders. In the meantime the Hurley squad licked its wounds and prepared for their season finale versus Washburn in a non-conference game.

Hurley completed its 1942 football season on October 24 with a 46 – 0 trouncing of Washburn. The Castle Guards simply had no chance as Dom Moselle wound up his Midget football career with runs of 42, 50, and 70 yards. Hurley playing only six games ended the season with a 5 – 1 mark. On Friday Night, October 23, Ashland proved they were no longer a pushover with a 12 – 7 victory over Superior East. Quietly the Purgolders won all three of their non-conference battles and dumped Wakefield earlier in the year for their lone conference win. Suddenly there was hope that the Purgolders could pull off a mighty upset in Bessemer. It seemed unlikely, but in the M-W, you just could not predict anything with accuracy.

On a windy and snowy Halloween in Bessemer, the Purgolders played "Trick or Treat" with Bessemer. Roy Melvin opened his bag of tricks and the unthinkable happened. Ashland defeated Bessemer 14 – 7 in a bitterly fought game. Roy Melvin delivered on his promise made in 1937. He proclaimed that upon the formation of the new league Hurley would win a conference championship by his twentieth year of coaching. At the time he did not foresee the strange circumstances upon which he made good on his prediction. Now in his twentieth year as a coach, he led Ashland to a rare win over Bessemer and handed Hurley their first ever conference title. The fact the title was shared with Bessemer did not matter. People in Hurley and Ashland had a glimpse of the future. The Michigan stranglehold on conference titles had come to an end. From here on out it was a level playing field and it would become increasingly tougher to gather wins in Michigan – Wisconsin Conference.

CHAPTER TWENTY THREE

———————

Carl Vergamini And Hurley:
The Perfect Match

Carl Vergamini could not have asked for a better start to his career in Hurley. With a football record of 5 – 1 with a share of the M – W Conference Championship he more than did his job. Still there were many who thought that he was just lucky to have inherited a talented group of athletes who had been shaped by Roy Melvin.

The comparisons were inevitable. On one side of the story was an unproven, young coach who now had 8 weeks of on the job experience. On the other was a beloved and iconic man who lived among the townspeople for 19 years. The Hurley fans were not being unfair; they just wanted to know what this Iowa man brought to the table. Would he be able to lead their beloved basketball team the same as Melvin had?

The short answer to that question was "no." Carl Vergamini would indeed lead his cagers, but not in the mold of Roy Melvin. Melvin was considered to be one of the best basketball minds in the north. He was strong in teaching the fundamentals of the game. Carl Vergamini would prove that he was a tremendous student of football and as such was a superior coach of that game. Basketball was another matter for him. Hurley's new coach never really played the game. As a freshman in high school, he stood among the many boys in his school to try out for basketball. As he looked around the gym, he saw the wrestling coach supervising the wrestling team. He was hooked. He quickly made his way to the other side of the gym. Carl Vergamini the football player became a wrestler instead of a basketball player. Basketball was a game he said he "hated."

While at the University of Iowa Carl Vergamini was called the "strongest man in two cities" in reference to his dominance in football and wrestling in the Council Bluffs, Iowa – Omaha, Nebraska area as a school boy. He was also feted for his "bone crushing tackles" as a Hawkeye. Carl Vergamini was a tough guy. He relished tough, physical sports to test his will and determination as well as his physical strength. Standing at 5' 10" tall and weighing in at about 220 pounds, the bigger and better the opponent, the more he liked it. Basketball was not, in his mind, a tough sport. At least that is what he thought at that time.

As the Vergamini family started to settle in their new life in Hurley, Carl developed a deep respect for the people there. He especially admired the miners and they were quick to adopt him as a native son. These hearty Italian immigrant souls were proud that their new coach was also Italian. It did not matter to them that he could not speak the language; he had the name. Like Roy Melvin, he also discovered that they followed the fortunes of their football and basketball teams closely. They were at every game. It wasn't just sports they followed; the high school was essentially the center of the town's attention. Plays, concerts, games, and exhibits always packed the house. "The school was the center of everything there (in Hurley)." stated Carl.

As much as the people of Hurley loved their sports teams, athletics were secondary to them. They were insistent that their kids receive a quality education and that they work hard at getting it. The new coach realized early on that this was the absolute number one priority. Parents did not waver in their commitment to education and their kids knew without a doubt what was expected. According to

Coach Vergamini, "Kids there were very well behaved. Parents were tough. Mr. Murphy and Mr. Conners had them toeing the line. They were well known for that." Under J.E. Murphy and Harold Conners Hurley had a reputation for educational excellence throughout the area and throughout Wisconsin. In 1997, Carl Vergamini proudly stated, "There were more kids there who graduated and went on to college, percentage wise, than any place I've ever heard of since."

On November 13, 1942, The Iron County News published a report from State Supervisor John Callahan in which Hurley High School received effusive praise. The report pointed out that there was only one new teacher at the school (Carl Vergamini) and 19 of them had been there for four or more years. This continuity made possible the remarkable success of the school and obviously reflected on the outstanding relationship Mr. Murphy and Mr. Conners had with their faculty. Their leadership was unquestionably the key to success.

The report went on to say that, "You have a staff of well trained mature individuals who possess power and stability." The report praised the curriculum for its superior vocational training opportunities while maintaining its focus on college preparation. It praised the library and encouraged its growth and usage. It praised the school's' maintenance and "immaculate" condition. It praised the new state-of-the-art gymnasium and recommend that the "old" gym be converted into a space for shop and music.

The school did turn the old gym into a shop space. To show that not every recommendation is well thought out, the school board did not include music in the shop space. The sounds of machinery, grinding, and pounding doesn't mix well with music classes. Later, at the conclusion of World War II, the library would come under the guidance of Miss Muriel Bino. Miss Bino left Hurley in 1942 to teach aeronautics to aspiring pilots at what is now the University of Wisconsin – Stout in Menomonie, Wisconsin. As one of the first licensed women pilots in the state of Wisconsin, she was qualified to teach five phases of the course. As nearly forty years of Hurley High graduates know, she also provided the students of Hurley with a fabulous library and her incredible mind, which was a repository of information. She was a reflection of the superb teachers who Carl Vergamini joined in 1942.

It was into this reality that Carl Vergamini found himself when he started handing out basketball uniforms to his potential cagers on November 2, 1942. The people of his new town expected their kids to absolutely work their tails off at school and at everything else they did. He knew then that he would adapt and become the best basketball coach he could possibly be.

What young Carl did not know at the time, was that he was about to get a basketball education that, coupled with his tough, no nonsense approach to sports, would fuel his teams to achieve excellence and greatness. In the fall of 1942 no one knew that Carl Vergamini would accomplish what no other basketball coach in Wisconsin, before or since, has ever done. For now he had to learn how to use his knowledge from coaching football and wrestling teams to prepare a basketball team for what would prove to be a long and grinding season.

CHAPTER TWENTY FOUR

A New Era Begins

During World War Two to "Keep Calm and Carry On" meant adjusting to the new realities brought on by the largest and most catastrophic war in human history. In Hurley and on The Range iron ore production was going full blast. Rationing was in full swing as commodities such as meat, butter, food oils, fat, oil, gas, rubber tires, and sugar were all rationed. Rationing ensured that not only the wealthy were able to buy scarce products. It worked well and all people and families adjusted. On one hand there was a sacrifice, but on the other hand unemployment all but disappeared. Wages were frozen in most industries, so employers started offering better and better "benefits" to lure workers. That worked out as more wages would not have increased consumption. There was little in the way of goods to be purchased. America was using virtually every resource to fight a vast two front war against very determined enemies.

When it came to sports, from professional to college to high school, everything was scrutinized to obtain maximum benefit for the war effort. This meant travel to and from events would be curtailed. Gas rationing included every entity including school districts. Getting kids to and from school was clearly the focus with all other activities having to cut back. On Tuesday evening, November 3, the M – W conference principals and coaches met in Ironwood to discuss the upcoming basketball season. They were under pressure to keep everything as normal as possible but they had limited fuel supplies available to them for transportation. They made a wise decision to have the conference expand its schedule to include three games versus every team in the conference instead of the usual two. Wakefield could not fully comply due to previous commitments, but the other four teams were all in on the arrangement. Regular non conference opponents were not scheduled due to the travel distance.   Instead two Catholic High Schools, Saint Ambrose of Ironwood and De Padua of Ashland, were scheduled by the M – W teams to fill out their schedule. Gas and the basketball season were saved.

While supervising his first basketball practice, Carl Vergamini literally rolled out the basketball unto the Hurley gym floor and told the boys to "show me what you have." As a licensed physical education teacher he did have a rudimentary knowledge of the game in his background. He understood the rules and had an idea of the level of conditioning required for players to succeed. Still, he did not know the intricacies of the game. What constituted good defense? What could a player do to get an open shot? How do you set a good screen? What foot work can a player use to gain rebounding position on a foe?

As he watched the first practice he saw Don Dick move his feet and garner most of the rebounds. He watched as Ted Thomas used a screen by Dom Moselle to get an open shot. He watched Don Dick on defense snuffing out play after play. He learned by watching and asking questions. If his players sensed that he was not as well versed in coaching basketball as he was at coaching football, they did not let on. They were a veteran squad with four returning starters and they were expected to have a good season again. They worked hard and they responded to the tough conditioning drills Vergamini instituted. They ran and then they ran some more. After running, their drills with the ball consisted of more running while dribbling left handed and then right handed. It was constant motion. This team would not lose because they were out of shape. They were being built to run other teams out of gas. They were gaining toughness and the mindset of never backing off. Iron sharpens iron.

It became clear that this team was going to play aggressively on both ends of the floor and every player had better be able to go hard for 32 minutes or find something else to do with their time. What Carl Vergamini learned as a wrestler was that your opponent would take advantage of any weakness you displayed. He taught his team to never show fear. He learned that wrestlers who could go hard for three 3 minute periods in a match against a superior opponent could frustrate him and win. Few sports require the mental and physical toughness wrestling does. Few sports require you to give every ounce of effort you have every second you are on the mat as wrestling does. One instant of a let up leads to defeat in wrestling. This wrestler coached these basketball players the only way he knew. He pushed them to the limits of their endurance and then asked them for more effort. Amazingly they responded with enthusiasm.

Above all, the new coach was a motivator. He pushed them hard for every minute of every practice. He may not have figured out all the nuances of basketball, but he certainly understood the competitive nature of athletes and pushed all the right buttons. When he spoke, he spoke of effort and a winning attitude. He spoke of how well served they would be in life if they learned the value of not limiting their talents to "good enough." Would this unrelenting approach work with the best group of players in the school's history to that point?

On Friday, November 13, the Saxon Knights traveled to Hurley. The new gym was not quite ready for play so the game took place in the old gym. Hurley fans had awaited the opening of the new facility with an anxious zeal so this was a bit of a disappointment. Undeterred, the Midgets played a solid game, substituted freely and came away with the 38 – 22 win as Don Dick scored 18 points and controlled the boards. Dom Moselle missed the game as he had been hampered by illness since the football season. Hurley fans were beginning to ask if their senior star football player would ever show the skills he flashed as a sophomore again. They would have their answer in 12 days.

On Wednesday, November 25, the Ironwood Red Devils became Hurley's first opponent in the new gymnasium. The brightly lit, spacious facility was gleaming. Some thought that the Saxon game could have been played in the new gym but that the powers that be wanted the opener to be against their arch rival. It may have been thought that the Midgets would need the extra spark against their rival.

With a new gym, a new coach, and a record crowd in Hurley what could go wrong? Well, it was Ironwood after all! Plenty could go wrong and it did. Ironwood scored first and then they scored again. They added a third tally and after 5 minutes they led 6 – 0. Finally Glenn Stenman dropped in a long shot from the wing to break the scoring drought for Hurley and with it had the honor of being the first Midget to score in the new gym. Moselle dropped in a free throw and then scored on a drive to the hoop. Dick dropped in another and then Moselle tallied again. The Midgets led at the end of the first quarter 9 – 7. In the second quarter Dick stifled the Red Devils inside game and the Midgets jumped all over the suddenly overmatched Red Devils. Ironwood was held the last eleven minutes of the half to just three free throws as the formidable Hurley defense smothered the Devils inside game. Hurley extended the lead to 20 – 9 at the half and never let the Devils get untracked in the second half as they cruised to the 39 – 22 victory. Dom Moselle proved that he was feeling much better and led the Hurley five with 15 points displaying a variety of drives and post-up shots. Hurley now had two dangerous scoring threats.

On that same evening, Ashland served notice to the conference that their basketball woes were a thing of the past. Roy Melvin led the rejuvenated Purgolders to a stunning 34 – 28 win over Bessemer as Red Nyland scored 20 points for Ashland. The Speed Boys looked more like the Pillsbury Dough Boys throughout the first half as Ashland spurted off to a 20 – 4 lead. It was a well executed ambush against the defending conference champions! After not winning a single game in the conference in the last season, Ashland turned the conference on its head with their astounding win. No one except the crafty Roy Melvin saw it coming. Wakefield played De Padua in a non conference game that night and won easily. The M – W conference play for 1942 – 1943 was off to an intriguing start with the two Wisconsin teams defeating two of the Michigan teams. No one could remember the last time that happened.

As the Range basketball fans reflected on the first week of conference play, the Ironwood Daily Globe had this to say about the new season. "With gasoline rationing keeping the conference teams busy playing themselves and with all of the clubs appearing to have strong teams it looks like the 1942 – 43 season may develop into one of the most unusual in conference history." The article went on to state that Bessemer, Wakefield, and Hurley had veteran teams with solid and experienced players. It said Ironwood's coach, Jack Kraemer would have a "job on his hands" rebuilding an Ironwood squad that was inexperienced and unknown. But it was Ironwood, and no one in Hurley felt sorry for the Red Devils. As a matter of fact, they did not trust anything about that report. When it came to Ashland, the article said all they ever needed was some "basketball sense" and now under Roy Melvin they had it. The prophecy of an "unusual" season would prove to be an understatement.

CHAPTER TWENTY FIVE

Nothing Is As Easy As It Looks

Basketball seasons unfold in layers like an onion. You peel one layer off and there is another. But unlike an onion, which will always be the same onion, basketball teams and basketball seasons are often vastly different at different stages of a season. Most teams get better, but sometimes they get worse. They play ragged, sloppy ball, and they play ball that can only be described as flawless. All too often that can happen in a space of just two games. Mostly it is a long slow process of grinding practices with endless drills, conditioning, and fine tuning offensive and defensive plays, followed by games. It is during those practices that a coach truly proves their value as a teacher, disciplinarian, motivator and innovator.

Teams go through growing pains. Players have to get used to playing together in different combinations. While your team is getting better, in theory, so should all the other teams. So improvement is not always seen in the scores. A team may lose a game early in the season to a rival by 12 points. Later in the season they may play that same rival again and lose by 12 points again. Most observers would agree that neither team improved when in fact both are much better. Winning is never easy. Winning against a familiar foe is even more difficult. The old saying, "Familiarity breeds contempt" was especially true in the whacky 1942 – 43 season in the old M - W. The season would be a five-way struggle, with each team writing their stories of improvement, disappointment and triumph. Iron sharpens iron.

On Friday, December 4, Hurley traveled to Wakefield to take on crafty Fred Trewyn's Cardinals. Like Hurley, Wakefield was now showing off their new state of the art gym. For the Cards it would not be a night to remember. Hurley took a 10 – 7 lead after one quarter and then they exploded offensively in the second quarter to take a 25 – 13 lead at the half. The stunned Wakefield team could not get any closer to the Midgets in the second half and Hurley prevailed 40 – 25. Don Dick had his usual steady, understated, and valuable game shutting down the Cardinals inside game on defense while gathering rebounds and scoring 10 points. For the second game in a row, Dom Moselle scored big, driving and slashing for 14 points. The rest of the team all chipped in and accolades were given to Steve Mrdjenovich for using his speed to disrupt the Wakefield boys.

About 100 miles to the west in the Superior East gym, Ashland pulled off their second big upset in a row by defeating East 23 – 22. Ashland, the team that could be described as a "dumpster fire" the previous year, had taken down one of the best teams in the state of Wisconsin on their own floor. Suddenly, Ashland and Roy Melvin were formidable. Never underestimate the influence of genuine leadership. Ashland was now a threat to everyone on their schedule.

Not to be outdone, Ironwood pulled off a stunning upset of their own in defeating Crystal Falls 37 – 32 in Crystal Falls. Their current star was a sophomore with the appropriate last name of "Hammerberg" who dropped in 28 of their 32 points. In Bessemer the Speed Boys rebounded from their stunning loss to Ashland and crushed De Padua 52 – 25.

With three straight wins things were looking good for the Midgets. Next up on the schedule were the Bessemer Speed Boys. Playing in front of their home crowd, Bessemer jumped out to a 26 – 16 lead at the end of the first half. The Speed Boys then demoralized Hurley in the second half in an absurdly easy 62 – 30 victory. For the Speed Boys it was a new scoring record for a single game in the M – W and the combined points were also the most ever in an M - W contest. For Hurley it was a disaster they wanted to forget as their vaunted defense was left in tatters. Suddenly they looked like a team with a fragile psyche when things got tough. To compound matters the high-flying Ashland Purgolders beat Ironwood 43 – 31 that night and they were now in the driver's seat of the conference. They were also Hurley's next opponent.

It was truly a time for the Midget squad to show what they were made of. Ashland was proving to be a top tier team in the conference and their win over Superior East got the attention of fans throughout Wisconsin. On Thursday, December 17 Ashland played host to the Midgets. Hurley was still smarting from the old fashioned beat down they experienced at the hands of Bessemer and needed to prove to themselves that it was in fact, an anomaly. They got off the bus at Dodd Gymnasium in Ashland ready to play some serious basketball. The quicker Midgets perplexed the Ashland five throughout the first half and took the lead 21 – 12. Dom Moselle was unstoppable as he rampaged for 17 of the 21 points the Midgets put up. Ashland had no answer for his strong drives and twisting shots. It appeared that young Carl Vergamini had pushed all the right buttons in preparing his team after a devastating defeat six days before. Hurley fans were breathing a sigh of relief. Meanwhile in the Ashland locker room, Roy Melvin started pushing some buttons of his own.

The game proved to be a tale of two halves. Hurley dominated the first and Ashland the second. The Purgolders closed the Hurley lead to 5 points at the end of the third quarter and finished with a flurry of points in the closing minutes to win the game 45 – 40. For undefeated Ashland it was their sixth straight win of the season and their third in a row in the conference. They went into the Christmas break as the clear cut team to beat. For Hurley it was an even more crushing defeat then the Bessemer game. It was a game that they were physically and emotionally prepared for. They dominated the best team in the area for most of the game only to see it slip away at the end. Their record was now 2 – 2 in the conference and 3 – 2 overall. Area basketball fans were buzzing once again about the twist of fate that landed Roy Melvin in Ashland.

The Ashland team was to be reckoned with. They were a tall and rangy team, just the type of big athletes Roy Melvin seldom had in Hurley. The prognosticators who predicted Ashland's turn-around with Melvin's arrival there were proudly saying "I told you so." For Hurley the buzz was about a wrestler who was coaching basketball. What did the school board see in this guy when they hired him?

CHAPTER TWENTY SIX

Another Tough Season Gets Tougher

What the Hurley School Board, J.E. Murphy and Harold Conners saw in Carl Vergamini was a young coach who, like their first hire, Roy Melvin, possessed self-confidence, a winning attitude and the ability to use athletics to help develop a young person's character. They wanted a coach and they wanted a teacher. He proved to be both. He also brought something else to the table and he brought it by the boatload. Carl Vergamini was a motivator! His practices became more and more focused and intense. He insisted even more than ever that the way to win was to work, work, and do more work!

During the Christmas break he began to tinker with his approach to the game and how to best use the talent on his team. Most of the team's scoring load had been carried by Moselle and Dick. Vergamini wanted more options than those two. Gerald Rosendahl was a junior on the team. What made him unique was that he was the tallest Hurley Midget on that team or any other Hurley team to that point. He was about 6' 4" tall or maybe 6' 6" tall, depending on which newspaper you read or the day you read it on. Gerald was a gangly collection of long arms and legs who, it was said, did not like basketball. That put him in good company as his coach didn't like the sport very much either. Thus was formed a strange kinship between Gerald and his coach based on their dislike for the game. Carl Vergamini coached basketball only because Hurley did not have a wrestling team. Gerald was expected to play simply because of his height. That made the game frightening rather than fun for the lanky lad. He was expected to not just be good, because of his height, people expected him to do what no other players had ever done! It was unfair.

Perhaps the coach and the tall boy saw themselves in one another when it came to basketball. The expectations were very unfair, but still Gerald played. As a coach Carl Vergamini had entered the arena of high school basketball in a place where the population was mad about the game. He inherited a good team and he was expected to win, despite his inexperience. The tall, shy, skinny boy and the stout, robust man were now joined at the hip. Together they would learn the game and they would grow more confident in their abilities.

Early on Carl Vergamini sensed that Gerald Rosendahl could be the key component on this Hurley team. Despite not being the best player on the team, he did add another dimension to an already talented bunch. These Hurley Midgets were not a small team but rather an average sized team for those days. With Rosendahl on the court Hurley could be more than a scrappy opponent; in fact they could be a scary team to play if the tall kid could contribute. The knock on the skinny boy was that he could barely leave his feet when he jumped. Still the coach was intrigued by the possibilities even if Gerald couldn't jump over a dime. A coach can teach and inspire in a lot of ways, but you just can't coach or teach them to be tall. He started the lad in several games and that enabled Don Dick to play forward. After a bit Coach would send in another guard for Gerald, and Dick would move back to center and Glenn Stenman would move to forward, making the Midgets an ultra fast team. He brought Gerald Rosendahl along a little more each practice and each game. As a result Hurley learned to play "tall ball" and "fire house basketball." At this point in the season it was a work in progress and the progress seemed to be painstakingly slow.

During the practice sessions during the break the team scrimmaged against a strong contingent of college players. Armand Cirilli of the Montreal River Miner reported that the Midgets more than held their own and even defeated the older players. It was hoped that the team would gel and get back on track. They were certainly working hard. With their coach exhorting them to shoot more often, Glen Stenman, Ted Thomas, and Steve Mrdjenovich were ready to contribute more in the scoring column. If Rosendahl could actually do what the coach thought he was capable of this would be a difficult team to stop.

Hurley resumed play on Friday night, January 8 against De Padua, a team that had been a punching bag for other M – W teams on their schedule. It was widely expected that Hurley would join in on the festivities and soundly defeat them as well. Only Armand Cirilli sounded the warning bell as he called the De Padua team "battlers who are above average cagers." His insight proved to be correct as De Padua battled Hurley on the Midgets home floor. They simply made the Hurley five look ragged, sloppy, and disinterested. Hurley squeezed out a fortunate win 25 – 23 in a game they should have easily won. That same night Wakefield turned the tables on Ashland and handed them a stunning 41 – 35 defeat in Ashland. Bessemer handed Ironwood its fourth conference loss in a row 40 – 33 in a game the Red Devils led after three quarters.

Hurley now had to face the resurgent Cardinals of Wakefield, and once again Armand Cirilli and the Montreal River Miner laid into the Hurley basketball team. He called the Midgets "pretty much a disappointment" and that "The fans are not very hopeful of any championship as the big game looms before the Midgets. The team is too erratic to hope for much." He continued saying the team reached a "new low" versus De Padua and that Coach Vergamini

"has trouble bringing his team around when they get into a slump."
He also suggested that he take a more "hard boiled attitude with his
players." No one in Hurley disagreed with Armand, but one has to
wonder just how "hardboiled" a coach should be. Carl Vergamini was
already one tough task master. Whatever the young coach thought
of those comments, he stayed the course and continued to work and
prepare his team for Wakefield.

Some teams just seem to play certain opponents well under any
circumstances. This Wakefield team was solid in every way and
certainly not easy pickings for anyone. Somehow Hurley had their
number. Playing at home the Midgets were quick on offense and
stubborn on defense as they rolled to an easy 47 – 29 win against the
tough Cards. Over in Ashland, the improving Ironwood Red Devils
nearly pulled off another upset, but Ashland again found a way to win
27 – 25.

The ship was back on course and the Midgets traveled to Ashland
for their next game. Don Dick did not make the trip as he was home
with the flu. Hurley once again jumped out to the lead and at the
half they led the Purgolders 22 – 15. Gerald Rosendahl had his best
game scoring 9 points and holding Ashland's big gun, Red Nyland
to 5 points. With their best player and the heart and soul of their
defense ailing at home, the Midgets again blew their lead in Ashland.
The Purgolders outscored the Midgets 26 – 7 in the second half and
cruised to the 41 – 29 win. The Midgets now had a record of 3 wins
and 3 losses in the conference with two non conference wins over
less than stellar smaller schools. Don Dick missed the game. Could
he have made that much of a difference? The answer to that question
was yes. Despite playing Ashland without one of the best players in

the area and the state, the wolves were howling louder than ever. What happened next became part of Hurley's basketball lore.

CHAPTER TWENTY SEVEN

———————

When The Going Gets Tough,
You Better Get Better!

The next game for Hurley would prove to be a make it or break it game. A fourth conference loss would in all likelihood put an end to the already fading title hopes the Midgets started the season with. The Bessemer Speed Boys loomed on the horizon on Friday, January 29. The game ended up being postponed due to a flu outbreak in Hurley which left 8 of the 10 players bedridden at home. Needless to say all practices were canceled too. The Hurley players would begin to get well and then play non conference games in the next week against two Catholic Schools, Saint Ambrose and De Padua.

With Don Dick still at home and the rest of the team still weakened by the flu, Hurley took on Saint Ambrose of Ironwood on February 3, and put on a dominating performance. Gerald Rosendahl again started at center for Hurley and again had a good game scoring 12 points before giving way to the subs. Lightning quick Steve Mrdjenovich thrilled the crowd as he swished one from the seated position beyond the free throw line after being knocked over. With the 52 – 29 win the flu-weakened Midgets seemed to be recovering nicely for De Padua, and De Padua was surely ready for them.

On Friday February 5, De Padua hosted Hurley in Ashland. Again, they had the Midgets' number and played flawlessly throughout the hard fought game. Don Dick was back in the lineup and the Midgets were at full strength numbers wise, but they were all still recovering from the effects of the flu. De Padua jumped out to an 11 – 4 lead after the first quarter and still led 18 – 15 at the half. In the third quarter with the game in the balance, Coach Vergamini showed his faith in Gerald Rosendahl as he inserted him into the game. The lanky lad proved his coach's hunch was correct and he quickly scored four baskets in rapid succession giving Hurley the lead 25 – 23 at the end of the third quarter. Rosendahl did not score another basket, but his spirited play lit the fire his team needed as they churned their way to the 36 – 33 win over a determined rival. The physically drained and recovering Midgets needed a spark and their unsung tall teammate gave it to them. As this basketball season unfolded for Hurley, this would be one of the defining moments. When things were at their worst, Gerald Rosendahl was at his best. This inconsistent team was now about to play the best basketball anyone in Hurley had ever seen.

Armand Cirilli, the erstwhile sports commentator and writer for the Montreal River Miner liked what he saw from the Hurley squad that week. Yes, Hurley won two games against weaker opponents, but under the conditions that was remarkable in itself. What he really liked was the fight the Midgets put up despite their weakened bodies. He said, "We believe that when the present Hurley team is at full strength and playing the ball it really can, it is the best team in the M – W League…..Ashland notwithstanding." There he said it, and he said it in print. A bold statement indeed!

The M-W standings looked like this on February 8: 1) Bessemer 4 – 1, 2) Ashland 5 – 2, 3) Wakefield 4 – 3, 4) Hurley 3 – 3, 5) Ironwood 0 – 7. Ashland's only defeats were handed to them by Wakefield. Bessemer's defeat was in the opener to Ashland, Wakefield had two defeats at the hands of Hurley and one to Bessemer, Hurley lost two to Ashland in Ashland, and the blowout to Bessemer. Once again the M – W was proving that on any given night, anything could and did happen. There was another factor that would change the league for the rest of the season.

Bessemer had 4 players graduate at the end of the semester, including Bill Lucas and Bill Velin, making them ineligible to continue playing high school sports. Bessemer was now missing four good players and their season was in a precarious place. Research shows that Bill Velin enlisted in the Navy and became a Corpsman (Medic) for the 3rd Marine Division, seeing heavy action in Guam. It was a scene that played out over and over again in the country as boys turning 18 could graduate early to join the service. Research turned up nothing about the other Bessemer boys, but it is thought that they too graduated and enlisted. Their selfless actions speak volumes about these young men and the hundreds of thousands of others who left high school early to answer their nation's call. Early graduation or not, virtually every boy who graduated from high school from 1941 - 1945 ended up in the service during WWII.

On February 12, Hurley ripped Bessemer 43 – 25, to the surprise of no one at all, given the circumstances. Dom Moselle scored 19 and Don Dick 14 to show they were recovered from their bout with the flu. Unfortunately Gerald Rosendahl was now out sick. That same night Hurley received help from the unlikeliest source; Ironwood bedeviled Ashland in a 36 – 32 upset. In the M – W anything can happen, and once again, it did. Ashland missed out on their chance to reclaim the M – W lead, instead leaving it in the hands of the Speed Boys. Four days later, on February 16, Hurley again defeated the Speed Boys 44 – 17 in the makeup game that was postponed due to the flu. Dick scored 13, Moselle 10, and Rosendahl tallied 8 for the victors. Ashland and Hurley were now tied atop the M – W with records of 5 –

3 while Wakefield and Bessemer were tied for second at 4 – 3. The Midgets were now at full strength and Armand Cirilli started to look like a prophet.

With a clear path to the conference championship in front of them, Hurley faced Ironwood in the Luther L. Wright gym. Ironwood was fresh off of their first conference win of the season and they were getting better by the day. Hurley had a history of blowing important games that had sent previous title hopes spiraling down the drain. Needless to say Ironwood was feeling pretty good about their chances to wreck another Midget season. But past history was of no concern to Carl Vergamini as he and this version of the Midgets set out to write their own chapter in the book. Hurley jumped all over the Red Devils leading 27 – 10 at the half and 40 – 14 after three quarters. Don Dick proved once and for all that he was healthy again scoring 21 points, playing stellar defense and passing the ball with precision to set up his teammates for easy scores. Gerald Rosendahl chipped in with ten points and also proved to be disruptive on defense as Ironwood could not score down low on the Hurley big man. Hurley now had to face Ashland for the third time.

This time the game was played in Hurley. The game proved to be a struggle for both teams as defense ruled the contest. Neither team could penetrate the other's defense and score inside with any regularity. Both teams displayed a crisp passing game but the defenses would not crack. The game was always within reach of both teams with four points being the biggest lead either team could muster. The game was thrilling for the fans. They witnessed two teams working so hard on defense that the other team could seldom get away with a clean shot. Glenn Stenman, Hurley's deadliest outside shooter dropped in four long range shots to boost the Midgets. Moselle and Thomas each scored 6 points and Dick tallied 4. Rosendahl and Joe Gosette both played but did not score.

On Friday, February 26, Ironwood came to Hurley to close out the conference schedule. A win by the Midgets would give them the undisputed M – W Conference Championship. The Hurley boys were now the hot team on The Range and they dismantled the Red Devils 39 – 25 with Don Dick pouring in 20 points, including hitting 8 of 8 free throws, and again shutting down Ironwood's inside game. The Midgets substituted freely as they coasted to the win. When the dust settled and all the conference games were played, the final standings had Hurley on top. Wakefield ended the conference season with only eight games played as they chose to forego the twelve game schedule at the beginning of the year and played each conference member only two times instead of three. 1) Hurley 8 – 3, 2) Ashland 7 – 4, 3) Wakefield 5 – 3, 4) Bessemer 4 – 7, 5) Ironwood 2 – 9.

In the Montreal River Miner, Armand Cirilli summed up the game and the season by saying,

> Those of us who have followed sports on the
> Gogebic Range never thought we would see the day
> when Hurley would approach an Ironwood game with
> anything but tremors. However, in the past few years
> the Midgets have taken Ironwood with regularity.
> This is a good thing for sports in general. It was
> heartbreaking for Hurley to see its kids splattered all
> over the football field by big Ironwood teams. The
> basketball defeats were discouraging, but at least
> more humane.

Then Armand inexplicably went on to write the following about Carl Vergamini and the Midgets. "Hurley fans have enjoyed their championship ways. It is too much to hope that they can continue. But, we have enjoyed it while it lasted." It seems Armand was preparing the populace for another disappointment. He was looking at past history, in which Hurley under Coach Melvin had a "long and sad story" of tournament failure. He also believed that Ashland's history of overachieving in the tournament would work against Hurley as they would meet for the fourth time in the season in the Regional Tournament opening game, which was, by the way, to be in Ashland where the Purgolders handed the Midgets two of their three losses. Dodd Gymnasium would be a tough nut for the Hurley boys to crack. Also waiting in the wings would be the Superior teams, East and Central, who also had more than their share of tournament success stories. The eight team regional affair was going to be competitive. What Armand did not know was that Carl Vergamini didn't give a damn what anyone thought about his team's chances! They would be ready to play--period!

With the regular season concluded, tournament time was upon the Wisconsin schools. The Michigan schools would conclude their season with non conference games before their tournaments began the following week. For the Michigan teams there would be no state tournament. To curtail travel and gas consumption there would be only regional tournaments with the winners receiving a certificate instead of a trophy to reduce the consumption of metal needed for the war effort.

The Wisconsin tournament would go on, but with a $25 War Bond going to the champions so they could purchase a trophy after the war. The boys on the winning team would receive a certificate they could exchange for medals in the future. The tournament would be compressed with teams who won the quarter final contests playing two games on Saturday of the regional semi-finals. The regional would be followed by the four "sectional" tournaments following closely behind the conclusion of the 16 regional tournaments. This format allowed for only four teams to make the trip to Madison. The most difficult thing about the format was that it was packing 7 games into eight days. All the changes were made to aid the war effort and conserve gas.

PHOTOGRAPHS | 1923 –1924

Superintendent
J.E. Murphy

Principal
H.F. Connors

Tom Hunt
Quarterback

Mario Giannunzio
Halfback

1948 Hurley Football Team
First row: *G. Sybeldon, Manager, J. Grasso, E. Martino, C. Corrigan, J. Kasper, R. Collins, J. Trier,*
G. Zell, F. Trier, J. Stremski, D. Voss, J. Trier, (water-boy)
Second row: *T. Vita, T. Cornols, J. Giovanini, H. Peterson, B. Thomas, R. Rainaldo, L. Negri*
J. Patritto, G. Aho, J. Forte, G. Baldowin, L. Pretti, R. Johnson, C. Rowe
Third row: *Assistant Coach Mario Gianunzio, B. Anonich, N. Mattei, J. Barton, F. Helinski,*
R. Hannula, L. Darin, R. Hill, R. Chiapusio, T. Erspamer, H. Peterson, A. Morzenti, C. Hermanson,
L. Kutz, Coach Carl Vergamini

135

PHOTOGRAPHS | 1942 –1943

Carl Vergamini

Dom Moselle

Don Dick

The New Home of the Hurley Midgets

Cheerleaders
B. Martini, R. Martini, V. McDonell, M. Erspamer, A. Friola, B. Swedberg, N. Debubeis, B. Francis

PHOTOGRAPHS | 1942 –1943

Basketball Team
Back: Mr. Vergamini, Coach, J. Mehnert, C. Kadletz, J. Muehl, E. Ciotti, M. Bonacci, T. Lopez, C. Mezzano, P. Barbara, M. Anonich, G. Van Hoof, B. Cattoi, J. Sealy, J. Reimer, B. Nelson
Front: V. Bottacin, L. Zanutto, E. Martino, J. Ciotti, T. Thomas, D. Moselle, D. Dick, G. Rosendahl, G. Stenman, J. Gosetti, S. Mrdjenovich, R. Zell, R. Tenlen, Manager

Football Team
Back: G. Stenman, Manager, Mr. Vergamini, Coach, D. Dick, Manager
Second: P. Freeman, D. Erspamer, J. Shea, T. Erspamer, L. Jordan, F. Fassino, A. De Rosso, J. Martino, P. Barbara, E. Gibbons, J. Becker, A. Penrose, E. Helin
Front: B. Zell, J. Ciatti, E. Martino, D. Moselle, T. Thomas, J. Gosetti, L. Zandi, J. Sybeldon, D. Trembath, V. Bottacin, G. Wallis, S. Mrdjenovich, J. Hunt
Front: M. Anonich, Manager

PHOTOGRAPHS | 1943 –1944

Eino Lefty Martino

Gerald Rosendahl

Ashland at Hurley... Hurley 45, Ashland 33

Cheerleaders
E. Slanzi, A. Brignoli, M. Lindberg, R. Martini, R. Friola, B. Swedberg, D. Balma, B. Philip

PHOTOGRAPHS | 1943 –1944

Home Nursing Club
Back: Smee, S. Wheeler, M. Schuier, F. Moehrke, B. A. Conhartoski, M. J. Conhartoski, W. Schwab, A. Vellenoweth, M. A. Conhartoski, M. Rota, G. Lennon, D. Gibbons, I. Calvi,
Front: E. Valle, B. Calligaro, R. A. Martini, P. Reader, H. M . Lake, R. Friola, R. Sealy, B. A. Swedberg, G. Levra, K. Domich

Surgical Dressing Club
Back: I. Koskell, M. Reinerio, E. Ijas, D. Bertagnoli, S. Rossi, E. Salo, D. Steiber, M. Bensoni, H. Uronen, E. Toivonen, S. Kivi, A. M. Popka, J. Trumph, J. Lindquest, L. Semberg.
Front: Miss Tipple, I. Hill, E. Ijas, E. Belmas, A. Frezell, E. Impola, C. Calgaro, B. Fedrizzi, Moccardini, P. Zandi, G. Upton

The Crowd

PHOTOGRAPHS | 1945 –1946

Cheerleaders
First Row: E. Martini, M. Lindberg, **Second Row:** M. Hockin, S. Wheeler, F. Glugla, B. Baima

Band
First Row: P. Formolo, F. Glugla, d. Gibbons, B. LaFave, V. Savant, M. Skaja, J. Penna,
F. Obertone, Mr. Swee, J. W. Soetebier, R. Sybeldon, D. Stremski, G. Luciano, C. Rubatt, I. Calvi,
V. Bruneau
Second Row: D. Zandi, J. Jelinski, B. Baima, J. Endrizzi, K. Bertolone, M. Schomisch, J. Marta,
V. Mattson, M. V. Bertolone, G. Calvi, E. Nygard, K. Canney, C. Julien, D. Ryan, G. richie, P. Trier
Third Row: E. Koski, L. Tabacchi, B. Williams, N. Luppino, P. Zandi, R. M. Endrizzi, E. Van Hoof,
M. Brack, D. Stremski, E. Gibbons, K. Domich, J. patritto, M. B. schlender, I. Lopez, B. Noren,
M. Tocci
Fourth Row: D. Moselle, J. Sullivan, J. Muehl, E. Lahti, R. Pearson, A. Fritz, L. Philip,
E. Verbunker, J. Rautio, B. Kuula, B. Williams, W. Julien, M. Penna, F. Krpan, B. Carlson,
M. Enkkeli

PHOTOGRAPHS | 1945 –1946

Basketball Team

First Row: M. Gianunzio, Coach, J. Darin, B. Canney, M. Brown, C. Mezzano, J. Muehl, W. Geach, B. Mioni, E. Van Hoof, L. Busch, Assistant Coach
Second Row: J. Dahl, C. Guenther, D. Johnson, J. Hermanson, C. Kaffine, D. Peterson, G. Mrdjenovich, C. Swanson, D. Gentile, D. Schomisch, D. Zell
Third Row: J. Rainaldo, J. Czech, J. Kubiak, B. Cattoi, T. Erspamer, J. Cattelino, G. Cisewski, D. Hoeft, J. Rainaldo, D. Zandi

Football Team

First Row: D. Gentile, G. Mrdjenovich, W. Webb, D. Zell, G. Gerry, B. Mioni, D. Smith, T. Erspamer, J. Muehl, D. Schomisch
Second Row: B. Barton, G. Aho, J. Hermanson, E. VerBunker, W. Anderson, A. Brunello, J. Sullivan, J. Nichols, B. Canney, E. Van Hoof, F. Barbara
Third Row: L. Busch, Assistant Coach, J. Grasso, C. Herman, D. Johnson, J. Cvengros, J. Dahl, J. Rainaldo, J. Czech, J. Rainaldo, M. Gianunzio, Coach

PHOTOGRAPHS | 1946 –1947

Eugene Van Hoff

Anton Brunello

Joe Darin

Cheerleaders
S. Wheeler, E. Martini, J. Kopacz, F. Espamer, F. Gluga, B. Biama, F. McDonell, M. Hockins

PHOTOGRAPHS | 1946 –1947

Basketball Team
Front Row: ML. Bartolutti, D. Gentile, C. Kaffine, W. Geach, J. Darin, E. Van Hoof, J. Rainaldo
Second Row: N. Bonacci, Manager, M. Giannunzio, Assistant Coach, J. Czech, J. Rainaldo,
C. Guenther, G. Cisewski, C. Vergamini, Coach A. Trolla

Football Team
Front Row: Assistant Coach M. Giannunzio, R. Collins, D. Johnson, G. Aho, N. Bonacci,
J. Hermanson, D. Smith, D. Schomisch, T. Erspamer, J. Rainaldo, t. Brunello, J. Dahl, C. Herman,
J. Forte, E. Celello, J. Grasso
Second Row: D. Gentile, Coach c. Vergamini, D. Zell, C. Corrigan, E. Martino, C. Hermanson,
M. White, A. Rigoni, R. Ademino, C. Swanson, A. Trolla, W. Paynter, N. Mattei, L. Pretti,
J. Baldowin, W. Van Hoof, J. Czech, T. Prospero
Third Row: F. Coxey, C. Rowe, J. Gemuenden, J. Perelli, B. Anonich, C. Peterson, C. Baron,
G. DeRosso, D. Hannula, R. Snarsi, D. Hoeft

PHOTOGRAPHS | 1947 –1948

Band Director
Oscar Swee

Cheerleaders
F. Mcdonell, G. Giannunzio, J. A. O'Berto, B. L. Baima,
F. Erspamer, M. Hockin, R. Pasqualucci

The Cafeteria

Basketball Team
Front Row: N. Mattei, D. Zandi, J. Hermanson, J. Rainaldo, E. Martino
Back Row: A. trolla, D. Hoeft, C. Hermanson, C. Guenther, W. Baron, L. Bartolutti,
Coach Carl Vergamin

Football Team
Front Row: L. Bartolutti, D. Hoeft, E. Martino, J. Rainaldo, J. Forte, G. Aho, A. Rigoni,
J. Hermanson, f. Trier, W. Kirby, D. Barnabo, C. Ramme, G. St. Catherine, J. Meade, R. Collins
Second Row: J. Kasper, C. Corrigan, F. Helinsik, D. Voss, d. Trembath, L. Negri, L. Pretti,
C. Rowe, W. Thomas, C. Calvi, G. Baldwin, J. Gemuenden
Third Row: A. Vida, R. Rainaldo, M. White, J. Grasso, R. Ademino, H. Peterson, T. Erspamer,
N. Mattei, W. Anich, C. Hermanson, W. Gemuenden

Cheerleaders
S. Wheeler, E. Martini, J. Kopacz, F. Espamer, F. Gluga, B. Biama, F. McDonell, M. Hockins

PHOTOGRAPHS | 1948 –1949

Basketball Team
Front Row: N. Mattei, W. Anich, R. Rainaldo, E. Martino, J. Tocci, C. Corrigan, P. Savant
Back Row: Coach Carl Vergamini, L. Bartolutti, T. Erspamer, W. Baron, C. Hermanson,
Manager J. Forte, Assistant Coach Mario Gianunzio

Football Team
Front Row: Manager G. Sybeldon, J. Grasso, E. Martino, C. Corrigan, J. Kasper, R. Collins,
J. Trier, G. Zeil, F. Trier, J. Stromski, d. Voss, J. Trier, T. Trier (water-boy)
Second Row: T. Vito, T. cornola, J. Giovanini, H. Peterson,B. thomas, R. Rainaldo, L. Negri,
J. Patritto, G. Aho, J. Forte, G. Baldowin, L. Pretti, R. Johnson, C. Rowe
Third Row: Assistant Coach Mario Gianunzio, B. Anonich, N. Mattei, J. Barton, F. Helinski,
R. Hannula, L. Dsrin, R. Hill, R. Chiiapusio, T. Erspamer, H. Peterson, A. Morzenti, C. Hermanson,
I. Kutz, Coach Carl Vergamini

147

Bartolutti's Block!

CHAPTER TWENTY EIGHT

History Is Neutral

Hurley entered tournament play on Friday March 5 with a shining 12 – 3 record. Of those three defeats, two came at the hands of Roy Melvin's Ashland team in Dodd Gymnasium. In both of those games, Hurley dominated play in the first half and then proceeded to fall apart in the second half. They got a measure of revenge by defeating the Purgolders in Hurley in the defensive slugfest in their third meeting. Ashland entered the tournament with an impressive record of 14 – 4. Other teams who traveled to the Ashland regional were Superior East, Superior Central, Park Falls, Phillips, Drummond and Prentice. Drummond and Prentice were there by virtue of winning their respective small school (enrollment under 210) district tournaments.

In the early games on Friday Park Falls defeated Drummond 36 -27, Central dumped Phillips 40 – 20, and East fought off a determined Prentice team 40 – 30. The last game of the night got underway at 9:00 PM. Those who studied basketball on the Range were sure that Ashland would win. Given they were playing on their home court, had handed Hurley two demoralizing loses there earlier in the season, and had the experienced coach, who could blame them? Add in Hurley's record for losing their biggest games of the year and there you have it; history was on Ashland's side.

Carl Vergamini had the Midgets ready to play. Hurley jumped out to lead 11- 6 after one quarter. By the half the lead swelled to 25 – 13. This time the Midgets showed up for the second half and continued to build their lead and it was 34 – 20 at the end of three quarters. The basketball mastermind, Roy Melvin, turned his now desperate quartet loose in the fourth quarter with racehorse tactics and dropped 15 points on the Midgets in the final stanza. The basketball apprentice, Carl Vergamini, had ensured the Midgets were ready for the onslaught and played Ashland's style. The Midgets countered with more than equal ferocity as they out raced Melvin's five by scoring 18 fourth quarter points and cruised to the 52 – 35 win over the stunned Purgolders. Glenn Stenman had his best game as a Midget as he dropped in nine free throws on his way to a 15 point effort to lead Hurley. Five other Midgets joined in on the balanced scoring, including Steve Mrdjenovich and Don Dick with 9 each, Dom Moselle with 8, Gerald Rosendahl with 7, and Ted Thomas with 4. This was the type of team Vergamini wanted. Now every player had to be accounted for and every player knew their coach believed in them.

On Saturday Superior Central again dumped Superior East from the tournament and Hurley ended Park Falls season 33 – 22 in the afternoon semi finals. That set up Superior Central and Hurley to play for the regional crown for the second straight season. Central was once again led by Bud Grant. The super sophomore was enjoying a season in which he was displaying his lethal "Johnny Kotz" shot. Kotz had popularized the one handed release while starring at the University of Wisconsin. Grant thought so much of the shot that he also perfected it. Playing in the tough Head of the Lakes Conference, he led the league in scoring. With the future NBA and NFL player leading the way, Central was poised to continue their season at the Midgets' expense. After all Hurley had never won the regional title.

History was not just smiling upon the Superior Central Vikings; it was beaming! These Vikings were Wisconsin High School basketball royalty. In this, the twenty-eighth year of the state tournament,

Superior Central had found its way to Madison a staggering 19 times, winning the State Championship four times, a mark that tied them with Fond Du Lac for the most at that time. Hurley, who had never advanced past the Regional Tournament, was all that stood in the way of the Vikings moving on to make their twentieth appearance in the state tourney.

On Saturday night the two excited but weary teams took to the court before a packed house in Ashland. While history was smiling upon Central, this Midget team was refusing to acknowledge it. This team was transformed during a rough stretch of the season that molded them into believers. Carl Vergamini had pushed this team in practice all year for this very moment. Playing their third game in less than 24 hours, they were in peak physical condition and they were ready to run and run hard. Over the last month they had stepped up their game, and with Glen Stenman and Gerald Rosendahl playing the best basketball of their lives they were no longer dependent on just Moselle and Dick for a scoring punch. The Midgets now had 8 players who had taken turns picking up the slack when needed. They were a team in every sense of the word. All the difficult times made them hard and sharp. Iron sharpens iron.

The game started slowly with Hurley clinging to a 6-5 lead at the end of the first quarter. At the half it was Hurley 17 – 10. Central fought back in a hard played third quarter to cut the Hurley lead to five points at 27 – 22. Central found themselves in the same position they were in during 1942 and, like in 1942, they fought back to within two points at 29 – 27 with three minutes to play. When Ted Thomas fouled out, it looked exactly like the 1942 game when Dick Guenther fouled out. Would history repeat itself? This time Gerald Rosendahl took over at center for Don Dick and Dick moved to forward. Then steady, hardnosed Joe Gosette entered the game to spell Rosendahl. Unlike the 1942 game Hurley had solutions for every problem Central threw at them.

Over the last three minutes the already smothering Hurley defense stepped it up still another notch and stifled the Vikings comeback. They proceeded to score 8 of the next 10 points and won the game 37 – 29. Dom Moselle led the Hurley offense with 14 points. Dick and Stenman chipped in with 7 each. On defense Don Dick led the way as usual and Central had a miserable time getting the ball down low. This Hurley team made their own history with the win. Everything this squad would do for the rest of the tournament was to be done in uncharted territory. The sectional format was new to the state. By winning both games at the Spooner Sectional tournament, Hurley would be one of 4 teams to play for the state championship in Madison. Until now history had always been against Hurley in the tournament. This team, this coach, and these boys were cut from a different cloth. By winning the regional tournament they put history back in its proper place as a neutral bystander. Hurley had defeated Ashland, their season nemesis, on their home court and then took down the vaunted Superior Central Vikings in a shocker. They were ready for the sectionals in Spooner. Iron sharpens iron.

CHAPTER TWENTY NINE

Living The Dream

There was no time to bask in the glow of winning the regional crown. On Monday afternoon, March 8, the team boarded a bus bound for Spooner. The games were scheduled to begin at 2:00 PM on Tuesday, March 9. Hurley of now one of 16 teams left in the tournament grinder. Each remaining team was now the reigning champion of one of the 16 regions in the state of Wisconsin. Each of the four Sectional Tournaments hosted four teams.

The Tournament would be a one day affair with Hurley playing Chippewa Falls in the second game. St. Croix Falls and Cumberland would tangle in the first game at 2 PM. The winners would meet in the championship game that same night after the losers of the first games played for third place. With that demanding schedule the four teams jumped from the frying pan into the fire. Most pundits expected the games to be close and hard fought affairs. All four teams were formidable with Chippewa Falls thought to be the best of them all after having a relatively easy time in winning their regional title in Eau Claire. As for history, Chippewa Falls had made five previous trips to the State Tournament while Cumberland and St. Croix Falls had each been there twice before. Only Hurley had never advanced that far.

The first game ended up as a blowout as the tall Cumberland Beavers jumped all over the St. Croix Falls Saints for a 23 – 6 halftime lead on their way to the 41 – 24 victory. Cumberland, winners of the Rice Lake regional title, would go on to the championship game at 9

PM. The River Falls region winners, St. Croix Falls, would play for third place at 8 PM.

Now Hurley would play Chippewa Falls in a game that featured Nate DeLong of Chippewa Falls going head to head against Don Dick, Hurley's defensive stopper. The 6' 7" DeLong was a scoring machine for the Cardinals, who regularly scored over 20 points in contests. He was a dominating player and explosive scorer who later, as a collegian at River Falls State Teachers College, would lead the entire nation in scoring. Chippewa Falls had a sterling record of 16 – 1 going into the game with their only loss to Menomonie. During the season they took down notable power teams Eau Claire and Superior East in games that were not very close. Hurley countered with their impressive 15 – 3 record and their big win over Superior Central that put them in Spooner.

The Midgets seized command of the situation with the first tick of the clock and never let up. Don Dick, known for his pressure defense kept DeLong "bottled up" throughout the first half as Hurley jumped off to a 10 – 0 lead at the end of one quarter. The rest of the team also caught "defense fever" as they methodically built the lead to 24 – 1 at the half. The Cardinals were caught completely off guard by the intense, swarming Hurley defense. That defense combined with constant motion and smooth passing ensured that the Midgets dominated both ends of the court. Chippewa Falls mounted a comeback as Don Dick fouled out early in the third quarter and they closed the lead to 29 – 17. The only Midget who could look big Nate DeLong in the eye was Gerald Rosendahl and he didn't flinch with the pressure now on him. DeLong fouled out in the fourth quarter as he now tried to keep Rosendahl in check. Hurley substituted freely down the stretch and claimed the 41 – 26 win. Delong scored 16 points, most of them after Dick fouled out, but the damage had long since been done.

Dom Moselle led the Hurley scoring with 12 points. Gerald Rosendahl had shown during the season that he was capable of scoring points in spurts and he did so again against the Cardinals, scoring 9. Glen Stenman also hit for 9. Dick, who played brilliantly on defense, showed that great players can affect the outcome of the game without scoring a lot. He scored 6 points, but was clearly the player of the game as he "nailed Delong's shoes to the floor." How good was Don Dick in that game? Well, in the consolation game Chippewa Falls blasted St. Croix Falls 60 – 32. All Nate Delong did was score 36 points and prove that he truly was the most dominating scorer in the state.

The Cumberland Beavers were a tall and talented bunch as they showed against St. Croix Falls in the first round. Hurley was poised for the showdown as both teams dreamed of earning a spot in the final four in Madison on Saturday. In previous years the State tournament had hosted between 8 and 16 teams. With World War II raging, gas rationing was in full effect and only 4 teams would get to punch their ticket to Madison.

Cumberland was led by high scoring Simon Lund who had tallied 51 points in the 3 regional games at the Rice Lake Regional. Hurley had the answer and put Don Dick on him. Hurley again methodically moved the ball with a crisp passing game that led to plenty of wide open shots. The Midgets were hitting on all cylinders on offense and defense. Dick kept Simon Lund in check, holding him to 3 points for the game. Gerald Rosendahl had his way in the low post scoring 13 points. Glen Stenman and Dom Moselle scored 12 and 11 respectively. The outcome was never in doubt after the first minutes.

Again Don Dick was the most outstanding player in the game as he again silenced the opponent's top scorer. He scored 5 points and controlled the boards for the second straight game. Hurley was an impressive winner 46 – 21.

When it was all said and done, the Chippewa Falls venerable coach, A. B. Paff was asked to comment about his team's game with Hurley. He simply stated, "No regrets. We lost to one of the best clubs in Wisconsin." The 1942 – 43 edition of the Hurley Midgets Basketball team had just put on the most dominating performance, considering the quality of the opponents, in their history. Two games, played within seven hours, that completely rewrote Hurley's basketball history. Hurley's Mighty Midgets were going to play for the Wisconsin State Championship; they were living the dream!

CHAPTER THIRTY

On The Big Stage

The whole town was buzzing. In every store, at every gas station, in every restaurant and bar, all anyone could talk about was the Hurley Midgets going to the state tournament. Two decades of athletic hopes and dreams were more than realized. Armand Cirilli was again leading the praises of the team and their young coach. "Superlatives are inadequate to describe this team. They are truly a swell bunch of fellows and a great cage organization." He also described the boys as "cool, deliberate, confident, and modest and cooperative in every respect." Armand now seemed to forget that he had earlier warned the populace to not get too excited about this team when they were preparing to take on Ashland in the regional tournament. Now he was touting them as potential state champions, writing that , "It is not at all impossible."

Of Carl Vergamini he wrote;

> Our praises to Coach Carl Vergamini, who through
> these crucial games has maintained his composure
> and given confidence and poise to his boys. The
> Hurley mentor came here pretty much on the spot.
> His material was exaggerated in football and even in
> basketball. With only limited experience in coaching,
> he was able to cope with the situation and give
> Hurley its greatest teams. Certainly, there have been
> no greater Hurley outfits

There can be no doubt about the effect Carl Vergamini had on this team. He wasn't afraid that they would break, and worked them harder and harder until they became a multi-faceted team. The coach would often claim that he did not like basketball. That may have been true at one time, and it's quite possible that even at the end of his first year of coaching it was true. But one thing about Carl Vergamini was that he had too much professional pride to not learn the game and give it his very best effort. He was above all a coach. No team, no matter how talented, will respond to lackluster or incompetent coaching. What Armand Cirilli mentioned many times in his coverage of the basketball teams was that this Hurley team passed the ball like no other. That selflessness would be the hallmark of all the teams Carl Vergamini coached. He also worked hard to develop the confidence of Gerald Rosendahl, Glen Stenman, Ted Thomas, Steve Mrdjenovich, Joe Gosette and the rest of the basketball team not named Dick or Moselle. With two stars getting most of the opposing teams' attention, the Midgets season took off when the other players stepped up and made huge contributions. Carl Vergamini molded a group of talented athletes into a selfless team. Opposing teams found that they could be beat by anyone on the squad if they decided to not pay attention to them.

The Hurley team left for Madison with a record of 17 wins and 3 losses and were riding a twelve game winning streak. The score was close in only three of those games. The determined De Padua squad (36 – 33), Ashland (24 – 20) and in the regional championship game, Superior Central (37 – 29) were the only teams to get within eleven points of the Midgets. The Midgets' average margin of victory in those twelve games was 16 points. Their three losses on the season were all avenged as they defeated Bessemer and Ashland twice each.

They clearly established themselves as the best team in Northern Wisconsin.

The University of Wisconsin Field House in Madison played host to the 28th Wisconsin State High School Basketball Tournament on Saturday, March 13, 1943. One can only imagine the excitement the boys from all four teams felt when walking into the place for the first time. It was vast, able to hold 13,800 spectators. It was the home of the Wisconsin Badgers, the 1941 NCAA Basketball Champions led by their hero, the great Johnny Kotz of Rhinelander, a two time All-American team selection.

The other three schools reaching the finals were Shawano, Reedsburg and Racine Washington Park. Shawano defeated Rhinelander in the Stevens Point Sectional Final 34 – 21 to punch their ticket to Madison, while Reedsburg won the Madison East Sectional by defeating Madison West 42 – 36. Racine Washington Park, like Hurley, overwhelmed their five tournament foes and only allowed a total of 98 points in the five games. They earned their berth in the Madison by beating the defending state champions, Shorewood High, 26 – 23 in the West Allis Nathan Hale sectional. All had sterling records and all were sporting impressive winning streaks. The format was the same as for the regional and sectional tournaments with two games to play in a single day to determine the champion. Hurley would play Racine in the opening game at 2 PM, with Shawano meeting Reedsburg following that clash.

Racine Washington Park, with their pressure defense and 20 – 3 overall record, was the pundits' pick to win the championship. Hurley looked to spoil their plans with their own solid defense and an offensive passing game that bewildered their previous tournament rivals. The two teams seemed to be mirror images of one another.

This would be the closest and most hard fought game of the entire tournament for either team. It was also the closest game of the finals in Madison by a long shot.

Several hundred Hurley fans were in the stands as the confident Hurley squad jumped out to a quick 3 – 0 lead. It should have been worse for Racine but the Hurley boys in their early excitement missed several wide open shots. Unfazed, Racine methodically fought back and led at the end of the first quarter 8 – 5. The game was as advertised: two fundamentally strong teams facing off without either giving an inch. Every point in this game would be earned only through hard work. There would be no quick scores, no easy shots, no rest. As the game progressed into the second quarter, the Racine team, who were considerably taller and bigger, also proved to be just a little quicker, just a little more precise on offense, and just a little tougher on defense as they expanded their lead to 17 – 9 at the half. The third quarter saw more of the same as the Midgets battled gamely to close the gap. In the end Racine Washington Park walked off the court with the 33 – 27 victory versus the plucky Midgets. Don Dick led Hurley with ten points, Ted Thomas scored 8, Rosendahl had 5, and Moselle 4. Racine's scoring was spread among seven players. They beat Hurley at their own game, making few errors, working hard on defense and never giving in to their determined opponent.

In the second semi-final game of the afternoon Shawano defeated Reedsburg 39 – 26 with an 18 point fourth quarter blitz that put the game away. Now Hurley would meet Reedsburg at 8 PM for third place while the championship game between Racine Washington and Shawano would follow.

The Reedsburg Beavers and Hurley would both prove to be strong contenders for the state title throughout the rest of the 1940's.

This would be the first of two times they would meet at the state tournament. Both teams had just felt the sting of defeat. Both teams wanted to prove they were better than they had just showed. One would salvage a win in Madison and the other would go home on a two game losing streak.

Hurley took the lead after one quarter by a count of 9 – 7. The Midgets expanded their lead to 15 – 9 in the second quarter and then Reedsburg exploded for 8 consecutive points and a 17 – 15 halftime lead. The Hurley five looked "dead on their feet". No one would have faulted the boys for being tired after the hard fought game versus the toughest team in the tournament. That is, no one but their coach. This team had worked hard for moments like this. Being tired was not going to be an excuse for mailing it in. Hard practices had prepared them to play hard even when tired.

Digging deep inside, the Hurley team doubled down on the defensive end of the court and held the befuddled Beavers scoreless in the third quarter as they pulled out to a 25 – 17 lead. There was no let up as the Midgets continued to grind away on defense and all Reedsburg could muster in the fourth quarter was four more points. Hurley took third place in their first ever tournament appearance 34 – 21.

In the final, Racine Washington Park proved once and for all that they were the best team in Wisconsin. With their methodical passing game working with precision, they played without an errant pass in the game. Shawano battled to a 10 – 10 tie after one period. They were then bulldozed by Racine's smothering defense. Growing impatient they launched many desperate shots that had no chance. They went scoreless in the second quarter while Racine built a 20 – 10 lead. Without missing a beat the Racine lads took what they wanted from the Shawano five in the second half. Racine played with machine like precision as they scored 10 points in each quarter of the game. After the first quarter Shawano could counter with only 13 points. With a near flawless game on offense and defense Racine Washington Park became the new Wisconsin State Basketball Champions by the score of 40 – 23.

As for the impression Hurley left at Madison, the Racine Journal Times wrote, "'Experts' who figured that the opening game between Park and Hurley was really the championship game weren't wrong." Shortly after the tournament the boys from Hurley learned they left a positive impression on none other than the Superior Central Vikings. Central players had a tradition of voting for their "All Opponents Team" at the end of each season, and this year 3 of the 5 members elected were from Hurley. Don Dick, Dom Moselle, and Glen Stenman were joined by one player from Duluth, Minnesota and another from LaCrosse. It was a great compliment from the traditional powerhouse team and a superb example of the sportsmanship their legendary coach, Harry Conley, imparted to his players.

As Carl Vergamini and his boys watched Racine dismantle Shawano, they looked on in admiration. They were happy with their progress and happy with being one of the best teams in the state. Hurley was proud but not satisfied. Carl Vergamini's basketball education had just begun. He had already proven he was already a master motivator and would go on to improve as a basketball coach. The road was about to take twists and turns that would slow down the drive, but the drive had begun and a new history would be written.

CHAPTER THIRTY ONE

September 1943: The End Of The Beginning

The United States was now locked into the middle of World War II. At least it was the middle as far as this country's involvement. It had been 21 months since Pearl Harbor. It would be another 24 months until the Japanese would sign the surrender documents in Tokyo Bay on the decks of the USS Missouri, ending the war.

The farther history brings us away from the days of World War II, the more it seems to newer generations that the outcome was inevitable. America and her Allies would win and peace would be restored. The truth is that in the days, weeks, and months following Pearl Harbor the Japanese and German forces ran roughshod. Germany and Mussolini's Italy controlled continental Europe and a large swath of North Africa with an iron fist. On the Eastern Front German forces pushed to within 20 miles of Moscow. Germany had conquered territory in which over 450,000,000 people lived. Japan had an easy time defeating the over matched Allied Forces in China, the Philippines, New Guinea, Viet Nam, Korea, Thailand, Laos, China, Indonesia, Singapore, Hong Kong, Malaysia, to name just some of the 28 conquered countries. They also controlled virtually every island and island chain in the Western Pacific. In all, over 28 countries with a population of nearly 500,000,000 people were now under the boot of the Rising Sun. Russia and England were perilously close to collapsing under the never ending onslaught of the Germans, while the Japanese were on the doorstep of Australia and New Zealand.

With so much conquered territory, the Axis nations began to pillage the resources of those nations. Japan now controlled most of the world's rubber resources, huge oil deposits and rich sources of ores to continue building their war machine. The Germans likewise squeezed their puppet governments for all of the same. In the middle of a "Total War" they increased war production exponentially. For Germany that was a massive undertaking when considering the continuous bombing attacks that were unleashed upon their industrial centers throughout the war. The Axis nations started the war with huge militaries that were well equipped with cutting edge weaponry, submarines, ships, and aircraft. They were well trained and experienced by the time the USA entered the war, so the thought that the outcome of this cataclysmic event was known from the outset is ill informed. The war, as we know, was protracted, bitterly fought, and changed the world forever.

Adam Bernard Woitkielewicz of Montreal became the first casualty of the war from Iron County. He is smiling in his picture on the front page of the March 20, 1942 edition of the Montreal River Miner. He was killed in action, "somewhere in the Pacific" on February 1, 1942, his 25th birthday. He was a graduate from Hurley High School and enlisted in the Navy on December 1, 1941, just six days before Pearl Harbor. He had been in the Navy for just two months when he was killed. With Adam's death, the reality of World War II hit home in Iron County.

Just below the news about Adam Woitkielewicz there was another picture. This one was of Corporal Kenneth P. Auger or Saxon. Corporal Auger was cited for bravery during the attack on Pearl Harbor and Hickam Airfield. He enlisted in the Army in September of 1940. Kenneth Auger survived the war.

The stories of two brave young men in the prime of their lives jumped off the front page. Similar stories would appear day after day in hometown newspapers throughout the United States. Valor was commonplace, but so were death and destruction.

Both of these Iron County men were fittingly hailed as heroes. In the home of Adam Woitkielewicz in Montreal there was unbearable grief as the Blue Star hanging in the window was replaced by a Gold Star. In the Auger home there was immense pride and the relief of knowing their son was safe for now. But that pride was fraught with the fear of having a son in the middle of the war. For all who fought and came home there would be the nagging and unanswered question, "Why did I live when so many others died?" That question still haunts those who are still with us some 75 years later.

Despite the sacrifice and pain America was indeed fortunate. The war was fought primarily in North Africa, Europe, China, Southeast Asia, in the jungles and on the beaches of islands scattered across the Pacific and above and below the waves of the world's oceans. Our nation was not invaded. The civilian population was 99.9999% safe. There were shortages of everything you can imagine, but there was no starvation or rampant diseases, no bombing raids upon our cities, factories, and schools.

Most people were 100 percent behind the war effort. The United States recycled everything. Kids and youth groups picked old tires from scrap heaps, the bottoms of rivers and lakes, and cleaned out garages. Every glass beverage bottle was recycled. It did not matter if it once held milk or beer; it was a precious commodity now. Scrap metal drives were held frequently. Tin cans were never thrown out. They were recycled and used for the war in a different form. Nothing was wasted and people saw value in any object.

By September of 1943, the U.S. Navy and Marine Corps had reversed the tide and were now on the offensive in the Pacific. The Battle of the Coral Sea, fought in May of 1942, stopped the Japanese from cutting the supply lines to Australia as the first ever naval engagement in history was fought without either fleet ever in sight of the other. Naval aviation now ruled the seas. In early June of 1942 the U. S. Navy lay in wait for the Japanese Fleet as it was bearing down on Midway Islands. The goal of the Japanese was to seize the islands and use it as a base of operation to take Hawaii. Had they been successful, the outcome of the war would have been much different. Fortunately the Navy had partially cracked the Japanese Navy's communications codes and pieced together what their plans were for Midway. With the only three aircraft carriers left in the Pacific, including the heavily battle damaged USS Yorktown, and with all the battleships sitting in the mud at the bottom of Pearl Harbor, the patched up task force surprised the Japanese Fleet. Navy torpedo planes found the Japanese fleet and attacked without fighter cover. The Japanese Zeros shot them to pieces as they attempted to attack from wave top level. Not one torpedo plane survived! Only one pilot from the entire squadron survived. The Japanese fleet remained unscathed. While the Japanese fighters were still hovering at wave top level after decimating the low flying torpedo planes, dive bombers from the American carriers arrived overhead and began their bombing runs. They came in unopposed by the Japanese fighters who had chased the torpedo planes at wave top level. They simply could not gain enough altitude quickly enough to stop the onslaught.

The Japanese carriers had recovered their aircraft that just attacked Midway. Their decks were full of bombs, torpedoes and fuel lines as they worked frantically to refuel and rearm the planes for another run. It was then the first dive bombers were spotted. Too late! Within five minutes three of the four carriers in their task force were burning. Explosion after explosion occurred as their bombs cooked off and the fuel laden planes erupted. The three carriers sank quickly. Later that afternoon the fourth carrier was spotted and sunk. The United States lost the USS Yorktown and was down to just two carriers. The Japanese invasion force, now without air cover, turned back for Japan.

The loss of the aircraft carriers, and even more so of precious aircraft and irreplaceable pilots, ensured that the Japanese would now spend the rest of the war on defense. The few times they tried to mount an offensive they failed. The tide of the Pacific War was turned. By September of 1943 it was clear that they could not replace their losses quickly as the US Navy submarine force now began to take a toll on their shipping. Japan would eventually be cut off of all raw materials by the "Silent Service." For the United States each day saw new ships and planes rolling out of shipyards and factories.

As for Germany and Italy, they too were being pushed back across all fronts by the Soviets. In February of 1943, German forces holding out in Stalingrad finally surrendered after 6 months of bitter fighting. It would be the largest land battle ever fought with about 2 million killed, wounded or captured. In North Africa the fighting ended in May of 1943 as the British and American forces finally subdued the Germans and Italians. By August they had taken Sicily. The Allies were knocking on the door to Italy. On September 3, 1943 the British and Americans landed. The bitter fight in Italy would last the rest of the war as the Germans refused to withdraw their forces even after Benito Mussolini and his regime were brought down and Italy surrendered.

It was into this world that high school graduates of 1943 walked. Don Dick would attend the university of Wisconsin and then end up at the Naval Academy training to become a naval officer while starring in basketball. Dom Moselle enlisted in the Army and the others scattered into the services. Only a few did not enter the service. Those who did not were either classified as "4F" (not suitable for military service due to physical conditions) or they possessed skills deemed needed on the home front.

With so many young men gone, women filled the void in the workforce. "Rosie the Riveter" was seen as strong and capable enough of doing a "man's work," and so she was! Rosie and the rest of the workforce produced war goods at a frenetic pace never seen before or since. Many men and women worked double shifts and overtime on a regular basis. The need for manpower both in the service and in industry was insatiable. As the war progressed, young men with families were drafted, as were older men with or without families. And as we saw with Bessemer's class of 1943, many high school boys graduated early to enlist. All across the country young men did the same. Seventeen year old boys who did not have enough credits to graduate early dropped out of school, had their parents sign for them, and enlisted. Most of them would complete high school after the war. Thousands of underage boys lied about their ages, falsified documents and "snuck" into the service as 15 and 16 year olds. Colleges graduated men early so they could be in the service. The service academies at West Point and Annapolis did the same. Celebrities and professional athletes were drafted and many volunteered. The ranks of the military would swell to over 16 million by the end of the war, including about 400,000 women. To put that into perspective, that was more than twelve percent of the population. About 24 percent of American males were in the service, one of every four men! Those who were not were forty years old or more, had "critical" war skills, were under 17 years old, or were disqualified for physical conditions. Almost an entire generation of young American men went to war. It is no wonder that the war was always on people's minds. They all knew someone dear who was in harm's way.

The middle of this war was difficult. The end was not in sight and the beginning seemed so long ago. Americans on the home front were indeed lucky to be spared having to experience the deprivations and viciousness of war, but they carried the fear of losing a beloved son, husband, brother, sister, or friend in a place that just two years earlier, they had never heard of. America and her allies had reversed the tide of Axis conquest. The war was now at the "end of the beginning."

CHAPTER THIRTY TWO

Another New Coach!

The manpower crunch in the fall of 1943 was acute. As more and more men were drafted, more and more men enlisted voluntarily. College educated men were particularly sought after as officers. Many saw the writing on the wall and volunteered; allowing them to choose their service branch and often times their jobs. After passing their physicals, they were commissioned into the Army, Navy, or Marine Corps Reserve and sent home to await orders. Many Hurley men experienced just that. In the fall of 1942 Ted Gentile knew he was about to be called up and continued to work as Carl Vergamini's assistant football coach until his orders arrived. Armand Cirilli of the Montreal River Miner was now called into the Navy, and now it was Carl Vergamini's turn to sit on pins and needles.

Since moving to Hurley, the Vergamini's had added another son to the family. On March 23, 1943, Ruth gave birth to Phil. March was one very busy month for the family! Around that time Carl began the process that would end with him as an officer in the Navy Reserve. At 5' 10" and about 220 pounds he was initially told he was "overweight". For most men that would be true, but for Carl Vergamini, former Iowa Hawkeye football lineman and star wrestler, it was not. The "strongest man in two cities" was big and strong and mostly muscle. The military doctors passed him on his physical and he went on the waiting list for orders.

For reserve officers a waiting list was necessary because there were ships being built that needed crews. They just were not ready for a crew yet. Once in the manpower pipeline the men were assigned to one of the new ships and then sent to train at a base near the shipyard. As the ship neared completion the crew was filled out. Once the ship was completed, it would be commissioned into the Navy's Active Fleet and the crew would take charge. It was a well laid plan that worked again and again during the war. It did leave the young officers in the position of not knowing when they would leave home and they usually needed to move quickly once they had their orders. Still not one person complained as they understood the gravity of the situation the nation was in.

In the fall of 1943 the coach handed out football uniforms to his players and began practice. Things were progressing and just as it looked as if Carl Vergamini might actually get his team through the shortened football season, his orders arrived. On September 13 he and Ruth loaded up their car and with the boys began the drive to her mother's house in West Branch, Iowa where she and the boys would wait for the return of their husband and dad. They had been in Hurley for scarcely one year and Ruth was heartbroken to be leaving. The family had fallen for the little mining community and its people. To be sure the people of Hurley had fallen for the Vergamini's as well. It was a bitter farewell.

In what would prove to be one of the most fortuitous decisions Harold Conners, J.E. Murphy, and the members of the Hurley school board would ever make, they decided to hold Carl Vergamini's job for him until after the war, if he still wanted it. In the interim they had an option that few people had seen as viable. A respected biology and science teacher in the school would become the physical education teacher and coach for the duration of the war. This unassuming and reserved man was a graduate of Hurley High, class of '27. He was a Hurley Midget through and through. When cut, he bled orange and black. Mario "Chief" Gianunzio was that man. Calm and almost demur in nature, he burned with a love of sports, teaching, and kids. Hurley's high school athletes and students knew him to be a superb biology teacher. They now were going to see him as a coach who could communicate and teach the fundamentals of sports, especially basketball, as well as anyone ever could. He would be assisted by another of Hurley's dedicated teachers, Leo Busch. Together they would shepherd the athletic department through the rest of the war. It was going to be quite a roller coaster ride!

CHAPTER THIRTY THREE

———————

A New Struggle

The Hurley Midgets football and basketball teams now inherited their third coach in three seasons. With the war effort requiring even more rationing, the decision had already been made to shorten the Hurley football season to four games. Ironwood and Ashland would play a full season of six games. Hurley would have played five games, except that Wakefield elected to suspend their football program until after the war. Then they entered the Western Upper Peninsula Conference for football until 1951. The Cardinals remained in the M – W Conference for basketball.

Chief Gianunzio took over for Carl Vergamini and had just five days to prepare for the Ashland Purgolders and Roy Melvin. This was more than a matchup of two football teams; it was also the student versus his teacher. Chief played for Roy Melvin and was on his first Hurley team. Melvin thought so highly of the pint sized halfback that he made him a four year starter. Chief would go on to the University of Wisconsin where he became quite a wrestler. Now he would have to match wits with his former mentor. To be fair Chief Gianunzio did not have the arsenal of players Melvin did. Hurley had been hit hard by graduation and had only four seniors on the team that would see significant playing time. It was a very green squad going up against the rejuvenated and experienced Purgolders.

The game started with Ashland taking the opening kickoff and then marching down to the Hurley two yard line before they fumbled. Hurley recovered and ended up punting the ball back to Ashland. It may have been a harbinger of things to come for the 1943 Hurley football team when in the first quarter, William Risku, the starting center, was lost for the season with a broken leg. Things went downhill from there as the tenacious Midgets fought tooth and nail only to have the bigger Ashland team methodically grind away to win 19 – 0. The game was not easy for Ashland. The small and inexperienced Hurley boys played them as well as possible and Ashland could not put the game away until the fourth quarter. The Montreal River Miner opined that "the old spirit is in this years' squad." It was also stated that it might be "5 – 10 years" before Hurley would see another championship in football. It was back to the same old thing: size!

The Midgets next game was away versus Park Falls, a team they dispatched with regularity in previous years. This Park Falls edition was a pretty darn good bunch. Hurley scored twice on the Cardinals but failed to convert an extra point. Park Falls also scored twice and nailed an extra point for the 13 – 12 win. Again the effort was there for the entire game. Coach Gianunzio's first two games showed that the Midgets had heart. They were gaining experience the old fashioned way, one bruise at a time!

While Hurley started the season with two consecutive losses, Ironwood was winning and winning big. They were standing on a perfect record and were un-scored upon while defeating Calumet 19 – 0, Iron River, 33 – 0, and Bessemer 15 – 0. Again they were big and this year they were also very fast. Hurley would make the short trip to Longyear Field in Ironwood on October 1 for a game under the lights. Nobody gave the Midgets a chance in this game. It was an expected blowout. Hurley was used to being undersized, but this year that discrepancy bordered on ridiculous.

For the third game in a row the overmatched Hurley 11 kept their opponent out of the end zone in the opening quarter of play. For the third game in a row, their opponent scored in the second quarter and then continued to grind the undersized team into dust. Only the tenacity of the small Hurley line kept the game from being ugly. Ironwood kept their un-scored upon streak going to four games as they defeated Hurley 19 – 0. The Montreal River Miner reminded everyone what their Midgets were up against with the story beginning, "Hurley Holds Red Devils to 19 – 0 Score." It was hard to fault this spirited squad for losing to what may have been Ironwood's greatest football team. Ironwood went on to beat Ashland 26 – 6 and Stambaugh 21 – 6 to end their season with a perfect 6 – 0 record. The Red Devils outscored their opponents 133 – 12! They were the M – W Conference champs and the Champs of Michigan's Upper Peninsula.

The last game of this painful season was versus Bessemer. To make a short story shorter, Bessemer won 13 – 0. The Midgets were so inept on offense that Eino Martino intercepted a pass and returned it 72 yards to the Bessemer 8 yard line. With the biggest break they had all season the Midgets still could not punch it into the end zone. Martino broke off many long runs in the season but reached the end zone only once, that in the Park Falls game. As for Park Falls, they upset Ashland 21 – 19 giving the Midgets the hope that they were not as bad as their record indicated. In reality that is true as no game was a blowout, but they were only really close in the Park Falls game. It was a tough season and the only season in which Hurley failed to win a game since records were kept in 1920. By all accounts this team gave everything they had. They just had too little experience, size, and football skill. The football season was over and according to the "experts," Hurley could expect the same miserable experience in basketball.

CHAPTER THIRTY FOUR

Refusing To Quit

The prognosticators selected Hurley to finish in fifth place in the M – W in the 1943 – 1944 basketball season. It was pointed out that the team returned only two players from the most successful team in Hurley's history. Only Gerald Rosendahl had played much. Eino "Lefty" Martino was the other letterman and he played sparingly. They would be joined by a promising sophomore, Charlie Mezzano. Seniors Cletus Kadletz, Tony Lopez, Bob Nelson, Bob Cattoi, juniors Lawrence Lewis, and Gerald Swetkovich, sophomore Jack Muehl, and a freshman by the name of Mickey Brown filled out the squad.

The team to beat looked like Ashland, who was returning most of last year's strong team. Wakefield was thought to be the one team that could knock off the Purgolders and claim the conference crown. Ironwood and Bessemer were the dark horses and Hurley would bring up the rear. The hometown newspaper asked the question, "Who will be the Mich – Wisc conference basketball champs this year?" Their answer was, "As we said last week, it won't be Hurley." That was the prevailing thought around the Range. Hurley's greatest group of senior athletes had graduated. The other conference teams could not wait to prey upon what was considered to be a weakened group.

This Hurley basketball team did not inherit their predecessors round ball acumen and skill; however, they did inherit 20 years of Hurley pride and Hurley character! They were ready to lace up their sneakers and play hard. What they found in their new coach was a man who was sure of his basketball knowledge and knew how to teach the fundamentals of the game. This college wrestler liked coaching basketball more than football. Mario "Chief" Gianunzio would prove to be a master at teaching the game. He was soft spoken but insistent in his methods. He was not a master motivator like Carl Vergamini, but rather he was a basketball professor.

So with most fans counting out Hurley before the first shot of the season had been taken, Ashland came to visit the Midgets for the opening game of the season. In a packed house in Hurley the Purgolders opened up a 12 – 8 lead in the first quarter. They stretched that lead to 21 – 16 at the half. Hurley was working hard to stay with the talented Ashland squad, but it was expected that the Purgolders would put the game away in the second half. The Midgets were overmatched in size, with the exception of Gerald Rosendahl, who was now properly listed at 6' 5" tall. The Ashland team held a significant edge in experience and it appeared in the first half that they also held the edge in skill as Hurley had to claw tooth and nail to stay in the game. Like the football season, the Midgets hung in the game for the first half, but in football they then were put into the grinder and worn down.

It was a good thing for Hurley that football and basketball are different games. Ashland could not block or tackle them; they had to run with them! Gerald Rosendahl and his partners took control of the game in the second half as Rosendahl caught fire on his way to a game high of 15 points. At the end of three quarters the Midgets had wrestled the lead from Ashland 24 – 23. It was the Purgolders who were being ground down by Hurley's pace and tempo. The Midgets extended the lead to 28 – 23 at one point, having outscored Melvin's team 12 – 1 to that point of the second half. Then the Purgolders came roaring back to tie it at 30 – 30. Clete Kadletz dropped in a free throw to give the Midgets the lead. The Purgolders missed on their next shot and Hurley had the ball. Lefty Martino was fouled and calmly dropped in the free toss and Hurley led 32 – 30 with three seconds on the clock. A desperate shot by Ashland wasn't close and the Midget faithful erupted with a roar of approval. Another M – W basketball season had begun and the same lesson was just re-learned. There are no easy teams in the conference--period!

The Wakefield Cardinals who were thought to be the second best team in the conference were thumped by De Padua 31 – 22 in Ashland. The "experts" had put their jinx on the top two teams in the conference. In the meanwhile the real experts, Roy Melvin of Ashland and Fred Trewyn of Wakefield, had the task of rebuilding the confidence of their powerful teams.

On Wednesday, November 24, Wakefield got back on track as they stifled the Midgets in Wakefield 39 – 25 after Hurley led 9 – 7 at the end of one quarter. Fred Trewyn was never going to let his boys wallow in self pity. They played a tremendous defensive game limiting Rosendahl to just 5 points. Ashland took out their frustrations by dominating the Bessemer Speed Boys 46 – 19. In the other game on the Range, Ironwood hosted the always good and always tough Rhinelander Hodags. The Red Devils were an unknown quantity while Rhinelander was highly regarded. In a thrilling double overtime contest, the Red Devils came away with a hard earned 29 – 27 win. The rest of the area teams sat up and took notice. The Devils appeared to be a team on the rise.

With the "experts" feeling good about their preseason picks once again, the Montreal River Miner added Ironwood to their mix of contenders with Ashland and Wakefield, while relegating Hurley and

Bessemer to the role of "villains." The Midgets just could not buy an ounce of respect. It was going to be a long season.

CHAPTER THIRTY FIVE

A Rocky Start

Sometimes the past haunts you. The expectations of others are based upon your past performances. Would this Hurley Midget athletic program sink back into hard times? Had they turned the corner to a new era? The up and down nature of high school sports is often tied to one simple thing: how many experienced seniors are on your team? Talented underclassmen are always a huge plus for any team, but seniors who have been through tough games and a long season are gold to any coach and any team. Seniors steady the ship in rough seas. The underclassmen look to them and imitate their behaviors on and off the playing fields and courts. Panicked seniors are seldom calmed by underclassmen, while panicked underclassmen are almost always calmed by calm seniors. Seniors set the tone in practice, in the locker room, and in games. On 90 percent of high school teams they are the leaders.

Shy Gerald Rosendahl and all conference football player Lefty Martino were lettermen from the State Tournament team. Tony Lopez, Cletus Kadletz, Bob Nelson and Bob Cattoi were the other seniors who were up from last year's "B" team. With the exception of Rosendahl they did not have much playing experience at the varsity level. What they did have was the superb work ethic passed on by the '42 – '43 team, and with Chief Gianunzio guiding them, those seniors led the charge. They did more than just lay the groundwork for the '43 – '44 season, they set the example for a talented group of sophomores and freshmen. It would be those freshmen who would rise to the occasion as seniors and make their hard working, scrappy mentors proud.

With two conference games played to start the season, the Midgets looked to the "easy" part of their schedule. The first game was against Mellen. The second was versus DePadua. DePadua had proven to be a tough opponent in the past for Hurley, and this year they were a very strong team favored by the Montreal River Miner to beat Hurley as they had Wakefield in the first game of the season. But first the Midgets took on Mellen in the Granite Diggers' little gym, which was packed with fans eager to see their little school take on the Hurley five. The game was an absolute dog fight! The tough Mellen kids took advantage of their tiny gym and smothered the Hurley offense. The Midgets wanted to push the pace but were stymied as there was no way to push the attack in the little box. Hurley squeaked out a 27 – 25 win and were glad to get out of town. The DePadua game was more of the same thing. Playing in Ashland on their very own tiny court DePadua held Hurley to 17 points and came away 19 – 17 victors.

The Midgets returned home to play the Bessemer Speed Boys on December 10. The two teams picked to be the bottom dwellers in the conference played each other tough. Gerald Rosendahl who had thus far supplied most of the offense for Hurley caught fire early scoring 13 points. But the game was a tale of two Bessemer teams. Hurley led three minutes into the third quarter 19 – 3 as the Speed Boys were tied in knots on offense. Then the game took a twist with Bessemer catching fire. The Midgets hung on 21 – 18 in a quirky game that was a slow paced defensive struggle.

Over in Ironwood, the Red Devils were undefeated at 3 – 0 after smacking Stambaugh 39 – 23. Remember, they won their first game versus Rhinelander 29 – 27 and then blitzed Crystal Falls 38 – 22. Crystal Falls would go on to win their sixth consecutive Michigan Class C State Championship in March. The Devils had put everyone on notice. After several down seasons, they were back and back with a vengeance! This was a very talented bunch. Coach Jack Kraemer had positioned his team well by scheduling tough opponents before playing a conference game. Next up for the Red Devils was that first conference game against Wakefield in the Cardinals gym. In another M – W nail biter Wakefield led the Devils 29 – 28 with just seconds left on the clock. A substitute player for Ironwood by the name of Bernard Skud, who had been in the game for about one minute, lofted a shot toward the basket and became an instant hero as the ball ripped through the net giving the Red Devils the 30 – 29 win and preserving their perfect record. And just like that the Devils were in first place in the M – W with a 1 – 0 record. Never a dull moment in the conference.

After the Christmas break school and basketball returned to the Range. Hurley took on Ashland at Dodd Gymnasium on January 7, and lost a heartbreaker 26 – 25. As usual the Midgets held the lead until the final seconds. The scrappy, overachieving Midgets shot themselves in the foot and right out of the game at the free throw line, making only 1 of 13 attempts! Ashland converted 10 of 14 charity shots for the win. The next Friday Hurley looked to use their home court advantage to right the ship versus the Bessemer Speed Boys who were mired in their worst season in years. Bessemer took out their season long frustration on the Midgets 22 – 19 handing them their first ever loss on their new gym floor after eleven straight wins. For the Speed boys it snapped a 12 game losing streak that dated back to the previous season. Making matters worse the Midgets were now holding a losing record of 3 – 4 in the season and 2 – 3 in the conference, which was now good for 4th place, just one game better than the last place Speed Boys.

They evened their overall record at 4 – 4 with a 32 – 23 win over Saint Ambrose as Rosendahl scored exactly zero points. According to the Montreal River Miner, he barely touched the ball as his teammates, particularly Charlie Mezzano were hitting on 20 foot shots. Since the break Hurley had blown a game to Ashland, was ambushed on their new gym floor by Bessemer, and beat a not so good Saint Ambrose team by not playing to their strength (get the ball down low to Rosendahl), and instead hitting a bushel of long set shots which they had not done before and would not replicate again that season. Their opponents found the key to beating Hurley was to play a zone defense and pack the defense around Rosendahl. By denying him the ball, they eliminated Hurley's best scoring threat. Things were about to get worse. Hurley had to travel to Ironwood to take on the red hot and undefeated Red Devils.

This should have been easy for the Red Devils. Hurley was a middle of the road team with a middle of the road record of 4 – 4. Ironwood was undefeated at 7 – 0 and were 4 – 0 in the M – W. They were playing on their home court, but it wasn't easy. The inspired Midgets made the Devils miserable all night long. At one point they led by ten points but, following a now familiar pattern, the Midgets crumbled as the Devils rallied. With 15 seconds to play, Kluklenski of the Devils hit a bomb from the deep corner, his only basket of the game to sink the Midgets 25 - 24. This team was now the "hard luck" Midgets. Of their five losses only Wakefield embarrassed Hurley. Their other four losses were by a total of 7 points. It was a team that everyone could see played hard. Would they ever catch a break?

CHAPTER THIRTY SIX

_____

Earning Respect

Chief Gianunzio had to rally his boys from the depths of despair. He surely made them aware of the fact that they had battled an undefeated team to the bitter end. He surely made them aware that they could easily have won 8 of the nine games they played but they did not finish games well. So the team went to work on the wings of a near miss against their arch rivals. If they could hang with Ironwood they could beat anyone! Hurley hit the reset button on their season.

In a very rare double header Hurley took on Mercer and Mellen in two Friday night games. Playing all his "A" and "B" team members Chief Gianunzio got the boys back on track by defeating Mercer 32 – 19 and Mellen 42 – 28. The wins were against two small district schools, but with the way the young "B" team members played it stoked the fire. There were five freshmen who saw extensive playing time in those games. It was a glimpse of the future while the team improved in the present.

When the Midgets resumed conference play on February 8, they were ready to get to work. The Midgets led early, in the middle, and finished strong to win at home against Wakefield 25 - 21, thus avenging their earlier loss to the Cards. Rosendahl got the ball down low early and often, scoring 14 to pace Hurley. The other seniors pitched in and sophomore Charlie Mezzano continued his fine play. Next they avenged their loss to Bessemer with a convincing 35 – 24 victory. With the game tied at 11 – 11 at halftime the Midgets showed their new found confidence as they seized control of the game. Lefty

Martino scored 11 and Charlie Mezzano 9 for the game. Gerald Rosendahl, who had a propensity for scoring big in spurts, dropped in 8 points, all in the second half. With two games to go in the regular season Hurley had now won five of their last six games, improving to 8 – 5 overall and 4 – 4 in the conference. The defining moment of their season was next. Ironwood was bringing their perfect 13 – 0 record to Hurley for the rematch.

The Hurley gym was filled to capacity and then some, as many people stood in the aisles and along the end lines. Others peered through the exit doors. The Red Devils were led by their big guns Joe Gotta and Siskonen. They were determined not to fall behind early against the Midgets again. They fought to an 8 – 5 lead at the end of the first quarter. With the crowd urging them on, the Midgets fought back to take the lead 16 – 14 at halftime. Ironwood had been finishing games with a flourish all season and looked to do it again. Hurley had only begun to figure out that formula for success. As expected there was a scoring explosion, but this time it was provided by Gerald Rosendahl as he showed off his "astonishing pivot shot." The Devils, refusing to play a zone defense, could not contain the big guy. He scored 12 points in the third quarter as the Midget lead grew to 31 - 25. Ironwood would not quit and stormed back to tie the game at 34 – 34. It was time to finish strong, and the Midgets took a page from the Red Devils' success story. It was they who finished strong while sprinting to the final buzzer for the 41 – 34 win. Charlie Mezzano scored five straight points in that final push and Gerald Rosendahl had the finest game of his high school career as he exploded for 23 points. The Hurley faithful in the packed gymnasium on 4th Avenue went home happy.

While Hurley was knocking off Ironwood, Ashland pulled off an upset of their own as they beat Superior Central 37 – 35 in Ashland. The Purgolders again were sending a message to the Vikings that they too would be reckoned with come tournament time. But first Hurley and Ashland had to square off in the last game of the season. Ironwood had now officially won the M – W Conference title so this game would be for second place. The Midgets picked up where they left off versus Ironwood as they sprinted out to an astounding 18 – 2 lead at the end of one quarter. But this was Ashland, and Melvin's team had a habit of crushing Hurley's hearts with big comeback wins. That's just what they set off to do again as they closed the gap to 21 – 14 at the half and to 30 – 27 at the end of the third quarter. The reeling Midgets fought off their weariness and dominated the fourth quarter to finish with the win 45 – 33. Rosendahl scored 18 points, Mezzano 9, Clete Kadletz 8, and Tony Lopez had 6 as the team showed some scoring punch.

The regular season was now completed. Ironwood claimed the conference championship with a 10 – 1 record and was 14 – 1 overall. Hurley finished second at 6 – 4 and 10 – 5 overall. Ashland was third at 6 – 5 and had big wins over both Superior teams. Wakefield was fourth at 4 – 6, and Bessemer suffered through a forgettable season finishing fifth at 1 – 10. It was certainly not the outcome the pundits had predicted.

The Wisconsin State Regional Tournaments were starting and Hurley traveled to Ashland again for a contest against a strong Park Falls team. The war time schedule was still in effect with the winners on the first day having to play 2 games the next day. In the opening game, the Cardinals proved to be a strong team as advertised. The game was tied at 6 – 6 after one period. The Midgets pulled ahead at the half 15 – 11 and then lengthened the lead to 23 – 17 after three periods. Gerald Rosendahl had 11 points and then fouled out of the game. Tony Lopez quickly followed him with his fourth and final foul. Park Falls took advantage and started to score down low. With Hurley leading 26 - 25 they were whistled for yet another foul with no time remaining on the clock. A Park Falls boy named Feet missed both free throws and Hurley could breathe again after nearly choking away the game.

In the other three games on the first day, Ashland had an easy time defeating Bayfield 36 – 13, Superior Central downed Phillips 42 – 30, and Superior East whipped Westboro 39 – 24. Hurley would play Ashland and the two Superior teams faced off in the afternoon games on March 4. For the Midgets it would be their fourth meeting with Ashland, and they had defeated them in two of the three previous meetings. Things were looking good until Ashland took a page from the smaller schools and played a zone defense against Hurley. Packing the key area around Rosendahl, the Purgolders dared the Midgets to take outside shots, which they just could not hit. With Rosendahl held to just seven points and his team mates unable to convert open shots from longer range, Ashland cruised to the 34 – 20 win. Superior Central topped Superior East 42 – 36 in the other semi final game.

The Midgets played East in the consolation game and earned a solid victory 33 – 25 to win 3rd place. The only two lettermen from the state tournament team the year before, Lefty Martino and Gerald Rosendahl each scored nine points in their last game in orange and black. Now all eyes were on Ashland after their convincing win over Hurley. Harry "Bud" Grant wasn't about to concede the game to the Purgolders. In this his third appearance in the Regional Tournament in three years The Montreal River Miner paid him tribute. "Grant is a natural leader. He is a coach's player and directs the team on the floor like Coach Conley would if he could." Grant would go on to score 13 points in Central's 29 – 27 win over the Purgolders in a double overtime cliff hanger. Roy Melvin was once again was so close he could taste it. Another season, another almost!

The 1943 - 1944 basketball season showed that Chief Gianunzio was an excellent coach. Quiet confidence is just as good as any other kind of confidence and Chief had it. The Montreal River Miner called him the "Coach of the Year" because "nobody thought he could do it." The Montreal River Miner also reported that it was Tommy "Runt" Hunt who hung Mario Gianunzio with the nickname "Chief" during the 1923 football season when Hunt was the senior quarterback who handed the ball off to the freshman he called "Chief." The season also meant that Hurley kids were as tough and competitive as ever. When the season hung in the balance, they and their coach hit another gear and finished with a flourish. For this group to compile a record of 12 wins and 6 losses took an extraordinary effort by the coach, his assistant Leo Busch, and especially the players who were on their third coach in three seasons. After suffering through a very disheartening and winless football season and then working so hard only to have a losing record of 4 – 5 at one point in the basketball season, they could have just packed it in. No one expected much of them from the get go anyway.

This Hurley team should always be remembered for what they accomplished. There was not a return to Madison or even a conference championship. There was plenty of the sweat, desire, and the indomitable work ethic that typified their town. They embodied the spirit of the Hurley Midgets, accomplishing more than anyone had a right to expect.

Eino "Lefty" Martino was considered to be the best athlete in the class of 1944 and one of Hurley's best ever. He was to the football team what Gerald Rosendahl was to the basketball team. Every defense was geared to stop him. Eino is most deservedly a proud member of the Hurley High School Athletic Hall of Fame. He later went on to teach and coach at Cornell High School in Wisconsin and is a member of The Wisconsin Track Coaches Hall Of Fame after leading Cornell to 17 conference championships, 5 WIAA Regional Championships, 11 WIAA Sectional Championships, and a 2nd Place finish at the State Championships. He also coached 10 individual state champions in track.

The '43 – '44 season also meant that Gerald Rosendahl was perhaps the most underappreciated athlete to ever play for Hurley. As Rosendahl went, so went the Midgets. It is very likely, that without the big kid, the Midgets would have been fortunate to win 5 games all year. In every single game opponents stacked their defenses to stop him. Hurley repeatedly saw zone defenses that packed their players in a perimeter around him. Still he led Hurley in scoring by a wide margin over Charlie Mezzano, the splendid sophomore. His value was seen in the Park Falls game as the Midgets fell apart when he fouled out. Gerald Rosendahl was the anchor to that team; without him they floundered. When you are tall, the expectations are always bigger than you play, no matter how well you play. So it was with Gerald Rosendahl. Instead of getting credit for playing well, he was expected to play even better. Win or lose, Gerald could not satisfy his critics. After enrolling at Wisconsin and then Marquette University, he left and joined the Air Force. Upon leaving the service, the University of Tulsa showed their appreciation for his talents and awarded him a scholarship to play basketball. Gerald, like his classmate Lefty, also deserves to be in the Hurley High School Athletic Hall of Fame.

There is still another chapter to the 1943 –'44 athletic seasons. A Hurley junior named Bob Sohl pulled off one of the most remarkable feats any Hurley athlete has ever accomplished. Bob was a swimmer and Hurley High did not have a pool. As a matter of fact, there wasn't a pool anywhere in Hurley. So Bob Sohl practiced in the Ironwood Memorial Building. Bob Sohl made Hurley proud by scoring 10 points in his events to give Hurley and their "one man swimming team" 7th place in the state meet held in Milwaukee on February 26, 1944.

That, however, is not the end of the Bob Sohl Story. He was the son of Dr. and Mrs. H. D. Baird of Montreal. Bob attended Hurley High for two years and then went to a boarding school, Mercersburg Academy in Pennsylvania (they had a pool and a swim team), where he graduated in 1945. Bob then went to the University of Michigan where he was on that school's powerhouse swim team. He made the U.S. Olympic Swim Team in 1948 and took the bronze medal in the 200 Meter Breaststroke, giving the American team a clean sweep in that event. Needless to say, Bob Sohl is also a member of the Hurley High School Athletic Hall of Fame! Wow!

CHAPTER THIRTY SEVEN

The Beginning Of The End

On Friday, May 26, 1944 Hurley High School bid farewell to the graduating class of 1944. As in the previous three years, most of the boys would end up in the Army, Navy, or Marines in a matter of weeks.

In just 11 days Hitler's "Fortress Europe" behind his vaunted Atlantic Wall would be assaulted by men, most of whom were barely older than the graduates that day. These weren't battle hardened men for the most part. Most of them would see combat for the first time on that morning, June 6, 1944. They stormed the beaches along with their British and Canadian allies. Many never made it to shore and never even had a chance to fire a single shot. On Omaha Beach the losses were especially catastrophic. Still these men, yesterday's boys, some who still hadn't ever shaved or kissed a girl, pushed forward into what was a wall of bullets and shrapnel. World War II Historian, Stephen E. Ambrose, wrote this:

> The Germans had taken four years to build the
> Atlantic Wall. They had poured thousands of tons
> of concrete, reinforced by hundreds of thousands
> of steel rods. They had dug hundreds of miles of
> trenches. They placed millions of mines and laid
> down thousands of kilometers of barbed wire. They
> had erected tens of thousands of beach obstacles. It
> was a colossal construction feat that had absorbed a

large percentage of Germany's material, manpower, and building capacity in Western Europe.

Four years of preparation for the assault. Four years of ensuring every inch of every beach was covered by machine gun, motor, and artillery fire. Four years of ensuring that no one could cross those beaches and live to tell the story. Hitler thought his Atlantic Wall was impenetrable. Like so many of his plans, this one too would prove to be flawed. This time it spelled doom for the Third Reich. Ambrose again:

> At Utah, the Atlantic Wall held up the U.S. 4th division
> for less than one hour. At Omaha, it had held up the
> U.S. 29th and 1st Divisions for less than one day.
> At Gold, Juno, and Sword, it had held up the British
> 50th, the Canadian 3rd, and the British 3rd divisions
> for about an hour. As there was absolutely no depth
> to the Atlantic Wall, once it had been penetrated,
> even if only by a kilometer, it was useless.

The Allies were now in France and began the difficult push toward Germany. Thousands had died that day and thousands more would sacrifice their lives to defeat the Nazis and the Japanese in the Pacific. America's first two and a half years in the war had laid the groundwork for the final push into the heart of Germany and to the shores of Japan. There had been casualties and numerous setbacks and defeats. Now the fighting would become constant, vicious, and intense. The casualty count would grow exponentially. In America, the War Department dispatched letters and telegrams delivered mostly by men in uniform. The news they contained was almost never good when delivered in person. Loved ones lived with the constant fear of receiving such a telegram or letter. A military vehicle or Western Union Telegram delivery man in the neighborhood spread panic among parents and families. They breathed a sigh of relief if their house was bypassed and then felt a stab of pain as a friend or neighbor had their lives shattered by the worst possible news, "The Navy Department regrets to inform you that your son, Petty Officer John Doe was killed in action in the performance of his duty and in the service to his country." That was the typical wording of the day. The telegram would continue to tell the wife or parent of the great sympathy all concerned extended to them. Some continued with the horrible reality that the body of their loved one "if recovered" cannot be returned at present. The telegram would also ask the parent or spouse not to divulge the name of the ship or unit so as not to give the enemy any information.

This was the terror unleashed by the dictators of the day. This was the reality of the world as it was in 1944. Into this reality, into this world, the class of 1944 took their first steps as adults. The most amazing thing of all is, like those who came before them, and those who would come after, they were ready and willing to answer their nation's call.

CHAPTER THIRTY EIGHT

The School Of Hard Knocks, Otto And EJS

The 1944 – 1945 edition of the Hurley Midgets football team was again expected to play their opponents tough and be much improved, with experienced players back from the previous year. The conference was to be decided by some very rare plays and odd bounces of the ball. The tone for the season was set when Bessemer played Iron River in their first game of the year. The Speed Boys' right tackle, Bruno Eppolite, did the unfathomable. He fell on a blocked punt to give Bessemer a 7 – 0 lead and then jumped on an Iron River fumble to score again in the Speed Boys' 13 – 0 win. A lineman scoring once in a career is rare. Scoring twice in one game has got to be some kind of record! The "experts" who predicted such things, chose Ashland to win the M – W title. The Montreal River Miner disagreed and chose Ironwood to repeat.

The Red Devils proved to be a good choice. They went six straight games into the season without giving up a touchdown. The only blemish on their undefeated conference season was a 0 – 0 tie with Bessemer in a game were both teams stoned the other on goal line stands. The Devils won versus Hurley 7 – 0, and Ashland 6 – 0. In both games blocked punts were recovered for touchdowns. Without those blocked punts, the bruising Red Devils would have had three scoreless ties in the M - W. As it was they won the conference title without scoring a single offensive touchdown! Bessemer beat Hurley 12 – 6 and Ashland 12 – 0. Ironwood and Bessemer tied for the conference title while Ashland was unpredictable all season long, and Hurley suffered through 5 more disappointing losses. They avoided a second straight winless season with a 14 − 13 win over Park Falls in the second game of the season.   The Midgets also lost two other non-conference games, losing to Rhinelander 20 − 0 and 38 − 6 to Superior Central as Bud Grant ran roughshod.

So what went wrong for Hurley? The crushing loss to Ironwood happened on a rare but opportunistic play by the Devils. They battled that superb team tooth and nail throughout the game. The Bessemer game was equally frustrating as they had opportunities to beat the Speed Boys.   There were also injuries along the defensive and offensive lines. Mickey Brown, an athletic but slightly built sophomore, was moved to center in hopes of stabilizing the banged up offensive line.   Matt Anich, the quarterback, was injured chopping wood and required stitches in his foot which sidelined him for the Ashland game and hindered him greatly in others.

The team again gave 100 percent effort and fell just short of teams that were just a little bit better. With the exception of the Superior Central game they were either in every contest or battled to the end. The School of Hard Knocks was in session.

The season did give us another chapter in the Hurley − Ironwood rivalry during game played in Hurley and in a pounding downpour. The Iron County Miner said it was a "Naval Battle" more than a football game. This time the gridiron warfare spilled over into the newspapers. Ed Sybeldon, known by the byline of "EJS" in the Iron County Miner, began a hilarious feud with an unknown writer for the Ironwood Times with the byline of "Otto Bounds." EJS and Otto sparred endlessly about anything. It was good natured, but not too good natured, and it got personal, in a funny sort of way. Each questioned the sanity of the other. Then Otto crossed the line! He called the Hurley football field, "a cow pasture."

The field in Hurley between 4th and 5th Avenues was once a hillside running east to west that was dug out and leveled off. The 4th Avenue entrance required one to descend a long set of steps to the playing field. When it rained, it retained water and the playing surface became a sea of mud. That was not so unusual for the times. It was the amount of water that soaked those hallowed grounds that was unusual. After all, water tends to run downhill. It could stay wet for days at a time and it did. Being the only field Hurley High had, it doubled as a practice field. By the second game of the season it was pretty beat up with little grass in the middle. So Otto Bounds was not too far off, especially when that field was surrounded by a snow fence that could be rolled up after the season. In 1944 that snow fence was painted red. It looked pretty nice too. Many of the diehard fans would forego the hard plank bench seating of the meager stands and lean on the snow fence to watch the game. But this year the paint was special! It never seemed to dry all the way. Maybe it was the wet field that kept it that way. Who knows? What we do know is that many fans ended up with their shirts and jackets sporting fresh red stripes! That was too much for Otto. He couldn't take it anymore.

Ed Sybeldon defended Hurley's honor by pointing out that Otto Bounds wrote with "poisoned ink" and that Ironwoods farmers seemed quite at home in Hurley's field. Otto simply stated that the splintery bleachers were good only for "braces for tomato plants and climbing beans." Ed pointed out that those bleachers were borrowed from the Ironwood field for the expected overflow crowd (they in fact were from Longyear Field). Otto further complained that the Ironwood fans got "wet." Ed pointed out that it would not be the last time people from Ironwood would come to Hurley to get "wet." He also stated that "our band is better than your band, our gym is better than your gym, and our faculty can lick your faculty."

Otto retaliated a few weeks later by saying that he called the field a "cow pasture with the worst of intentions." He simply could not come up with a better term. He then reiterated, "Hurley has a cow pasture, Hurley has a cow pasture." Hurley people deluged the Miner with letters in response. Most were humorous. One writer prophesied by saying; "Thanks Otto for your cow pasture story, as it may be the beginning of a movement to get Hurley a stadium comparable to the gymnasium." With that Otto Bounds announced his retirement (he returned briefly to take a couple of more pot shots at Hurley and Ed Sybeldon) to Tula, Michigan, a ghost town about 15 miles east of Wakefield. EJS missed him and wondered if the "Tula Tulip" would make a return.

Just as an Ironwood sports writer gave Hurley its mascot in 1924, another Ironwood writer sparked Hurley's desire to build a new football field. Construction started in 1947 and Memorial Field was ready for the 1951 season. It took four years of work and filling in the swamp at the north end of 5th avenue to create the new field. They did the job right! Memorial Field is still in use today as Hurley High's football team, under coach Scott Erickson, dominates their opponents there. Thanks Otto, and thanks Ironwood!

In the time between football and basketball seasons, Carl Vergamini returned home to Hurley on leave. After Ruth and the boys moved back to Iowa, her mother took ill and passed away. Ruth packed up the boys and her younger brother, Carl "Dutch" Holland and returned to Hurley, the place she now considered home. When Carl Vergamini was in town it was learned that his newly built ship, LST 546 (LST's in WW II were not named due to the vast numbers of them produced), lacked a movie projector that would allow the crew to enjoy movies. A total of $453 dollars was collected to be used for that purchase. The people of Hurley gave the gift of "Hollywood" to the crew. It no doubt was used at every opportunity as LST 546 transited the Panama Canal and entered the Pacific. The article went on to say that the projector would be returned to Hurley at the end of the war, owned jointly by the Chamber of Commerce and the city. It would be kept at the Memorial Building.

On Friday, November 17 the Montreal River Miner repeated a blurb from the Bessemer Herald. In reading it the people of Hurley and Ashland were reminded of the dominance of the Michigan teams, particularly Bessemer and Ironwood. In football, Bessemer or Ironwood had won or tied for the M – W title every year since the league began in 1937. Only Hurley in 1943 was able to gain a tie for the title with Bessemer. Hurley also won the 1943 title in basketball, with Bessemer and Ironwood taking the rest. Although the gap had closed between the Wisconsin and Michigan teams, there was only one year in which a Wisconsin team could be called champions. With a new basketball season just starting, that was about to change.

Hurley traveled to Ashland on that night of November 17 to take on the favored Purgolders. Hurley had one regular returning from the previous year. Charles Mezzano was now a junior and would be one of the team leaders. Gerald Swetkovich, a senior, did not get much playing time the previous year, but would prove to be a solid contributor. Ashland was not only experienced but also big, with five of their top six players standing over 6' tall. The sixth was 5'11". The untried and unknown Midgets went down in flames against the senior laden Purgolders 38 - 23. Added to Ashland's roster of savvy seniors was a junior by the name of Dick Axness. Axness played his 9th and 10th grade years at Mason High School. Like many other schools of the time it only went through 10th grade. Axness had a choice to enroll at Ashland or Drummond to finish high school. He decided on Ashland. Standing at 6' 3" tall, Axness would prove to be the icing on the Purgolders' cake. In his debut against the Midgets he scored 8 points in a balanced Ashland offense in which 7 Purgolders scored. For Hurley only three players scored. Gerald Swetkovich had 10, Charles Mezzano 9, and sophomore Mickey Brown 4.

The Midgets defeated Eagle River 30 – 14 and Wakefield 22 – 21 in the next two games. Coach Gianunzio played several sophomores in both games. Joining Mickey Brown in getting some playing time were his classmates Carl Kaffine and Willard "Bud" Geach. Charlie Mezzano continued to play well. The two wins were then followed by a loss to Park Falls 18 – 14 and the Midgets suddenly looked punch drunk. Next up they had Bessemer, a team that would typically kick the Midgets when they were down and not think twice about it. The Speed Boys had just played Ashland wire to wire losing to them 26 – 24. Things did not look good for Hurley, so in the usual way of things in conference basketball, the Midgets played an inspired game winning 28 – 27 in overtime. The up and down Hurley squad was up again and looked to stay up heading into the holidays. On December 20, they were ready to open an early Christmas present when they played the downtrodden St. Ambrose Ramblers at home. It was indeed a Merry Christmas--for the Ramblers! They edged Hurley 25 – 24. The Midgets proved that they were consistently inconsistent with their 3 – 3 record.

So what causes inconsistent play? Young players have a tendency to be inconsistent and the Midgets were a very young team. In a nutshell that's it. Gerald Swetkovich was the only senior starter and the only senior who saw considerable playing time although Matt Anich did play some, but not consistently. The rest of the team were juniors and sophomores. The future looked bright, but the present was clouded by inexperience.

After the Christmas break it was more of the same for the Midgets. They split two games with DePadua and lost again to Ashland, then beat Eagle River for the second time in the season. Hurley's record for the season was an even 5 – 5. They proceeded to lose their next four games to Ironwood, Park Falls, Bessemer, and Ironwood again before finally defeating Wakefield in the last game of the regular season. Their record stood at 6 wins and 9 losses. There were close games, and the young Midgets worked hard to stay in games against superior opponents, only to lose at the end. Charlie Mezzano, the team's best scorer, broke his ankle and missed five games. The Midgets lost four of them, all in conference. Still they nearly pulled out several close games with a lineup of sophomores teamed up with Swetkovich.

The Wisconsin State Basketball Tournament playoffs were next. Ashland was a perfect 17 – 0 on the season and ranked #2 in the state, but had to overcome the loss of one of its starters. Jake Konkel caught a bus to Milwaukee and joined the Army after the Rhinelander game early in the season. The Purgolders were still more than formidable with Dick Axness getting used to playing with his new teammates. Superior Central again was, well, superior! They sported a sterling 15 – 2 won – loss record with their only two defeats coming at the hands of Ashland. They were ranked #12 in the state. Superior East, Park Falls, and Phillips rounded out the field. Hurley was scheduled to take on Superior Central in the mismatch of the tournament and Ashland would meet Phillips in the first round games. Park Falls and Superior East drew first round byes and met the winners of the first games.

As expected Ashland had an easy time of it in knocking off Phillips 42 – 23. In the second game everyone thought it would be another slaughter as Central was expected to brush off the Midgets with little resistance. There was resistance, and more than that, Hurley gave their fans a look at the future as sophomores Bud Geach and Mickey Brown came to life against Bud Grant and the Vikings. The game went back and forth with neither team gaining more than a two point lead. With Hurley leading 27 – 26 Brown missed a shot that rolled around the rim for an eternity before falling out. Brown did get two free throws and the young gun missed both. With Central leading 28 – 27 Brown hit another shot, but it was waved off as he was called for traveling. Grant than secured the win with a bucket. Central added another late score for the 32 – 27 win. For the young Hurley five it was a bitter pill to swallow. They came within a whisker of upsetting a ranked team. With new found confidence they won third place in the regional by defeating Phillips 30 – 18 and then Superior East 19 – 18. Geach and Brown were revelations and the hope of better things to come. On the year the Midgets finished with a record of 8 wins and 10 losses. If not for the loss of Charlie Mezzano for five games, that record would easily be reversed. It turned out to be Hurley's only losing record in basketball from 1940 – 1965.

As for Roy Melvin and his Ashland quintet, they won the regional title with a 30 – 28 win against Central on a last second shot that ended the Vikings dreams. The Purgolders then crushed Park Falls 43 – 28. Superior Central lost only three games all season. Only Ashland could defeat them. Park Falls lost only four games all season. Three of those were to Ashland. The Purgolders were the cream of the far north crop. Now they were on to Spooner for the Sectional Meet. Ashland was then rocked by the news that Les Howard would have to depart for basic training in the Navy. He thought when he enlisted that he would not be called up until after the state tournament. Ashland lost a key player in Howard who was their fourth leading scorer, a superb defender, and a rugged rebounder. They went on to blow away Drummond 45 – 7 and Spooner 61 – 24 to win the right to go to Madison with a perfect 22 – 0 record. In Madison the Purgolders missed the tough, hardnosed Howard as they lost in the opening round and again in the consolation finals. For Roy Melvin and the Ore Dock city, they were left to wonder what might have been. They finished their greatest season at 23 wins and 2 losses.

CHAPTER THIRTY NINE

The War Ends

At the end of May, graduating classes across the Range stepped across stages to receive their high school diplomas and step into the world. Their futures were once again filled with uncertainty and danger. In the Pacific the United States began landing 180,000 soldiers and marines on Okinawa on April 1, 1945. One Iron County man who fought there was Warren Buccanero of Iron Belt. After making history, he would go on to teach history at Iron Belt High and then Hurley High School for 35 years.

The Battle of Okinawa would be one of the bloodiest battles of the war and it was still raging when the War in Europe ended on May 8th. The Battle of Okinawa continued until June 22, 1945. It was this horrific battle that brought the forces of the United States to Japan's front door. The writing was on the wall for the Japanese, and yet they were adamant that they would never surrender. America was now preparing for the invasion of Japan itself. This invasion would be on a much larger scale than the D-Day invasion of Normandy, and would cost America more casualties than any battle ever fought in the history of this planet. For the Japanese people the cost would turn out to be even more horrific. Starvation, disease, homelessness and exposure to the elements would claim a huge portion of their population. The planners had a sense of foreboding and dread. Time and again the numbers were crunched, and time and again, the numbers told the grisly story of such a large scale invasion.

Lieutenant (Junior Grade) Carl Vergamini was now the Supply Officer on LST-546. An LST was a U.S. Navy Amphibious ship, in this case a Landing Ship Tank (LST). These ships were about 320 feet long and were built with a flat bottom and with a bow that opened like saloon doors to disgorge its cargo of tanks, half-tracks, trucks, jeeps and men right onto the shore. Over one thousand were built for the Navy and our allies. With huge diesel engines powering them, their sole purpose was to drive up to the beach and unload. It was a thankless and dangerous task. On the open ocean an LST was slow, making an average of about 9 knots cruising speed. Their crews called them Large Slow Targets, and they were only half-kidding. In the summer of 1945 LST-546, with a crew of about 117 men and carrying about 175 marines and equipment, completed its training and entered the Pacific Ocean via the Panama Canal to make its laborious journey to the shores of Japan.

The casualty reports from Okinawa were making the rounds throughout the military. Every soldier, airman, marine and sailor knew what that meant. If Okinawa was so bloody, how much more so would the invasion of Japan itself be? The civilian population of Okinawa was about 300,000 of which over 100,000 were killed during the hostilities. About 12,000 Americans were killed in action in the Okinawa campaign. Japanese military casualties were about 110,000 killed and about 16,000 surrendered. It was the only time in the war that Japanese surrendered in large numbers. The population of Japan was about 35,000,000. The bulk of their military forces were still there. One can do the math. Multiply those casualty numbers by about 115 and there you have it.

On August 6, and again on August 9, 1945, the U.S. dropped atomic bombs on the Japanese cities of Hiroshima and Nagasaki. So fervent were some of the Japanese hardliners that they attempted a coup rather than surrender! The coup failed and on August 15, Japan announced that they would surrender. As the word spread throughout the world, spontaneous celebrations took place. Onboard LST-546, which was transiting from Guam to Okinawa, the crew opened up with all anti-aircraft batteries firing in celebration! They and countless others would be spared. Carl Vergamini had stood the mid-watch the previous night and was sleeping in his quarters when all hell broke loose. Thinking the ship was under attack, he ran to his General Quarters station on the main deck ready for action. It's a good thing for him no action was required as he found himself standing among the joyous crew in his underwear!

In Hurley and on the Range, the celebrations took place on Tuesday evening, August 14, after the 6 PM news broadcast. Amid church bells, sirens, and steam whistles blaring, the people of Hurley went to town, turning up on Silver Street in record numbers. A bonfire was started at the intersection of Silver Street and 4th Avenue which became the focal point of the celebration. Miners were given the next day off and they too showed up. People congregated in restaurants, taverns, and the street. Churches all opened their doors and they were packed with people offering thanks and praying for their loved ones. Restaurants ran out of food. Three high school boys started playing music and a street dance began. The boys were the recipients of the princely sum of over twenty dollars in donations for their efforts. Over in Gogebic County, the authorities closed all the taverns, leaving those who wanted to celebrate with an alcoholic libation one clear alternative: Hurley! As Silver Street was becoming deluged with revelers from both sides of the state line, the mayor ordered Hurley's bars closed too. They did so, with all closing the front doors while a few kept the back doors open with a wink and a smile.

At least one woman did not go to town. A neighbor called out to her as she was working in her garden and told her the war was over. The woman blessed herself, wiped away tears, and went back to tending her tomatoes.

And then there is this. What are the chances of a sailor, in Hurley, on V - J Day, not drinking alcohol? It happened! A sailor was seen sitting in a car while drinking a bottle of milk as he explained that he could not find anything stronger with the bars closed. And finally, the Montreal River Miner concluded, "Most people turned out to watch the other people. It was a case of a lot of spectators and few actors. But those intoxicated with joy or otherwise did put on a good performance."

On September 2, 1945, Japan signed the surrender documents on board the USS Missouri in Tokyo Bay. While the world rejoiced, reality set in. The cost of this war was beyond comprehension. How can you begin to tally the cost? Here are some of the facts.

There were fifty nine countries involved in WWII (depending on what one considers involvement). For the first time naval warfare was conducted above, below, and on the surface of all the oceans of the world. Warfare was conducted mainly on the continents of Asia, Europe, and Africa. Australia was attacked from the air and sea but no land battles took place there. No battle took place in North or South America but there were clandestine operations on both continents. Antarctica was left alone. Historians have not been able to conclude just how many people died in WWII. It is estimated that 50 – 70 million perished. After the war many more people died of starvation, disease, and exposure to the elements. Those numbers were also in the millions and no one knows with certainty the exact number. No one knows just how many children were orphaned with estimates ranging from one million to thirteen million. The United States had 416,800 soldiers, sailors, airmen, and marines killed in action and another 2.8 million received non-fatal wounds. The cost of the war was about 5 trillion dollars. In today's world that works out to about 20 trillion dollars.

All those numbers are numbing. So numbing, that human beings tend to see only the massive statistics and forget the individual toll. When brought to a personal level the numbers mean so much more than we want to imagine. Here are the more personal numbers. In Iron County well over 1,000 men and women served. The exact number is also unknown because many young people from Iron County were living, working, or attending college elsewhere at the start of the war. When they joined the service they were counted in among those from their new location. Forty-three men from Iron County were killed in action during the war. An unknown number were wounded. The tiny towns of Iron County were filled with houses displaying a blue star for every member of their family in the service. Forty three of those homes displayed a gold star for their beloved son or husband who gave their lives. Almost everyone in every town knew those men. They were yesterday's boys. Only a few short years before, they ran through the neighborhoods playing tag, hide and seek, and sports. They cut their neighbors' grass, shoveled snow for the elderly, and ran errands to the grocery stores where they were well known. Most of their parents knew each other. They lived down the block or next door. They were long remembered as a best friend, the boy next door, a first date, a first kiss, the kid who built the tree house, had snowball fights, and as ball players. They loved and were loved in return. They were sons, brothers, fathers, nephews, cousins, friends, babies, kids, boys and men. They answered the call to defend their country, their communities, and their families. They and those who returned home truly saved the world. They were ordinary people who lived in extraordinary times and acted with extraordinary bravery and resolve.

The end of the war did not end the uncertainty for many families. Many would wait for weeks and months to learn the fate of their loved ones. They were listed as "missing in action," and/or "presumed dead." One incident late in the war affected three Iron County families in this way. On July 30 the USS Indianapolis was torpedoed by a Japanese submarine after delivering the first atomic bomb to Saipan. Gilbert Chart of Montreal, Charles Bruno of Hurley, and Lloyd Barto of Gile were crewmembers and shipmates on that ill fated cruiser. For weeks their fate was unknown to anyone. Both Gilbert Chart and Charles Bruno were killed in action on that night. Of the crew of 1,195 only 316 survived the sinking and subsequent ordeal of floating on the ocean for over 96 hours. Lloyd Barto was among those survivors. At the war's end many families were reunited with a serviceman who was listed in that category but were unreported prisoners of war. Most of them, however, never returned. There are still some 72,000 World War II service members listed as "Missing in Action" to this day.

As service members returned home over the next 18 months, life returned to "normal." These boys and girls were now men and women. They took jobs, went to college, and started building a peacetime nation. They seldom spoke of their experiences in war, preferring to focus instead on living in peace. They became friends, co-workers, and neighbors to people who never knew they were in the company of a hero.

Most people know that the Medal of Honor is the highest recognition bestowed upon a member of the United States Armed Forces for valor in combat. Iron County did not have a recipient during World War II. They are rarely awarded and most are awarded posthumously. Each branch of the service may award the second highest award for valor. They are The Navy Cross, the Distinguished Service Cross (Army), and the Air Force Cross. Iron County had at least four recipients during World War II. They were, Lieutenant David R. Rautio, U.S. Army Air Corps from Hurley, Sergeant William E. Kero, U.S. Army, from Saxon, Lieutenant Emil B. Stella, U.S. Navy, from Hurley, and Private First Class James L. Geach, also from Hurley. Their citations are lengthy but here is the gist of their brave actions.

David Rautio was a co-pilot on a severely crippled bomber that suffered numerous flak hits over Germany. With the pilot severely wounded, two of the four engines destroyed, the windscreen shattered, and the cockpit instrument panel wrecked, LT Rautio flew the crippled bomber back to England while enduring frostbitten hands. He landed the "lopsided" bomber without incident saving the pilot and crew. He completed over 30 bombing missions during the war.

William Kero was killed in action in Holland during Operation Market Garden. He was a paratrooper with the 82 Airborne. He was also awarded the "Ridder vierde klasse der Militaire Willems Orde" by the Dutch government, the highest honor that nation bestows for "conspicuous acts of bravery, leadership, and extreme devotion to duty in the presence of the enemy."

Emil Stella was a U.S. Navy dive bomber pilot. During the Battle of Leyte Gulf, the largest naval engagement in history, he scored a direct hit on a Japanese battleship and then ten days later scored another direct hit on a Japanese cruiser. Both were sunk. He earned the Navy Cross for the hit on the battleship and the Silver Star for the hit on the cruiser.

Jim Geach had never fired a bazooka before he used one on July 5, 1944 against a German tank in France. He missed three shots but sent the tank into retreat. He then sent the German infantry troops with that tank running. He did not miss with his rifle. That doesn't sound extraordinary until you find that he did it while he was alone! He then located U.S. tanks and led them to the Germans, who were then routed. Before that, while in action in Italy, he won the Silver Star for heroism.

Hurley's long time dentist, Leno C. Odorizzi, won the Silver Star for evacuating wounded from the aid stations in Belgium. Acting with disregard for his own personal safety he repeatedly passed over terrain subjected to direct enemy machine gun and artillery fire. Doctor Odorizzi saved the lives of many wounded men that day.

The Silver Star is the third highest award for bravery for U.S. Service members. Jim Geach and Emil Stella both were awarded the second and third highest awards for valor during World War II. There were many from Iron County who earned Bronze Stars, the fourth highest award for valor and other citations for exemplary actions. How someone determines the difference between these acts of gallantry is beyond my scope. I am in awe of every one of their actions. Veterans know that those who earned these medals were heroes, but they will also tell you that there were so many others who acted with courage time and again and those actions went unnoticed or unreported.

If you are wondering why this is included in the story about Hurley High's sports teams, there is a reason. The story of Hurley High School sports is a reflection of the character of the town and its people. World War II was as real as it gets. For the people who lived through it, whether they were in the military or on the home front, it became the seminal point in their lives. They divided their lives into three parts: "before the war, during the war, and after the war." Most of their stories and recollections start off with one of those three introductions. Our World War II generation not only lived through that great cataclysm but they also endured the Great Depression as the sons and daughters of miners and those living in a mining community. The people of Hurley and the Range knew great heartache as many miners were killed on the job. Others lost their lives in a myriad of industrial and farm accidents. They knew the ravages of diseases that had no prevention or cure at the time. Even in good economic times, most people lived frugally and wasted nothing. Children did not have many toys and those they did have were well cared for. They did not expect to be entertained, but rather provided their own entertainment in the company of one another. Their friendships ran deep, and their respect for each other was deeper still. As strong and tough as that made them, it also made them kind hearted like their immigrant parents and grandparents. They found joy and happiness in simple pleasures. A ball game, a concert, or a play at the school was a big occasion. Most Hurley people were proud, determined, quick to share, and their big hearts ached with the desire to provide their children with a better life than they had. The school and the kids of Hurley were the center of their universe. The soldiers, sailors, airmen and marines from Iron County were already tough and strong willed before the war started.

There are other factors that made the people of Hurley, and of the entire Range for that matter, unique in many ways. The work they did in the mines was difficult and dangerous even by the standards of those days. Farmers in the region had short growing seasons which required even more work from them. One of the standing jokes of the day was that these farmers cultivated a lot of rocks. Once they cleared a field of trees, the real work of removing the rocks began. There are many homesteads and farms in the area that to this day that are surrounded by walls of rocks piled up and stretching from one end of the property line to the other. They were placed there one at a time. Railroaders, construction workers, tradesmen, clerks, accountants, lawyers, doctors, nurses, business owners, lumberjacks, and others knew what hard work was and they went about their days with the pride that comes with accomplishment.

Geography also conspired to make this area unique. While technically located in the "Midwest," the Range was at the farthest reaches of the northern Midwest. So far north, that people from 100 miles to the south and further began to refer to the area as "Up North." It was settled later than the rest of the Midwest. It became a frontier far removed from the population centers of Michigan and Wisconsin. The people who settled there had a frontier mentality long after it had disappeared from those who lived south of this piece of heaven.

The Range has Lake Superior to thank for its weather. The big lake is vast, deep, and the water is very cold. It keeps the area air conditioned on most summer days. In the winter it causes some deep freezes that would make a penguin happy to live there. Oh yeah, it snows there a lot too. It comes early in most years and stays as late as it pleases. Travel 20 miles to the south and you will find less than half the snow that the Range has. Ashland is spared the amount of snow the rest of the Range gets, but they also have a colder spring as the town is built right on the lake. The inhabitants of the Range do complain about the weather, but it is usually with a smile. Being a tough place to live is what made it s special place to grow up in. Shared experiences bring people together. The tougher and more difficult the experience, the closer the bond becomes. All the hardships, compounded by the Great Depression and then World War II, cemented that bond for all time.

CHAPTER FORTY

No Easy Days!

The end of the war was the most welcome news of the twentieth century. It also brought with it many changes and adjustments. Wartime industries were converted to peacetime industries. America now had the largest and most robust economy on the planet. Still the period just after the war was uncertain. Sixteen million men and women were being demobilized, and were returning to civilian life wanting civilian jobs. It was widely thought that the United States would roll back into another depression with high unemployment rates and high inflation, but that did not happen.

The unemployment rate did double from 1.9 percent to 3.9 percent from 1945 to 1946, but that was a far cry from the double digit unemployment that plagued the nation during most of the Great Depression. It was in fact similar to the unemployment rates prior to 1930. The fact that America was the only industrialized nation on the planet that had escaped the destruction of its manufacturing hubs was one reason for employment rates to remain low. The retooling of industry to peacetime mode began immediately. New jobs producing consumer goods replaced those building war machines. Farm production remained high as America sought to feed the starving masses of Europe and Asia.

With the return of sixteen million men over the next two years, many married women working in the war industries began to return to the home as their husbands re-entered the workplace. People were married in record numbers during and soon after the war. They did not wait to start their families. The United States still has not seen anything like the Baby Boom generation from 1946 – 1964. Young American men and women wanted to make up for the time the war had stolen from them and they did just that! With so many children, mothers tended to stay at home. That too contributed to the low unemployment rate.

Finally, the G.I. Bill provided veterans with the opportunity to continue their education after the war. Almost 8 million of them did, attending colleges, trade schools, business schools, agricultural training schools, and other job training programs. By 1947, 49 percent of all college attendees were veterans using the G.I. Bill. Armed with new skills and abilities they helped grow the nation's economy over the next five decades. By being in college they helped keep the unemployment rate low immediately after the war.

America's success in maintaining high employment rates and raising the standard of living after World War II did not extend to the Range. America continued to produce steel, but iron ore production did not keep pace. Instead the steel producers began to utilize more scrap iron and steel. It was more cost effective and it was abundant now that the war was over. Ships, tanks, and other war materials were scraped, melted down, and re-used. You can make thousands of washing machines and dryers from the scrap of just one tank. Ships were dismantled with cutting torches and sold for scrap. Many former sailors ended up shaving with razor blades made from the scrap of their old ships. Before long two-thirds of all steel produced was from recycled scrap. Iron ore production continued, but at a reduced rate. The one thing that saved the iron ore mining industry in the area for the time being was the fact that much of the rest of the world's steel producers had been bombed out of existence during the war and, for now, America was helping rebuild the demolished cities of Europe and Japan with its steel production.

The post war population loss on the Range was profound. Iron County lost 13.3% of its population between 1940 and 1950, mostly after the war. Ironwood lost 14.4%, Bessemer lost 14%, Wakefield lost 7 %, and Ashland, which produced no iron ore but was a shipping hub for that ore, lost 4.2% of her population over that time. Another reason for the downturn in iron ore production on the range was that the ore found on the Minnesota Iron Range north of Duluth was less pure than the ore found on the Gogebic Range. The ore on the Gogebic Range required underground mining, with many mines deeper than 4,000 feet and some over 5,000 feet below the surface. The surface ore in Minnesota although not as pure, was plentiful and could be mined from open pits, a less expensive method. Also these ores, known as taconite, were magnetic. By grinding the taconite ore into dust the iron could be extracted with powerful magnets and formed into pellets for shipping, whereas the more pure ores of the Gogebic range were not conducive to making pellets. Mining in Minnesota became more and more surface mining until all the underground mines closed in favor of the open pits. The population on Minnesota's Iron Range remained steady throughout the 1940's and then boomed from 1950 – 1960 by 12.4 % due to taconite processing.

Minnesota's taconite boom contributed to the demise of mining on the Gogebic Range. The Gogebic Range did not run out of ore because it was too pure. It's hard to imagine that a superior ore would be too good to mine, but the economics of the situation have made it so. There is a lot still there waiting for the time when it will be economically feasible to mine once again.

The Gogebic Range people who could not find work in the area did find it in places like Detroit, Milwaukee, Chicago, and other postwar boom towns. The economic bleed out on the Range was not caused by one major blow, but rather by 10,000 tiny, irritating paper cuts. The big blows would come later in the late 1950's and early 1960's when the mines began closing. The postwar population decline would not be reversed. As Hurley's youth graduated from high school, most traveled south seeking jobs or going to college. Most would return only to visit as the slow, almost imperceptible decline had begun. A large number of Hurley's graduates had always left the area to seek opportunities elsewhere. They found that they were welcomed by employers with open arms. The Range had a reputation for producing people of high character, with a strong work ethic and dependability that was off the charts. Hurley and the rest of the Range would change dramatically, but first there was going to be one more cause for celebration.

CHAPTER FORTY ONE

The Journey Of A Thousand Miles

The end of the war brought a new optimism to America. As noted, Americans were now in a hurry to make up for lost time. They were also quick to turn their attention back to the simple pleasures. As always the Range turned its attention to a new school year and a new football season. Shortly after Chief Gianunzio welcomed his football players to their first practice, Carl Vergamini and the crew of LST 546 were assigned the task of ferrying Japanese soldiers from China and Korea back to Japan. It was clear to the crew that they were not going back to the States for awhile. Chief and his assistant, Leo Busch would again coach the Hurley football team.

Things started going south for Hurley before the season even got started. Mickey Brown was scheduled to make the move from center to quarterback where his athleticism would trigger the offense. When he and his friend and teammate Bruno Mioni were injured in a car accident in August, those plans were scrapped. Mioni would be cleared to play in a few weeks, but Brown was out for the season with a neck injury. To further complicate matters, Ed Sybeldon wrote that he noticed a genuine lack of commitment from the senior members of the team as they reported to practice well after the practice schedule was put out. Worse, they made no effort to contact their coach as to why they did so. Only 23 boys reported to the first week of practice. Sybeldon thought there was an attitude issue, calling the older boys "prima donnas." He continued his rant, flatly predicting Hurley would not win a single game unless they played the game because they liked the game. This former Midget was beside himself. In all the research found for this book, he never, ever sounded angry or upset in any of his other writings. This group definitely put him on the spin cycle. He was furious!

The end of the war brought about Wakefield's re-entry into the football world. They remained out of the M-W Conference in football and choose instead to schedule schools their size. Hurley was their size but the Cardinals would not play them again until 1951 when they re-entered the M-W for football.

One thing did go Chief Gianunzio's way as the practice sessions started. He recruited one of Hurley's greatest linemen ever. Tony Brunello lived on a farm in Kimball, just west of Hurley. The area was called "Dago Valley" a name the inhabitants wholeheartedly embraced as they said, "Hard work makes the Day Go." Tony Brunello was all about hard work. He did not play football in his freshman or sophomore years because it was eight miles from the school to his farm. He also felt he should be there after school to help with the chores. He had to ride the bus home right after school. After talking with Chief about football he and his father decided he should play. To get home, he would leave practice early when Chief had the players run laps. Tony ran home every night. There was not an entitled bone or a hint of being a "prima donna" in his body or character! Tony was also a big kid. Farm work left him finely chiseled and strong as a bull. Without ever playing a down of football before in his life he became the starting left tackle. He dominated his opponents, all of them, every game!

The season went as Ed Sybeldon had predicted. He wanted the boys to prove him wrong, but it never happened. The losing habit was ingrained upon them, or at least upon the older boys. They give Ashland a tough time of it in the season opener as Ashland beat the

Midgets 12 – 0. The Midgets put up a fight until George Mrdjenovich broke his ankle on a long run and was lost for the season. With Brown and Mrdjenovich sidelined, points were hard to come by. After squeezing out a tie with Park Falls, the hammer fell when Ironwood crushed the Midgets 42 – 0. Ironwood, for the third year in a row, was the class of the M-W and the Upper Peninsula. They overpowered opponents with their size and speed. They had it all. With the score 35 – 0 and Hurley having been kicked all over the field, the Red Devils came out throwing the ball, as their starters remained in the game and tried to run up the score. There were 105 boys out for football that year at Ironwood. The lack of substitutions was a fact not lost on the Hurley players. One player in particular was steaming, but he was steaming at what he saw in the team.

In the middle of this lost season, the scene in the Hurley locker room after the game was predictable. The players shook their heads. They spoke of how they could never beat Ironwood. How unfair it was to play such a big school in football. It was pretty much a pity party. And then the reserved junior, the new kid on the team, had heard enough. Tony Brunello stood and addressed his teammates. He asked them to dedicate themselves to beating Ironwood in 1946; to dedicate themselves starting at that very moment. The seniors shook their heads and said it couldn't be done. But Tony wasn't sending his message to the seniors. He was sending it to the juniors and sophomores, who nodded their agreement. The Red Devils had just pulverized them and after Tony Brunello spoke they wanted payback! The Midgets found their leader and a true pillar of strength. The kid from Dago Valley, the very kid who ran 8 miles each night to get home from practice had earned their respect. Things were going to be different. For the rest of the season the Midgets played better despite a rising rash of injuries. They did not win a game, but they rallied around their new found leader and improved each step of the way. Juniors Tony Brunello and Don Zell were selected to the All Conference team, with Brunello named the captain of the second team. Not bad for a guy who had never played before. The football season was not a complete loss. The table was set and pride was restored to Hurley football.

Fall began to give way to winter and basketball season was upon the Range. EJS predicted Hurley would finish first or second in the conference based upon the play of juniors Mickey Brown, now recovered from his neck injury, and Bud Geach. Those two, added to the return of two seniors, high scoring Chuck Mezzano and tough Jack Muehl, gave Midget fans high hopes. Chief Gianunzio would continue to be the coach and Ted Gentile, now released from the Army, was back to assist him as Leo Busch took a leave of absence to take care of his health. As the Hurley boys practiced in preparation for the season, Carl Vergamini's thoughts were not on basketball.

On the other side of the world some 6000 miles from Hurley, LST 546 pulled into Tokyo Bay and disembarked hundreds of Japanese soldiers who were stranded in Korea at the end of the war. Before making another trip across the Sea of Japan to return Korean nationals who were enslaved during the war, Lieutenant (Junior Grade) Vergamini and a couple of friends were able to latch onto a jeep. The group drove to Nagasaki. The ride there was filled with small talk as they wondered what they would see at the scene of the city which had the second atomic bomb dropped on it. Upon their arrival on a hillside overlooking the city, all talk ceased. They stared out at the devastation in stunned silence. After a few minutes and with only a nod, the men, now alone with their own thoughts, jumped back into the jeep and silently returned to their ship. It would be decades before Carl Vergamini spoke of that day to his sons, and then it was with the word "devastation" repeated again and again. The basketball season would play out before Carl returned home. Sports and games seemed to be light years away, in another universe.

On November 16 the 1945 – 46 edition of Hurley basketball got underway in Eagle River, WI. Eagle River had a pretty tough team and they were especially difficult to play on their home court. It was another throwback to the 1910's with a low ceiling and a short court that enabled the defenses to establish position quickly. At the half it was 19 – 18 in favor of Hurley. It was the third quarter that would decide the game as the Midgets pulled ahead 34 – 23 and then cruised to the 43 – 36 win over the stubborn Eagle River five. Chief Gianunzio played 13 boys in the game but only five scored. Charlie Mezzano and Mickey Brown led the way with 14 and 12 points with Bud Geach and Jack Muehl chipping in with 8 each. Senior Bill "Kaiser" Canney scored the remaining point.

Two new rules went into effect with the new basketball season. The first was that teams now had ten seconds to advance the ball past the half-court line after a change of possession. That greatly increased the speed of play as teams could no longer fiddle around to slow the game down far away from their own basket. The second rule allowed for a player to accrue five fouls before being disqualified from the game. The game was starting to look more like the modern basketball we know today.

Ashland was next on the schedule in the M-W conference opener for both teams. Ashland served notice by belting the always good Rhinelander Hodags 35 – 20 in their first game of the season. The Purgolders were left seemingly threadbare by the graduation of the bulk of the state tournament team from the previous year. But they still had Dick Axness and he was better than ever. Roy Melvin tried to explain to people that he had nothing other than Axness, but they explained to him that Axness might be all he needed. He was clearly one of the best players, if not the very best, in the state of Wisconsin.

Playing on Hurley's court, the Purgolders trailed the Midgets until late. Mezzano and Brown again carried Hurley with 17 and 16 points. Geach scored 4 and Muehl 2. For Ashland it was the Dick Axness show. The big, quick, and tough center scored 22 points including Ashland's last six points on put backs off his teammates' missed shots. He fouled out with five fouls with 15 seconds to play, but the Midgets could not take advantage as the Purgolders held on for the 41 – 39 win. As in the recent past, Ashland continued to dominate the Midgets with the game on the line. It was becoming disheartening to lose to the Purgolders time and again in that way.

The loss to Ashland was followed by good and historic news. Hurley would host the Regional Tournament for the first time ever. Hurley had tried for 25 years to host the tournament but to no avail. Now, four years after Hurley High built the best gym on the Range, the townspeople felt it was about time! All the previous regional tournaments had been in Superior or Ashland.

The third game of the season was played in Ashland on DePadua's cigar box sized basketball court. Following their same formula, the Bruins played a zone defense and had to run only a few feet to get back on defense. As usual the Bruins turned the game into a slow crawl. Hurley was able to overcome the tactics and the cramped court to pull out the 23 – 18 non-conference victory.

Coinciding with the Hurley win was a message from "Otto Bounds" writing for the Ironwood Times and reprinted by Ed Sybeldon in the Miner. It seems Otto was fed up with "poor sportsmanship" around the Range and pointed to Hurley as an example of what good sportsmanship looked like. Otto said, "They should see a Hurley game and follow their example in sportsmanship. Hurley's got the best bunch of cheerleaders and the best organized student body in this part of the country." That was not to say Hurley was a quiet place to play. The fans were as loud as they were numerous. Sellout followed sellout as the new gym was jammed to the rafters with spectators. The cheerleaders really were that good, and the student body participated in every organized cheer with full throated gusto. It was good old fashioned "spirit" and it was fun for everyone. Hurley High had a "Pep" club that along with the cheerleaders ensured everyone got involved. They were organized, loud, clean, and intimidating for other teams. Otto also said this, "Another thing, Hurley never uses that vulgar yell either that has been so prominent in the Upper Peninsula these last two years." Otto was right about that. With J.E. Murphy and Harold Conners at the helm of the school, that would never happen. It wasn't that the student body was afraid of them. It was because they admired and respected them. It was a case of choosing to do the right thing because they did not want to disappoint those who placed their trust in them. Of course they also would have had to face their parents. There was tough love for sure, but it was even-handed and genuine. The Hurley kids knew it and they respected that fact also.

So after two years of quibbling, Ed and Otto finally agreed on at least one thing. Ed also pointed out that the organized cheering wasn't just for the students but that the adults joined in with just as much enthusiasm. Finally Ed praised the Hurley band for their part. They were always in full uniform at the games and put on brilliant halftime shows that pumped up the crowds even more. Hurley basketball was truly more than a game. It was an event that the entire town participated in. The fans expended every ounce of their energy, just as the players did.

The Midgets had won both non-conference games and lost to Ashland in the conference. Their next game was against Bessemer and they needed a win or risked falling out of contention for the title early in the season. Hurley started strong and had an 18 – 5 lead at the half. Bessemer fought back in the second half and closed the gap but could not make up the early deficit. Hurley 32 – Bessemer 24 was the final score. A week later they blasted Wakefield 50 – 25 for another conference win and then followed that up with a 34 – 19 win over a good St. Ambrose team. Hurley's two headed scoring monster of Mezzano and Brown again led the team in all three of those games. Hurley headed into the Christmas break with a record of 5 – 1. The Red Devils from Ironwood were standing by to help them greet 1946 with a game on January 4 in Ironwood.

The Devils had only one loss on the season, which was by just two points to Ashland, just like Hurley. The game was expected to be close and it was. It was also a sad display by both teams. The Midgets were understandably embarrassed by the 42 – 0 shellacking the Big Red Devils handed them during the football season. They came out with a chip on their shoulders. The Ironwood boys were not about to let the Midgets dictate the tempo and pace of the game. The result was a bitter battle low-lighted by 36 personal fouls, 23 on Ironwood and 13 on Hurley. Bud Geach and Ironwood's Winkowski were both ejected in the second quarter. They didn't exactly fight, no big punches were thrown, but they did engage in a two man, "wild melee." To add insult to their ejections, they both proceeded to miss their free throws that resulted from the double foul before being banished to an early shower. As far as basketball went, there wasn't much of it played. Mazurak of Ironwood ended up losing a tooth at some point due to the rough play, and that was one of the few plays in which the whistle did not blow. Whistle after whistle resulted in a complete lack of cohesion or rhythm for both teams. Both coaches were red faced at the display, but remained calm. The crowd of over 2000 was loud, but well behaved as noted by Ed Sybeldon in the Miner. He had nothing but praise for the spectators regarding their sportsmanship. "Not a program was tossed – not a boo – not a jeer." Ed went on to give the coaches and the fans a grade of 100. He failed both teams on that same exam. Ironwood ended up winning the game 29 – 27. The rivalry went from red hot to boiling over.

No season is ever easy. If you are a good team, every other team takes aim and hits you with their best game. If you are a bad team you work like a dog to get better. It's a long season and it's filled with ups and downs. Hurley was about to head into a valley. They were talented, but almost all their scoring punch came from two players. Jack Muehl was beginning to show some scoring touch and Bud Geach chipped in some too. There were several juniors who showed real promise, but they were not scoring. It was a bit of a problem. It was a bigger problem now that Hurley had to travel to Ashland to face high scoring Dick Axness and his Purgolder teammates. Axness was averaging over 24 points per game and was the focal point of the Ashland offense. The Ashland 5 was undefeated in the conference and had lost only to a superb Superior Central team. The Midgets broke with tradition and played a zone defense in effort to bottle up Axness. It worked to perfection in that the Ashland center was held to just one point in the first half. The zone didn't work against Ashland's other players as they sniped away from the outside to give the Purgolders an 18 – 10 lead. In the second half, those snipers went dormant and

Axness came to life with ten more points in Ashland's 34 – 27 win. It wasn't as close as the score indicates, as the Midgets scored six straight points to close the game. Again Mezzano and Brown led the scoring with only two others dropping in any points. Hurley now was 2 – 3 in the M-W and 5 – 3 overall. The once promising season was heading south in a hurry and the wheels were falling off the bus.

A frustrated Ed Sybeldon wrote that this was one of Hurley's most talented teams "(individually)." He then proceeded to say that each player was "good on his own merits" but they were not a good team. It was clearly now a season that hung in the balance.

The Eagle River Team Hurley beat in the season opener at Eagle River was the next opponent. This time the game was on Hurley's regulation sized court. And the difference in the speed of the game was amazing! Eagle River was a rarity. They were a small school team that played fast and loose where most other small schools slowed down the game versus bigger schools. Hurley and Eagle River both showed well offensively, but Hurley put in more effort on defense and won easily 65 – 45. For the first time all season a player not named Brown or Mezzano led the team in scoring. Tall Joe Darin, a junior, scored 17 points and Bud Geach pitched in with 12. Chief Gianunzio played 13 boys and none of the starters played more than half the game. For Joe Darin it turned out to be the finest game of his high school career. He had another career in mind. He became a world renowned doctor who did ground breaking research in the field of liver disease.

Ironwood was the next opponent, this time in Hurley. This time they would forget about football and play basketball. An overflow crowd was expected and special bleachers were erected on the band stage to seat more fans. The run up to the game was electric. The last "brawl game" had enticed the most casual of fans to seek a seat for the game. Ironwood still had only one loss on the season and was firmly entrenched in second place in the league. Hurley could not take another conference loss and hope for anything more than third place or less. Ironwood still could knock off Ashland and claim the league title. Losing to Hurley meant that Ashland would probably win its second straight title. It was the moment of truth for both teams.

On Friday evening, January 25, the temperature in Hurley was about 20 below zero. Inside the gymnasium it was closer to 90 degrees. The place was jam packed. The game had an 8:30 start time. People started lining up outside at 6:15. According to Ed Sybeldon, "At 7:15 there was standing room only. At 7:45 there was just hanging room – from the rafters." Ed guessed the crowd to be about 1700. It was probably greater as they never reported that people jammed the end lines behind each basket as well. Not bad for a gym that supposedly was built to hold 1500 spectators. As players from both teams took the court, Oscar Swee, the Hurley band director, had his charges playing, "Who's Afraid of the Big Bad Wolf" to the delight of the Hurley fans. As stated previously in this chapter, Hurley basketball was an event the town participated in. This game was the proof of that. With the organized cheering, the band playing, and the cheerleaders whipping up the crowd, the place was rocking!

The game was the antithesis of the first clash. Both teams showed up to play basketball and play it clean and hard. Ironwood tied the score early in the second period at 7 – 7 as their fans roared in approval. Hurley went on to score the next eight points to take a 15 – 7 lead and the Hurley fans nearly blew the top off the gym, it was so loud. The Devils got two back just before halftime to trail by 15 – 9.

With every score, every sweet pass, every rebound or steal the gym erupted. This heated rivalry had reached a new level of passion.

As the second half began, the crowd again rose and urged on the boys. It was the Hurley 5 who then channeled the crowd's energy. Playing the best ball seen by a Midget team since 1943, they were flawless in the third quarter as they picked apart the Red Devil defense with precision passes, and quick drives that led to open shots. When the dust settled as the quarter ended they had opened up a 31 – 16 lead! This was what Ed Sybeldon and the Hurley fans had waited all year to see from this team. Hurley continued to play stellar defense and won handily 39 – 21. The visitors section of the gym began to empty before the end of the game. The decibel level however, was higher than at any point in the game as the Hurley faithful roared with excitement. Who's afraid of the big bad wolf? No, no, no, not the Midgets!

With the fires now lit and burning the Midgets dispatched DePadua 32 – 21. The Bruins again tried to slow the game to a crawl, but the Midgets remained patient and were able to get good shots over the zone defense. Three days later the Midgets put on a scoring spurt to beat Park Falls 58 – 45. Jack Muehl who had improved his play throughout the season went off for 22 points and Charlie Mezzano notched 20 more. In Ashland on that same night, Ironwood downed the Purgolders 33 – 28. One week later, the red hot Bessemer Speed Boys took down Ashland 42 – 36, while Hurley dumped Wakefield 41 – 20 behind the scoring of Charlie Mezzano, Jack Muehl, and Mickey Brown. The conference standings were now 1) Ashland 5 – 2, 2) Ironwood 4- 2, 3) Hurley 4 – 3, 4) Bessemer 3 – 3, and 5) Wakefield 0 – 6.

The Midgets finished their conference play on February 15 in Bessemer. The Speed Boys were coached this year by Paul Santini, the former Midget star who agreed to guide them until they could hire a full time coach. Hurley had been through three coaches since Roy Melvin departed and Chief Gianunzio had taken the helm for the Midgets since Carl Vergamini was called to duty. Bessemer had four coaches in the past four years. Under Santini they started slowly, but now they were a team to be reckoned with and even Ed Sybeldon sang their praises and thought they could beat Hurley. So the two hottest teams on the Range collided, not to decide first place, but third place. The Midgets again rose to the occasion and handled the Speed Boys 36 – 25 in a game they played with consistent pressure on defense and sharp, clean passing on offense. Best of all, the five starters all scored in the most balanced offense they had shown all year.

The Midgets played their last game of the regular season with a return match in Park Falls where they downed the Cardinals 39 – 31. The Midgets finished their regular season with a record of 12 wins and 3 losses while finishing in third place in the M-W with a conference record of 5 – 3. The very next night in Wakefield Dick Axness made history as he led Ashland to a 71 – 42 win. All he did was score 53 points! The previous record for points in a game by a Wisconsin school boy was 42 points held by four others. He did not break the record as much as he shattered it. Further, Axness now had 407 points in a 17 game season which broke the old record of 403 held by Johnny Kotz of Rhinelander. He also shattered the M-W conference record by scoring 203 points versus conference foes. The former record was held by Ernie Kivisto of Ironwood with 129. The 71 points by Ashland represented the highest point total by a team in conference history for one game. You can argue about who the best player in the M-W was up until 1946, but no one can make an argument that Dick Axness was not the most dominating player in league history. Who stopped him?

Ashland's win over Wakefield and Ironwood's 36 – 28 triumph two days later over Bessemer ended the season for everyone in the conference. The Bessemer – Ironwood contest was another foul fest with a total of 40 fouls called. The Ironwood Daily Globe gave this description. "Science and precision were tossed out the window last night as the two teams staged a slam bang battle that frequently left players scattered about the floor like ten-pins." With that another season in the Michigan-Wisconsin Conference was now in the books. Ashland and Ironwood tied for the title with records of 6 – 2. Hurley was next at 5 – 3 with deep regrets about giving away the first Ashland game and playing football instead of basketball in the first Ironwood game. Bessemer ended up at 3 – 5, for fourth place, and Wakefield had their second winless conference season in a row to finish 0 – 8. For Ironwood, it was their second title in three years and Ashland had their second in a row.

With the regular season in the books, the people of Hurley were in near hysteria as the long awaited regional tournament was about to start on their school's home court. For the first time ever there was going to be a "Hurley" Regional Tournament.

CHAPTER FORTY TWO

History In Madison

The 1946 Hurley Regional Tournament was an experiment by the Wisconsin Interscholastic Athletic Association (WIAA). Superior and Ashland had been the only other schools to host it until then. Would Hurley draw the fans? That was a silly question for the WIAA to ask. Every home game was a sell-out, it was just a matter of how many people would fill the gym when there were many who would stand in the aisles, along the end lines, or hang from the rafters. The Hurley Regional was in fact played in front of capacity plus crowds, to the delight of every team and the WIAA.

In 1945 the WIAA instituted a new (and better) format for the tournament. It is best explained in Carlo Kumpula's book, When All Roads Led to Spooner.

> It was a five part process: 1) Not every team made the
> tournament. 2) Committees met in four cities to select
> entrants for 30 district tournaments (small schools)
> and 17 regional tournaments (large schools), with
> the dividing point being an enrollment of 210. 3) The
> Board of Control met to confirm the appointments
> and resolve disputes. 4) After the district and regional
> tournaments were played, the 30 district winners
> were cut to 15 via sub-sectional playoff games; which
> when added to the 17 regional winners left 32 teams.
> 5) Those 32 teams were assigned, on a mileage
> basis, to eight sectionals of four teams each, with

each sectional sending one team to the state finals in Madison. This district/regional format remained in place until the mid 1960's.

About 350 teams were dreaming of becoming the new state champion. In district play each of the 30 Districts had a field of 6 or 8 teams. Of the 17 regional tournaments, 16 had 8 teams each and the Hurley regional had 6 teams due to the paucity of larger school teams in the area. Those six teams were Superior Central (with a record of 15 – 2), Superior East (8 – 6) Ashland (11 – 6), Phillips 9-6, Park Falls (11-4) and Hurley (12 – 3). The prognosticators agreed that Superior Central was the class of the field, but they also agreed that any of the other five teams had more than a fighting chance to win. The tournament was to begin on Thursday evening February 28 with Ashland playing Superior East and Superior Central taking on Hurley. Phillips and Park Falls drew byes and would meet the winners of Thursday's games on Friday evening.

This regional tournament, like so many before, would feature close, nail biting contests. In the opening game Ashland avenged two regular season losses to Superior East by a 24 – 22 tally. As usual, Dick Axness was responsible for 60% of Ashland's scoring as he dropped in 15 points. The Purgolders fell behind early and then scrambled to take a five point lead. East then closed the gap as the overflow crowd looked on. East ran out of time and Ashland moved on to play the winner of the Hurley – Superior Central game.

That game started at 8:30 as people stood outside the gym hoping enough people would leave after the first game so they could get seats, or at least have standing room to watch what was figured to be another close one. The Ironwood Daily Globe estimated the crowd to be over 1700. The Iron County Miner estimated it at 2000 as the standing room only crowd was standing eight deep. The game started slowly with each team passing the ball around the key looking for a soft spot in the other's defense. There were few of those and the first quarter ended with Central on top 6 – 4. The Vikings then found the range and outscored the Midgets 12 – 7 to take an 18 – 11 advantage into halftime. Hurley did a fine job in containing Central's high scoring Don Bredahl but the talented Vikings were not a one man show and Gene O'Brien picked up the scoring slack.

As the second half opened, Hurley worked relentlessly to close the gap to 18 – 17 as Jack Muehl and Charlie Mezzano combined for the six unanswered points. Central clung to the lead and upped it to four points on several occasions only to have the Midgets battle back to within one point twice. With 30 seconds left in the game, Central had the ball and a two point lead. Hurley fouled, but with the rules of that time, the Vikings chose to take the ball out rather than shoot free throws. They ran out the clock and left the court exhausted but victorious by a 28 – 26 score.

Hurley would play Superior East in the consolation round in Friday's first game. Phillips would take on Park Falls and Ashland was set to meet Central for the third time of the season in the semifinals. In this regional meet every team had a winning record, which is not only rare but nearly impossible. This high school basketball tournament was a treat for fans.

Hurley and Superior East tangled in the opening game on Friday, and keeping with the theme of hotly contested games, neither team could gain a large lead. It went back and forth with East taking the lead after three quarters by a 20 – 18 mark. The defenses tightened, and with the style of ball played in those times, both teams probed the other's defenses with a movement passing game. The players weaved in and out catching a pass and flicking a pass within a tick of the clock. Good shots were few and made shots fewer yet. Finally with less than two minutes left in the game, East took the lead 23 – 22. With about one minute to go Jack Muehl dropped in a long bomb from the corner to put the Midgets back on top 24 – 23. East could not connect and Hurley rebounded and started to run out the clock. East fouled but Hurley declined the free throw and retained possession on the inbounds play. This time they ran the clock out and advanced to the Saturday consolation game versus the loser of the Phillips – Park Falls contest. Charlie Mezzano continued to be Hurley's big gun on offense as he scored 11 points.

The crowd stayed right where it was and took in the second game. Park Falls opened a huge lead on Phillips and it looked as if after three games the tournament was finally going to see a game won by a comfortable margin. Park Falls completely dominated the Loggers and after three quarters the score was 29 – 15. Many fans decided it would be a good time to step out for a quick smoke break. That was the wrong move! Phillips turned the tables on the Cardinals scoring from every spot on the court. Park Falls tried everything in the book to slow down the rampaging Phillips five. In the end the clock ran out on the Loggers with Park Falls clinging desperately to a 35 – 33 win. The Cards survived the Phillips power surge to play the winner of the next game between Central and Ashland on Saturday night for the regional championship.

Four games had been played in two nights so far and each had ended up with a one or two point margin. The next game seemed like it might end the same way. Superior Central had beaten Ashland twice in the regular season. Most fervent fans thought they would make it three in a row. Central started the game by methodically building a 12 – 6 lead after one quarter. They were patient and it paid off as they dropped in 6 of the seven shots they took. Ashland was playing their tight zone defense but Coach Harry Conley's Vikings were able to solve it. It was then that Conley decided he wanted to "break" Ashland's zone by freezing the ball. Central took only two shots in five minutes as they chose to run the clock in an effort to force Roy Melvin's team to play a man-to-man defense. What happened instead was that Ashland remained stubborn and stayed in the zone. The hot shooting Vikings cooled off. By the time Conley instructed his players to play their normal offense they couldn't hit water if they fell out of a boat. Ashland managed to score four points to Central's two in the second quarter and the first half ended with the score 14 – 10 in favor of the Vikings.

A lot of ink and newsprint was used to question Coach Conley's decision. It certainly was questionable. However there is no question about what happened in the third quarter. Dick Axness happened! The Purgolders outscored the Vikings 14 – 0 in that decisive stanza with Axness scoring 12 of those points. Ashland now had a commanding 24 – 14 lead with the final 8 minutes left to play. Central finally found the range again against the tough Purgolder zone defense as they fought to get back into the game. Axness and his four friends kept pace and the game ended with Ashland cruising to the 35 – 27 win.

The Saturday lineup of games was now known. Hurley was to play Phillips in the third place game to start the night. Then another treat for the fans was on tap. The Drummond Fire Brigade, winners of the Ashland District Tournament was playing Tripoli, the winners of the Phillips District Tournament. The winner of that one would go to the Spooner Sectional Tournament along with the Winner of the third game between Ashland and Park Falls.

With Charlie Mezzano, Jack Muehl, and Bill Canney starting and playing in their last games in their beloved Hurley gym, the Midgets and Loggers game tipped off. It proved to be a game of ebbs and flows. At the end of the third quarter it seemed that Hurley was in control as they held a 23 – 18 lead over the stubborn Phillips boys. Then Phillips started another fourth quarter rally. With just fifteen seconds to go in the game Phillips missed a shot and Jack Muehl rebounded. Hurley held the lead 29 – 28 and one would have expected Hurley to hold the ball and wait to be fouled. Muehl decided to take off like a man on a mission, driving the length of the court in an attempt to score. Instead he ran over a Phillips defender and was called for the foul. The rules at that time allowed for one free throw on every non-shooting foul unless they declined the free throw for the opportunity to take the ball. Phillips gladly chose to shoot the free throw and made it. Hurley was now locked into an overtime game. Phillips' shooting went cold in overtime and Hurley scored four to secure the win 33 – 29 victory. The Midgets ended the season with a record of 14 – 4. Ed Sybeldon and most others in town believed Hurley to be the most talented team in the area. They also believed Hurley, led by Mickey Brown would be formidable next year as well. Sadly, it looked much like Hurley's other talented teams that "almost" made it to the sectionals or state tournaments in years gone by. It began to seem as if the 1943 team would be the only Hurley team that would ever get that far.

The second game was indeed fun to watch as Newman Benson of Drummond proved to be on heck of a player. Drummond was averaging over 55 points a game and scored over 80 points in a game three times that season. That would be the equivalent of scoring well over 100 points a game in modern times. The Fire Brigade had little trouble dispatching Tripoli and rolled to a 43 – 28 win.

The championship game between Ashland and Park Falls was a tightly contested defensive struggle. Park Falls managed to hold Dick Axness to just six points in the first three quarters and found themselves down 20 – 18 at that point. Then Axness happened again! He scored four quick points and then when Park Falls closed the gap he scored again. The Ashland defense did their job, Axness scored 6 points in the decisive fourth quarter and the Purgolders won 28 – 23 to advance with Drummond to the Spooner Sectional.

The first ever regional tournament hosted by Hurley was a raging success. The games were close, the teams carried themselves with class, and the fan support was off the charts. The gate receipts exceeded $2600, over $700 more than in Ashland the previous year. The WIAA took notice and from then on Hurley was in the yearly rotation with Superior and Ashland to host the tournament.

Ashland went on to Spooner and destroyed Rice Lake in the opening round 46 – 28. Drummond with their record of 17 – 2 met Clayton with their sparkling 19 – 1 record. Clayton defeated Drummond 48 – 46 in a game where the Fire Brigade once led 33 – 23. In the sectional championship game against little Clayton the Purgolders found themselves down by a point at halftime 16 – 15. Then Axness happened yet again! He exploded for 32 of Ashland's 43 points scored in the half and the Purgolders ran away with the 58 – 41 win. Axness added another record to his resume by scoring 41 points in the game, a sectional record that stood for 12 years. Ashland was going to their second straight state tournament in Madison where this year, history would be made!

The 1946 Wisconsin State Basketball Tournament was a pleasant surprise for state basketball fans who loved cheering for the lovable underdog. Tiny Reedsville High School, in a town with a population of just over 700, became the darling of the state when they stunned mighty Racine Park 30 - 28 in the opening round. Also in that round, Ashland lost to Eau Claire 38 – 33. The Purgolders rebounded in the consolation round the next night to beat Beaver Dam 29 – 28 and then lost the consolation title on Saturday night to Racine Park 37 – 29 as Dick Axness scored 24 of his team's 29 points. Axness led all scorers in the tournament with 63 points, one short of the record set in 1939 by Johnny Kotz. Ashland finished their season with a record of 16 – 8. In the 1945 – 1946 season Dick Axness was the most dominant player in Wisconsin.

Little Reedsville was the big story of the tournament. On the second night of play they overcame a superb Wisconsin Rapids team 47 – 43 to reach the finals against Eau Claire. Never had a school enrollment discrepancy been so vast. Eau Claire had one of the largest, if not the largest, enrollments in the state with over 1600 students. Reedsville boasted 87. Somehow, someway, Reedsville crushed the giant 48 – 39 to become the smallest school to ever win a Wisconsin State Championship in the one class era. With multiple classes since 1972, it is a record that will never be broken!

CHAPTER FORTY THREE

Achieving Excellence

In March of 1946, as Reedsville was celebrating their remarkable state championship, Carl Vergamini returned to Hurley. With his return came the question of who would coach the basketball team. Well, the answer was easy. Mario Gianunzio was a man of incredible class and integrity. He stepped away and returned to the science and biology classroom. There was little doubt that "Verg" was the better football coach, but it was also clear that Chief knew his business when it came to basketball.

On the surface it seemed no two men could be more different. Carl Vergamini was gregarious and comfortable in a crowd. Chief was reserved, quiet, and eschewed the limelight. But both men loved to hunt and fish. Both loved the sport of wrestling with a passion. Both burned with a competitive fire and both of them loved coaching. They held their teams to the highest standards of conduct and integrity. Both were complete gentlemen who were quick to praise and encourage their students and players. Both were respected deeply by their students and players. Both were devoted to their families and to their professions. It was no wonder they became best of friends. This lack of friction, lack of ego, and the desire to have Hurley achieve excellence became a key ingredient to the remarkable story about to unfold.

Chief became Carl's assistant coach in football and basketball. He was patient and insistent; the ultimate teacher on the field and court. He took charge of the "B" teams as the Junior Varsity was called in those days and he was perfect for the job. On game days he was right next to Carl, lending his experience and observations to the head coach. Together they complemented each other's skills and strengths. Chief burned with a desire to achieve perfection through teaching. Under his guidance players learned to think like champions. He fed their minds. Carl Vergamini burned with the desire to achieve perfection through hard work and limitless dedication. He was the master motivator, demanding everything they had physically. They learned to push beyond their limits. They learned to work like champions. He fed their hearts. Together these two men created an environment where athletes learned to meld the physical and mental aspects of sports and more importantly, of living, into lifelong habits of success. Together they fed the souls of a generation of Hurley athletes.

Hurley opened football practice in August of 1946, more than a week earlier than ever before. The WIAA had loosened the practice restrictions so the boys could begin conditioning drills two weeks before the start of the school year. 35 hopefuls showed up for practice led by Tony Brunello and Mickey Brown. Don Zell was back and the hard running fullback was looking good. Also back were many former Midgets just returned from the service. Dom Moselle was among them and he along with the others were working out to the side and keeping a watchful eye on this new crop of footballers. Carl Vergamini was back in charge and the players knew it immediately. His idea of conditioning was very different from most coaches. Carl pushed his players to the brink of exhaustion in the conditioning drills and then brought them back down. Then he pushed them to the limit again and again. With each movement they became more and more exhausted. With each movement they became stronger and stronger. They were learning to push beyond their inherent comfort zones. They were discovering their untapped reservoir of physical and mental strength. After three seasons in which they won only one game they would need that strength to right the ship. The boys were fully onboard that ship and willingly worked harder than ever before in their lives. They wanted to win and they wanted to turn Tony Brunello, their rock of stability, into a prophet. They wanted Ironwood! They wanted the Red Devils like no Hurley team ever before. Their craving for absolution for the 42 – 0 loss the previous season was insatiable. If it was absolution they wanted, Carl Vergamini knew what it would take to attain it. He laid it out there for them and they pushed themselves.

When J.E. Murphy found out that Tony Brunello was running 8 miles to go home after practice each evening, he picked up the phone. Next he called Tony into his office. The superintendent had arranged for Tony to "hop" a train leaving Hurley each evening heading toward Ashland and beyond. Further the train would slow down as it neared Dago Valley for Tony to "hop off." His days of running 8 miles a day after practice were over. Now think about how that would fly in today's world!

On Monday night, September 16, Hurley kicked off the 1946 football season in Ashland versus the Purgolders. The unusual starting date was because Ashland had a polio outbreak and the game was pushed back ten days as Ashland closed the schools until proper medical authority gave the okay. The Ironwood Daily Globe reported that the Purple and Gold were "completely outclassed by the less experienced Midgets." With the score 12 -7 in the fourth quarter, Hurley twice drove inside the Ashland 20 yard line only to be stopped. Ashland scored two touchdowns off of Hurley fumbles as the Midgets managed to push Ashland around only to drop the game into the Purgolders lap. Hurley scored in the fourth quarter on a 15 yard shovel pass from Brown to Cotton Van Hoof. It was another bitter defeat on the gridiron, but the Midgets refused to have a pity party. They were on a mission of redemption and this was a bump in the road.

With a new attitude, the team continued their work. They steamrolled DePadua 33 – 2 on the Hurley field with Van Hoof, Don Zell, and sophomore John Hermanson running wild on the hapless Bruins. Next up was Park Falls and again the Midgets showed strong as they handily beat the Cardinals 31 – 7. The night before Hurley beat Park Falls, Ashland pulled off a stunning upset. Wausau High School had one of the greatest high school football teams in the state of Wisconsin or any state. From 1937 until the early 1950's they lost but one game and arrived in Ashland with a 46 game winning streak and a 64 game unbeaten streak. They left Ashland dazed and bewildered as the boys from the Ore Dock City beat them 13 – 7 ending an almost ten year unbeaten string. Ashland's win had every team from Up North feeling pretty good about the football they played.

October 5, 1946, the date Tony Brunello and his team mates circled in red on the calendar when the schedule came out, was fast approaching. Ironwood was coming to Hurley's "cow pasture" to take on the Midgets. Ed Sybeldon was impressed with the Red Devil squad, but thought they could be beaten and predicted that they would lose two games in this year. The Devils' just man handled a strong Bessemer team 20 – 7 and again looked like a power house. To bring things to a boil, Ironwood had offered Hurley the opportunity to shift the game to Ironwood and promised a 50 – 50 split of the gate to the Midgets. Of course, that was taken as an insult to Hurley rather than a gesture of good will. The VFW was hosting a convention in Hurley and as part of the festivities the members were going to attend "The Game." Ironwood offered their field as it held more spectators and was indeed a better venue. Hurley was having none of it and told the Devils and their supporters that they just would have to suck it up and play in Hurley. Of course there was a packed house as the spectators stood all around the field of play and leaned upon the dreaded red fence. Bessemer came to the aid of the Midget faithful as they lent their bleachers for the game so at least half of the people there could sit. Of course Bessemer wanted Hurley to win so they would still have a chance to win the conference title, but a gift is a gift even if it wasn't exactly from the depths of their wonderful Speed Boy hearts!

The game started with Ironwood kicking off. The kick went right to Tony Brunello who was in for his blocking rather than running prowess. What could the big fellow do but run with the ball? He did, and he did not get far. But it was the Ironwood tacklers who suffered for their kicker's inaccuracy. As the two would be tacklers drew a bead on the Hurley lineman they had a head of steam. Tony was big, but not slow, and he too had a head of steam. The two Devils were on a collision course with this Midget locomotive. Brunello lowered his shoulder and split between them as the three collided at full speed. In the words of Bill Cattoi (Hurley '47), who was in the stands, it was "the biggest clash you ever heard. Like two trucks that piled into each other." The sound of the shoulder pads cracking each other was heard throughout the field and beyond. The crowd fell silent. Then Brunello jumped to his feet and went to the huddle. One Ironwood player got up slowly and the other stayed down. By the time he recovered and took to his feet, the message was clear. This was not going to be a repeat performance of last year's game. On the second play of the game someone on the Devils' defense called Brunello a "farmer" in a derisive way. Now Tony was very proud to be a farmer and he decided to take it in stride. Instead of fuming he dominated the line of scrimmage as he and his mates opened huge holes in the Devil defense. He was serving "pancakes" to the Ironwood linemen all afternoon. Nothing but the finest in "farm food" for them!

From their own 20 yard line, Hurley ran the ball five straight plays for five straight first downs and 71 yards. The Ironwood defense recovered from the shock and stoned the Midgets' next two run attempts and then Mickey Brown threw an incomplete pass. On fourth down from the nine yard line, Brown floated a pass to Dom Gentile who leapt sideways among four Devil defenders to snare the pass as he fell into the end zone. Don Zell kicked the extra point and Hurley lead 7 – 0. From there it was the Hurley defense that played an inspired game. Ironwood did not cross the 50 yard line in the game. The Midgets went on several drives that ended up short but they controlled the ball and the game. The frustrated Red Devils went down to their first defeat of the season. Don Zell and John Czech gained most of Hurley's yards with several runs over ten yards and first downs. The Devils contained Cotton Van Hoof, but quarterback Mickey Brown was able to read their intentions, faking hand-offs to Van Hoof and pitching it instead to the others. When Van Hoof left the game with an injury, the Midgets continued to grind away and control the ball. When the Devils asserted themselves later in the game, Don Zell came up with a 70 yard quick kick on third down that rolled the Devils back to their own 1 yard line. Hurley thoroughly outplayed the area's biggest and best team over the three past seasons and were rewarded with the 7 – 0 win!

Over 2,700 fans had crammed into the Hurley ball field. That was a record. On Sunday afternoon, the VFW Convention held a parade. Tony Brunello and fellow Hurley tackle Jim Dahl proudly carried a huge banner that proclaimed, "HURLEY 7 IRONWOOD 0." The crowd cheered wildly as they walked that banner the length of Silver Street. The victory was as sweet as any ever scored over an Ironwood team.

The modus operandi for the Midgets had been to lose to Bessemer, no matter how strong the football team was. Bessemer was not a pushover, but after handling the Devils, Hurley was favored to win. Instead, they lost in another heartbreaker to the Speed Boys, 7 – 6. By the time the game was played, Don Zell was running on a badly sprained ankle that would get better and then get worse. Cotton Van Hoof was lost for the season with a broken collar bone.

Hurley led most of the way 6 – 0 before the Speed Boys punched in a touchdown in the fourth quarter. Hurley also had fumbled the ball back to Bessemer when they only needed five yards for another score. Then in the waning seconds of the fourth quarter Brown connected with Dom Gentile for what appeared to be a touchdown. Gentile was called "out of bounds" and the pass incomplete. The Hurley partisans went bonkers, pointing to where the feet landed. After the game all three officials of this all-Duluth trio admitted that the call was incorrect. Bessemer had a hex on the Hurley eleven, even when all was lost they found a way to win.

Hurley thumped Phillips 24 – 0 the following week as Brown completed 18 of 23 passes to make up for their lack of running backs that were out with injuries. They went into their last game of the season against Superior Central with a record of 4 - 2. The banged up Midgets had a MASH unit sized list of injuries going into the game. They showed up and gave the Vikings a tussle in a game played at Duluth's Wade Stadium. The tough Midgets fought tooth and nail with the Vikings and were tied at 0 – 0. Then Superior went on a 56 yard drive to score to end the first half. Central led 7 – 0. The Midgets came out passing the ball in the third quarter and drove to the Viking 29 yard line where the drive stalled. The Midget defense which had held the Vikings offense in check for most of the game crumbled as Central drove 71 yards for a 14 – 0 lead. Then the worst case scenario became reality. With Mickey Brown passing the ball with ease and confidence, he was hit hard and he stayed down. He left the game with a broken collar bone. With him went the Midgets chances for a comeback. Central defeated Hurley 21 – 6. For the season Hurley made a comeback to football prominence with a 4 – 3 record that easily could have been a no loss or one loss season with some luck on the injury front, or so lamented EJS. Don Zell was nominated for the All State team along with Mickey Brown. Tony Brunello was named to the all conference team for the second consecutive year. When Carl Vergamini called him to the office to give him the news, he handed Tony a star to put on his letter sweater. Tony was perplexed and asked why he was given a star. His coach told him that he was voted in as the "Captain" of the M-W All Conference Team. Not only did he prove to be Hurley's leader, the other teams wanted him to be theirs too. Respect for a farmer who never played before his junior year--not bad at all!

As far as the M-W Conference standings went, Ashland enjoyed their best season ever defeating Ironwood 15 – 6, ending a 25 year losing streak to the Red Devils. They then defeated Bessemer 7 – 6 to lock up the title. EJS predicted Ironwood would lose twice and they did. Ed Sybeldon's crystal ball was getting to be pretty accurate.

The sports cycle continued as fall started to ebb and another northern winter was knocking at the door. The boys quickly traded in their football uniforms and those who played basketball were outfitted quickly. There were 50 boys trying out for basketball. That was more than 25 percent of the male enrollment and was 15 more than showed up for the first football practice. Some people say that basketball never eclipsed football in popularity. The fans and boys of Hurley would have begged to differ!

It was known now that Mickey Brown would be out until after Christmas with his broken collar bone. The question was could the team weather the storm without their most explosive scorer? EJS was unsure what the season would bring for the Midgets as he pointed out that Mezzano, Muehl, and Canney were graduated, leaving Willard "Bud" Geach as the only starter from last year until Brown returned. Perhaps Ed's crystal ball was foggy, but at the Hurley practices players were quietly confident in their abilities. Carl Kaffine remembers that they spoke of Brown's injury only briefly and decided they would "hold on until Mickey gets back." They were "not concerned" about the season. They just wanted to play ball. This group of players were among the first participants to play in the Iron County League and the season ending Iron County Grade School Tournament as 7th and 8th graders in 1942 and 1943. They were exposed to high expectations as 12 and 13 year olds. Large crowds did not bother them one iota. They knew each other as grade school teammates and also competitors. The fact that, of them, only Geach and Brown had amassed any real playing time the year before was unimportant. They grew up believing in each other and they now were licking their chops at the opportunity to represent the Orange and Black. As Carl Kaffine said, "It didn't dawn on us that we couldn't win."

The boys were sorted out and the Varsity, "B" team and the freshman teams were formed. The coaches went to work and so did the players. They ran because they scrimmaged continually. They moved their feet and moved them fast or they would sit and watch. Constant motion on offense and defense was the Hurley way. Defense was "in your face" and offense was ball control until there was an open shot and then you had better take it. Being caught "flat footed" was not acceptable. When the other team had the ball the Midgets were expected to hustle back on defense and establish position. Fast break points by opponents were the kiss of death and to get on the court you better play the game on your toes. Carl Vergamini wanted scoring to come from any player at any time to keep defenses from keying on one player. Just as he worked Gerald Rosendahl into the 1943 team's offense, he did the same now with seniors Carl Kaffine, Bud Geach, Dom Gentile, Cotton Van Hoof, Joe Darin, and junior Jim "Smokey" Rainaldo. Those players would see the bulk of the playing time. They were joined by seniors John Czech and John Rainaldo and two sophomores, best friends and neighbors, Charles Guenther and Len Bartolutti, both of whom decided to try out for the team even though they had not played organized basketball prior. With each practice and with each scrimmage the team gained confidence and they gained the stamina necessary to play the style of ball Vergamini insisted upon. This team was going to grind down their opponents with relentless defensive and offensive pressure until they cracked.

On Friday, November 15, the season got underway. DePadua was coming to Hurley and they too were very excited about their season. They were returning all but one member of their very good team from the year before. They also had a habit of playing at a snail's pace and were good at it. They could "muck it up" and try a team's patience with their tough zone defense. How good was this DePadua team? Well good enough for the soothsayer EJS to predict that they would beat Hurley on Hurley's floor!

The game was as expected. DePadua held the ball, tried the Midget's patience, and generally drove everyone, including the fans, crazy. Rather than fall for the Bruins' tactics and force themselves into mistakes, the Midgets went with the flow and built a 22 – 11 lead early in the fourth quarter. Then Darin, Van Hoof, and Gentile fouled out in rapid succession and the Bruins made their move. It was too little too late and Hurley held on for the ugly 23 – 19 win over the tough Catholic School. Carl Kaffine and Bud Geach paced Hurley with 7 points each and Dom Gentile hit for 5. It wasn't pretty, but it was a victory over a determined team.

The Ashland Purgolders played host to Hurley the following Friday and again EJS sounded the warning bells by touting the Ashland team as being very good, despite Roy Melvin's crying about losing Axness to graduation. He still had most of his best players back. EJS proved to be correct. Ashland was tough and they jumped all over the stunned Midgets to seize the lead at the end of the first quarter 14 – 2. At the half it was 19 – 9 as Hurley showed they missed the scoring ability Mickey Brown brought to the table. Next was the scene that would be replayed over and over again in the Hurley locker room. Coach Vergamini started his exhortations and instructions, finishing with a flourish of "Who's going to be our center?" "Our forwards" "Our guards?" With each starter replying, "I will," the din they and their teammates created echoed off the locker room walls. They did not take the court to start the third period; they stormed it! At the end of three periods it was a 26 – 23 Ashland lead. Then the Midgets defense became impassioned as they denied the Purgolders a clean shot at the basket. Finally Dom Gentile and Smokey Rainaldo scored for the Midgets and they held the 27 – 26 lead. With 3 minutes and 45 seconds left in the game, Ashland continued to play a zone defense. The Hurley five put on a clinic in stalling the ball. For the next two

250

minutes and 15 seconds they held the ball daring Ashland to play man-to-man. When Dom Gentile drove to the basket he charged into the Purgolder defender and Ashland converted the free throw for the 27 – 27 tie. With one minute to play Bud Geach scored and the Midgets regained the lead 29 – 27. Ashland then scored on a free throw. Then the resourceful Midgets ran out the clock with a beautiful passing game. Dodd Gymnasium was as quiet as a library as the Midgets ran off the court with the 29 – 28 comeback win.

With two straight road wins against the Ashland teams, Hurley again traveled for their third game of the season. This time they were visiting Bessemer, which was always a troublesome place to play. The Midgets had no trouble this time and they walloped the Speed Boys on their home floor 48 – 19 behind the scoring power of Bud Geach with 14 points and Cotton Van Hoof with 13. Carl Kaffine contributed 8 and Jim Rainaldo was inserted into the starting lineup and produced 7 more points. Finally, after three straight road games the Midgets would get the chance to play in front of the home crowd on Wednesday night, December 11. Their opponent was the Park Falls Cardinals and they were sporting their strongest team in years, perhaps ever. The Park Falls five consisted of several returning stars and their three "Macs," Coach McDonald and his two star players, MacGregor and McGinnis. The Cardinals were riding high with a perfect record of 4 – 0, including a 55 – 42 beat down of Ashland in a game that was not as close as the score would indicate. The Park Falls High school closed at noon and a caravan of over 500 fans arrived in Hurley to watch their boys take on the undefeated Midgets.

The gym was packed as the excited fans for both teams anticipated another win. The game was fast paced, too fast, actually. Both teams were ragged, sloppy, and seemingly disorganized. The Cardinals led by 3 points at the end of the first quarter and then maintained the lead heading into the fourth quarter 26 – 24. In the third stanza, Bud Geach fouled out of the game and then Dom Gentile fouled out in the fourth. Park Falls behind their two tall Macs pulled away for the 38 – 31 win. EJS conceded that it was Park Falls who was the class of the region by virtue of their wins over Ashland and Hurley. The folks in Park Falls were ecstatic!

With no time to lick their wounds, Hurley made still another road trip, this time to Wakefield to take on the other Cardinals. Wakefield played inspired ball on their home floor and held the Midgets to a 22 – 21 lead after three quarters. Then Hurley erupted for 16 points of offense and held the Cards to just four points in the last quarter as they steamed to a 38 – 25 win. Jim Rainaldo led the balanced Hurley attack with 11 points. The Midgets were now 3 – 0 in the conference and 4 – 1 overall. On Friday, December 20, the Phillips Loggers came to call in the Hurley gym to tangle with the Midgets. The game started fast and both teams showed scoring punch. Hurley gained the early lead and was never thwarted as the Loggers could never close the gap. Hurley won by six, 48 – 42. Geach, Kaffine, and Van Hoof scored 14, 13 and 11 points respectively for the Hurley five. The highlight of the evening was not the basketball game, but rather the halftime show. With Santa Claus (Oscar Swee) directing the band, little six year old Jimmie Thom brought down the house with his rendition of "Silent Night." The Hurley cheerleaders ran through the stands to escort community members and teachers to the band stage to sing along with the band and soon, the whole gym, including the Phillips fans were joining in the festive merry making. It was basketball fever, Hurley style!

Heading into the Christmas break, the Ironwood Daily Globe lamented the fall of the Michigan teams to the Wisconsin competition. Hurley, Ashland, and Park Falls had spent the first weeks of the season blistering their Michigan cousins on the hardwood as none of the area Michigan teams could claim a victory over a Wisconsin squad. The writer also went on to heap praise on the high flying Park Falls team who just kept on winning. Despite the accolades for the Wisconsin teams, Hurley kept a wary eye to the east. After the break, the Ironwood Red Devils were coming to Hurley and they intended to correct their Wisconsin problem.

Friday, January 3, 1947. The Red Devils are the underdogs. They want revenge and they want to beat a Wisconsin team to break the hex. And now, EJS goes out and claims that "Hurley could just about clinch the conference crown tonight, with the season not even at the halfway mark." Thanks, Ed. Talk about putting the cart before the horse! Now Ironwood was really fuming and they wanted a piece of the Midgets. The ink on that missive was barely dry by the time the Hurley gym was packed. By 7:30 PM the overflow crowd exceeded 2,000 with hundreds more being turned away at the doors. The radio station in Ironwood, WJMS, broadcast that people should stay away because they could not get into the gym. It was all on the line. State pride, revenge for a football loss, and most importantly, it was Hurley versus Ironwood and that really was all that mattered to the players.

The one thing we know for sure about the game was that both the Ironwood Daily Globe and Montreal River Miner reporters witnessed the same game. They even had the same headlines. The Globe said it was "one of the weirdest exhibitions of modern basketball played on a local court in years." The Miner said, "The 2,000 odd fans witnessed a game which will go in history as the weirdest, most confusing, unorthodox, and a great display of how basketball should not be played." It literally started at the tip off. Bud Geach pushed the opening tip to Cotton Van Hoof who went uncontested to score the basket. He then scored again ten seconds later but the tally was waived off as he was called for a travelling violation. Then it got confusing! The officials stopped the game and had a discussion. All ten players on the court assumed Hurley had the north basket and Ironwood the south basket. The only problem was the centers, Geach and Smetana of Ironwood faced the wrong baskets. Van Hoof scored, but for the Red Devils! The question was did it matter where the players warmed up or which way the centers were facing? So ten players, two coaches, two officials, and 2,000 spectators were all unaware something was afoot. The officials conferred and made the call. Ironwood led 2 – 0. That was just the beginning. The Devils led after one period 10 – 7. Hurley rallied and actually played the best stretch of ball all night in the second quarter to take 15 – 12 lead at halftime. The game had proceeded at a frantic pace with both teams missing easy shots, taking bad shots, turning the ball over on terrible passes and just running hard, but aimlessly. It was a spirited track meet with no finish line and no definitive rules. It was rough play at times, but with no hard fouls or cheap shots. The crowd was amused, but disappointed with the ragged play. The third quarter started after Coaches Vergamini and Kraemer spent the intermission trying to calm their boys down and get them to concentrate. That didn't go as planned either. Each team managed to score three points in the third period and Hurley led 18 – 15. The race horse pace continued and neither team could hit the broad side of a barn. In the fourth quarter Dom Gentile fouled out for the fifth time in seven games and Hurley was without one of their best ball handlers and defenders. Dom had a habit of playing every second of every game like it would be his last and now it was costing him playing time. With the score 23 – 21 Hurley went into a stall. Ironwood fouled Carl Kaffine, Hurley's best free throw shooter with ten seconds to play. The decision was made to take the free throw and take a three point lead. A great decision on most nights. But this was not most nights and Carl missed the free throw. Ironwood's Begalle pushed the ball the length of the floor, catching the normally fleet Midgets flat footed, something that also rarely happened, for an uncontested layup that would tie the game. It was one of those nights and Begalle missed it! Somehow the Midgets won the game that both teams seemingly kept trying to lose.

Every improbable thing had occurred during that game. Dozens of opportunities to win the game were wasted by both teams. There were 32 fouls called in the game. 21 of them were on Ironwood. It wasn't a repeat of the "Brawl Game" of the previous season. It was two teams running at full speed the entire game, much like a NASCAR race with demolition derby rules, and there were bound to be a few 3 and 4 car pile-ups. The only positive was the intensity and hustle of both teams and that the crowd was again loud and superbly sportsman-like. Two exhausted teams and 2,000 bewildered fans walked out of the gym wondering what in the name of John Naismith they had just witnessed.

Ed Sybeldon had spent a lot of time being right in his predictions. Now he predicted that Ashland would beat Hurley on January 10 on Hurley's floor. It seems Ed was miffed by the poor play exhibited by the Midgets versus Ironwood and he believed Roy Melvin was capable of walking on water. Hurley blew out the Purgolders 37 – 20 in a game that Sybeldon said could have been much, much worse for Ashland. Carl Kaffine kept up his fine play scoring 12 points and Dom Gentile reigned in his breakneck style of play and committed only two fouls. Behind Kaffine was a balanced score sheet. Ed's predictions again went wrong and his foggy crystal ball now appeared to be painted black!

On Jan 17, Hurley travelled to Phillips to take on the tough Loggers for the second time in the season. The Mickey Brown-less Midgets hit their stride that evening as they walloped Phillips 47 – 27 after a slow start. Gentile committed but one foul and scored 8 points. Kaffine was becoming a downright dangerous scorer as he poured in 15 points. Again the scoring punch came from many and Hurley with an 8 – 1 record was starting to be noticed outside of Iron County. Park Falls continued their fine play and was ranked as number 12 in the state. Hurley and Superior East were named "honorable mention." And just when you think you know something about high school basketball, here comes an upset. Saint Ambrose, the little Catholic high school in Ironwood, was playing some pretty good ball themselves. Park Falls had the misfortune of running headlong into that dandy little buzz saw and lost to the Ramblers 43 – 34. It was Saint Ambrose that broke the hex Wisconsin teams held over Michigan teams that season. No one saw that coming.

Of course Saint Ambrose was next on Hurley's schedule and the two hottest teams in the area squared off on a Tuesday night, January 22. The Ramblers had lost only once all year and had an imposing group of tall, rangy players. The game was everything it should have been with several lead changes in a see-saw affair. With four minutes left in the game Saint Ambrose was clinging to a 32 – 30 lead. Cotton Van Hoof hit a free throw for Hurley to cut the lead to one point. Then Dom Gentile slashed his way to the basket as he split the Rambler defense for the layup. Hurley now was clinging to a one point lead. After an errant Rambler shot, the Midgets rebounded and went into their now well-practiced stall. Hurley refused the free throws and continued to hold the ball each time Saint Ambrose fouled and the game ended with Hurley winning 33 – 32 for their ninth win in ten games.

Mickey Brown had been working out and was now ready to play. He was actually ready to play a few weeks before but WIAA rules required him to be inactive for 90 days from his injury due to their insurance company's rules. That Mickey was Hurley's best basketball player was not in doubt. As an athlete he could always make difficult things look routine. That this team had won 9 of 10 with him sitting on the bench was a surprise to many, the normally astute EJS included. What these folks had missed was that you just can't see what is in a team's heart. This team had it. They all proved to be superb players in their own right and they played together with the precision of a Swiss watch, if you discounted the Ironwood game, of course. Now it was up to Mickey Brown to fit into this team after previously being the centerpiece. Brown's first basketball game of the season would be against Ironwood in the Devils' gym on January 24.

Ironwood was now fighting for their lives in the conference. Another loss would give them zero chance at the title and even if they did win it was a long shot. Still in this rivalry a win meant a meaningful season and bragging rights. They were ready to play. So were the Midgets. This game would be a classic for all the right reasons. Both teams left the ragged, hair on fire style of play in the locker room and this time the fans were treated to a basketball game.

Carl Vergamini did not waste any time inserting Mickey Brown into the game. He started him as Smokey Rainaldo took his place on the bench. The Hurley five was now an all senior quintet. The Hurley fans were ecstatic by the possibilities, so of course, the Devils jumped on top 4 – 0 before you could say lickity split. With the Ironwood gym crammed to the rafters, it became intense. Hurley battled back to take a slim 8 -7 lead after one period. The game remained tight with both teams playing well. Ironwood was however prone to fouling as for the second time in the season they hacked the Midgets 21 times. Hurley converted 16 of 25 free throws and they needed every one of them. With the clock running out and the Midgets ahead by 34 – 32, Begalle of Ironwood had the ball with 8 seconds to go. The same guy who missed the potential tying layup as time expired in the first meeting was non-pulsed as he swished a long shot to tie the game. This game was going to overtime.

Hurley played only six players in the game as Dom Gentile once again remained in control and totaled only one foul. Rainaldo spelled Brown for a while and that was it. In the overtime period Ironwood took the lead 35 – 34 as they converted an early free throw. Bud Geach hit one from the corner to put the Midgets back up by one point. Ironwood could not get a good shot and Hurley had the ball; and again they went into their constant motion stall. The Ironwood players chased the ball frantically trying to solve this passing game. Now exhausted, they finally cracked as Dom Gentile found a lane and drove for an easy layup. Ironwood could not convert again, and the Midgets escaped with the 38 – 35 win that assured the Midgets at least a tie for the M-W Conference title. They were 6 – 0 in the league and now 10 – 1 overall. It would take losses to Wakefield, and Bessemer and Ashland winning three consecutive games in conference to force the tie.

A tie for the championship was just not in the making. Ironwood took out their frustration on the Purgolders the next week with a convincing 42 – 28 win that handed Hurley the title outright. Hurley then went out and dismantled Wakefield 41 – 32 as Brown scored 10 points in another balanced attack as eight Midgets scored and all played. Now Hurley hit the road for a trip to Park Falls, the only team that had beat them in the season. The high flying Cards proved tough yet again but the Midgets were more than their equals as they forged a 33 – 30 lead by the end of the third quarter. Then the Midgets launched a furious offensive in which they scored 20 points in the final quarter for a 53 – 42 victory. They had avenged their only loss of the season. Four players scored big for Hurley with Gentile dropping in 16, Kaffine 13, and Geach and Brown netting 10 apiece.

The Midgets were red hot! With a record of 12 – 1 and still undefeated in conference play, Bessemer came to town to try and knock the Midgets off their lofty perch. The Speed Boys were playing some good ball in the late season after stumbling over the first half of the season. They come out with a chip on their shoulders. In the second quarter the Bessemer five looked like they could pull off the upset as they spurted into the lead for a minute. Hurley regained the lead 19 – 17 at the intermission and then Carl Vergamini went into one of his motivational masterpieces. The spirited exhortations had the desired results and at the end of three quarters the Midgets held a 33 – 20 lead. The final score was 43 – 32. Mickey Brown and Bud Geach led the balanced attack with 12 and 11 points. Hurley had won the conference title with a perfect 8 – 0 record and they stood at 13 – 1 for the year. Ashland was second in the MW with at 5-3, Ironwood was third at 4-4, Bessemer was 2 – 6 and Wakefield was 1 – 7. Another big test for Hurley was on the schedule. They were on a collision course with Superior East and they were going to play in Superior! The two teams were tied in the state rankings in 16th place.

It was a much anticipated contest as it was now clear that these two teams were the favorites in the fast approaching Superior Regional Tournament. East took a 6 – 3 lead after one quarter and then held onto the lead at the half 13 – 11. Enter Coach Vergamini. After another motivational work of art the Midgets took the court in the third period breathing fire. At the end of three they led East 27 – 21. Hurley was making a habit of exploding in the third quarter. In the fourth quarter there was no explosion by either team. The Midgets could garner only four more points, but they matched East's defensive intensity and went home 31 – 27 winners. Their record was the best in school history at 14 – 1 with one game left in the regular season. Those pesky DePadua Bruins were coming to town. In another hard fought game Hurley ended the regular season the way they started it; with a 4 point win of the Bruins, 40 - 36. This was a very good DePadua team and Hurley was only too happy to be finished with them. Mickey Brown again paced Hurley in scoring as he dropped in 12 points. Dom Gentile and Carl Kaffine had 10 and 9 respectively. Hurley finished their regular season with a record of 15 wins and 1 loss. The regional tournament was about to start in Superior. Regular season records meant little at this point. A team either had to win or it was the end of their season. The Midgets got right to work.

On Wednesday, February 26, 1947 Hurley had even more reason to be proud. Bob Sohl, the "one man swim team" is pictured in the Ironwood Daily Globe with his two University of Michigan teammates who had just set the world record in the 300 yard medley relay. Bob swam the breaststroke, the same event in which he would win an Olympic Bronze medal in just about 17 more months.

CHAPTER FORTY FOUR

Win Or Go Home

The history of high school basketball is filled with stories of how a team mired in season long ineptitude reversed their fortunes in the tournament. In football most states did not have a tournament until the 1980's and then not every team was entered. Teams with poor regular season records were left out. In basketball it was everyone into the pool! A team with a record of say, 5 wins and 11 losses could upset a team with a record of 13 wins and 3 losses and it happened more than one would think. There have been great teams who won state championships with perfect undefeated records who barely escaped a team who had just experienced a miserable season. Many others have seen their fortunes fall altogether after losing their only game of the year to an also-ran during the tournament. In the tournament, no one cares about the win - loss record. The next game is all you look forward to. It is do or die! Win or go home! Your season continues or it comes to a sudden and painful stop.

The boys on this Hurley team had known the heartbreak of losing in the previous three regional tournaments in the first game. The last two years Superior Central downed the Midgets by scant margins. Both times the Midgets were the underdogs. This year they won 9 of 10 games with their best player nursing an injury. Now with Mickey Brown back in form, they were an even greater force to be reckoned with. These Midgets were ranked 13th in the state by those who guess at such things. They were confident but not cocky. They respected their opponents, but they had no fear of them. They had the best Chief Gianunzio could give them, and now they had a head coach who oozed confidence. This team reflected the best of both men. They played smart, heady ball, and they played with unmatched passion. Superior East would be the first team to stand in their way. Superior Central, ranked number 3 in the state was still the best team in the Northland, and most people thought it wasn't even close. They and the tough Park Falls Cardinals were scheduled to play the first game on Thursday evening and then Superior East would take on Hurley. Ashland and Phillips were given byes.

In the opening game Superior Central jumped off to a big lead as they handled their business in defeating the Cardinals of Park Falls 44 – 33. The Cards seemed overwhelmed at the size of the Field House at Superior State Teachers College where the tournament was hosted. They were used to their tiny gym in their mill town. By the time they awakened the Vikings had already built a strong lead. The East – Hurley match was next. East scored first and then relinquished the lead to the Midgets. Early in the third period East jumped ahead again. The Midgets recovered and surged into a five point lead at the end of the third period 28 – 23. The fourth quarter was just like the first meeting between these two teams. East scored 5 points, Hurley 4, and ball control became the weapon of choice for the Midgets as they won 32 – 28. Bud Geach played well on both ends of the floor and netted 14 points for the Midgets. Brown added 10, Gentile 6, and Kaffine had 2. Hurley won in the first round for the first time since 1943. In other regional matches on that same night, three schools ranked in the top ten in the state, Menasha, Madison Central, and South Milwaukee had their dreams shot down in flames. It was tournament time once again. Win or go home!

For the third year in a row, the Vikings stood in Hurley's path. They cast a giant shadow across the basketball landscape in the north and this year they were better than just good. They had not tasted defeat! The game started with the best team out-working the other. At the end of the first quarter it was 9 – 5 in favor of the best team. At halftime the best team had harried the other into uncharacteristic turnovers and sloppy play and they led 18 – 9. In the third quarter the Vikings finally came around and played better. Hurley still led 26 – 20 at the end of the third period but Central was ready to make their final move. Win or go home!

In the fourth quarter Central gave Hurley a dose of their own medicine with a smothering defense that kept the Midgets from scoring from the field. All they could muster was a single free throw as they went ice cold. Central did just enough on offense to tie the game at 27 – 27 to end regulation time. Central had it going their way and they clearly had momentum on their side. In the overtime period, the Midgets got back on track and Hurley took a 31 – 27 lead with a minute to play. Then Dom Gentile fouled out with 55 seconds to go in the overtime and Smokey Rainaldo replaced him. They missed Dom's defense. Central scored two baskets in the final 45 seconds to tie the game again at 31 – 31.

The second overtime period served up more twists and turns. The large crowd was hysterical as the two toughest teams from "Up North" traded blows. The Central star, Sherman Moe put the Vikings up 33 – 31 and things were looking bleak for the Midgets. Win or go home! The Mighty Midgets then exploded with three baskets in quick succession as Cotton Van Hoof, Hurley's most underrated player, scored on a nifty shot to tie it up again. Brown followed with another from short range and then Geach drilled one from medium range to put the Midgets up by 4. After clearing a Viking missed shot the Hurley boys went into their trusty stall. In this, their eighteenth game of the season, they were well conditioned and drilled. Hard practice after hard practice had taught them how to play and play well when they were tired. Their weariness faded away as they deftly snapped off precision passes and kept their feet moving the whole time. Five times the frantic Vikings fouled and five times the Midgets declined the free throws to retain possession. The game ended without the Midgets relinquishing the ball. The scoring for the Midgets was evenly distributed as Brown, Kaffine, and Geach all scored 9 points in the win. In a season marked by resilience and toughness, this was what they had worked so hard for. They defeated a great Superior Central team. More importantly they also defeated fatigue; the silent assassin that repeatedly kills the dreams of would-be champions.

With the win, Hurley earned the right to play the winner of the Ashland – Phillips game for the championship on Saturday night. That game immediately followed the heart stopping Central – Hurley match. The fans had just caught their breath as the game tipped off. Ashland started fast and wore down the Loggers. After halftime the game was no longer in doubt and the Purgolders walked away with an easy 39 – 25 win. The stage was now set for Saturday. The two Wisconsin teams from the M-W were going to face off for supremacy of the North.

Ashland was thinking that Hurley was not "that" good. They only beat the Purgolders in November by one slim point. It's true the Midgets pounded them 37 – 20 in the rematch, but the Midgets also barely won two tight games against Ironwood, a team the Purgolders crushed in their second meeting. They had the most experienced coach and a seasoned team with players who had been to the state finals in Madison the previous two years. History showed that other than 1943, Hurley had wilted in big games, while the Purgolders become stronger. They also had something else. They had Hurley's kryptonite, one of the most smothering zone defenses in the state.

Since the days of Gerald Rosendahl in 1943 – 44, the word on the street was Hurley could not handle a good zone defense. History was somewhat on the side of that reasoning as teams continued to throw the zone at the Midgets even after Rosendahl graduated and Hurley became a small team again. What history also showed was that the Midgets, when presented with a zone defense had learned to become very patient on offense. They were willing to engage in a low scoring game rather than launch low percentage shots from deep. This season had been full of examples of that as Hurley overcame the zones from all those who bought into the theory. Still a Roy Melvin coached zone defense was a real threat to the Midgets' dreams.

After Superior East toppled Phillips in overtime to win the third place honors in the region, Ashland and Hurley took the court. Well over 400 Hurley fans made the trip to Superior to watch the game. The rest of the town took to their radios and yelled themselves hoarse throughout the game.

Ashland did in fact play the dreaded zone defense and the Midgets were stymied by it as the Purgolders held the 5 – 2 edge after the first quarter. The sluggish start may have had more to do with the fact that Ashland had played only one game in the tournament so far and that was the easy win over Phillips. Hurley had the most grueling road to the championship game, having to play and beat both Superior teams in hotly contested games, especially the double overtime classic of the night before versus Central. In those games, Hurley had played their starters almost the entire time with Smokey Rainaldo spelling them briefly. This was the third game in three nights. Fatigue hovered over the Midgets like a vulture waiting to descend and pick them clean.

Fatigue and a stifling zone defense created high hopes for Ashland and their fans. But this was a different Midget team than Roy Melvin had previously coached against. They had the mental toughness to both ignore the vulture and charge full speed ahead. In the second quarter they came to life as they outscored Ashland 8 – 3. It appeared they had solved Melvin's mystery zone as they entered halftime up by two points 10 – 8. Armed with the challenges issued by Carl Vergamini they stormed the court to start the second half. They remained patient but aggressive on offense with their precision passing game flummoxing the Ashland five. In possession after possession the Midgets made the Purgolders move their feet more than they wanted to. On defense it was they who smothered the Purgolder offense. By the end of the third quarter the Midgets held the lead 19 – 10. It was then Melvin changed tactics and started to play the Midgets straight up. The Purgolders scored most of their 11 points in the fourth stanza after the game was decided. Hurley won 28 – 21 as the Midget subs finished the game. Brown scored ten points and Kaffine had 9 to pace Hurley. The Midgets won and moved on. The other five teams in the region lost and went home. Of the well over 350 high school basketball teams in the state, only 32 were left standing. Hurley now had a record of 18 – 1. That was the most wins in a season by a Midget team, tying the 1943 team who finished with a record of 18 – 4.

The Spooner Sectional Tournament was set to get underway on Friday, March 7. One of the other three teams making the cut was the Drummond Fire Brigade, the Ashland District champions for the third year in a row. They then won the right to be in the sectionals by beating Milltown 50 - 45 in the sub-sectionals for class C teams. Drummond would quiet the doubters in this sectional. They belonged as much as any larger school team ever did. Rice Lake earned their way to Spooner by blasting Cumberland 60 – 34 in their regional championship game. They also twice defeated a very strong Bloomer team late in the year and in the regional opener 49 – 35. They were a hot team. St. Croix Falls entered the Spooner Sectional with a 14 – 4 record after defeating River Falls 45 – 41 in their regional final. Four superb basketball teams all knowing they had to win or go home

On Friday morning, after a rousing pep rally that sent the student body into frenzy of full throated cheers, the Midget team and coaches departed for Spooner. The caravan to the Rail City would soon follow.

The first game of the evening pitted Drummond against Rice Lake. Drummond had a population of about 300 and there were less than 100 students in the high school which drew from a large rural area. Rice Lake no sooner got done licking their chops at the thought of winning big when the Fire Brigade jumped all over the Warriors, fighting them to a 22 – 22 halftime tie. While many observers thought Rice Lake would take advantage of the small school in the second half, Drummond had other ideas. They continued to play strong fundamental basketball. Suddenly the Fire Brigade broke loose from long range as they scored from deep again and again. When the dust settled, Drummond had downed the Warriors 50 – 42 in an impressive performance.

Hurley versus St. Croix Falls was the next game on tap. The very tall Saints squad had an impressive season. Hurley was favored by the pundits who knew any team that could beat Superior Central should be favored. The Midgets charged out to a 15 – 5 lead only to have the Saints fight back behind their star, Jim Beattie. At half time the Midgets were clinging to a two point lead, 18 – 16. Following their season-long formula, the Midgets again opened the second half on fire and they did not let up. They outscored the Saints 26 –

11 in the second half of the game and dominated both ends of the floor.   Mickey Brown scored 16 points and played solid defense. Dom Gentile and Bud Geach scored 9 and 7 points each. Hurley ran away with the game 44 – 27. At the end of the night only sixteen teams remained in the tournament field. By the end of the next night there would be only eight. Win or go home!

When Drummond faced off versus Hurley it was with the same mindset that the Midgets had. They respected their opponents, but did not fear them. Under their coach, Morris Vesperman, they were fundamentally sound and tougher than a sack of nails. One might wonder how Drummond might have fared the two previous years if Dick Axness had decided to finish high school at Drummond instead of Ashland. Along with Newman Benson, it is not unthinkable that Drummond would have been in the finals at Madison and could have won it all. Bud Grant, the former Superior Central star had thought that Benson was the toughest player he had seen in high school and he had played against Axness! To the credit of the Fire Brigade, they did not complain about their misfortune, they instead became a force in Northern Wisconsin basketball. The Hurley Midgets knew they were good and they prepared for a hard fought game.

The game started with Hurley grabbing a 4 – 1 lead on baskets by Gentile and Brown. Drummond fought back to tie it at 6 – 6. By the end of the first quarter the Fire Brigade held the lead 9 – 8. In the second period Brown drilled one from the side and tied the game at 10 – 10. A minute later Kaffine scored from that same spot to give Hurley the lead at 12 – 10. By half time the Midgets held the lead 22 – 18 and they knew they were in a dog fight. Win or go home! Drummond knew Hurley was a strong second half team and they were prepared to weather the coming storm. Hurley did not blow them away at any point of the third quarter. The Midgets just played ball the way Drummond did. Both teams were giving 100 percent plus effort and Hurley simply had a little more scoring punch and just a little more defense. At the end of three quarters the Midgets led by eight points, 37 – 29. The scrappy Fire Brigade continued to play hard and well, but just could not match the Midgets' talent. Hurley finally was able to put some distance between them and the scrappy Drummond boys and won the game 48 – 35. Drummond was so sound up until the fourth quarter that they left a lasting impression on the Iron County News and the Montreal River Miner. Both papers heaped praise on the gutsy Fire Brigade. Hurley played near perfect ball. It was a good thing too, as Drummond just refused to give in. Again the Midgets showed balanced scoring with Brown, Kaffine and Geach scoring 14, 11, and 10 points in the victory. Hurley had a seventeen game winning streak and for the season boasted their best record in school history at 20 – 1.

The Midgets were going to Madison. The sectional championship was easy in comparison to winning the regional tournament. That showed the power of the northern basketball programs. Central, Hurley and Ashland typically won the sectional by big scores in the 40's. The prevailing thought became, "Win the region and you will win the sectional." It was a dangerous thought, but the northern teams felt they could back it up, and in most years they were correct.

The Midgets felt well prepared by a tough conference schedule and by having to play in a very difficult region in which it was not uncommon to have two or three teams highly ranked in the state. Since 1942 only Eau Claire in 1944 had broken the string of domination by Central, Hurley, and Ashland. For the M-W Conference, both of their

Wisconsin teams had now gained the state finals twice apiece and a total of four times in the past five years. Iron sharpens iron.

The state tournament field was now set. Stevens Point with their record of 20 - 2 was ranked number 1 in the state and was going to play Neenah who was 16 – 7 in the first game on Thursday. The second game pitted Hurley against Tomah, 21 – 3, who had played the season as a member of two conferences, winning both the Gateway and West Central Conference titles. They were playing in their fourth state tournament in a row and had a savvy veteran team led by the incomparable 5' 7" Tom Curry, who inch for inch may have been the best basketball player in the state. Tomah also had Dick Davis, who along with Curry, were appearing in their fourth state tournament. Dwight Dickinson was playing in his third in a row, and high scoring John Schedler, his second in a row. The third game of the opening round had Blair, 23 – 2 against West Allis Central, 18 – 5, and the fourth and last game of the day Madison East, 14 – 8 against Beloit 15 – 6. Beloit and Madison East tied for the Big Eight Conference title with Madison West and Madison Central and were facing each other for the third time in the season. They had each won against the other on their home courts. Tomah, Neenah, and Beloit were appearing in their eleventh state tournaments. Neenah, Stevens Point, and Beloit all had won the tournament previously, with Beloit being a four time champion.

The road to Madison was similar for each team as they had to beat strong teams in the regional and sectional tournaments. Hurley did have a unique road that none of the other teams could claim to have taken, and that is meant in the literal sense.

The Midgets had by far, the longest trip to make to get to Madison. The decision was made to take a train. Since no trains ran from Hurley to Madison and connections were not going to be easy to make, the boys piled into cars driven by the willing townspeople to take them to Woodruff, some fifty miles south of Hurley. There they would catch the train to Madison. The coaches, players and team managers said their goodbyes to their drivers and entered the Woodruff depot. They then found out that Woodruff did not have service to Madison either! Service to Madison was available only from Minocqua which was just over a mile away. With the drivers already heading back to Hurley, the party of marooned Midgets grabbed their suitcases and started walking down the tracks in the cold and snow. They arrived at the Minocqua depot in time to board their train. The journey of a thousand miles begins with a single step--and erroneous information!

Stevens Point found that being the top dog in the tournament came with a price. The Neenah Rockets were more than just a match for them. With only eight teams still playing, they all got to Madison by believing they would be the champions. None of them had any fear. The Pointers escaped with a 46 – 45 win over the Rockets in overtime. With the crowd still buzzing about the non-stop action of the first game, Tomah and Hurley took the court. Tomah was riding a ten game winning streak and were tournament tested. This was a lightning quick squad with speed to spare. Like Hurley, they ran hard all the time and played defense as if they were possessed.

The game started out with both teams displaying sharp passing, but generally poor shooting. After the first quarter Tomah led 10 – 7. Then in the second quarter Hurley went ice cold and managed only two points. Tomah now led at the half 19 – 9. It appeared now that Hurley had met their match as the Indians used their ultra quickness to befuddle them. But Hurley had been in this position before and was now in the locker room figuring out how to solve the problems

Tomah presented. Keeping to their season long script, Hurley owned the third quarter. Mickey Brown led the way. Described by his team mate Carl Kaffine as a "man among boys," Brown caught fire. His torrid shooting helped the Midgets close the gap to 26 – 24 at the end of the third quarter. The other Midgets all contributed, and Geach was an anchor on defense as he gathered the Tomah misses and gave them no opportunity for an easy put back off a rebound. In the decisive fourth quarter Tomah increased their lead to four points on a long shot by Davis. Brown countered with another basket from deep and Geach dropped in a free throw to cut the lead to one. Schedler of Tomah dropped in a short one to put Tomah up 30 – 27. Then in rapid succession Kaffine buried a short one and Brown did the same. Hurley now had the 31 – 30 lead. A Tomah free throw tied it at 31 apiece and then Schedler struck again to give the Indians the 33 – 31 lead. Hurley had to score or risk a Tomah stall. They did as Brown came through again burying another long bomb. With the score knotted at 33 Tomah was stymied and Hurley had the ball. With the defense keying on the red hot Brown, Bud Geach took the shot and missed. The Hurley pivot man then did what he had done in practice thousands of times before; he followed his own shot, and tipped the miss in for the basket with five seconds to go. Tomah could not get a shot off and Hurley had escaped the first round of play with the 35 – 33 win in a comeback for the ages. Mickey Brown scored 14 of his 19 points in the second half as he carried his beleaguered team mates to the semi – final round versus the mighty Stevens Point quintet.

In the other two opening round games that night, Blair, the small school team with tall talented players fell to West Allis Central 40 – 38. Beloit than beat back their conference rivals, Madison East 45 – 38. There were four teams left. Win or go home!

Steven Point 21 – 2 versus Hurley 21 – 1. Nobody predicted that Hurley would win. Everybody was wrong. Point took the early 1 – 0 lead and Bud Geach tied it at 1-1. That would be the last lead and last tie score for Stevens Point in the game. Geach then scored on a nifty hook shot and Hurley had the lead 3 – 1. The Midgets kept their foot on the gas pedal all the way and dismantled the Pointers 51 – 30. Carl Kaffine led all scorers with 21 points and Dom Gentile scored 9. Mickey Brown scored 10, but it was Kaffine and Gentile that were called by many the "best guard tandem" in the tournament. They simply controlled the game. The high flying Stevens Point five could not solve Hurley's defense at any point of the game as the Midget lead increased every quarter. The best team in the state in the minds of the sports writers was shot down in flames. In the other semi-final game Beloit put on a scoring clinic versus West Allis Central as they completely outclassed the Bulldogs 64 – 30 and set the single game scoring record for the tournament. Now there were two.

While Carl Kaffine and Dom Gentile won plaudits for their superb play against Steven Point, it was a diminutive little Hurley cheerleader who stole the show and the hearts of the Friday night crowd. Joanne Kopacz, a little red haired sophomore was the only Hurley cheerleader to get to the game as the others were fighting their way south during another winter storm. Joanne was given a ride by her uncle and arrived on time. The others caught rides later in the day and ended up not getting through till after the game. Not only was Joanne small, but she was very shy and relied on her cheer team to overcome her nervousness. They were not there and her emotional safety net was gone. Before the game the Stevens Point cheering section was brought to life by their cheerleaders. Then all eyes were on Joanne! With her knees shaking and her voice trembling she took the court to lead Hurley's fans in cheering. Sensing her nervousness, they got behind her and cheered like they never had before. In a 1997 interview Joanne remembered the Hurley student body and the large group of parents who attended the games as being like a "big family." When she needed that family the most, they came through for her. Carl Kaffine looked on in admiration. He also could not help but notice that she received a spirited and appreciative cheer from the non Hurley fans as she completed the routine.

With each timeout and break in the action Joanne led the Hurley cheers. The well-rehearsed, organized cheers grew louder each time as more and more people joined in with the Hurley fans. Finally, Joanne had the entire crowd up and cheering for Hurley! Carl Kaffine was the hero of the game but it was Joanne Kopacz who stole the hearts of the near capacity crowd of 13,000. Hurley was now the sentimental favorite to win the championship. Later in life, with both Carl and Joanne married and raising kids, they became neighbors in Gile until the mines closed, and Carl moved his family to Eveleth, Minnesota. Carl, now 90 years old, says, "I can still picture Joanne out there, all alone." In fact, she was standing alone, together, with her Hurley family.

After the Stevens Point game the duo of J.E. Murphy and Harold Conners began to pull strings to get the Hurley band to Madison for the championship game. Finally in the early hours of Saturday morning they found a bus and the band was off. Hurley took on the appearance of a ghost town as half the population piled into cars heading south on US 51.

Saturday night brought about the matchup between large school and small school, north versus south, a team from the Michigan border and a team from the Illinois border. The Beloit State Liners and Hurley had won close games in the opening round and then crushed their opponents in the semi-finals. The crowd leaned heavily toward Hurley as they wanted the little school to beat the big guys. Beloit had other ideas and they and their 6'5" center Bob Wegner jumped all over the Midgets to take an 11 – 0 lead before the stunned Hurley squad could blink. Five of Beloit's top six players stood over 6 feet tall. Their size was not surprising, but the speed of those big guys caught Hurley off guard. Then it was the Midgets who made their case as they battled back by the end of the first quarter to trail only by 12 – 11. Bud Geach buried a shot to start the second quarter and Hurley had the lead 13 – 12. The first ever capacity crowd at the state tournament roared their approval. Not all of the 13,800 fans were cheering for Hurley, but it sure seemed that way. Then Beloit again flexed their muscles and took the lead at halftime 28 – 22. The Midgets stayed within striking distance through the third quarter and closed the gap to 29 – 26 at one point. Beloit continued to grind away at the Midgets and they again pulled away. At the end of the third quarter it was Beloit 39, Hurley 30. By this time the game looked like the Hurley – Drummond match in the sectional final. Everyone could see that Hurley was fundamentally sound, tough, and game. It was also evident that Beloit was bigger, faster, and just as sound, tough, and just as game. The Midgets could find no holes in the Beloit team and the State Liners methodically put the game on ice. The final score was 56 – 37, but like the Drummond game, it seemed much closer.

For Hurley, it was a tough pill to swallow, but the boys knew that they gave it all and then some. Carl Kaffine scored 14 points in the championship game to pace Hurley again. He simply says, "Beloit was just too big for us to handle." There were no ifs, ands, or buts about it. Beloit was the best team in the state. They deserved the championship.

There was plenty of drama for Hurley in this tournament. But there was even more than met the eye. The most difficult thing for the team was that Mickey Brown did not want to go to Madison. His older brother, Bill, a World War II veteran, had taken a terrible fall down a flight of stairs and was in critical condition. Mickey idolized Bill. Mickey's mother, May Brown, told Mickey to get on the train because "That's what Bill would want you to do." Mickey did. Bill passed away shortly after the team left. May Brown insisted that no one tell Mickey until after the tournament saying, "That's what Bill would want." With the whole town aware of the situation, no one spoke a word of it out of respect for the Browns. After the game Carl Vergamini had his most difficult assignment ever as a head coach. It was he who told Mickey the news that broke his young heart.

The disappointment of losing quickly dissipated and the town embraced their team with an even more pride than ever. Hurley now had been to the state tournament twice and had a third and second place trophy to show for their stellar work. The people were proud of "their" boys and proud of their town. They knew that they had a championship caliber basketball team. They also knew they had a championship school and their kids were the embodiment of the values they held dear. Hurley kids went into the world with an astounding work ethic, respectful behavior, and a character that was uncommonly strong. The parents and the school district were doing their jobs and it showed.

CHAPTER FORTY FIVE

Exceeding Expectations

Most coaches are good coaches. They are dedicated and committed to their athletes and their sports. When it comes to coaches Hurley was fortunate. Since 1923 they had been led in athletics by Roy Melvin and Carl Vergamini. They were doubly lucky to have found a third coach in Mario Gianunzio, who not only impacted the lives of his players but who also preferred to be an assistant coach and teach younger players the intricacies of the game at the freshmen and "B" team levels. Many players stayed in touch with these men and they formed a lifelong bond of friendship and respect. Roy Melvin happened along at just the right time when J.E. Murphy and Harold Conners wanted to raise Hurley's physical education and athletics standards. When he left for Ashland, Carl Vergamini was hired sight unseen. His resume and recommendations must have been solid gold. To have found three good coaches in a row isn't rare. What is rare is that they were all so incredibly good at what they did. All three were superb communicators and all three built their relationships based upon mutual trust and respect. They were genuine and sincere. That is what made them great coaches. In the 1947 – 48 school year the people of Hurley would clearly see just how good the tandem of "Verg and "Chief" could be.

The 1947 football season would see the Midgets compile a record of 3 wins and 5 losses. Four of those losses would be by one score. It would turn out to be the only   losing season Hurley would have while Carl Vergamini was their coach. The team that greeted the coach for the first practice sessions of the year was young and inexperienced.

14 seniors who saw significant playing time the year before were graduated leaving a squad with only 7 current seniors, a load of juniors, and a few sophomores with real promise. One of those sophomores was a bruising fullback, Eugene "Smocky" Martino, younger brother of Eino "Lefty" Martino. A talented group of freshmen practiced hard with the team and did get a little playing time, including Florian Helinski, who would go on to be a star quarterback for the University of Indiana and Francis "Red" Trier who would become one of the best linemen in Hurley's football history. Trier began to pick up more and more playing time as the season progressed as he developed into a sure tackler on defense.

The Midgets started the season with a disappointing loss to Calumet 6 – 0. It was the virtue of charity that Hurley displayed that day as they turned the ball over on fumbles five times. For the game Hurley outgained the Cooper Kings by a 2 – 1 margin and also compiled twice as many first downs. Carl Vergamini played 22 of the 27 Midgets that made the trip to the Keweenaw Peninsula. The game displayed that Hurley had some talent, but they, like most young teams just exposed to varsity football, were prone to mistakes. With lessons to be learned, the next game would be even worse.

Park Falls turned the table on Hurley in 1947 as they cruised to a 26 – 0 win on their field to avenge the 31 – 6 loss the Midgets inflicted upon them in '46. In over 20 years of play between the two teams, it was the most lopsided win by Park Falls. Hurley tallied three first downs in the first quarter on three good runs of 10 yards by Martino. After that, it was nothing! Finally, the subs took the field and it was a bright spot for the Midgets days. With the lightning-quick freshman quarterback Florian Helinski passing the ball, the Midgets tallied their only first downs since the first quarter. Coach MacDonald of the

Cardinals reinserted his starters rather than give Hurley something to cheer about and that ended the threat. Vergamini played every player in that game. That was sign that he was looking for someone to step up and produce. It's also a sign of a very green squad. With two games and zero points put on the scoreboard. Coach Carl went back to the drawing board.

The next game on the schedule was against Phillips with the Loggers coming to Hurley on a bright and warm Saturday afternoon. Phillips started the game like gangbusters as they moved 59 yards on four plays to the Hurley 21 yard line. Just when it looked like this game would be a repeat of the first two, the Midget defense threw the Loggers back with several devastating tackles. Having thwarted the Loggers, the Hurley offense started to show signs of life. The Midgets moved the ball with good runs bys Martino and Noel Mattei. They continued to move the chains and then Jim Rainaldo hit Carl Hermanson in the end zone to get the Midgets on the scoreboard for the first time in the season. Mattei later intercepted an errant Logger pass and returned it to the 10 yard line. He then swept around the left end and scored. Hurley was up 13 – 0. They added a score in the third and fourth quarters to win 25 – 0. Phillips moved the ball well at times, but a fumble, two costly interceptions, and their inability to gain critical first downs left them short of the goal line the entire game.

The Montreal River Miner had welcomed back Armand Cirilli from the Army and he took over the sports editor job for the paper. Ed Sybeldon gave up his typewriter and devoted himself to teaching at the high school. He then took up doing a sports column for the Iron County News. The one thing they both liked to do was make predictions. Sometimes they were surprisingly good at it. Now with a win under their belt, Armand, who was writing the Comment on

Sports as "Sir Riley," heaped praise on the football team for their win. He remarked that it did not seem as if the team that played Park Falls was the same one that played Phillips. That much was true to be sure. He should have left it at that and not made any predictions. One such comment was, "They may still lose all their games from now on, but at least they'll be hard to beat." He went on to predict that Ashland and Ironwood would be the teams to beat in the conference and Bessemer could be the dark horse. Nothing unusual about that, as that was the case most years. But then Sir Riley predicted that Roy Melvin would have a bag of tricks to throw at the "green Midgets." That Armand and Roy Melvin were friends was well known. That Ashland beat Park Falls earlier in the season was a fact. But a young coach preparing his team for the Purgolders did not care one iota about any of that. He was brewing up something special for Ashland.

Hurley scrimmaged their alumni on Tuesday and played well. When asked on Wednesday if they could beat Ashland the players all said yes. Then Carl Vergamini was asked if they would beat the Purgolders. He also said "yes." Most coaches won't come out and say that to the press or to anyone else. He was confident for a reason. His team of inexperienced players was improving by the day.

After starting the game with both teams punting to the other, Hurley again held Ashland without a first down. The Purgolders punted for the second time and it was taken by halfback John Hermanson at the 50. He cut back looking for blockers as two Ashland players descended upon him looking to bust his chops. Instead little brother Carl Hermanson took out both Purgolders with one powerful block, knocking them back to the Ashland County line. John finished the job and sprinted into the end zone. The Miner described the block this way, "It was here that Brother Carl threw one of the most brutal blocks ever seen on Lincoln field as he mowed down his two adversaries in one scythe-like move." Sir Riley wrote, "Those fans who did not see the block, surely must have heard it as the thud reverberated all over the field as he flattened two Purgolders."

The Purgolders played the rest of the game as if they had been bitten by a snake. They fumbled, missed blocks, and tossed the ball to the Hurley defense. Jim Rainaldo scored in the fourth quarter on a two yard quarterback sneak and then intercepted an Ashland pass on the dead run and took it to the end zone from 30 yards away. Hurley won 21 – 0. Ashland did not move the ball past their forty yard line until the Hurley reserves took over in the fourth quarter. They then moved to the Hurley 40 and fumbled. The freshman Red Trier pounced on it to quell the Purgolders last scoring threat.

Sir Riley heaped praise upon the lads and then started to eat a little crow. Not only did Hurley beat Ashland, they did it convincingly. The failed soothsayer then ate a second helping because Bessemer beat Ironwood, the other co–favorite and conference bully, 20 – 7. It was shaping up to be a strange season.

Of course Hurley was looking great and Ironwood looked very vulnerable. Everyone knew that in this rivalry anything could happen. So the Red Devils defeated Hurley 6 – 0. The Devils scored in the first quarter after John Hermanson fumbled a punt on the Hurley 12 yard line. Speedy George Kolak took it over from the three yard line a few plays later and the Devils had their due. The game saw Ironwood gain 9 first downs to Hurley's 8. Hurley gained 128 yards from scrimmage and Ironwood had 127 yards. Hurley threatened to score three times but they were stopped each time. In an up and down season, you need look no further than this. When you fumble, you lose. When you do not fumble, you win. With three loses, two of them were directly caused by fumbles.

Hurley rebounded nicely in the next game versus DePadua as they blasted the overmatched Bruins 40 – 13. It took the Midgets until the third quarter to get untracked after leading at halftime 14 – 13. That set up the next game versus Bessemer. With a win Hurley could end up with a tie for the conference title. A Bessemer win would assure them of a tie for the title and if they could beat Ashland the following week they would win it outright.

Hurley played a very strong game and but it was Bessemer who led 7 – 0 as they scored just before the half on a drive that featured two 15 yard penalties on Hurley that became first downs after the Speed Boys were stymied. The Miner stated that the calls "reeked to heaven." Hurley finally punched through the Speed Boy defense for a score just as the fourth quarter got underway and then stunned the Bessemer crowd by doing it again to take a 12 – 7 lead. The first Hurley score came on a two yard pass from Rainaldo to Joe Grasso. Matt Anichs' point after kick hit the crossbar and bounced back. Later in the quarter John Hermanson took the pitch from Rainaldo and turned the corner to see open field in front of him. He turned on the afterburners and sprinted 85 yards for the score. The stunned Speed Boys then took a short kick off and in the next four plays they were in the end zone for the 13 – 12 win over the Midgets. The following Friday night the Speed Boys did make Armand Cirilli look good in his predictions as they defeated Ashland 13 – 0 in the Ore Dock City to win the conference title. Hurley in the meantime was given absolutely no chance to beat a powerful and mammoth Superior Central team. Armand Cirilli, not content to have been correct about Bessemer's chance to win the conference now urged the Midgets to never schedule Central again. So Hurley took the opening kickoff 70 yards on 11 plays to take a 6 – 0 lead against the bewildered Vikings. But Central recovered their senses and scored twice in the bitterly fought game to win 13 – 6. The statistics were close in all categories. Hurley again played another team of behemoths evenly for the most part. The Vikings left Hurley with a deeper respect as the little scrappers left them drained. Carl Vergamini continued to schedule them through the 1952 season and the Midgets won three of the last four meetings.

So Armand did end up eating a little humble pie. It must have been pretty good, because he was going to continue the prediction business. To be fair, he was pretty good at it, as was Ed Sybeldon. They hit on about 50% of their prognostications, just like the weatherman! That's a good percentage considering that high school sports are much more unpredictable than the weather will ever be.

With winter approaching and the autumn leaves all off the trees, the people of Hurley began buzzing about the prospects of their basketball team. Gone was the fabulous senior class of ball players that made the 1946 – 47 team the best in history. Back from the previous year was senior Jim "Smokey" Rainaldo, who saw plenty of playing time when Mickey Brown was hurt and then was a valuable player coming off the bench later in the season. Len Bartolutti and Charles Guenther were on the varsity as seldom used sophomores the year before. That was it for experience; there were no returning starters and only three players from the year before. The team would be filled out by seniors Don Zandi, Don Hoeft, and Joe Cattelino, juniors Bill Anich, John Hermanson, Noel Mattei, and Wayland Baron, along with sophomore Carl Hermanson. All of them were promoted from the junior varsity team that compiled a 14 – 3 record the previous year. The Hermanson brothers were for purposes of athletics, going to be ineligible to play in their senior years because of Wisconsin's age limit. That meant that John was playing in his last season and Carl had only two more seasons.

Never let it be said that Armand Cirilli was timid about making predictions. Right or wrong, they flowed forth. Of the upcoming Hurley Basketball season he said this, "On paper, it doesn't look like he (Vergamini) has the stuff there to set the world on fire – or even the Michigan – Wisconsin league. Nor does it seem he has the material to defeat the Hodags of Rhinelander, tutored by Russell Leskell, a former Ironwood star." Yes, Carl Vergamini scheduled the always good Rhinelander Hodags for the first game of the season. To Carl Vergamini a strong schedule meant developing a strong team. He would continue to schedule as many tough opponents as he could find every single season.

The season kicked off in the Hurley gym as Russ Leskell led his Hodags onto the floor. Rhinelander had seven returning lettermen including "Moose" Lytle, from a strong team. Hurley countered with Smokey Rainaldo and the inexperienced quartet of John and Carl Hermanson, Len Bartolutti, and Noel Mattei as starters. Sir Riley was right to think this was a mismatch and he wasn't the only one to believe that. Fortunately, the Hurley players forgot to read the predictions. They pounced on the Hodags like a lion on a steak and ran off to an 11 – 1 lead. Rhineland regained their poise and battled back to tie the game at 22 – 22 early in the fourth quarter. Carl Hermanson then took over and dropped in two consecutive baskets. With Rhinelander not able to connect and Hurley controlling the rebounds the Midgets went into their stall with Rainaldo holding the ball as much as possible. Why? Because he made free throws! When the dust settled Hurley pulled off the improbable win 34 – 25. Smokey Rainaldo scored 7 points, all on free throws and the Hermanson brothers combined for 17 more points. Len Bartolutti also contributed 7 points while Noel Mattei had 3 and Bill Anich scored 1.

Sir Riley was not yet ready to partake of another piece of humble pie as he wrote that "Hurley looked good in spots" and that people "were surprised at the weakness of the Hodags." As the season progressed, Rhinelander would prove to be anything but weak, and Hurley would look good in spots--a whole lot of spots!

The second game of the season was on tap on Friday, November 21. The Ashland Purgolders were in Hurley and they had something to prove. This was another big squad for Roy Melvin and he had them ready to play. Ashland rolled to an early lead and was hanging on to it throughout the game. The Midgets were out rebounded terribly by the big Purgolders but they were tenacious and refused to crack. Ashland could no more solve the Hurley defense than Hurley could the Purgolders. With three minutes to go in this tight and mistake filled game, Ashland lead 19 – 14. It was then that Smokey Rainaldo scored on a free throw, a field goal, and another free throw to bring the score to 19 – 18. Two Hurley substitutes, the string beans, Wayland Baron and Charles Guenther, then broke through with baskets to give the Midgets a 22 – 19 lead. Ashland scored on a free throw to make it 22 – 20. Hurley then went into its deadly stall. Ashland fouled repeatedly, but the Midgets declined the free throws to maintain possession until the final buzzer. Yes it was an ugly win, but it was over a tough Ashland team and that was a thing of beauty!

Hurley played its third straight home game of the season against Phillips. The game started off with Hurley holding a 14 – 7 lead after the first quarter. Then halfway through the second stanza, the Midgets exploded. Time and again the Midgets let loose with quick, long outlet passes off of rebounds that caught the Loggers by surprise. The Miner called it "Race Horse" basketball. Today we know it as the "fast break." Ten of the eleven Midgets scored in the game as Hurley did in fact race to the 68 – 27 win. Perhaps the strangest thing to come out of this game was that Len Bartolutti, one of the very best and most disciplined players to ever put on a Hurley uniform, fouled out of the game in the first quarter!

Bessemer was next up for Hurley. The Speed Boys were coming off a fourth place finish in the M-W in 1947 with a 2 – 6 conference record. Showing vast improvement over the course of the season they pulled off two major upsets in defeating the powerful Stambough Hilltoppers 37 – 35 and ended the regular season with a 44 – 33 win over traditional powerhouse Iron River. In the Michigan U.P. Tournament the Speed Boys continued to gel as they ran all the way to the Class B championship game where they defeated Lake Linden 46 – 45 for their first ever Class B championship. Now this collection of Speed Boy basketball players was back almost intact. This was a big and fast team that had plenty of scoring punch, experience, and confidence. Sir Riley wrote that they were the favorites for the M-W tile along with Ashland; the same Ashland that just lost to Hurley. Well, he turned out to be half right.

Bessemer was favored to win the game. So the Midgets defied logic and played their best game of the year. At the end of the first quarter Hurley led 15 – 7. The crowd at Hurley's fourth straight home game was again at capacity and again they were loud and proud. Bessemer recovered and closed the gap to 20 – 19 at the half. The Speed Boys used their size advantage to take the lead in the third quarter, which they maintained up until late in the fourth when the

Midgets had several opportunities to tie the game. Inexplicably, Hurley blew two wide open shots from underneath. Then Smokey Rainaldo and Noel Mattei fouled out. Now it was Hurley's turn to chase down and foul Bessemer as the Speed Boys went into their stall to ice the game 39 – 35. The Speed Boys showed they were a classy team that would be reckoned with all year. The young Hurley squad learned from their experienced foes that night. If you want to win, you take care of the ball all game long. Bessemer did. Hurley did too. It was a great game.

The talented but sputtering Park Falls team was next up. The experienced senior-laden Cardinals found themselves to be sputter free versus Hurley. They took an early 10 – 6 lead and never relinquished it. The Midgets for the second game in a row played well in defeat but lost to a better team on that night. Park Falls made few mistakes and stayed in control. Hurley was also calm and controlled but the Cardinals never relented. It was clear that for Hurley to be a factor in the conference and in the region they had to improve and do it quickly. Teams like Bessemer and Park Falls with a bevy of experienced seniors were not going to beat themselves. Hurley's strong contingent of juniors needed to start playing like seniors or it was going to be a frustrating season.

With the "other" Cardinals coming to Hurley for a conference game the Hurley five needed to get back on track. The Cardinals were experiencing a frustrating season so far and they also wanted to get a precious win. They started the game by taking an 11 – 7 lead after one period and still led the 14 – 13 at halftime. The Midgets, rather than trying to take what they wanted, took what the Wakefield defense gave them in the third quarter to wrest the lead away from the Cards 22 – 17. Since the opening quarter the Midget defense was stifling as Cardinals offense ground nearly to a halt. In the fourth quarter the dam burst as Charles Guenther and Smokey Rainaldo scored almost at will. The Midgets blew the game wide open and coasted to victory 41 – 24. Guenther scored 11, Rainaldo 9, and Len Bartolutti netted 7 to pace the Midgets. All eleven players saw action and 9 of them scored.

The last game before the Christmas break was a non conference tilt versus the DePadua Bruins. DePadua was winless in the season but had just taken Park Falls into overtime before losing by three points. As usual, DePadua played Hurley a tough as one could hope for. Noel Mattei caught fire in this game and canned 17 points to give the Midgets an early Christmas present with the 37 – 28 win. Hurley was now 5 – 2 on the season including 2-1 in the conference. The "B" team was rolling along with a perfect 7 – 0 record and was being led by Pete "Pupsy" Savant, a junior who possessed a strange high arching shot that somehow went in more than anyone could believe. Rather than mess with correcting it, the two coaches decided that he would not be the same player if he tried to change it. It would turn out to be one of the best decisions they ever made.

With eleven games remaining in the regular season, Hurley had to leave the confines of the Lincoln gym and travel for eight of them. Their inexperienced team would have to hit their stride playing in hostile environments, if they were to hit their stride at all. The first game after the break was in the most inhospitable place any Midget team could play in: Ironwood! The Devils were undefeated in the conference after defeating Ashland and Wakefield, good for a first place tie with Bessemer. The Speed Boys of course were still undefeated on the season and the only game that was even close was their win versus Hurley. Surprisingly, Ashland had not won a conference game and was tied for last place with Wakefield at 0 – 3. The Purgolders were still considered to be very tough and proved it with wins over Park Falls and a superb Superior East squad. So with the break over, Sir Riley heaped praise upon this edition of the Hurley Midgets, saying that they "are a nice bunch of youngsters. They play hard and have a world of courage." He used words like "stick-to-itiveness" to describe their stubborn refusal to lose to Ashland in the second game of the season. This was an astute observation rather than a prediction. He also urged the fans to get out and continue to support the team as the hard part was just beginning. He was right about that and he was right about them having courage and "stick-to-itiveness."

In the packed to capacity L.L. Wright gym in Ironwood, the Devils and Midgets resumed their rivalry. Ironwood was favored to win the game by those who followed the Range teams closely. From the opening tip, the Devils dominated the first quarter of action as they jumped off to a 7 – 0 lead and then kept pace for the remainder of the period for an 11 – 4 lead. The Midgets battled back to close within two points at halftime and it was 17 – 15. The game was called "pell-mell" by the Miner, and "race horse" by the Ironwood Daily Globe. No matter the description, it was intense. Hurley was whistled for 25 fouls and ironwood for 20. The fouls were a matter of hustle and effort without the players putting on the brakes at the right times. That intensity was the key and the Midgets turned up the heat in the third quarter. Carl Hermanson controlled the boards giving Ironwood no chance for a second shot. Noel Mattei erupted for the second game in a row and the Hurley offense and defense were clicking as the Midgets were now playing their best ball of the season. Hurley scored 16 points in the third stanza to Ironwood's 6 for a 31 – 23 lead. The Devils' vaunted passing attack went to pieces as the Midgets turned into ball hawks, intercepting passes and scoring easy buckets.

The fourth quarter saw the Devils tally 13 points, but they had no answer for Mattei and Hurley scored 14 more for the 45 – 36 win. Mattei led all scorers with 19 points. Carl Hermanson had 7 as did Len Bartolutti.

Hurley looked like they had figured things out. Now they had to play Ashland at Dodd gymnasium in Ashland. The Ashland Press writer, Jim Goeltz, had started to refer to the Ashland teams as the Oredockers and the name was beginning to stick. Ashland was previously known as the Oredockers before the name was dropped in favor of the Purgolds after their school colors. The Oredockers took to the court in brand new uniforms, and with a new but still unofficial name they were ready to play. Hurley got off to a 3 – 0 lead but then the Ashland five took control of the game scoring 14 unanswered points. The Midgets battled back like men possessed but could not find the range as they missed shot after shot. The Oredockers' stubborn defense refused to yield the lead and they held on for the 40 – 32 win. Len Bartolutti and Wayland Baron were the two bright spots on the Midget offense with 10 and 9 points each. Hurley was now 6 – 3 for the season and 3 – 2 in the M - W. Ashland climbed out of the M – W cellar with the win. The on again, off again Hurley team was off again.

As expected by everyone who cared about basketball in the area, Hurley defeated Phillips on their own court 49 – 34. Smokey Rainaldo returned to form scoring 16 points and Noel Mattei netted 9 in the victory. The next test would be much more difficult with Ironwood invading the Hurley gym on Friday night, January 23.

This contest was played with more crispness than the first encounter. The game was close for the first three quarters with Hurley leading 24 – 20 at that point. Ironwood tried in vain to close the gap but could gain only one point on the Midgets before the final buzzer sounded giving Hurley the 38 – 35 triumph. Carl Hermanson played a near perfect game on both ends of the court as he scored 15 points and held Ironwoods high scoring big man Smetana to just six points. Hurley was on again. This time they would stay on.

There was a pattern to successful Hurley basketball seasons. They would start out okay, win a few, lose a key game or two and then go on a strong run to finish the season. It was especially true under Carl Vergamini, now in his third season with the Midgets. You can speculate on the reasons why that was, but the results were astounding. Year after year, nobody wanted to play Hurley late in the season, and for good reason. They simply kept getting better as each season progressed. A lot better! With the win over Ironwood, Hurley was about to go on another patented run down the stretch. In short order they blasted St. Ambrose 58 – 38, beat a strong Superior East squad 38 – 34, defeated Wakefield 46 – 25, and then avenged their early season loss to Park Falls 39 – 21. All games were blowouts except the game versus East who had a record of 12 – 4 going into the game. The scoring was balanced over that stretch with occasional explosions by different players. Rainaldo scored 17 against St. Ambrose, five players scored between 6 and 9 points apiece in the win over East, Carl Hermanson and Wayland Baron led the charge against Wakefield with 13 and 11 points respectively and John Hermanson led the scoring against Park Falls with 11 points.

With multiple scoring threats in the starting lineup and on the bench, Hurley was primed to take on the undefeated Bessemer Speed Boys who had just defeated Superior East 43 – 40. Bessemer was at 6 – 0 in the conference and Hurley was 5 – 2. This was the last conference game for Hurley, and Bessemer still needed to play Ironwood. They were playing for pride. Bessemer wanted that undefeated conference season! Hurley wanted to prove they were Bessemer's better. They wanted to give the Devils a chance to knock the Speed Boys into a tie for first place with Hurley. The game was in Bessemer with a capacity crowd waiting to witness what most felt was the only remaining threat to the Speed Boys' season. Only Hurley had come close to beating this group, but that was on Hurley's court.

Only February 13, Friday the thirteenth, to be exact, Hurley took to the court in Bessemer. Traditionally, it was a house of horrors for most teams to play in. The game was a torrid affair with the Speed Boys jumping out front 11 – 6 after one quarter. The raucous Bessemer fans were then silenced in the second period as Hurley fought back to gain an 18 – 18 tie at the half. The atmosphere in the Bessemer gym was electric with anticipation. The Speed Boys scored three baskets in 45 seconds to open the second half and the Bessemer faithful were going through the roof with joy. Hurley played scrappy ball to come back to tie it again. The game remained tight and tense with Bessemer now gaining the slim lead until the last three minutes of the third quarter when the Midgets finally jumped out in front. The beginning of the fourth quarter saw Hurley holding fast to a one point lead 30 - 29. The Speed Boys kept pace with Hurley throughout the fourth quarter and then with less than a minute to go they took the lead 39 – 38. With four seconds left Len Bartolutti drove towards the basket and was fouled by Bessemer star Ray Kangas. Bartolutti took the ball and despite the Bessemer fans urgings to miss, he calmly swished the free throw to tie the game. Overtime!

In the overtime period John Hermanson converted a free throw to give Hurley the lead 40 – 39. The Midgets regained possession of the ball on a missed shot by Bessemer and went into their stall. Bessemer had to foul. Hurley elected to shoot the free throw and Noel Mattei converted it for a 41 – 39 lead. Again Bessemer could not score and again Hurley controlled the rebound. Again Hurley stalled and Bessemer fouled. John Hermanson sank the free one and Hurley led by 42 – 39. The scene repeated itself and Hurley was fouled again. Bartolutti converted the charity toss and Hurley led 43 – 39. That was how it ended. Bessemer was knocked out of the ranks of the undefeated and Hurley avenged their loss to the Speed Boys in Hurley. John Hermanson scored 12 and Smokey Rainaldo scored 11 for the Midgets. The seniors looked polished and cool. Carl Hermanson added 9, Wayland Baron 5, and Bartolutti and Mattei each had 3 for Hurley. The young guns for the Midgets were now confident and equally as cool under pressure.

Hurley was 6 – 2 in the conference and Bessemer was 6 – 1. A week later, the Ironwood Red Devils did all they could to beat the Speed Boys but they fell just short in a spirited game won by Bessemer 52 – 47. The Midgets had to settle for second place in the M-W. Bessemer was the league champion and the favorite to win the Michigan U. P. Class B title for the second year in a row. This year Michigan changed its format for the tournament and the U.P. champion would play in the state quarter-finals to qualify for the state tournament in Lansing. The Speed Boys would be there!

The last game of the regular season was against DePadua in Hurley. DePadua played a great first quarter and led 11 – 10. Then the wheels fell off the Bruins' cart and the Midgets ran away with a 57 – 33 win. Every player on the Hurley roster played and everyone scored. Hurley finished the regular season with a 14 – 3 record. They were on an eight game winning streak. In a season filled with question marks, the Hurley boys and their mentors found all the right answers. The Midgets now turned their attention to the regional tournament. This year it was hosted by the Ashland Oredockers at Dodd Gymnasium. It would be memorable.

CHAPTER FORTY SIX

How Strong? M – W Strong!

The Ashland Regional Tournament got underway on Wednesday, February 25 with Hurley playing Superior Central in the first game. The Vikings had endured a down season winning only seven games but you wouldn't have known that if you watched this game. As usual Central played with intensity. It was a seesaw first quarter with the score tied three times as both teams dug in and refused to yield. Central took a one point lead 7 – 6 at the end of the quarter. The score was knotted up twice more in the second quarter before Hurley could cobble a three point lead at halftime 14 – 11.

The key to beating this Hurley team was to not allow them to get the lead going into the fourth quarter. The vaunted Hurley passing game and stall were now well recognized as the "seal of doom" to any team trailing the Midgets late. Other teams racked up fouls as they chased the lightning quick Hurley five around the court in desperation. Looking to seize the initiative Central battled like banshees in the third quarter and took the lead for a brief moment. The Midgets recovered and then withstood the Viking onslaught, and increased the lead by another point to take the 24 – 20 advantage into the fourth quarter. Once again Central tightened the screws and on two occasions closed the gap to within two points of Hurley only to have the Midgets respond with scores. As the clock wound down, the Midgets snapped off pass after pinpoint pass as the ultra quick boys from Iron County flashed their stall. Central had no choice but to foul and foul again. It was over for the frustrated Vikings. The final score was Hurley 32 – Superior Central 26. Smokey Rainaldo paced Hurley with 11 points and the Hermanson brothers contributed 16 between them. Wayland Baron scored 3 and Len Bartolutti had 2. Noel Mattei did not score, but his ball handling and defense were key ingredients in the victory.

In the second game Ashland took a 17 – 4 lead against Superior East. East had only 4 free throws to show for the first half of play as Ashland completely dominated play. East had to be frustrated. They lost only six games on the season and had regularly defeated the teams from Duluth and the western Wisconsin area. Four of those defeats came against M-W opponents. They had lost to Ashland twice, once to Hurley, and once to Bessemer. Playing for pride, they mounted a rousing comeback against the Oredockers. In the last minute they tied the game at 26 – 26 to force overtime. The overtime period was spirited but without a single basket from the field. Don Jensen of Ashland converted a free throw for the only score and Ashland escaped with their third triumph of the season over East, 27 – 26.

Hurley would go against Ashland on Friday night while Park Falls subdued Phillips in the sub-regional game on Thursday in Phillips to earn the right to play for the regional title on Saturday night. The Hurley – Ashland encounter pitted the two M-W rivals for the third time in the season. They had split the two previous games. Now one of them would ruin the others dream. Hurley was ranked as the number 10 team in the state behind Rhinelander who was number 9. Wisconsin Rapids was ranked number 1. Hurley was favored to beat Ashland, but only by the narrowest of margins.

The game was as advertised. At the end of one quarter Hurley led 7 – 6 as an inspired John Hermanson netted six of those points. It was a bruising, physical game with both teams refusing to give the other an inch. It was body on body with plenty of bumps and contact and more than just a couple of loose elbows. Hockey players call this type of game "chippy." It wasn't dirty, but there was more of an edge to the play. Fouls were hard but not cheap. Gaining position for rebounds was a tough proposition as the players were unafraid to put their bodies on the line. Hurley was able to find just enough room to maneuver to take a four point lead at halftime 15 – 11. In the third period both teams found the basket for eight points and the score was 23 – 19 in favor of Hurley going into the final stanza. Ashland now made their biggest push of the game as they surged into a 25 – 23 lead. Len Bartolutti connected on a free throw to cut the lead to one point and Miller of Ashland hit shortly after giving the Oredockers the 27 – 24 lead. John Hermanson swished another free throw for Hurley and Jerry Hinds scored again for Ashland on a push shot. With 2:55 left in the game Ashland had the lead 29 – 25 and things looked very grim for the Midgets. On the next possession, Hurley snapped off several nice passes and found John Hermanson open for a shot. He was fouled. He sank the first toss and then the second, his seventh consecutive free throw without a miss, and the Oredocker lead was just two points. Ashland could not answer and Hurley cut the lead to one point as Smokey Rainaldo sank another free throw. There was now 1:30 left to play. Ashland again could not score and Hurley was wheeling and dealing the ball until Rainaldo got loose for a little hook shot in the lane to put the Midgets up 30 – 29. 55 seconds were left in the game.

It was at this point the game went from chippy to rough as told by Jim Goeltz of the Ashland Press. The Ironwood Daily Globe reported that it got out of control only after the final buzzer. In any case, during the last 55 seconds, Ashland became Crashland as bumps became collisions, working for position against an opponent became a shoving match, and in general the play became desperate. When told about the Ashland Press account Wayland Baron stated it was a "tough, rough game." After another Ashland miss, Hurley had the ball and the lead. That of course brought out the stall. Ashland fouled but Hurley chose to retain possession of the ball. With only a tick left on the clock, Baron took a pass from a team mate. Don Jensen of Ashland crashed into him with a football rolling block as the final buzzer sounded. Baron recalled the scene. "In those days we didn't stand around after the game. Everybody, both teams, just ran to the locker room. The refs came into the locker room and told me to get up to the court to shoot two free throws." The scene that greeted "Mop" Baron was not a pretty picture. The crowd had rushed the court and some say that the players threw fists at each other. Baron and Len Bartolutti dispute that to this day as neither saw any player from either team swinging at another. Baron was adamant that both teams ran off the court to the locker room. Now with both teams back on the court and the fans back in the stands with the help of three Ashland police officers, Baron stepped to the line for his free throws. There was no time left on the clock and the outcome was already certain. With the crowd booing, screaming and shrieking and nothing on the line, Baron shot both free throws as quick as he could and again he ran to the locker room. This time the game was over. Oh yeah, he missed both shots and he didn't care one iota! John Hermanson was the big gun for Hurley that night as he scored 13 points. Hurley had its 16th win of the year and Ashland fell to 12 – 6 with five of those losses to M-W teams.

On Saturday, March 1, Park Falls and Hurley met for the regional title. This was their third meeting of the year as well, and they had split the previous two games. The Cardinals were a solid team but had played inconsistently for the most part. Hurley jumped out to an early lead and held through the first half. In the third quarter the Midgets built the lead to nine points at 23 – 14. Park Falls finally came to life and scored six straight to cut the advantage to three points. Hurley pulled away once again but Park Falls kept plugging away to keep it within striking range. With 45 seconds to play and holding the lead 36 – 29, Vergamini sent in the reserves. Don Zandi and Eugene Martino both scored baskets before the end of the game and Hurley was the Regional Champion for the second year in a row. Rainaldo scored 11, John Hermanson 9, and Bartolutti 8 to pace Hurley. Carl Hermanson managed only three points but was the game's dominant rebounder. On defense he held the Cardinals' rangy and high scoring center, McGinnis, to only two points. His efforts did not go unnoticed as he and Rainaldo were named to the all –tournament first team. John Hermanson was named to the second team.

The Midgets and their fans made plans for the trip to the Spooner Sectional. Hurley was joined in the sectionals by St. Croix Falls, who had the best record of the four teams there at 22 – 1. Bloomer was the surprise team. They had two juniors, both standing at least 6'3" tall. Both were agile and both were strong. Burt Hable and Don Barlow were a potent 1 – 2 scoring punch. After leading the Blackhawks to victories over Spooner and Hayward, they shocked Rice Lake in the regional finals. Rice Lake had defeated Bloomer twice that season in the "Heart O' North" conference play and were ranked 13th in the state before the Blackhawks turned the tables on them 47 – 44. The fourth team in the section was Shell Lake, who dumped Drummond 50 – 47 in the Spooner district finals the prior week.

Most pundits saw the Hurley – St. Croix Falls game as the "real" championship of the sectional tournament. The Saints were led by Bill Addington and Paul Morrow, a 6'7" sophomore. While the Midgets got off to a good start leading 14 – 9 after one period of play, the

Saints tightened the game up as they closed the gap to 23 – 20 at the half. While St. Croix Falls had the size advantage, it was clear that Hurley had much better floor play and ball handling skills. At the end of three quarters the score was 35 – 29 in favor of Hurley. The Saints could not close the gap and finally saw their chances slip away as the Midgets deftly passed their way to the 46 – 36 win. Len Bartolutti scored 16 points with his smooth shooting. Smokey Rainaldo had 9, John Hermanson netted 8, brother Carl 6, Wayland Baron 5, and Noel Mattei had 2.

Bloomer knocked off Shell Lake 42 – 30 in the next game as Hable and Barlow combined for 28 points. This duo was just starting to flex their basketball muscles. They would continue to terrorize teams for the next year. The stage was set for a showdown between Hurley, winners of 12 straight games, and the red hot Bloomer five. Both teams carried themselves with confidence and both teams would play like champions Saturday night in Spooner.

Bloomer took the early lead as Hable and Barlow went to work. The big Bloomer boys used their size and strength to fashion an 11 – 5 lead going into the second quarter. Then Bloomer flexed their muscles again and built the lead to 18 – 6. Hurley seemed to have no answer for the two Bloomer big men. Carl Hermanson, Smokey Rainaldo, and Mop Baron committed fouls by the boatload trying to stop the dynamic duo. Just when it looked like Bloomer was poised for a blowout win, the Midgets rallied to cut the lead to 22 – 16 at the half. It was encouraging, but Hurley's front line players were all in danger of fouling out of the game. It was going to be an uphill battle for the Midgets to contain Bloomer's two scorers.

With foul trouble the reality of the day, Carl Vergamini shuffled the deck and the defensive assignments changed. He also inserted junior reserve center Charles Guenther into the game to get some relief to the other Midgets front liners. The strategy worked and the Midgets plugged away until they closed the gap to 30 – 27 going into the fourth quarter. Carl Hermanson fouled out of the game but with the Midgets getting scoring from Bartolutti, Baron, and Guenther they surged yet again and claimed the lead 36 – 34. A Bloomer free throw cut it to 36 – 35 and then Smokey Rainaldo who had been playing with three fouls since early in the game scored on a free throw for his first point of the game but also fouled his opponent on the same play. The Bloomer kid sank his shot as well and the score was 37 – 36. Rainaldo dropped in a shot in close to put Hurley up 39 – 36. Seconds later he committed his fifth foul and Burt Hable sank the free throw and it was 39 – 37. With time running out, Bloomer got the ball back for one last shot. Hable took it and dropped it in the bucket as time expired to knot the game at 39 apiece. To this point Hable and Barlow combined for 31 of Bloomer's 39 points. They had been nearly unstoppable.

Hurley entered the overtime period with Carl Hermanson and Rainaldo banished to the bench. It was up to the two string bean juniors, Guenther and Baron, to hold down the fort defensively on the inside against the rugged Bloomer duo during overtime. The teams slowed the pace looking for a good shot. The Midget defense swarmed the interior to cut off Hable and Barlow, daring Bloomer to shoot from outside. He didn't. With about one minute to play Len Bartolutti scored on a runner in the lane and Hurley led 41 – 39. Bloomer could not score, Hurley rebounded, and to no one's surprise they whipped the ball around the bigger Blackhawks to run out the clock. Hable scored 19 and Barlow 12 for Bloomer in the game. Hurley's juniors countered in force with five of them getting into the scoring column and all of them playing a key role in the game. Baron had 11 points and Bartolutti 8. Guenther came off the bench for 6 critical points. Carl Hermanson scored 6 before fouling out and Noel Mattei added three. It was a good thing the juniors stepped up as John Hermanson and Rainaldo came up with only 7 points between them. Hurley was going to Madison again. Bloomer was going home to plot their course for next season. They had served notice. They were a force to be reckoned with.

While the Wisconsin Sectional Tournaments were being played, in Michigan it was district tournament time. Bessemer was the smallest school in Class B. They were moved to Class C the next year due to their smaller enrollment. The Speed Boys were not intimidated. They knocked out Ironwood 54 – 40 and then thumped Stambaugh 45 – 36 to win the Stambaugh district title. The Speed Boys had every intention of winning the U.P. title for the second year in a row and then moving on to the Michigan state tournament. They were off to the races.

Hurley was no longer a surprise team to state basketball fans. They were good and everyone knew it. They had a 13 game winning streak which included blowouts and overtime wins against tough opponents. Their overall record was now 19 – 3. The Eau Claire Old Abes (17 – 5) would be their opponent in the opening game on Thursday afternoon, March 11. The LaCrosse Logan Rangers (21 – 4) were back in Madison and were taking on the Janesville Battlin' Bluebirds (18 – 5) in the second game. The third game pitted the Monroe Silver Streaks (23 – 2) against the number two ranked team in the state, the Wauwatosa Red Raiders (21 – 2). The last game of the opening round had the Menasha Blue Jays (21 – 1) tackling the number 1 ranked team in the state, the Wisconsin Rapids Red Raiders (23 – 2).

When Hurley took the court versus the Old Abes, they were looking up at their tall opponents. Seven of the ten Eau Claire players stood at 6 feet tall or better. Two were 6' 4. Hurley countered with a starting lineup of two 6 footers and three players standing at 5' 9" tall. It was nothing new for the Midgets as they scrapped their way to a 12 - 5 lead. Then Art Anderson, the big Eau Claire, center got loose for a couple of easy hook shots and the first quarter ended 12 – 10 in favor of Hurley. The Old Abes continued to put pressure on the undersized Hurley squad scoring from the pivot. At 5'9" Smokey Rainaldo was doing all he could to stem the tide but ended up in foul trouble. Still the Midgets were refusing to yield and Eau Claire could manage only a one point lead at the half 21 to 20.

In the third quarter, the Midgets tied the game at 23 apiece. Then the train wreck occurred. The Midgets had been struggling to score all game. Now they went totally cold as the Old Abes reeled off eleven straight points to take the lead 34 – 23. Nothing was going in for Hurley. It was as if the basket had a lid on it. Hurley fought back with all they could muster in the fourth quarter and outplayed the Old Abes, but they could not overcome their shooting woes. The final score was 39 – 31. Hurley was going to play for the consolation honors while Eau Claire would advance. For the game the Midgets connected on only 9 shots out of 66 attempts from the field. Their free throw shooting was good, but they could not buy a basket with lottery money. That sealed their fate. Eau Claire's shooting was nothing to brag about either. They did manage to hit on 14 of 63 tries and 11 free throws. If only a couple of more shots had dropped, if only.

Menasha pulled off the upset of the night and of the tournament when they not only beat the top ranked Wisconsin Rapids squad, but crushed them, 63 – 51 behind the shooting of guard Charles Block who torched the Red Raiders for 25 points. Janesville upended LaCrosse Logan 35 – 30 and in the closest game of the opening round Wauwatosa squeaked past Monroe 48 – 46 as the Silver Streaks late game comeback fell short. The next round of games pitted Hurley against Lacrosse Logan and Wisconsin Rapids versus Monroe in the consolation semifinals. In the championship semifinals, it was Eau Claire against Janesville and Wauwatosa taking on Charles Block and his Menasha teammates.

Hurley picked up against LaCrosse Logan where they left off against Eau Claire. They couldn't hit the broad side of a barn! Fortunately the Midget defense was as intense as the Rangers and the first quarter ended in a 3 – 3 tie. All six points were scored on free throws. Shooting the ball was an exercise in futility for both teams. In the second canto things heated up as the Midgets found the range early and often, outscoring the Rangers 16 – 6 and they led at the half 19 – 9. Hurley stretched the lead to 41 – 22 at one point in the fourth quarter before LaCrosse closed the gap against the Midget subs to 45 – 30 in a hopeless attempt to make the game look close. Seldom used Don Zandi, a senior reserve guard and sophomore Eugene Martino were rewarded for their yearlong effort with playing time. They closed out the Midget scoring as Hurley cruised to the 48 – 30 win. Smokey Rainaldo again led Hurley with 14 points. John Hermanson added 11 and Len Bartolutti and Noel Mattei added seven each from their guard positions. Don Zandi may have been the happiest Midget of all as he scored 3 points on 3 free throws in the closing moments of the game.

Wisconsin Rapids build a big lead against Monroe in the second game of the consolation round and then hung on for dear life as the

Silver Streaks lived up to their nickname by scoring 26 points in the fourth quarter, narrowly missing out on what may have been the greatest comeback in tournament history. Their amazing efforts fell short as Rapids escaped with the win 59 – 56. Hurley would play The Red Raiders for the Consolation Championship.

In the championship round Eau Claire rolled to a 47 – 40 win over Janesville setting up the title game with Wauwatosa who pulled away from the tough Menasha Blue Jays in the fourth period to win 56 – 45.

In 1947 Hurley crushed the top ranked team in the state when they beat Stevens Point 51 – 30 in the tournament. This year they would play Wisconsin Rapids who went into the state tournament ranked number 1 in the state. This game was not a blowout win for Hurley but it also was not as close as the 39 – 35 score would indicate. The Midgets kept the Red Raiders offense off-balance all night as it was their turn to feel the misery of a poor shooting performance. Hurley fared slightly better shooting from the field but they cashed in on their free throws while the Rapids squad did not. Len Bartolutti and Wayland Baron led the Midgets with 12 and 10 points. Hurley was the Consolation Championship winner meaning they were the fifth best team in the state. In three trips to Madison Hurley had finished third, second, and fifth. They ached for that elusive championship.

The Wauwatosa Red Raiders and Eau Claire Old Abes met in the championship round for the state title. Tosa built a 25 – 16 lead at the half and the game looked like it might be over. The third quarter belonged to the Old Abes as they battled back to enter the fourth quarter with a fighting chance now down only three points 30 – 27. The Red Raiders fought to maintain their lead but Eau Claire shaved it to two points at 35 – 33. Tosa's Bob Wolff hit from the corner to push the lead back to four and Art Anderson of Eau Claire cut it back to two with a shot from the pivot. The Red Raiders went into a stall and Bill Buechl found an opening for an easy layup, not once, but twice to seal the game 41 - 35. The Wauwatosa Red Raiders were the 1948 state champions. This was a team that had made the first of five consecutive state tournaments. They would be back and they would be remembered.

Meanwhile in Michigan, Bessemer kept on winning! They dumped Ishpeming 43 – 35 and Lake Linden 44 – 43 to take their second U.P. Class B title in a row. They were now set to play Rodgers City in the state quarter-finals. With Ray Kangas going off for 30 points the Speed Boys sprinted to an easy 43 – 31 win. In Lansing they lost to the eventual state champions, Saint Joseph 60 – 49. They received a hero's welcome back in Bessemer and deservedly so. The Range was proud of the Speed Boys and the Midgets. Two teams from the same conference representing that conference in two separate state tournaments has to be extremely rare if not some sort of record.

70 years later Mop Baron remembered that Bessemer team. "Weber, Kangas, and Skowr and the rest of them were great, great players. What a tough bunch." Len Bartolutti stated that Don Skowr was the" toughest ball player" he ever went up against. Both men were proud to have played in the M - W conference. Range basketball teams played for keeps. The level of competition would continue to reach new heights. Iron sharpens iron!

CHAPTER FORTY SEVEN

Practice, Practice, Practice, Play!

In late August of 1948, Armand Cirilli, aka, Sir Riley, took a walk down to the Hurley football field to get a glimpse of the talent in the opening days of practice. He spied the freshmen and hoped they would grow. He thought the team could be good but was worried about the reserves if the injury bug hit again. He liked what he saw of Carl Hermanson, Henry Peterson, and Ted Erspamer who he called "huge, but not cumbersome." In 1948 Ted was pretty big, but huge was a stretch. He was huge by Hurley standards, but if he played for Ironwood or Ashland he would be just another big guy. Glen Aho also caught the scribe's eye. He made suggestions to Carl Vergamini on who should play fullback and halfback. He then noted that a coach's job was tougher than a miner's. "When you leave the 22nd level you leave it until the next shift. But a coach takes his job to bed with him." That probably made Carl chuckle a little. Carl loved Hurley's miners and knew they were among the toughest men on the planet. He was friends with many miners as they shared fishing and hunting trips with him and Chief Gianunzio. As much as he respected those men, I doubt that he would ever want to do their job over his.

Ted Erspamer was all about playing football. He loved football and he tolerated basketball. When the 1948 football season began he was slated to be a starting offensive tackle and a starting defensive end. Ted was big, strong, and he loved contact. Every Hurley football and basketball player from that era will tell you that practices were tough. Ted said, "Carl was not easy on any player, ever! But he was fair, tough and fun to play for." Fair, tough, and fun is not an easy combination to put together, but Carl Vergamini got results because his players knew that he always had their best interest in mind. They would hang on his every word and work hard to improve. He was quick to praise and reinforce the positives and just as quick to provide them with more challenges. When a player made a mistake, Carl corrected them and worked with them until they got it right. As he began his fourth year as the Midget head coach, and his third in a row, the players trusted and respected him without reservation. Carl Vergamini was a developer. He developed teams, he developed character, and he developed young men. He made every effort to set up his players for success and that began on the practice field.

The work ethic the people of Hurley had amazed the coach. He called them "a hearty type person, tough people. They had to be tough to do the work they did." As far as the kids who played on his teams were concerned, he said this, "They were rugged, very rugged. They came from hearty, hearty, people." He continued with this story.

> I had a friend of mine come visit from Iowa, I did
> my athletics in Council Bluffs and we played on the
> same football team. I said to him, if you want to see
> some real football players tonight, come down to
> practice. He was amazed at how hard they worked!
> I said that's typical around here. Not just this year,
> every year! That's the way they play, every game
> is played like that! All up and down the Range that's
> how they play!

As far as any discipline problems were concerned, the coach had this to say, "They had the background of coming from iron mining people. In all my time in Hurley, I can say that we never had to take drastic action with kids, ever. That element (Silver Street's lower block) didn't have any influence on them at all. They were mostly church going and well behaved. Very well behaved." Hurley kids were truly a reflection of their parents, their teachers, and their community. Who could blame Coach Vergamini and Chief Gianunzio for loving their jobs?

The expectations were running high for this football season as Hurley was returning several quality starters from the year before. Armand Cirilli cautioned that Ironwood was looking "big, rough, fast and potentially strong." That just sounded like every other year since the turn of the century! Of course Roy Melvin was again telling everyone that Ashland was bereft of players. Hurley had 38 boys out for the team that fall. Ironwood had over 70 and both Ashland and Bessemer had over 60.

Amid high hopes, Hurley was ready to play. The opening game was a rematch of the last year's opener in Calumet, except this time the game was in Hurley. Eugene "Smocky" Martino set the tone for the season when he took the Copper Kings' kickoff at the 10 yard line and burst through a hole for 65 yards to the Calumet 25. Six plays later Hurley scored when a Joe Forte pass found Carl Hermanson alone in the end zone. Hurley was up 6 – 0. The lead was short lived as Calumet drove down the field to score and the game was tied at 6 – 6. The Midget defense put up little resistance on that drive. In the second quarter the Midgets scored twice after Calumet fumbled twice to take the lead with Martino scoring on a 2 yard plunge and Forte hitting Tony Vita with a pass for the other score. Hurley was up 19 – 6. Florian Helinski scored from 1 yard out early in the fourth quarter to push the lead to 26 – 6. The Cooper Kings tallied late in the game for the final score of 26 – 13. It was a good start.

Against Park Falls the Midgets came out passing the ball. After throwing 15 times against Calumet, Hurley put it up 20 times against the Cardinals at Hurley's dusty field. Ray Collins scored on a 1 yard sweep late in the first quarter for the only score of the game. It was the Hurley defense that shined that Saturday afternoon as the Cardinals crossed mid-field only three times in the game. Two times in the fourth quarter, Hurley passes ended up in the hands of Park Falls defenders in Hurley territory. Both times the defense held. The game saw Florian Helinski pin the Cardinals on the 1, 2, and 5 yard line with perfect punts. Hurley was their own worst enemy committing 9 penalties, one of which nullified a 30 yard interception return for a touchdown by Forte. Ashland was next on the schedule and the Midgets needed to tidy up their game.

With a capacity crowd on hand in Ashland, Roy Melvin's team greeted their visitors with a stout defense and a boatload of hard knocks. In the second quarter, Ashland nearly scored first after marching to the Midgets 6 yard line where the Hurley defense held. The Midgets then went on a drive that pushed the ball to the Ashland 10 yard line but time ran out and the half ended in a 0 – 0 tie. The second half was a repeat of the first with yards hard to come by as both defenses played with passion. Players were often slow to get up and on several occasions needed help to get off the field. This was a bruising and bitter battle. After a scoreless third period Hurley put together the best drive of the game. Behind great blocking by the Hurley line, powerful little Smocky Martino blasted away at the Oredocker defense for three consecutive first downs. With the ball on the ten yard line Hurley gained nothing on two more plays. Then "Flinging" Florian Helinski found Tony Vita running free to the left of the end zone and hit him with a perfect strike. He then found Carl Hermanson for the extra point and the Midgets led 7 – 0 with five minutes to play. In a game where the Oredockers could gain only 90 yards on offense they were desperate to score. Putting the ball into the air they started to move. Then Martino jumped in front of an Ashland receiver and picked off a pass. He sprinted down the sideline until he was knocked out of bounds at the Ashland 15 yard line with about one minute to play. Game over!

After the bitter and brutal game against Ashland, the Midgets would get a week off from play and resume their season versus Ironwood on Lincoln Field. The game featured two goal line stands by the tough Hurley defense. Glen Aho, Ted Erspamer, and Carl Hermanson formed the nucleus of the Midget front wall and they bent some, but they refused to break. In the first quarter Ironwood put together a drive that positioned them inside the Hurley five yard line. The Midget defense then rose to the occasion and denied the Red Devils on four consecutive plays. The Devils controlled the ball for most of the first half but could not score. The second half saw the Hurley offense come to life as they controlled the ball most of the time, but the Red Devil defense refused to crack. Finally in the fourth quarter the Hurley offense cobbled together a drive that pushed the ball to the Ironwood 21 yard line. It was from there that Helinski found Carl Hermanson open for the first score of the game. Ironwood then caught fire! After the kick-off the Devils ran off 8 plays that gained 77 yards and pushed the ball to the Hurley 2 yard line. With the Red Devils power surge and the game on the line the Hurley defense was gassed! It was here and now that the grueling August practices began to pay off for the Midgets. The boys had learned to play hard when they were tired. On first down Hurley stopped the Ironwood fullback, Molenda, for no gain. On second down Leppi, their halfback, was thrown for a five yard loss back to the seven yard line. On third down the Devils ran for 1 yard. On fourth down the Midgets' harried quarterback Carlson into throwing an incomplete pass. The Midgets took over but the Devil defense held again. Hurley had to punt and Florian Helinski hit a beauty that floated out to the mid field stripe. From there the Hurley defense held again and then the offense kept possession of the ball until time expired. Hurley 7, Ironwood 0. The Midgets had won four in a row and had three consecutive shutouts by the same 7 – 0 score.

Hurley had only experienced one five game winning streak in football. That happened when the Midgets won their last game of the 1940 season and the first four of the 1941 season. They had a seven game undefeated streak that included three tie games in 1931 and 1932, but never had they won five in a row in a season. To accomplish this feat they needed to beat Phillips in Phillips. The Midgets scored the first two times they had the ball and after five minutes they held a 14 – 0 lead. It was homecoming for the Loggers and they had pride. They scored in the first period and then again in the second to work the score to 14 – 13 at halftime. The spirited Loggers did what no one had done for a month. They scored on Hurley's defense, not once, but twice! The game was played in a continuous drizzle. Phillips' first score came when Phillips punted and the slippery ball went through the hands of Noel Mattei on the two yard line. Four plays later the Loggers were able to punch it into the end zone. In the third quarter Martino scored his second touchdown of the game. In the fourth quarter Hurley went on a long sustained drive that put the game away. Freshman halfback Robert Johnson sparked the drive and took it to the end zone to ice the game 27 – 13.

Since 1940 the Midgets had battled the Red Devils on even terms with each team winning four, losing four and sharing one in the 1940 6 – 6 tie game. While the Devils were the arch rivals, Hurley was beguiled by the Bessemer Speed Boys who they had not defeated since 1937. It was the Speed Boys who completely wrecked several Midgets' bids for the M – W football crown and often did so in the most excruciating ways.   These Speed boys were Hurley's new boogeyman on the field. So who should be standing in their way once again? Those same Speed Boys!

A capacity crowd filled Lincoln Field on that Saturday afternoon. The Hurley faithful wanted to see an end to eleven years of pain and misery at the hands of their tormentors. The Bessemer fans were all for Hurley's pain to continue. After a scoreless first quarter, the Midgets got the first break of the game when a Bessemer punt went nowhere and the Midgets set up shop on their own 30 yard line. Five plays later Martino scored from the one yard line and Bill "Wyoming" Anich kicked the extra point for the 7 – 0 lead. Bessemer kicked off to start the second half and Hurley's lightning bug, Florian Helinski, fielded the kick on the 25 yard line. He turned up field and was gone in a flash. Just like that the Midget lead was 14 – 0. After Bessemer punted again, Hurley marched down the field and scored again. 21 – 0! The subs took over and the game ended by that score. Hurley won the conference championship and put together a six game winning streak, the longest in school history.

Bessemer managed just one first down until Carl Vergamini pulled his starters. Then Bessemer ran off three on one drive late in the game. Many Midget fans started yelling for him to put the starters back in to preserve the shutout. It seems they had noticed that no conference team had scored on Hurley and they wanted to keep that record intact. The way a coach views a game and the way fans view it are so different. Carl wanted to reward his young players and give them some experience. It did not matter to him what the fans wanted.

Those boys had been pouring their hearts and souls into the team as much as any starter. This is where the character of the coach stood out. He said, "They won't score, have some faith in them." He then added, "Well, it turns out, they might have scored, but they fumbled and we recovered." Carl Vergamini, confidence builder. Over 70 years later his son, Jerry Vergamini still remembered that day.

The following week Hurley played Superior Central in that harbor city. After a scoreless first half, the Viking big boys broke through for a third period touchdown. They scored twice more in the final quarter as their massive line kept pounding away at the lighter Hurley defense. Central ended Hurley's bid for an undefeated season 18 – 0. The boys went home disappointed but proud of their efforts. They were the undisputed champs of the M – W and in their lone loss of the year they gave the big city Central boys all they could handle. Many Hurley fans wanted Vergamini to stop scheduling Central. He did not grant that wish. The two teams would meet again for the next four seasons. Hurley would win three of those contests.

The football team had their best season since 1942 and was probably the best team Hurley had ever put on the field to that time. The tone was set for the upcoming basketball season. Expectations were through the roof! The Midgets were returning five lettermen from the previous year. They were returning starters Len "Beppi" Bartolutti, Noel Mattei, Carl Hermanson and Wayland "Mop" Baron who started about half the games. Smocky Martino was also returning after being promoted to the varsity for the tournament games. Those players, coupled with players from the B team that won 19 games while losing only one the previous year, had the fan base excited. Pete "Pupsy" Savant was a senior up from that team. He could have sat on the varsity bench in '47-48, but Verg and Chief insisted that he needed to be on the B team where he could play and gain experience. He wasn't happy about that, but the plan worked. He improved and he gained confidence. The coaches coaxed Ted Erspamer into playing basketball that year. Ted did it for the team but he really didn't care much for the game. His team mates saw him as their protector and enforcer in case things got chippy. He didn't play much but he was on call when needed. The roster was filled out with John Tocci, a hardnosed junior with a nice scoring touch, senior Bill Wyoming Anich who also had a nose for the basket, Bob "Buckwheat" Rainaldo, and Clayton Corrigan, a junior, who was the eleventh man and played on both B and A teams during the season. Charles Guenther started out with the team and then decided to drop basketball, or the team would have been even more formidable. With this much talent, it was hard for the town to temper the expectations. Even the players felt it.

Len Bartolutti said it as simply as this, "After going to Madison in '47, I just thought it was natural that we would keep going to state. The thought that we wouldn't go to state never even occurred to me." It wasn't that he was a naïve kid, Len and his teammates expected to be good and expected to win. Wayland Baron remembers the attitude of the team. "The attitude we had was that you aren't gonna beat us! It was in our minds that we just would never quit, never give up, we just would not lose, and that we would do what it takes to win." Pupsy Savant was asked when he knew the team was championship caliber. He said, "Oh, I knew we had a team! I knew that!" And he knew it from day one. Every other player knew it too, and every player went to work to meet their own high expectations. They were on a mission!

The football team had 38 players on it. That is counting all the players in all grades. When basketball practice started over 50 boys showed up. 43 of them ended up on the freshman team, B Team, or A Team. That is unusual for any school and especially unusual for those days when football teams were always larger than any other school team. It wasn't the first time it happened in Hurley, and it would not be the last time either.

Carl Vergamini said that the team was "fair" this year when quoted by the Montreal River Miner. He must have taken lessons in the art of understatement from Roy Melvin who never started a season with anything more than lamentations. With the season getting underway in Rhinelander on Friday night, November 12, the Midgets took the long ride to visit the Hodags. This was another team primed for a banner season. Rhinelander also returned six lettermen including Arnold "Moose," Lytle their tall and rugged high scoring center. Two anxious fan bases packed the Hodags gym. The prognosticator gave a slight edge to the Hodags since they were the home team in a pretty even match.

The Midgets started slowly, but played well, applying a strong defense to the Hodags' scheme. Carl Hermanson worked especially hard to contain the explosive Moose Lytle and gave the big man little room to operate. Getting help from Mop Baron and Len Bartolutti, Hermanson and his friends gave Rhinelander only a precious few rebounds. The Midget scoring came early and often from Pupsy Savant who drilled five of his patented high arching shots from the corners. He added two free throws to make his total 12 points. Noel Mattei was the man designated to feed the other players and play back on offense to prevent fast breaks. He was stellar in that role. Baron and Hermanson fouled out of the game in their efforts to contain Lytle. They held the Hodags' big gun to ten points. Baron exited with 7 points, Hermanson had 3 and together they kept Rhinelander from threatening the Midget lead. At one point the game was 26 – 14 in favor of Hurley. Vergamini sent in the reserves and the Hodags closed the gap to the final score of 30 – 24. It was a convincing win over a quality team.

This Hurley team wasn't catching anybody by surprise. Everyone in the area and most across the state knew this was a quality team. The shoe was now on the other foot for the Midgets. They were the hunted and as such, every team the Midgets played was going to give their best effort. Unfortunately for most of their foes, their best efforts would not be enough. Every boy on this team was talented and most would be full time starters for many of their opponents' teams had they lived in those towns. These players had a wealth of basketball experience and even greater quantities of self discipline. They would need plenty of both to get through the first part of their demanding schedule.

Carl Vergamini sensed that his team was on the cusp of greatness and hammered out a tough non-conference schedule for the Midgets. Seven of the first nine games of the year were to be played on the road. Having scheduled Rhinelander for the first game of the year, he then he worked out a deal with Roy Melvin and the Ashland Oredockers to share transportation costs to Merrill and Antigo, Wisconsin after Christmas to take on two more tough opponents from "downstate." Then for good measure he included Superior East and Superior Central to the regular season schedule. St. Ambrose, who would have a history making season of their own, was included and along with the M – W teams, there was going to be fireworks. This was more than a basketball schedule; it was a basketball gauntlet.

Before the next game another highly anticipated Hurley tradition was scheduled. On Thursday evening, November 18 the annual senior class play had a slightly new twist. It would be three one act plays this year. There was a drama, "Unto Us the Living," a comic mystery, "Grand Cham's Diamond," and a comedy, "The Happy Journey." The casts included several athletes and cheerleaders, including Ted Erspamer, who found time to rehearse for the play and get to basketball practice for several weeks. Miss Helen Weiser, an English teacher, directed the plays. In typical Hurley fashion the auditorium was packed full. Also in typical Hurley fashion the aspiring actors and actresses delighted the audience and brought down the house with their performance. As Carl Vergamini stated, "The school was the center of everything." The term "everything" includes, well everything, and Carl was not wrong.

With the rousing performance of the night before in their memory banks, the basketball team turned their thoughts back to the game. In short order the Midgets traveled to Ashland, Phillips, and Bessemer for the next three games. In Ashland the Oredockers put up a real battle before succumbing to the Midgets 29 – 24. Ashland held the early lead and then Hurley took charge in the second quarter to gain the lead that they would not relinquish. Again "Pistol Pete" Savant led Hurley in scoring with ten points and was awarded still another nickname by Sir Riley. Hurley then traveled to Phillips where they overwhelmed the Loggers, 62 – 30. Hurley substituted early as 7 players scored at least 6 points and Len Bartolutti led the way with 11. All the players saw extensive time on the court and 9 of the eleven tallied. Against Bessemer it looked like the Midgets and Speed Boys would pick up where they left off the year before. After Hurley jumped out to a first quarter lead, Bessemer closed the game to within a point at 9 – 8 early in the second stanza. Sadly for the Speed Boys, this Bessemer team was not ready for this Hurley team. Only Don Skwor remained from the Michigan State Tournament semi-finalist team of the year before. Skwor did all he could to rally his team, scoring 13 points and playing his usual solid game. The Midgets ran off nine straight points after the Speed Boy rally and it was lights out. Carl Vergamini again played the entire varsity roster, this time twelve players, with Bartolutti scoring 15 points and Baron going for 12 in the 47 – 27 blowout. Hurley had played four games on the road and dominated their opponents. Now they would get to play in front of an excited home crowd. The town was buzzing. The people of Hurley had basketball fever and the only cure was to get to the gym.

Park Falls handed Hurley one defeat in each of their last two seasons. Each time Hurley had avenged the loss by defeating the Cardinals in the late season rematch. Nobody was taking Park Falls for granted. In front of another capacity crowd in the Hurley gym, the Midgets went on a scoring rampage. At the half they led 33 – 18. Points were coming from everybody and from all over the court. All twelve of the Hurley players saw action and eleven of them scored. Carl Hermanson broke out of his early season scoring slump to tally 12 points to pace Hurley. Bartolutti continued his scoring pace with 11, Savant scored 10, Baron 9, John Tocci and Noel Mattei each had 5, Bob Rainaldo 4, and Clayton Corrigan, Wyoming Anich, Ted Erspamer and Smocky Martino all scored a bucket. Not to be outdone, the B team under Chief Gianunzio also remained undefeated as they racked up their fifth straight win 45 – 28 over the Cardinals B's. Nineteen players saw action for Hurley in that game with twelve of them finding the hoop.

The Wakefield Cardinals had a four year string of miserable records in the M – W. Since the 1944 – '45 season they had won one game against their M – W brethren. With a loss to Bessemer in this season they now had a record of 1 win and 32 losses over that period. The Cards held their own against opposition from outside the conference, but within the neighborhood they could not catch a break. With Hurley coming to pay the Cardinals a visit, things looked bleak for the Wakefield bunch. Roman Yatchat was now Wakefield's coach and he was building a competitive team. The Cards had 2 wins over non conference foes, including a convincing win versus St. Ambrose. Still no one expected the Cards to beat Hurley.

Carl Vergamini then gave the Cardinals hope. On Friday, December 10, he suspended Mop Baron and Noel Mattei for one game for breaking team "training rules." In a proper display of leadership, he did not speak a word of what the specific infraction was to anyone other than Chief Gianunzio. After the suspension he put the boys back on the team and proceeded to work their tails off. During the suspension they were sorely missed. Still this was Hurley, and the team was loaded with good ball players. Juniors Smocky Marino and John Tooci were given starts. So Hurley could have had a pity party, but Wakefield deserved one too. They were without the services of Rudy Valesano, their leading scorer. To be fair it was a wash, but there were no pity parties, just high school basketball at its best.

Hurley showed that they were indeed formidable even with two starters sitting out the game. Wakefield served notice that they would not be intimidated even with their best scorer unable to play. At the half Hurley held a 22 – 17 lead and all seemed well with the Midgets. In the third quarter there was a defensive clinic put on. This clinic was taught by the Wakefield Cardinals and their young core of juniors. Their reluctant students were held to just three points in the third quarter as the Wakefield five spurted into the lead 29 – 25 at the end of three quarters of play. The Cards continued to pressure and harass Hurley into more sloppy offensive basketball in the fourth quarter.

When the dust settled Wakefield had pulled off the stunning upset 38 – 33. Their record was now 3 – 1 while Hurley dropped to 5 – 1 for the season. The scrappy Cards usurped Hurley's role as giant killers and won a game that would remain fresh in the memories of the Wakefield faithful for decades. And so an inexperienced team from a town that had won just one conference game in four years schooled an experienced team that had a recent history of wild success. That's high school basketball. That was the M – W Conference. It makes perfect sense!

With some hard life lessons learned, the Midgets licked their wounds and returned to the court in Hurley to take on St. Ambrose. This Rambler team had lost only to Wakefield in this young season. Their two star players, Ray McKay and Gordon Kennedy, were both 6' 4" tall. They were also very good basketball players. Two of Hurley's 6' starters were assigned to guard them. Carl Hermanson drew McKay and Len Bartolutti took on Kennedy. In the words of Mop Baron, Bartolutti was "so tough on defense. He had really long arms and was able to intercept passes and knock down passes. Guys had a hard time shooting over him." It was those long arms that allowed the Montreal kid to hold Kennedy to just 6 points for the game. McKay and Hermanson staged a brilliant battle all night long as they worked hard to score on each other with regularity. McKay ended the game with 15 points. Hermanson would gather 17. The game started out with Hurley playing their aggressive defense and running hard. The Ramblers kept pace and then surged into the lead. At halftime they led 16 - 15 as they showed Hurley they could run hard and play defense too.

In the third quarter the Midgets came out on fire defensively. After gaining a 21 – 20 advantage, they kept on sprinting and closed the deal with steals, interceptions, and easy baskets. St. Ambrose could no longer keep pace with the tireless Hurley bunch. At the end of three quarters it was 28 – 22. Hurley exploded for 20 fourth quarter points as the Ramblers were running on fumes. The subs finished the game and Hurley rebounded from the Wakefield game to win 48 – 35. Hermanson led all scoring with 17 points and Mop Baron tallied 13 and controlled the boards. Pupsy Savant tallied 10 for Hurley and Len Bartolutti made his contribution on defense. In a time when there were no statistics kept for steals, blocked shots, rebounds, and assists, Bartolutti was lauded for all of those things in the win. The Hermanson and Baron duo had an uncanny knack for outplaying their taller opponents. It had been going on for over a season and it was not about to stop. The bigger the opponents, the bigger this duo played. With steady Noel Mattei setting the offensive tempo and stopping the fast break, and sharp shooting Pistol Pete Savant, the Midgets were a team without a glaring weakness.

The road trip Carl Vergamini had set up for the Christmas break was now a reality. When the bus carrying Roy Melvin and the Ashland pulled up outside the Hurley gym, the Hurley boys boarded. There they saw the faces of their basketball foes; the same boys they beat earlier in the season. Many of the same boys were on the Ashland team the year before when all hell broke loose in the Ashland Regional Tournament game between the two teams. Did they like each other? Not really. Did they hate each other? No. Did they respect each other? Yes. So they took a trip south together. They mostly kept to themselves, with each team claiming a piece of the bus. The coaches, all friends, sat up front and conversed. Mop Baron remembered the trip and when asked if Roy Melvin and Carl Vergamini thought up this trip as a way of teaching the boys to get along, he said "I don't think so. I think it was an economic decision. They pretty much stayed on their part of the bus and we stayed on ours".

For the Oredockers and Midgets the trip proved to be well worth the effort. The bus traveled 133 miles south to Antigo. There a rare doubleheader was on the docket. Hurley was to play Antigo and Ashland would take on Merrill. These two teams were members of the Wisconsin Valley Conference. This conference boasted Stevens Point and Wisconsin Rapids, who had been to the Wisconsin State tournament in 1947 and 1948. Hurley defeated both teams in Madison after they had been ranked as the top teams in the state. Rhinelander was a perennial powerhouse in that conference as well. The Midgets had dispatched them in the opening games of the past two seasons.

In the games played on December 29, Ashland tipped Merrill 45 – 44. Hurley throttled Antigo 57 – 32. Carl Hermanson powered his way to 15 points while Pupsy Savant, Noel Mattei, Len Bartolutti, and Mop Baron hit for 10, 9, 8, and 7 points respectively. All the reserves saw action as the Hurley five ran Antigo off their feet.

The next night the action shifted to Merrill where the teams swapped opponents. Ashland thumped Antigo 55 – 40 and Hurley took down Merrill 49 – 35 giving the M – W a clean sweep of the Wisconsin Valley Fives. Len Bartolutti led the way with 13 points and Eugene "Smocky" Martino came off the bench to pour in 10 more. Once again Coach Vergamini emptied his bench as 10 of the 11 Midgets scored. The Ashland and Hurley boys boarded the bus and headed north. No one in Central Wisconsin was sad to see them go. In a twist of fate, the next game for the two teams was scheduled for Jan 7 in Hurley. They would play each other. After watching each other play two games and having played earlier in the season, they knew each other quite well.

While Hurley and Ashland were continuing their winning ways, St. Ambrose took a little trip of their own to Escanaba, Michigan to compete in the Upper Peninsula Parochial Tournament. Coach John Shea's Ramblers ran away with the championship as they defeated St. Joseph in the finals 40 – 34 behind 22 points by lanky Gordon Kennedy. The Ramblers were now 8 – 2 on the season with their only two losses being to Wakefield and Hurley. Their finest moments were still to come.

On the line for the Ashland – Hurley matchup was sole possession of first place in the M-W. The winner would have a record of 3 – 1 in the league and the loser would drop to 2 – 2 and a tie for second place with Ironwood. With seven of their first nine games played on the road, Midget fans were happy to stay in Hurley to watch their boys in action. As usual the place was packed even before the B teams started play.

The game started at a slow pace and after a quarter of play Hurley led 9 – 5. Then the Midgets defense sparked the offense. Using what the Ironwood Daily Globe described as "harassing tactics," Pupsy Savant, Smocky Martino, and Noel Mattei proved to be terrific ball hawks as the Midgets stole the ball and intercepted Oredocker passes to key easy fast break points. "Harassing tactics" was a term the reporter used to describe what we now call "the full court press." At the half the score was 27 – 13 in favor of Hurley. At the end of three quarters it was 39 – 21. In came the reserves and they preserved the win. Hurley 47 – Ashland 31 was the final score. Len Bartolutti continued to be the hot shooter as he scored 12 points. Baron, Hermanson, Savant, Martino and Erspamer scored 8, 7, 6, 5, and 3 respectively. It was the defense, however, that befuddled the Oredockers as they were swarmed under by an agitated band of Hurley hornets.

Mop Baron described the team's attitude toward playing defense. "We would guard our man closely even if they didn't have the ball. We were right there up on them. We were taught to force them toward the sideline and make them pick up their dribble. The sideline acted as another defender and they would be trapped by the sideline and the defensive player. That's how we forced bad passes." When it came to playing defense, the Midgets had a "mean streak" in them. They took playing a fierce team defense to level that few teams could match. The intensity level caught opponents by surprise. Mop Baron again says, "Most teams would take it easy on defense to conserve energy for playing offense. We were just the opposite. Most teams didn't press in those days. We did it all the time. Other teams couldn't handle the pressure."

For Len Bartolutti playing defense came down to pride. "Verg emphasized defense. We worked hard at it. I took pride in being a strong defender." Len played guard on offense but often drew taller players to cover on defense because of his long reach and quick hands. Armand Cirilli called Len a "sweet boy." He was polite, studious, athletic, strong, good natured, friendly, and just a nice kid. That described him off the basketball court. On the court he was all business. Len was a complete player who was a superb ball handler, exceptional defensive player, a strong scorer and a ferocious rebounder. Like his scrappy teammates, he had the heart of a lion. Hurley's opponents would never have described him as a "sweet boy" after playing against him.

About his back court mate, Len said, "Noel Mattei played back on offense to prevent the fast break. He didn't get beat. He was so quick, not very tall, but very quick. He couldn't jump much but he never got beat." Wayland Baron said, "Noel hustled back there. He just didn't get beat on a break. He was too fast, too quick on his feet. Nobody really wore knee pads back then, it was rare. Noel always wore one on each knee. He would dive for balls all the time."

Carl Hermanson and Pete Savant were every bit as intense on the defensive end of the court as the other starters. Both were fast and had amazing lateral quickness. Hermanson had the added advantage of being very strong. Savant was opportunistic and had his fair share of steals and intercepted passes. He also worked hard in the rebounding department. Carl Hermanson was an agile ball hawk. He would normally be assigned to guard the other team's tallest player. There was never a game when he was taller than his opponent. He used his smarts and agility to keep himself positioned to deny an entry pass to his opponent. There is a long list of players who were frustrated time and again by Carl. He was also a great rebounder.

The most unappreciated aspect of basketball is rebounding. Whether on offense or defense, the team that gets the most rebounds usually wins the game. When you rebound your teammates' missed shots, you get a second chance to score. On defense when you rebound your opponents' shots, you deny them a second chance to score. It's the job players seldom get credit for. It's the job that must be done to be successful. Len Bartolutti stated, "Rebounding has little to do with height. It's work." Mop Baron agreed, "In rebounding you're working your tail off. You have to get position. You have to know where to go when the shot is taken." He went on to describe how to judge the angle of the shot and get to where the miss would most likely carom off the hoop or backboard. "There was a lot of contact underneath the basket when rebounding. You never get credit for being a good rebounder."

Hermanson, Baron, and Bartolutti were more than willing to mix it up with the mass of humanity under the hoop and they became stellar rebounders. They were often lauded for their board work by reporters. When your team is continually shorter than your opponent and you continually out rebound them, people who know the game of basketball notice. Hurley made up for their lack of height by being technicians as rebounders. They knew how to work themselves into rebounding position. They were also relentless and tenacious, refusing to be pushed around or elbowed out of position by taller and bigger players. Hurley time and again shocked opponents and their fans with their "team rebounding" because all five of them would "crash the boards" on defense and four of them would do the same when on offense. The exception was that Noel Mattei would often stay in position near mid court to prevent a fast break.

Hurley's defense and rebounding was the bread and butter of their game plan. That leaves us to examine the offense. The five starters were all listed at between 5' 10" and 6' tall. Individually they had diverse strengths and few weaknesses when it came to the game of basketball. The frontcourt of Hermanson, Savant, and Baron were all very good ball handlers. They could dribble, pass, and move like guards. The backcourt of Bartolutti and Mattei were exceptional ball handlers and could rebound like forwards are expected to. The Midgets on offense were interchangeable parts with guards sometimes playing the high post like a center and the forwards playing back and feeding the ball. They ran a motion offense. There were screens and cuts and constant movement. All five players were capable scorers including Noel Mattei who sacrificed shots to set up his team mates and to stay in position to "play back." As a junior, Mattei scored 19 points versus Ironwood and 17 versus Phillips. He could be explosive. In this season all five starters all would end up leading the team in scoring in at least one game. They simply ran their offense and hit the open man. They all were unafraid to take a shot and they all had a knack for scoring at a critical juncture of a game. If an opposing team decided to double team a hot shooter, one or more of the others would immediately pick up the slack.

The biggest improvement in the 1948 – 49 team over the 1947 – 48 team was in shooting the ball. Pete Savant gave the team a real shot in the arm with his unorthodox but accurate rainbow. All the others were improved shooters. The 9 for 66 shooting display in the previous year versus Eau Claire in Madison was a thing of the past. Most importantly, this was a T-E-A-M! No one cared who scored the most points. They all pretty much knew from practicing under Chief Gianunzio and Carl Vergamini for nearly four years that winning started with defense and rebounding. Of course they liked to shoot and they loved to score, but they also were quick to praise each other for doing the dirty work of basketball. They fed off each other's hard work. They played for each other, they played for their coaches, and they played for Hurley!

As a team, they had proven that they could play at breakneck speed or beat an opponent who slowed the game to a crawl. They often just wore other teams out. The pressure defense and constant motion of offense required incredible stamina. Practices under Carl Vergamini were mostly full out scrimmages with little rest. Starters did not just go against the reserves. Often the practice pitted starter versus starter in an effort to push them harder. Wayland Baron faced off against Carl Hermanson every single day. He said Carl was the "toughest player I ever went up against." Hermanson was solidly built and very strong. Baron was a string bean with quickness and agility. Carl had to learn to move fast to keep up with his friend and Wayland had to get tough and learn how to get position in order to match Carl's rebounding power. Practice after practice they pushed each other harder than any opponent ever could. Practice after practice they continued to improve, and after practice they would find a new bruise courtesy of the toughest player either of them ever went up against.

On Friday, January 14 another overflow crowd jammed into the Hurley gym. Superior Central with their record of 8 – 1 was on a collision course with Hurley at 9 – 1. There was no doubt that this game was for Northern Wisconsin basketball supremacy. It was also a preview of what many thought would be the regional tournament championship. That tournament would be played in Hurley. But for now it was the regular season and both teams were looking to make a statement to the other.

The game was not particularly smooth sailing for either team as the defenses applied pressure from the opening tip. Hurley managed to take the early lead and maintained it throughout the first half as they entered the intermission with an 18 – 15 lead. Central tied the score at 18 to open the third quarter. Just when it looked like the Vikings were ready to roll, the Hurley defense showed up. Forcing turnovers and missed shots the Midget defense caused Central to go ice cold. During that third quarter stretch Hurley methodically scored 9 unanswered points to lead 27 – 18. By the end of the third quarter the score stood at 30 – 21. Central rallied in the fourth stanza but Hurley had enough gas in the tank to take the win 39 – 34. Len Bartolutti paced the Midgets with 14 points while holding Central's high scoring Sharon Craker to three points. Carl Hermanson scored

10 and Wayland Baron had 9 points. Pistol Pete Savant was held scoreless as his rainbow shot couldn't connect with the pot of gold. All in all it was a hard fought game against a high quality opponent. It was noticed around the state.

On Tuesday, January 18th the WIAA basketball ranking came out for the first time of the season. There were two rankings. The "Big Sixteen" ranked schools with enrollments of 210 or more. The "Little Sixteen" ranked schools with enrollments of 209 or less. Hurley was ranked 7th in the state while Superior Central was 12th. St. Croix Falls and Bloomer, both in the Spooner Sectional, were ranked 3rd and 6th. In the Little Sixteen the undefeated Washburn Castle Guards were ranked 16th. A well meaning fan wandered into the Hurley practice to inform Carl Vergamini of Hurley's lofty ranking. Upon receiving the information the coach just nodded. The fan then told Verg that Wauwatosa was ranked number one and everyone thought they would win another state title. Now the big man bristled. He looked right at the messenger and vehemently exclaimed, **"Wauwatosa! Wauwatosa!** Let me tell you something! This team can beat Wauwatosa anytime, anyplace and don't you ever forget it!"

Carl Vergamini had done it. He put the cart before the horse, but he wasn't alone. The players seemed to be of a like mind. On the other side of the river, Ironwood, under their new coach, the 6' 7" Stretch Goedde, was working on a plan to stop the rampaging Midgets. The Devils' season had started with inconsistent to average play, but now they were hot and playing with confidence. The arch rivals clashed in Hurley on January 21. Carl Hermanson did not start for Hurley that night. He weakened by a bout of tonsillitis, so John Tocci started in his place. Hermanson relieved Tocci but was largely ineffective. Ironwood took an early lead only to see the Midgets battle back. Nine times the Devils led and nine times Hurley tied the game. At halftime Ironwood had a slender 21 – 19 lead. Then the defense rode to the rescue, but it was the Red Devil defense. With continuous pressure and relentless pursuit the Devils jumped all over the Midgets as they sprinted out to a 35 – 24 lead as the third period ended. The Midgets fought back, but Ironwood was not about to crack. It was they who controlled the rebounds and played quick and loose on defense. It was they who ran the Hurley five into the ground. When the final buzzer sounded they walked off the court with the victory 47 – 37. With the win the Devils vaulted into the M – W Conference lead with a record of 3 – 1. Hurley fell to 3 – 2 and into second place. The Midgets crashed back to earth and began to lick their wounds. One of the wounds was that in the next WIAA Big Sixteen rankings Hurley was dropped completely out.

CHAPTER FORTY EIGHT

_____

Learning Basketball, Learning Life

There is a fine line between victory and defeat. Where do confidence and self assurance end and where does arrogance begin? When you win as much as Hurley had been winning under Coach Vergamini, it is easy to fall into a trap. That trap is the line between expecting to win and feeling entitled to win. In the middle of his fourth season as Hurley's basketball coach the Midgets had compiled a win – loss record of 71 – 12 and were in the Wisconsin State Tournament all three previous years. What Carl Vergamini may have once lacked in basketball acumen was a thing of the past. He did understand the game and he understood teenage boys even more. He understood that he wielded influence. It was the kind of influence that the boys willingly accepted and even craved. They trusted him.

The loss to Ironwood was surely not the end of the world. It could have been nothing more than a hiccup or a blip on a radar screen. But it was more than that. The way they lost was uncharacteristic of this team. They were out rebounded, out shot, out hustled, and out worked. They were beat by a team who played like them. Every team has a "stinker" of a game during the season. The Ironwood game certainly fit that description. It was now up to the Coach to ensure his boys got back on track. If there ever was a sense of entitlement on the part of his players, it was now gone. Everyone was asking, "What's wrong with Hurley?" The short and correct answer was "nothing." They lost a game to an inspired arch rival. The players were not immune to criticism. It hurt. They knew they had their butts handed to them by the Red Devils. They did a double take on themselves and on their team. They looked inside and they found that they were human. Very human! Knowing they were not invincible brought them back around to the fundamentals of basketball and also to the fundamentals of life. These boys knew their individual and collective strengths. Now they also understood their individual and collective weaknesses. They had never put themselves above each other but now, in defeat, they learned there is more to team building than putting your ego aside. More than ever they would depend upon each other. They had been humbled, but they refused to be humiliated. Instead they raised their collective efforts. They raised each other. The final lesson was now learned, courtesy of the Ironwood Red Devils. If there ever was a "good" defeat, then this was it. The Hurley Midgets' play was now not just sharp; they were razor sharp. They were not just focused; they were laser focused. They were inspired and they inspired the entire community.

Pity the Phillips Loggers of 1949. Earlier in the season they lost to Hurley 62 – 30. This time Carl Vergamini decided to reward the reserves with some well deserved playing time. The only regular starter was Len Bartolutti. He was joined by Eugene Martino, John Tocci, Bob Rainaldo and Clayton Corrigan. With four reserves starting it looked like the game could be closer than the first meeting and it was. After one quarter Phillips led 8 – 7. Then the subs came to life. Hurley won 61 – 31 as Bartolutti scored 20, Tocci 16, Martino 11, Rainaldo 5, and Corrigan 3. The four senior starters played only in the last minutes of the game as the reserves had their shining moment.

As the Midgets downed the Loggers, there was some serious basketball action on the other side of the river. Ashland took down Ironwood 50 – 45 to claim first place in the M-W with a conference record of 4 - 2. Those two defeats were both to Hurley who was now tied with Ironwood for second place with a record of 3 − 2 in conference play. That was big news, but the night belonged to St. Ambrose. Mass, Michigan was the defending Michigan Class D State Champion and also the U. P. Class D Champs in 1947. They were sporting a 59 game winning streak, the longest in Michigan history to that point. They had not lost a game since 1946. The Ramblers invaded the Rockets' court and played the game of their lives. At the end of the third quarter, Mass held an eleven point lead, 42 − 31 and it looked like they would win their 60th consecutive game. The Ramblers then took off like they were rockets as they scorched the nets for 27 fourth quarter points. With the score tied in the final seconds, Ray McKay scored the winning basket as the St. Ambrose upset the dazed Rockets 58 − 56. They still were not done. Their season gets better!

Wakefield was next up for Hurley. Both the Midgets and Cardinals needed a win to stay in the race for the title. Hurley was 3 − 2 in conference play and Wakefield was 2 − 3. With the game in Hurley, a capacity crowd saw the Hurley B team remain undefeated by beating the Cardinals B team 49 − 36. With the warm up game complete, the fans were revved up for the main event. The starting lineup for Hurley was a shocker for the fans. Carl Vergamini was impressed by their performances against Phillips, so John Tocci started at center for Carl Hermanson who was still battling tonsillitis, and Smocky Martino started in place of the slumping shooter Pete Savant. Wayland Baron, Noel Mattei, and Len Bartolutti rounded out the lineup. It turns out that the coach pushed all the right buttons in this move. Tocci and Martino scored early and often for the Midgets. The lead was lengthened throughout the game and it ended without drama with Hurley avenging the December loss to the Cards, 60 − 37. Tocci scored 16, Martino 14, Bartolutti 13, Mattei 8, and Baron 5 for the Midgets. Savant was able to drop in two free throws and Hermanson scored 2 in relief of Tocci. It was a convincing win for the Midgets and their new starting lineup.

Now tied with Ashland for the M – W league lead, Hurley was primed to invade Ironwood. The Devils trailed Hurley and Ashland by one game and were desperate to win or drop to the middle of the pack. Of course the gym was packed to the rafters in another standing room only contest. Coach Vergamini again opted to start Tocci and Martino for Hermanson and Savant. From the opening tip it again looked like Ironwood was clearly better than Hurley. The Devils were quick to the loose balls, and took advantage of their height advantage by scoring inside. The Devils held a 14 – 6 lead after one quarter. This is where Carl Hermanson and Pupsy Savant were inserted into the game. The slumping duo along with Mop Baron, himself mired in a bit of a scoring funk, erupted. Savant drilled four long range rainbows and Hermanson hit 5 of 6 free throws in that second quarter. The Midgets erupted on defense too, generating turnovers and controlling the rebounds with Baron and Hermanson leading the way. By halftime Hurley led 25 – 22. The onslaught continued in the third quarter as the freshly tuned Hurley engine was hitting on all cylinders, offense, defense, and rebounding. The Midgets pulled away to a 40 – 25 lead and by the beginning of the final quarter it was 40 – 27. The tough Red Devils were not ready to concede the game and mounted a furious late rally. It was a matter of too little, too late as Hurley avenged the loss three weeks prior 49 – 42. Pupsy Savant again became "Pistol Pete" as he knocked down 15 points to lead the Midgets. Hermanson and Baron each scored 10, and Mattei and Bartolutti had 7 and 6 points. More important than the points was the defense and rebounding. The Hurley Midgets were back to cooking their favorite recipe. Iron sharpens iron.

High school basketball seasons are predictably unpredictable. St. Ambrose was cruising along with only two losses on the year after their rousing comeback win versus Mass. Those losses were Wakefield, 44 – 42 in overtime and to Hurley 48 – 35. The Ramblers were now looking for a measure of revenge against the Cardinals. Their twin towers of McKay and Kennedy were red hot and the team was even hotter. But in high school basketball nothing makes sense. Wakefield had the Ramblers' number. Of course Wakefield was a much improved team themselves. They had given everyone outside of the M – W fits all season long, and they upset Hurley in December. Still this St. Ambrose team should have handled the tough Cards. They just couldn't do it. Wakefield defeated them for the second time in the season 38 – 33. It was a setback, but the Ramblers weren't done shocking area fans.

Lost in the shuffle of a long season, another Iron County high school was on a hot streak. The Saxon Knights, with a school enrollment of 50 students, were starting to pile up wins after an up and down start to the season. With a record of 5 wins and four losses the Knights were pretty good. They had a new coach named Sy Castagna, a Hurley native. Sy was a graduate of Ferris Institute in Big Rapids, Michigan; he had been working in the Ben Franklin 5 & 10 Store in Hurley. Saxon needed a teacher and a coach, and they hired Sy for both jobs even though he had never taught or coached before. Sy earned his teaching certificate and went to work in the fall of 1948. Little did he realize that he and the 1949 Saxon Knights would end up in the Hurley High School Athletic Hall of Fame.

Of the 18 boys in the school, 13 played basketball. One of them was the ultra talented Ron Peterson. Playing in the Indianhead Conference it took awhile for the Saxon boys to hit their stride. In January of '49 they took on the undefeated Washburn Castle Guards and sent them to their first loss of the year. They followed up that huge upset win with a close loss to second place Drummond. Their record stood at 6 – 5. That would be their last loss of the regular season. They were about to catch fire and set the small schools in Northern Wisconsin on their ears. Saxon, among the tiniest of the small schools, was about to make some history of their own.

Washburn had quite a story to tell too. Their school burned to the ground in February of 1948. Construction on their new school was ongoing and would not be completed until the start of the next school year. In the meanwhile the school was moved into a club house. After school the basketball players moved all the tables and chairs out of the room and practiced and played their home games right there. It didn't hurt the Castle Guards one bit as they finished 1947 - 48 with a record of 18 – 3 and had won eleven straight games in the 1948 - 49 season before Saxon upended them. Now that's some serious dedication and commitment!

With three games left in the regular season Hurley had a record of 13 – 2. Park Falls was due to have a rematch with the Midgets on their brand new gym floor. Hurley was provided with scoring punch from Noel Mattei and Len Bartolutti as the backcourt mates drained 12 and 10 points. The defense was again superb and all the Midgets played in the game. It was never close as the Midgets jumped out to a 17 – 5 lead and cleared their bench. The final score was Hurley 48, Park Falls 30. Noel Mattei became the sixth player to lead the team in scoring in a game during the season. While Hurley was in

Park Falls, Wakefield continued their resurgent season by clipping Ironwood by 50 – 42 destroying the last hopes the Red Devils had of gaining a tie for the M – W title. They and the Cardinals were now both 3 – 4 with one conference game left to play. Hurley and Ashland sat atop of the league with records of 5 – 2. Ashland now had to face the suddenly formidable Wakefield five while Hurley had to take on Bessemer and high scoring Don Skwor on Friday Feb 11.

Bessemer was mired in a miserable season and Skwor was their only bright spot. The Midgets took full advantage of Bessemer and crushed the Speed boys 64 – 41. Hurley scored 25 fourth quarter points and Bessemer tallied 17 for one of the biggest one quarter explosions in M - W history. The Hurley reserves got in plenty of action. Eugene Martino and Pete Savant each scored 14 points to pace the Midgets while Noel Mattei had 12 and Len Bartolutti netted 10. Martino became the seventh Midget to pace the team in scoring during the season. Don Skwor continued to shine for the Speed Boys by dropping in 17 points for his team. He would end up leading the conference in scoring for the season. The win assured Hurley of at least a tie for the championship with a record of 6 – 2 pending the outcome of the Ashland – Wakefield game on the following Tuesday.

It's always tough when you want another team to help you. When Wakefield derailed Hurley in December, it ruined the Midgets' fast start to the season. They could now make it all up to the Midgets with a win over Ashland. The Cardinals did just that as they thumped the Oredockers 38 – 31 to wreck their dreams of a tie for M – W championship. Wakefield handed Hurley one of their two defeats on the year and then gift wrapped the title for them. Hurley became the undisputed champions of the conference for the second time in three years.

There was still one more game to play before tournament time. Superior East, led by 6' 5" center Louis Shears, had been tormenting Wisconsin and Minnesota teams all season. They just claimed a huge victory over the high flying Duluth Central Trojans 41 – 35. They were ranked as the seventh best team in Wisconsin in the WIAA's Big Sixteen with a record of 15 – 1. Their only loss was to their arch rivals, the Superior Central Vikings. Hurley was ranked number 10 as the two teams collided in Hurley on February 18. With both teams playing well, the first quarter ended in a 13 all tie. Paced by sharp shooting Len Bartolutti and Pete Savant, Hurley scored eight straight points to start the second quarter before East could tally a basket. Hurley led 29 – 21 at halftime and then in the third quarter East scored first. Hurley then tallied 7 straight points by Savant and Bartolutti and that ended the threat from East. Hurley went on to score the 47 – 35 win in convincing fashion. Bartolutti pumped in 17 points and Savant 14 to pace the Hurley offense. The Midgets ended the regular season with 16 wins and 2 losses. Superior Central, Superior East, Ashland and Hurley now prepared to take each other on in the Hurley Regional Tournament beginning the following Wednesday evening.

The day before the Hurley Regional Tournament there was a rematch of the Mass – St. Ambrose game in the Ironwood gym, where the Ramblers played their "home games." Mass was primed to avenge the two point loss to the Ramblers. With every basketball fan in the area wanting to see the game, somehow over 2,000 fans squeezed their way into the gym. The fire marshal must have been on vacation. The game was expected to be another barn burner and most of the crowd expected that the Rockets would claim the victory and begin another march to the Class D championship. The game was never close after the first few minutes. The Ramblers' Ray McKay could not find his usual scoring touch and ended the game without a point. His teammates however picked up the slack, and they picked up all the slack en-route to a lopsided and shocking 60 – 30 win! The Ramblers finished their regular season with a glittering 16 - 3 record. They were truly a basketball weapon of Mass destruction!

The area boosted the surprising St. Ambrose team and now they were joined by the high flying Saxon Knights. The Knights finished their season at 13 – 5, including a tie for third place in the Indianhead Conference with Mellen, both with 10 – 5 records in the league. Washburn and Drummond tied for the conference lead with identical 13 – 2 records. The word on the street at the start of the Ashland District Tournament was that Drummond would easily win their 5th straight district title and their 7th in nine years with only Washburn being a serious threat to them. The boys from Saxon were chomping at the bit to prove them all wrong.

There was still another team that had the Range buzzing with excitement. The Hurley B team completed the season with a perfect 17 – 0 record and now had a 27 game winning streak over two seasons. In the 1947 – 48 season they finished with a record of 19 – 1. In the 1946 – 47 season they were 14 – 3. Under Chief Gianunzio the Hurley B team had a record of 50 wins and 4 losses in three years. They were so exciting that fans packed gyms for the B games before every varsity tilt.

The thirty district tournaments got underway a week before the big schools began the 17 regional tournaments. About 240 small schools began to pursue their dream of winning their district and then winning another pairing to propel them into the sectional tournaments against the big schools. They all wanted to follow in the footsteps of Reedsville, the 1946 state champions. To be honest, most small schools thought of winning the district championship as being the apex of a season. Getting to the sectionals was akin to a state championship and just getting to Madison was the top of the basketball mountain. What Reedsville accomplished was a once in history event. It was possible, yes, but most unlikely. What Reedsville did was inject those dreams with reality. Little schools can and in fact did win a single class championship!

In Ashland, Saxon started the tournament by running over Ondossagon 43 – 29. The next night they were locked in a titanic struggle with Port Wing (now known as South Shore High School) before pulling out a razor thin 41 - 40 victory. In the championship game the Knights not only beat Drummond, but led throughout the game as they won 49 – 45. The final score was misleading; Drummond scored late to make it closer than it really was. Ron Peterson and Bill Nordberg led the Knights with 12 points apiece and Roy Kero dropped in 11 more in the win. Saxon had done the improbable. They won the Ashland District Championship and they left no doubt in anyone's mind that they were the best team in that tournament. The Knights now would face Prentice, winners of the Phillips District, for the right to play in the Spooner Sectional Tournament.

The Hurley Regional Tournament began on Wednesday evening, February 23 with Ashland tackling Superior Central. Ashland lost 7 games during the regular season including two each to Superior East, Superior Central, and Hurley. The other was to Wakefield. Central was still Central and dealt East one of their two losses on the season. Ashland's Roy Melvin had a history of coming up with surprises in big games. In this one he had his Oredockers playing a zone defense against the bigger Vikings. Both teams proceeded with caution as the score remained close. It wasn't until the fourth quarter that Ashland finally took the lead 33 – 32 with about one minute to play. Central's Anderson put the Vikings back up 34 – 33 shortly after with a nifty shot. The Oredockers couldn't score and Central stalled out the last fifteen seconds for the thrilling win. The next game would be even better!

The Superior East team that showed up in Hurley that night was transformed after their showing on the same court the previous Friday. They came to play and show the WIAA why they would go to Madison. The game was a whirlwind of ups and downs for the 2100 fans jammed into the Hurley gym. Hurley took a 13 – 11 lead after one quarter of play and then scored five straight points to start the second quarter. It began to look like the first game between the two teams until East applied pressure of their own and held the Midgets scoreless for the rest of the quarter while scoring 11 unanswered points. At the intermission East led 22 – 18. The third quarter saw yet another dramatic reversal as Hurley outscored East 11 – 4. Disaster struck Hurley with one minute to go in this period as Carl Hermanson fouled out in his effort to contain big Louis Shears. From then on it was up to John Tocci, the back-up center who was only 5'10" tall, and Mop Baron to hold the fort. At the end of three quarters the score was Hurley 29, East 26. The fourth quarter saw the East five battle back as both defenses began to apply the squeeze on the offenses. Baron and Tocci ensured Shears did not break loose. Tocci ended up picking up four fouls of his own in the effort. East found scoring from Don Dodge and Stromko as they closed the gap to 31 – 30. With 15 seconds to go the Midgets led 33 – 31. Stromko was fouled in the act of shooting. He calmly sank both shots to tie the game at 33 apiece and force overtime.

The atmosphere in the Hurley gym was electric with fans now on their feet. Len Bartolutti wasted no time as he scored before the overtime period was fifteen seconds old to give Hurley the lead 35 – 33. Midget fans caught their breath and then held it yet again as East tied the game on two charity tosses by Dodge. Bartolutti put Hurley back in front on a free throw, 36 – 35 with 45 seconds to go. With 20 seconds on the clock, Leland of East was fouled and awarded two shots. He made the first one to tie the game yet again. His second attempt missed and Hurley rebounded. The East defense was now tighter than ever and Hurley could not get an open shot at the hoop. As time slipped away the ball was headed out of bounds. Pupsy Savant who had not scored a single point in the game retrieved it from the furthest reaches of the corner and in one motion fired his patented rainbow shot from behind his right ear as he was falling backwards. The ball arched toward the rafters and cleared the edge of the backboard and swished through the net. The roar of the crowd told Pupsy that the shot went in. Len Bartolutti recalled that shot 70 years later. "I was in the perfect position to see that shot. He was falling out of bounds as he shot it from behind his ear over his right shoulder. From where I was I could see the ball clear the backboard and I knew it was going in." He then added, "Only Pupsy could make that shot. He did things like that all the time. We all saw it in practice." Bartolutti scored 15 points including those timely baskets down the stretch in the fourth quarter and overtime. Hermanson scored 10 before he fouled out. Baron notched 7 more. John Tocci did not score but he helped hold Shears to just 8 points for the game after Hermanson exited. Pupsy Savant would live his life knowing that he would always be remembered as the one who made "The Shot." Hurley was set for the next game versus Central for the sub-regional title.

On Thursday night Ashland dumped East in the consolation game 31 – 29. The Superior Central Vikings and Hurley Midgets found themselves in familiar territory as they again faced off for the sub-regional title. The winner would be taking on Park Falls as they had just won their sub-region. It was Central who jumped out to the early lead at 8 – 5 with three minutes to go in the first quarter. Hurley then countered with three quick baskets and a free throw to take the lead 12 – 10 going into the second period. The second quarter saw the offenses slow down as the defenses picked up in intensity. Points were hard to come by but Pupsy Savant hit two from long range and Len Bartolutti also drained one from outside. John Tocci added a free throw. Central's offense managed 9 points against the swarming Midgets and the half ended in a 19 – 19 tie. Pug Polgase, Central's star started the third quarter with a basket and then Wayland Baron scored at close range to tie it at 21. Hurley made a run and took the lead 29 – 24 but Anderson of Central connected on two shots to make it 29 – 28. Savant scored again with five seconds left in the quarter to put Hurley up 31 – 28 heading into the fourth period. In the fourth it was Bartolutti and Savant who combined for 6 points and Baron scored the last two. Central could not close the narrow gap and after Baron's basket put Hurley up 39 – 36 with 90 seconds to go, Central could only manage a free throw. The Midgets ran out the clock for the 39 – 37 victory. Savant rang up 13 points and Bartolutti had 9. Carl Hermanson, Wayland Baron, Noel Mattei and John Tocci contributed 7, 6, 3 and 1 point respectively.

On Saturday evening Ashland blasted Medford 61 – 25 for the regional consolation crown. Hurley and Park Falls were meeting for the third time of the season for the right to play in the Spooner Sectional Tournament. Coming off of two hard fought wins against the Superior teams, the Midgets were in no mood to let the Cardinals hang around. The score after one period of play was 11 – 8 in favor of Hurley. Then the sky fell on Park Falls as Hurley scored repeatedly from everywhere. Savant, Hermanson and Bartolutti led the scoring frenzy in the second quarter and by the half they held the lead 31 – 15. The Cards held their own in the third period and then Hurley exploded again with 19 fourth quarter points to coast to the 59 – 34 win. Savant, Hermanson, and Bartolutti all scored in double figures with 17, 14, and 10 points for Hurley.

Down in Phillips almost the entire population of Saxon traveled to see their miracle workers take on the highly touted and favored Prentice Hawks. The Hawks jumped out to a 5 – 0 lead and at the end of one period they led the Knights 12 – 6. Saxon closed the gap to 17 – 16 at the end of two quarters and then took the lead in the third. The two teams continued to play their hearts out and Saxon led 34 – 31 going into the final period. Saxon maintained their slight margin until the final buzzer and won 50 – 48 behind Ron Peterson's brilliant 28 point performance. The Knights were joining the Midgets in Spooner, one of just 32 teams left playing of the nearly 360 that started on the road to Madison. Not only did they make it to Spooner, they would play their bigger neighbors in the opening game. Saxon was by far the smallest school left in the tournament. All of Iron County now had basketball fever.

Sy Castagna and the Saxon boys had the undivided attention of Carl Vergamini. Getting one colossal upset in a tournament means you are a darn good team. Doing it twice meant that it really isn't an upset anymore. Facts are facts. Saxon had gelled into a great team. They beat Washburn and battled Drummond to the wire to start the ball rolling in January. Since then they had won 11 straight games including the big games in the tournament when they outplayed and outworked two great teams in Drummond and Prentice. The Hurley coach was doing everything he could think of to keep his players focused on Saxon. The other two teams in the Spooner Sectional were Luck, with their 16 – 7 record taking on Bloomer, the Heart O' North conference champions and the Rice Lake Regional winners. The Blackhawks were again led by Burt Hable and Don Barlow and sported a record of 21 – 1 and the number 8 ranking in the state. Hurley and Bloomer were heavy favorites to meet for the championship and the trip to Madison.

The Knights showed the fans who packed the Spooner gym just why Carl Vergamini was leery of them. With tough defense and timely shooting the Saxon boys battled the Midgets on equal terms and took a 10 – 9 lead into the second quarter. That's when Hurley's fast paced, in-your-face defense took over. Hurley had an extra gear and they now shifted into it. The undermanned Knights could not keep pace and Hurley led at the intermission by 25 – 15. The third quarter was the back breaker for Saxon as the Midgets keep up the pressure defense. After three quarters the score was 40 – 21 and Vergamini played the subs the rest of the way to the 61 – 34 win. Wayland Baron used some nifty head fakes on his way to scoring 16 points and Carl Hermanson and Pete Savant canned 13 and 12 points. Len Bartolutti held the explosive Ron Peterson to 5 points for the game. In all nine players scored for the Midgets. Tim Sullivan led the Knights with 12 points.

Bloomer had nothing but trouble with Luck in the second game. The Blackhawks looked safe holding the 29 – 13 halftime lead against the plucky Cardinals. After an evenly played third quarter the Luck five could only cut the lead to eleven, 35 – 24. Then the Blackhawks saw that lead evaporate before their eyes. Hable fouled out in the final quarter and back came the Cardinals. In the end it was two critical baskets by Hable's replacement, Don Burghardt that spelled doom for Luck. The final score was 41 – 37 as Bloomer escaped the trap.

On Saturday evening, March 5 Bloomer and Hurley teed off for the second time in two years for the right to go to Madison. The Midgets won in overtime the year before and Bloomer was still feeling the sting of that loss. If anything the tandem of Hable and Barlow was even more intimidating then the year before. They had simply dominated their foes throughout the season. On the opening tip of the game Barlow tapped the ball to Hable who waltzed in for the easy layup and the 2 – 0 lead. Hurley regained their composure and jumped back into the lead at the end of one quarter 12 – 6. With two minutes to go in the second quarter Bloomer broke out the old Hurley nemesis, the zone defense, after the Midgets extended the lead to 19 - 10. The Blackhawks then scored four quick points to get back into the game 19 – 14 as the half closed. With Hurley employing full court pressure and Bloomer playing a tight zone, the two defenses continued to grow in intensity. Bloomer was just more intense. The Blackhawks worked the score to 22 – 21 and then Hurley scored on a free throw for a two point lead. Hable scored and the game was tied. Barlow scored on a put back and Bloomer lead 25 – 23. Wayland Baron dropped in a charity toss and it was 25 – 24. As the clock wound down in the third period Len Bartolutti fired a shot from deep in the corner that hit nothing but net. Hurley led 26 – 25.

The fourth quarter started with Hable hitting on a free throw to tie the game at 26 each. A short time later Hable was again fouled and again he drained the free throw. Bloomer led again 27 – 26. Then the Hurley fans let out a collective groan as Carl Hermanson picked up his fifth foul and went to the bench. Seconds later Barlow scored on a tip-in and Bloomer added a free throw. The Blackhawks led 30 – 26 and Hurley was without their starting center and bulldog rebounder. Things looked bleak as everyone thought that two Bloomer big men would exploit the Midgets' weakened interior defense. It never happened. Pupsy Savant cranked up his rainbow maker and dropped in two long bombs to tie the game at 30 – 30. Hable then broke out of a scrum and scored on a lay-up, putting Bloomer back in the lead yet again. Then it was the Bloomer fans' turn to groan as Hable picked up his fifth foul as he hacked Bartolutti in the act of shooting. Bartolutti dropped the first toss through and the lead was cut to one point. He then missed the second shot, but Wayland Baron worked his way in front of the Blackhawk defenders for the tip-in and Hurley now led 33 – 32. The now red hot Savant connected on yet another long shot and the lead grew to 35 – 32. John Tocci dropped in a free throw and Stienmetz of Bloomer calmly dropped in two charity tosses and it was 36 – 34 with the clock winding down. Hurley ran their stall and Tooci was fouled just as the game ended. He hit the free throw and Hurley narrowly defeated Bloomer for the second year in a row. The Midgets were going to the state tournament for the third year in a row! For Bloomer it was another bitter pill to swallow as they ended their remarkable season with 22 wins and only 2 losses. Hable and Barlow netted 18 and 10 points for Bloomer, which accounted for all but six points. Steinmetz scored 5, all on free throws. Burghardt scored the remaining point for the Blackhawks. For Hurley, Savant and Bartolutti scored 13 and 10 points. Baron came up with the biggest rebound of the game when he tipped in Bartolutti's missed free throw to give the Midgets the lead late in the game. All seven Hurley players who got in the game scored. It was a fiercely contested game against a most worthy opponent. The battle-tested Hurley squad was ready to represent their community in Madison.

CHAPTER FORTY NINE

Iron Men

Len "Beppi" Bartolutti's hero was his dad. Giuseppi Bartolutti was an immigrant. He came to the Hurley area to work in the iron mines like so many others. He found a job working at the Montreal Mine. Giuseppe worked so hard and was so dependable that he became a foreman. Len remembered that Giuseppe would go to work before the sun came up and would come home after it went down. Len's friends nicknamed him "Beppi," which was his father's nickname. "I considered it an honor to have that nickname," said Len. It's easy to see where Len's work ethic comes from. In the summer between his junior and senior year of high school Len went to work in the Montreal mine too. Giuseppe worked in shaft number six on Tremble Hill in Montreal. Len went to work in shaft number 4 in Gile. What struck him about working in a mine? "It was hotter than hell down there. You would think it would be cool that far down. Let me tell you, it wasn't." Len worked at an average depth of over 3000 feet below the surface and on occasion worked up to 5000 feet below. On one occasion he and the rest of the crew were in the cable operated cage ready to ascend to the surface when rocks began to fall and pelt the cage. The men waited, but the rocks kept coming. Later they just were told to walk to shaft number 5 which was about a mile away. They did, passing beneath the West Branch of the Montreal River to shaft 5 and rode the cage there to the surface. Such was the life of a miner.

Wayland "Mop" Baron lost his father as a young boy. His mother was left to raise her three boys alone. Wayland was the middle boy.

His brothers were Don and Leon. Times were hard for the Baron family. His mother Aggie was well known as a good worker and she tried to piece odd jobs into a living. It wasn't easy. Ted Erspamer was his best friend. He said, "Nobody had much in those days, but my God, the Barons were poor. I think they were the poorest people in town." When asked about growing up poor Wayland simply says, "I know now that it was an advantage. It was the best thing that ever happened, growing up poor. It puts some starch in you. It makes you appreciate everything you have." Now you know how Wayland developed his "you will never beat us" attitude.

Carl Hermanson's dad passed away the year before, when both he and his brother John were starters on the '48 team. The boys played through the pain of that loss as their classmates rallied around them. That may have been one of the reasons he and Wayland Baron developed such respect for one another. There was an unspoken bond between them. In many games it was as if they could read each other's mind. Carl also was an easy going and funny. Often he was funny without trying to be. Carl was an undersized center who continually guarded the other team's biggest player. He never backed down and more often than not, he gained the upper hand. His work ethic and relentlessness were evident in every practice and in every game. Selflessness describes Carl to a tee.

Pete "Pupsy" Savant was a rascal in every sense of the word. Now Pete was truly a good kid, but he had energy to burn. Sitting still was impossible for him. He became what athletes today call a "gym rat." Sports were a godsend to such a boy as Pupsy. He directed all that energy into playing ball. As a gym rat Pupsy would work tirelessly on shooting that unorthodox shot of his. When he got bored he would experiment by taking shots from impossible angles. He shot until there were no more impossible angles. Like Carl Hermanson Pupsy was easy going and funny. Unlike Carl, he tried to be funny, and most often he was. It's told that during halftime of a game the Midgets were losing Coach Vergamini said, "Okay, what's going on out there?" Pupsy replied in all sincerity, "We don't even know ourselves." As was often the case with Pupsy, it's not what he said, but how he said it. The team had a good laugh and then they went out and won the game. Pete recalled his childhood, "I didn't know I was poor. None of us did. We knew that we didn't have some things, but we just wanted to have fun and play ball all the time. I delivered newspapers for some money. Most of us worked or helped parents, but I didn't think we were poor." Pupsy was right. When you have a family, good friends, and a sense of humor, you're never poor.

Noel Mattei grew up in Pence, one mile west of Montreal. He was another kid who just wanted to play ball. He did that every chance he could. He was also very shrewd. Noel would be said to have a high basketball IQ in today's parlance. He could sense where another player would go before he actually went. He was quick to anticipate an opponent's every move. He stopped the fast break before any opponent could get it started. His quick hands and feet drove his foes to frustration time and again. He was the facilitator on offense. When Noel started his engine, good things happened. He was clever and smart, but didn't particularly like school. His smarts later translated into a business acumen that would serve him and his family well. In 1949 it served his basketball team well. Noel also loved his coach. The discipline Carl Vergamini brought to him and his teammates was a critical contribution to his life.

These senior five boys, the starting unit, all good kids, and all on the cusp of manhood were going to Madison. You had better believe they were on a mission. The reserves were ready too of course, but Carl Vergamini was going to ride his starters as much as he possibly could. Carl took a calculated risk as the tournament started. He moved Clayton Corrigan, a ball handling guard, to the roster in place of Ted Erspamer, the big reserve enforcer. Ted was hurt by the move, but he sucked it up and said nothing. He traveled with the team throughout the tournament and offered support and encouragement. This was a team that would not be divided and it became a team that would not be conquered.

On Wednesday, March 9, 1949 the Midgets boarded the train to Madison. Upon arrival at their hotel Carl Vergamini and Chief Gianunzio told them to store their suitcases in their rooms and meet in the lobby. At the meeting the coaches gave the boys one hour to walk around the downtown area and check out the stores. Carl Hermanson suggested that they all should "simonize" their watches. The boys were sent on their way and the two men broke into hysterical laughter. If you don't get it, Google "simonize" and "synchronize." There was a time when people spent some time "simonizing," but it wasn't a watch that got that kind of attention. It was a story told by the two men throughout their lives and they laughed hard every time they told it.

Eight teams, the winners of each sectional tournament, were in Madison. The tournament schedule was set. On Thursday afternoon at 2:00 PM the largest school in the tournament, the Eau Claire Old Abes (17 – 6), were set to take on the smallest school, the Cuba City Cubans (24 – 1). The Cubans earned the right to play in Madison by knocking off 5 time champions, Beloit 34 – 31 and Brodhead 33 – 31 in the Monroe Sectional. In the 3:15 PM game it was the LaCrosse Logan Rangers (20 – 2) versus Kimberley Papermakers (18 – 2). The evening slate pitted the Reedsburg Beavers (24 – 1) against Hurley (21 – 2). The nightcap was the main event with the two top ranked teams in the state facing off. The Red Raiders of Wauwatosa (24 – 0) were ranked number 1 in the state and winners of 38 consecutive games, a state record. They were playing Red Raiders of Wisconsin Rapids (24 – 0) ranked number 2. Of course those who make predictions predicted that this game would be the "real" championship game.

In the opener, Cuba City pushed the much taller Eau Claire five all over the court until a late surge by the Old Abes finally subdued the Cubans 38 – 36. LaCrosse Logan then defeated Kimberly 53 – 41 after trailing at halftime 21 – 17. Merlin Nehring paced Logan with 21 points while Ralph Twite had 14 and lanky Jim Thomas had 9.

In the third game, Reedsburg jumped all over Hurley in the opening minutes to take a quick 6 – 1 lead. The Midgets regrouped and rattled off seven consecutive points to take an 8 – 6 lead. The see-saw game was knotted after one period at 12 – 12. Reedsburg took the lead at 13 – 12 and the Midgets promptly replied with a barrage to take a 22 – 16 lead. Reedsburg answered with four more and it was 22 – 20. Hurley then scored the last four points of the half to lead 26 – 20 at the break. The Midgets were getting scoring from everyone to that point. In the third quarter that scoring continued to come as Len Bartolutti hit from the corners. Pupsy Savant and Wayland Baron added free throws and Noel Mattei tallied. The defense stifled Reedsburg and at the end of three periods Hurley lead 38 – 28. Bill Frazier scored the Beavers' last five points of the third quarter and he picked up where he left off scoring ten more in the fourth quarter. The big lead evaporated as Frazier was unable to miss. Finally, with the score 46 – 44 in favor of Hurley, Len Bartolutti sunk the shot that sunk the Beavers 48 - 44. Reedsburg's tremendous rally fell short and the Midgets gladly left the court knowing they would not see Bill Frazier again in this tournament. The five Hurley senior starters played the entire game.

The much anticipated Wauwatosa – Wisconsin Rapids showdown was the final game of the opening round. Wisconsin Rapids used their speed against the superior height of the Wauwatosa five. Playing fast and loose they held the lead at halftime 28 – 22. In the third quarter 'Tosa came roaring back to cut the Rapids' lead to one point at 29 – 28. Both Red Raider teams continued to battle with Rapids staying in front. With Rapids in front 34 – 31, 'Tosa's high octane offense struck with lightning quickness. In a blink of an eye, they scored six straight points to take the lead 37 - 34. Although Wauwatosa was the much taller team, they did not sacrifice speed for height as they now began to match Wisconsin Rapids step for step. Rapids scored just before the end of the quarter and the score was 37 – 36 in favor of 'Tosa as the fourth stanza started. The tight contest continued. With 'Tosa leading 42 – 41, Ray Kotz and Dick Schwab erupted to put on a dazzling shooting display for Wauwatosa. The dam had burst and Wisconsin Rapids could not keep up. Wauwatosa was pushed hard but the defending state champions pushed back for the 55 – 49 win. It was their 39th consecutive win. The champs were on their game.

The Wisconsin State Journal had a sports writer by the name of Roundy who did a column called "Roundy Says". Roundy did not use punctuation nor did he use proper grammar, which was probably why he was so popular. He said this about Hurley's win against the Beavers, "The Hurley team they had the old drive and zip they weren't fooling they were pepped up like a guy full of summer vegetables they played a beautiful game." Roundy went on to praise the rebounding, especially Carl Hermanson, saying "Brother was he ever a star." Of Len Bartolutti he wrote, "he's one of the best players in this tournament that's a cinch." Of course he noticed Pupsy Savant's shot and commented, "I had to laff at that Pete Savant he has got that high arch shot the ball goes up near the rafters and sees if there are any robins in town and did he ever hit five beautiful baskets." On Wayland Baron, "he played a beautiful game he's smart out there he knows what it's all about he's got good height too and he's a honey of a ball player." Noel Mattei's understated game did not escape Roundy. The man knew what Noel's role on the team was and said this, "Noel Mattei he's a very good guard for Hurley he was a good leader out there he knows what it's all about." The thing that stood out in Roundy's column was that he praised a lot of the teams and their players, but Hurley and Wauwatosa were the only two teams that had five players getting Roundy's ink. Interesting!

The Semi-final matchups were now set for Friday evening. LaCrosse Logan was to meet Eau Claire and Hurley had the tall task of tackling Wauwatosa. In the Friday afternoon consolation round Reedsburg recovered from their tough loss to Hurley by edging Wisconsin Rapids 41 – 39 on a last second shot by Jim Arenz. Kimberley downed little Cuba City 45 – 39 in a game the Cubans led until the last few minutes.

In the first evening match, LaCrosse Logan and Eau Claire were meeting for the third time of the season. Logan won the two previous games 40 – 39 and 31 – 27. This game followed the same pattern, as Merlin Nehring again led Logan to victory 37 – 33 over the Old Abes. All that was left was for Logan to wait and see just how badly Wauwatosa would beat Hurley. None of the sports writers gave Hurley a chance. Only two high school coaches who were queried gave the Midgets a fighting chance. One went unnamed. The other was Madison East's Milt Diehl who said, "If I were a betting man, I'd wager on Hurley."

How did the Wauwatosa Red Raiders become the current bluebloods of Wisconsin high school basketball? For one, nobody had defeated them in 39 games. Two, they were very talented, very tall, and very fast. Their roster was chalk full of players who would go on to play at the University of Wisconsin, Marquette and other big schools in college. They also had an innovative coach. Bill Walters was both a superb shop teacher and basketball coach at Wauwatosa High School. One task he gave his students was to make a wooden fan-shaped basketball backboard, just like the one's hanging in gymnasiums all over the country. The Wauwatosa kids took to that task with gusto. Soon these works of art were hanging on garages throughout the city. The result was that the clever Walters honed both the woodworking skills and basketball skills of his boys at the same time. Wauwatosa became a hotbed for high school basketball. This was the second of five consecutive state tournaments that they would participate in. Sitting in the stands the night Hurley and Wauwatosa played was a 9th grader from 'Tosa named Roy Wolff. He and his friends grew up playing basketball in the alleys where all those backboards were hung. He says, "No matter where you looked, there was a basketball hoop hanging on one of those backboards. They were in every alley on almost every garage."

So it was suburban Wauwatosa, the Milwaukee area's basketball royalty, versus little Hurley who carried the hopes and dreams of the Range to Madison with them. Two powerhouse teams representing two communities that were stricken with basketball fever would face each other. The fans in the state took notice of this game and it was a sell out with people turned away at the doors. The Wauwatosa cheering section was big and loud. Hurley's, by comparison, was small, even though nearly a thousand people made the long trip. The sentimental favorite was the little team from the north. In the Hurley locker room prior to the game, the sentiment was simple. Len Bartolutti recalled their resolve. "We just weren't going to let them win another championship – they had enough!"

As the teams positioned themselves for the opening tip-off it was clear that the Hurley Midgets were indeed the smaller team. Tosa was led by their high scoring trio of 6'3" Ray Kotz, 6'1 Dick Schwab, and 5' 9" Walt Zitske. The icing on the cake was their talented and rangy center, 6' 6" Gene Kvitle. In all they had 7 of their ten players standing more than 6 feet tall. Hurley had 7 players listed at 5"10" or shorter. Skinny Wayland Baron was listed at 6' 1" and Carl Hermanson at 6' even. Len Bartolutti was also listed at 6' 1" but that may have been a tad generous as in team pictures he is not as tall as Baron. But as Len stated, "Rebounding has little to do with height. It's work."

Carl Vergamini knew that to win the elusive state title, the road would take him to a meeting with Wauwatosa. His bristling rebuttal to the Hurley fan bringing him the news that Hurley was ranked number 7 in the state and Tosa was number 1 back in January was telling. Now he upped the ante. The Wisconsin State Journal reported

> Coach Carl Vergamini wasn't one bit pessimistic
> over his team's chances of beating Wauwatosa.
> Asked by the writer to bring his team into the press
> tent after the game, if the Midgets won, Vergamini
> readily replied, "We'll be there." Coach Bill Walters of
> Wauwatosa wasn't that optimistic, however, his reply
> was, "Maybe."

Dick Schwab shot Tosa into the early lead 2 – 0 but two long shots from Savant and Baron put Hurley up 4 – 2.   Kvitle and Schwab gave the Red Raiders a 7 – 4 lead and Bartolutti hit from long range to make it 7 – 6. With the score 11 – 9 in favor of 'Tosa, Hermanson and Mattei tallied to put the Midgets up 13 – 11 going into period number two. The second period saw both teams continue to race up and down the court. Most basketball minds believed Hurley was playing into the hands of Wauwatosa. Throughout the season the high scoring Red Raiders had worn their opponents to a frazzle. Not one team could keep up with their running style. Vergamini had been warned by his fellow coaches, "Don't try to keep up with the race horse tactics of that team. They'll run you into the floor. Make 'em play your game." With both teams pushing the pace, Coach Walters substituted for his starters with players nearly every bit as good. Hurley stuck with their five starting seniors. In what the 'Tosa fans had hoped would be a repeat of so many other games, they waited for Hurley to crack. As the first half ended it was still the Hurley Midgets in the driver's seat by a single point 30 – 29.

As the third quarter started it was clear that Carl Vergamini's Midgets were indeed going to continue running with 'Tosa. He took half of the advice given to him and decided to "make 'em play your game." Hurley's game all year long had been to run, run, run, and then run some more. If that was also Wauwatosa's game, then so be it!

Noel Mattei scored to open the second half and 'Tosa responded. Baron tallied and 'Tosa did too. Finally the Red Raiders tied the game at 34 – 34. The teams exchanged free throws and it was knotted again at 35 – 35. It was then that the first crack appeared in the running game for either team. It was the Red Raiders who flinched. Led by the rebounding and scoring of Hermanson and Baron, the Midgets scored 11 of the next 12 points in the third period. Wauwatosa could not stop the onslaught until Schwab tallied just before the end of the third quarter. The crowd was now breathless and stunned by the torrid shooting of Hurley. The Capitol Times stated that 90 percent of the crowd of nearly 14,000 was cheering for Hurley. Everybody loves the underdog. In the closing minutes of the third period and throughout the fourth, Wauwatosa fouled and fouled again. Once Hurley had opened the lead they began to whip the ball around on offense waiting for a good shot. It was the same formula they employed all year. In desperation the Red Raiders chased and lunged after the ball. Hurley dropped in ten free throws during this critical run to the finish line. When they did get a good shot, they drilled it. Wauwatosa was damned if they fouled and damned if they didn't. All the Midgets were sizzling hot. With the score at 60 – 44 and time running down, Hurley took their foot off the gas pedal and 'Tosa scored 6 of the last eight points of the game. With 22 seconds to play the starters left the game to a standing ovation. The final score was 62 – 50. The Midgets were paced by the rugged rebounding of Hermanson and Baron. The defense was ferocious as Wauwatosa jacked up an absurd 85 shots in 32 minutes. They continued to run with break neck speed on offense. Only the Hurley defense had matched them in this season. Offensively the Midgets were led by Baron and Hermanson with 18 and 17 points respectively. Savant had 11, Bartolutti 9, and Mattei 7. Once again playing a much taller opponent brought out the best in Baron and Hermanson. Hurley, it was reported, had just pulled off the greatest upset in Wisconsin basketball history. To Carl Vergamini it was not an upset at all. He knew it all along.

Roy Wolff, the Wauwatosa 9th grader and his friends went back to Wauwatosa feeling down. The next day they did what boys always do in a situation like that. They went into the alley and played basketball. This time they imitated the one opposing player in the tournament who caught their eye. They started to launch the rainbow shot of Pupsy Savant toward the hoop. Roy never forgot that shot. Roy never forgot the sting of his beloved Red Raiders loss that night to Hurley, either. Over six decades later he was sitting in a coffee shop in St. Paul, MN when he over head a conversation between a married couple who were acquaintances of his. They were talking about a visit they planned to Hurley. Roy, huffed, "Did you say you're going to Hurley? I hate Hurley!" The man who is a psychologist asked why that was. Roy explained. His friend urged him to make a trip to Hurley himself and try to contact Pupsy Savant. Surprisingly Roy did just that. Roy and Pupsy met and Pupsy gave Roy a Hurley Midgets cap. During my interviews with Roy, he proudly wore that cap. He and Pupsy became friends. Roy still calls Pupsy, who is now in the Sky View assisted living facility in Hurley. Roy's friend wrote an article for a local St. Paul neighborhood paper about the interaction between Pupsy and Roy. He changed the names of the teams and towns in the story. Basketball is both a heart breaker and a heart mender.

At 5:00 AM on Saturday morning, March 12, the Hurley High School band boarded a bus for the state championship game. They were already in their full uniforms. Traveling by school bus meant traveling slow. Gloria Stremski Fillion, Hurley '49, made that trip. "I don't think the bus went over 35 miles per hour." They stopped briefly for lunch at a Lutheran church in Stevens Point. Finally 12 hours after the journey started they were at the University of Wisconsin Field House. As the band members walked into the cavernous building, still shaking off a case of "bus legs," they were immediately mesmerized by the immensity of the place. They were also impressed by the basketball court's raised floor. Within a few hours they were going to play the

Hurley fight song like it had never been played before. The fans back home on the Range were treated to Tod Hogan's introduction of the championship game with the Hurley fight song playing in the background. It was magnificent!

On that evening Reedsburg dispatched Kimberly 62 – 52 to win the consolation honors. The crowd was now in their seats waiting for the championship game. LaCrosse Logan was the number 3 ranked team in the state and they were expecting to meet Wauwatosa for the championship. They were feeling good about becoming the next state champions now that the Red Raiders had been sent home. The Red Raiders were intimidating. Hurley just wasn't. They were not bigger or stronger.

During the warm-ups prior to the championship game the cheerleaders for both teams took turns on the raised basketball court. With each turn the fans grew louder until the field house was rocking. The five Hurley cheerleaders led the choreographed cheers that everyone in Hurley knew by heart. They found a rhythm with those cheers and more and more unaffiliated fans joined in. It soon became clear that the underdog Midgets were the fan favorites. The cheerleaders, Joanne Kopacz, Gloria Gianunzio, Loretta Cortichiato, Jeanne O'Berto, and Rosemarie Pacqualucci had set the stage. The rest was up to the boys.

LaCrosse Logan had what was called in those days a "rangy" team. Today the word sportscaster's use is "long." No matter which term you choose, they were tall and they were good. It was Logan that scored first when their star, Merlin Nehring, tallied. Hurley started slow but then scored and scored again to take a 6 – 5 lead. It would be the only time in a long time they would have the advantage. Nehring broke loose for two more baskets and then the Rangers 6'5" center

Jim Thomas scored three more in rapid succession to give Logan a 15 – 8 lead at the end of one period of play. Hurley tried in vain to get their offense on track but to little avail. They could manage only 5 points in the second stanza. Fortunately the defensive intensity made its return and LaCrosse Logan could manage but 7 points. At the intermission the Rangers held the lead at 22 – 13 and Hurley looked like they had left their game behind them. They played like their legs were encased in cement. The sports writers and broadcasters, as they always do in these situations, speculated that the Hurley five was finally out of gas after their Herculean effort the previous night. They certainly looked dead on their feet compared to the previous two games. Fatigue, the silent assassin, was lurking. Carl Vergamini had the solution for fatigue.

Roy Melvin and Carl Vergamini were friends. They liked and respected each other and they admired each other's professionalism. How much did they trust one another? Carl allowed Roy to be in the locker room at halftime and again after the game. We will never know how many coaches allow that, but the numbers have got to be pretty small. Roy didn't speak; he just listened. His place was coaching Ashland and he did not interfere with Carl's game plan, speeches, or tactics. Hurley was his home for 19 years and he wanted to see the Midgets take the championship trophy. Before Carl Vergamini and Chief Gianunzio entered the locker room, Pupsy Savant and Mop Baron exhorted their teammates to take and make better shots. They just were not hitting anything to that point. A minute later the big coach stepped into the middle of the room. The three men Hurley athletes admired and respected the most stood before them. Roy Melvin, the designer of the locomotive, the one who brought hope to a moribund and downtrodden program looked on. Mario Gianunzio, the man who cared for and maintained that locomotive when the designer and engineer were not there, stood by. Now Carl Vergamini, the head engineer, the one who knew every intricate moving part and every valve, stood over his exhausted engine. He had made his decision. He was not going to alter the game plan or the style of play due to fatigue. He was going to throw every last chunk of coal there was on the fire and get the engine running even hotter. He looked his team over once, then twice, and shook his head. Then he admonished his boys. They were the same boys who had given their coach, team, school, and community every ounce of energy in their bodies. After a season in which they practiced at breakneck speed every day, he knew they had just a little more in them. He knew that they would need every molecule of adrenaline in their bodies to pull this game out. He quietly said, "I'm ashamed to walk out there with you guys." With that he turned and walked out the door. With a nod of agreement, Chief Gianunzio and Roy Melvin both followed him. The challenge had been thrown down. You could have heard a pin drop.

Hurley scored first in the third quarter. Wayland Baron dropped one in from the side. 22 – 15. Hermanson then split the defense for a layup. 22 – 17. Bartolutti swished a free throw. 22 – 18. Baron connected again from the corner and then canned a free throw. 22 – 21. Carl Hermanson collected a missed shot by Savant and put it back up for two more. Hurley took the lead 23 – 22. Bartolutti sank another free throw and the Midgets led 24 – 22. Hurley had come all the way back to take the lead scoring 11 unanswered points in less than four minutes. A free throw by Jim Thomas snapped the streak and pulled the Rangers to within one point. Bartolutti sank his third free throw of the quarter to get the lead back to two at 25 – 23. Thomas once again wiggled his way in for a tip-in on a team mates miss to tie it at 25 each. Savant dropped in a long rainbow from the top of the key to put the Midgets back on top 27 – 25. Ralph Twite connected on a free throw for Logan and it was 27 – 26. Baron took a pass underneath the basket. He was covered. He gave a head fake and then another in rapid succession. The defender left his feet in anticipation and Baron slipped under him for an easy bucket. 29 – 26. With time running down in the period Baron took a pass in the lane, gave another head fake and popped in an 8 foot shot that went uncontested through the hoop. 31 - 26. When the buzzer sounded to end the third period the Hurley boys ran to the bench with vigor. LaCrosse Logan was stunned. They had just been outscored 18 – 4 in the quarter. Their nine point lead turned into a 5 point deficit.

These Rangers were every bit as resilient and tough as the Midgets. They did not hang their heads. There was no pity party. No blame assessed. They rallied around each other like champions always do. Like a punch drunk heavyweight boxer they were saved by the bell. In the precious minute or so between periods they recovered their basketball senses. This was it.

When watching the black and white video of the game one of the first things you notice was how seamlessly the Midgets switched men when playing man-to-man defense. This defense was the fuel that propelled the Midget engine. Logan repeatedly was forced to a sideline. It was rare that they could take advantage of the middle of the defense. Time and again they were forced to take bad shots. In the fourth quarter the Rangers defense came back to life and started doing the same thing to the Midgets. Nehring scored twice off of steals and the score was 31 – 30 in favor of Hurley. Then Twite found the bottom of the net from outside and the Rangers had made their way back to take the lead 32 -31. A double foul was called as Baron and Thomas tangled beneath the Hurley basket for a rebound. Baron missed his free throw and Thomas drained his. Logan now led 33

– 31. Fatigue hovered above both teams looking for a victim. Again both teams pushed the pace. Baron took another pass inside and pump faked, then head faked. The defenders did not bite. One more head fake and one defender left his feet. Baron wheeled and sank another short shot to tie the game at 33 – 33.

With the clock winding down in this tight contest it was Carl Hermanson who was a bearcat on the boards. He cleared rebound after rebound not giving Logan a second chance to score. His front court partner, Wayland Baron was providing the offense as he had scored the Midgets last six points. They were doing what they did best. They controlled the inside on defense and offense. In game after game against taller opposition they seemed to play like they were six inches taller. Yes, big Jim Thomas was scoring a lot of points, but Hermanson beat him more often than not to rebounds.

Baron sank yet another shot from close range and Hurley had the lead again at 35 – 33. There were 2 minutes and 54 seconds left to play. Fatigue for once failed and was shown the door. Both teams were playing with focus and intensity. Then Jim Thomas struck again. He used every inch of his tall body and long arms to tip in a missed free throw by Nehring. It was a real hustle play. The score was 35 – 35. With one minute and 40 seconds left in the game Baron was fouled away from the basket as the defender reached too far and smacked him. That was the wrong guy to foul. The kid they called Mop was scorching hot. He calmly sank the free throw to give the Midgets the lead 36 – 35. You just could not find two more evenly matched teams. Despite most of the fans cheering for the Midgets, the Rangers were nonplussed. When Bartolutti fouled Nehring, the Logan star sank the free throw. 36 – 36. Over the next minute of play both teams missed shots and each had a turnover. The field house was now a pressure cooker!

With 41 seconds to go, Baron was fouled as he tried to receive a pass from Noel Mattei. After a timeout was called he stepped to the free throw line at the north end of the court. It was fitting that he was facing north toward Hurley. Wayland Baron had little in the way of material things in his life. He felt fortunate to have food on the table, yet he had everything that mattered. He had family, his friends, his teammates and his community. The man who stated that growing up poor "puts starch in you" and that the best thing that ever happened to him was growing up poor, was the boy who over seventy years ago had 28,000 eyes looking right at him. The slightly built lad stood at the free throw facing home, with the hopes and dreams of all those who had ever walked the halls of Hurley's Lincoln High School in his hands. Back on the Range even people who never cared about basketball cared about this game. They were glued to their radios as Tod Hogan brought the game into their living rooms, restaurants, taverns, and even into the mines. Every fan, every band member, every youth coach, volunteer county league referees, every student, every parent, every immigrant, every miner, every single person in the community was standing at the free throw line with Mop Baron. For every humiliating defeat ever administered to the little Hurley teams, there was a new hope; the hope that all their blood, sweat and tears were important. It was the sense that they too, in some measure, contributed to the steady growth of Hurley athletics. It was the knowledge that their selfless hard work, their wins, their losses, and most of all, their Hurley pride helped get this team to this place in time. In the stands Aggie Baron turned to the fans behind her and said, "That's my son, that's my son." As if he didn't have a care in the world, Wayland Baron took the ball from the referee and in one smooth motion sent it toward the hoop. A clean swish! 37 – 36.

The field house was now a madhouse, a cacophony of sound. The atmosphere was super charged and electric. The players played on without being able to hear anything except the chaotic exhortations of nearly 14,000 fans. 41 seconds to go in the game. Logan moved the ball quickly up-court. Not a single newspaper accounts tells us what happened next. As always they used their ink to talk about shooting and scoring. They left out the most important defensive play of the game, the most important defensive play in Midget history! The video and Tod Hogan's audio tell us exactly what came next. With about 30 seconds on the clock, Nehring took a pass in the corner and turned to take the shot. He was Logan's deadliest shooter. Len Bartolutti, who took such pride in playing defense made the timeliest defensive play of his life. As Nehring released the shot, the boy they called Beppi did what hard working miners do, he gave it his all as he stretched out his long arms and nearly jumped out of his shoes. Using every centimeter of his height and every micrometer of his long arms, he did what the reporters found unworthy of mention. He tipped the ball as it was released! He then turned and recovered the ball after it bounced from hand to hand of players on both sides. He started up court and was fouled by Nehring to stop the clock. Hurley refused the free throw and took the ball out of bounds. With less than 25 seconds to go, Nehring fouled Savant and again the Midgets elected to take the ball out of bounds. There was no keeping up with Hurley's snappy passing, and again Logan fouled. Again Hurley declined the free throws and inbounded the ball. For over fifteen seconds they played catch and release, snapping off crisp, clean passes without hesitation. The Rangers lunged and reached to no avail. The boys were dialed in. Not one of them even glanced at the clock. They were

100 percent focused on the task at hand. That task was the Midget stall. It was flawless, just as it had been over the past two seasons. Once it started no other team could break it without fouling. The seconds ticked off the clock. The excitement in Tod Hogan's voice on the radio broadcast was palpable as he announced the final 15 seconds, his voice cracking. These are his words.

> Taken out by Savant, in to Bartolutti, back to Savant
> in the corner, back to mid-court to Bartolutti, he turns
> around, far side pass to Hermanson, 37 – 36 state
> championship, Hurley leads, Mattei has that ball!
> Bartolutti has that ball! Mattei has it a mid-court, the
> ball game is over, Hurley leads, Oh, Hurley won the
> ball game! You won't believe it unless you were out
> here to see what happened! The Hurley High School
> Midgets are the new state champions of Wisconsin!

The scene in the field house was a sight to behold. The scenes in living rooms, establishments, and in the mines of the area were every bit as joyous. A half a mile beneath the earth's surface, in the Montreal and Cary Mines, some of the toughest, strongest, and hardest working men in the world shouted, shook hands, and embraced. In homes all across the Gogebic Rang, they celebrated. Doris Thompson Morello, Hurley '49, and her mother listened to the game in their farm home. The normally reserved Mrs. Thompson "was pounding so hard she literally broke the arm off the couch."

As the Championship trophy was about to be awarded to the Hurley Midgets, Tod Hogan acknowledged the LaCrosse Logan Rangers. He saw them standing there, looking lost and sad. He said, "We can all feel terribly sorry for the Lacrosse Logan team out there, because you should see the group of boys out there as a team, they're really feeling down." LaCrosse Logan's boys were now experiencing a sad reality. John R. Tunis wrote his book, "Yea! Wildcats"

> No rush for the showers. No shouts, no yells this evening. No yippees and whoopees. No songs….no bear hugs. No hollering of young voices. No shrieks of joy back and forth. It's quiet in the dressing room of the team that loses.

> It's lonesome, almost. The photographers have suddenly deserted them. So have the newspapermen and the agreeable, smiling sports writers who came to life after their earlier victories……They have gone, all of them…..its empty now and almost lonely.

What happens when a team comes so close to winning a championship only to come up short? The initial pain is terrific. That pain through time yields to a sense of pride. There is only one champion and there are so many worthy teams. Hurley left a trail of tattered dreams in their wake on the road to the state championship. It took an overtime session and Pupsy Savant's miracle shot to send Superior East home for the season. Superior Central played their hearts out only to lose by two points. Park Falls dreamed the dream, so did tiny Saxon. Bloomer felt the sting of another close loss in Spooner. Reedsburg was a superb team who came up just short. Wauwatosa had dreamed big; they wanted two in a row. Lacrosse Logan was as good as any team in Wisconsin. The players who have their season end in a loss can only wonder what might have been if only. There is but one champion and yet we play on. We play for fun. We play for the love of the game. We play for pride. We play for each other. We sweat together, work together, dream together.

We forge life-long friendships. We learn that dreams don't always come true. We learn to continue dreaming. Losing a basketball game often means learning to win in the game of life. With time we all learn to appreciate the opportunity to compete, to strive, to achieve. If we come up short, we come back and lace them up again. In our efforts to find perfection, we all fall short, but in doing so we achieve excellence. Sports should always be a window on life. We live and we learn. With only one champion every competitor knows defeat at some time. Ask any of them if they would do it all again. Was it all worthwhile? We know the answer to that.

And now the Hurley Midgets were called out onto the court. The announcer mentioned that they, as Logan was now, were the runner up in '47, consolation champions in '48, and now the 1949 Wisconsin State Champions! Wayland Baron remembers the moment. "It was great! We were happy. In those days we didn't stand around and gloat and carry on. Once we were handed the trophy, we just walked to the locker room. There was none of this stuff they do now. We went to the locker room to celebrate. We celebrated together."

Newspapers statewide had called the Hurley team the "Iron Men" after playing their five starters all the way versus Reedsburg and within 22 seconds of the final horn in the spectacular win over Wauwatosa. In the championship game versus LaCrosse Logan, juniors Smocky Martino and John Tocci played sparingly in the second quarter as Carl Vergamini tried to inject some life into his exhausted squad. Now the name stuck to the boys like glue. They were feted in pictures and written accounts and were always referred to as Hurley's Iron Men. No name could have described them better. No one could have possibly been more proud of that nickname than Carl Vergamini. As a member of the 1938 and 1939 Iowa Hawkeye football teams, Verg and his teammates were referred to as the "Iowa Iron Men" because they played both offense and defense without substitutions. Ten years later his team was again the "Iron Men"

Accolades followed the Hurley Midgets as newspapers named their "All tournament" teams. Depending on the paper, four of the five Midgets received that honor. Only Noel Mattei did not. Carl Vergamini heaped praise on his formidable point guard right after the game in an interview with Tod Hogan.

> Mattei is one of the top ballplayers around here
> although he won't get a lot of ratings, because he
> doesn't score much. But that boy is one of the finest
> athletes Hurley has ever had.

His team mates all agreed with their coach.

When the boys had calmed down and showered they went back to their hotel. At noon the next day, they boarded a charter Greyhound Bus for Hurley. The long ride north on US Highway 51 took them through the very heart of Wisconsin. As the highway gave way to the towns and villages along the route, the bus would slow and pass through such places as Portage, Westfield, Plover, Stevens Point, Wausau, Tomahawk, and Minocqua. Once they passed through the bus would accelerate once again until the next town's posted speed limit impeded their progress.

The sun set and the bus pushed on through the darkness. The jubilant tone of the passengers gave way to hushed voices, quiet smiles, and the strange, sweet satisfaction of total exhaustion. Moving ever northward, the towns were further and further apart. The farms gave way to the wilderness of Northern Wisconsin. Moving northward also brought a noticeable drop in the outside temperature. It wasn't a harsh, deep winter cold, but it was bitter even by Northern Wisconsin standards. Although signs of early spring appeared in the southern part of the state, in the extreme north, winter hung on tenaciously.

The steady drone of the bus engine was broken once more, this time only 22 miles shy of Hurley. Sleep and drowsy thoughts of meeting families and having a home cooked meal were interrupted as the bus slowed down upon approaching the tiny resort town of Mercer. At least they were back in Iron County. They would sleep in their own beds tonight. Thoughts turned to readying themselves to get off the bus at the high school. Only about 30 minutes to go now. They wanted to get home, but the bus was coming to a stop. They could now see the commotion. More people were standing along the main street of Mercer than anyone from Hurley could have believed. They were holding signs and cheering. The people of Mercer were giving a hero's welcome to the Wisconsin State Basketball Champions. A short speech was made and the boys were wished Godspeed. The bus began to roll forward again.

Twenty one miles later, less than one mile from town, the bus rolled to a stop yet again. At the bottom of the hill, just north of the bluff, between 200 – 300 cars waited. In the cold night air the boys left the bus and were put into convertibles. The tops were down. The joyous caravan began to ascend the hill toward Hurley. They had traveled nearly 300 miles. Home was a breath away.

As the first car crested the hill and began its descent, US 51 gave way to Second Avenue. On Silver Street the crowd had begun gathering two hours earlier. A throng of about 10,000 shivering men, women, and children were packed tightly along the parade route on Silver Street. While they waited, a sound truck played the last two minutes of the championship game broadcast over and over.

At about 9:45 PM a shout cut through the night, "Here they come!" The caravan turned left onto Silver Street. The huge crowd roared for their Midgets amid blaring sirens. The high school band struck up the Hurley fight song. The caravan reached the end of Silver Street and turned around going through town again. The joyous noise did not cease. The parade crossed the river into Ironwood. For the first time in history the Ironwood High School band played the Hurley fight song with smiles on their faces, the family feud forgotten (until the next game). The streets of Ironwood were teeming with people shouting the praises of the Hurley Midgets. In 1997 Carl Vergamini remembered the homecoming.

> I'll tell you it was an exhilarating experience, believe me. Nobody expected it. I got a hint of it when we got to Mercer and they stopped the bus…. The whole town of Mercer as out in the streets there, cheering and hollering and screaming and we were trying to sleep (laughs). It had been a long ride home. We were met outside of town by this huge caravan of cars, police, fire trucks and everything. They put us out of the bus and onto convertibles and it was cold, believe me it was cold. When we got to Hurley it went right down the street and over to Ironwood, circled around Ironwood, and there was talk about Bessemer and Wakefield, and I said no, I'd have froze to death by the time we got back to Hurley.

The support Hurley received was illustrated in a banner cared for by Doris Valle Soine, Hurley '49. During our interview in 1997 she unfurled it. On that canvass HURLEY was written in large orange letters. It had hung in the field house in Madison during the tournament. It also hung in Hurley during the regional tournament and Spooner in the sectional tournament. It was well travelled. It was signed by the members of the Superior East and Saxon basketball teams. The head usher at the state tournament signed it. People from Hurley signed it. People no one in Hurley had ever heard of signed it. The Hurley team also signed it.

As hundreds of telegrams poured in from seven states, they celebrated. Many Hurley fans felt something deeper in the celebration. Anna Kangas Gertz shared this memory. "It was wall to wall people. There was barely room for those cars to get through....I'd never seen people in town like that, right from the buildings all the way to the streets, so that there was just room for the convertibles with the players on them to get through. I was crying. It had never been done before."

Doris Thompson Morello was also crying. In 1997 she and Anna explained why those emotions flowed so freely.

> I think the war had a lot to do with it, and you know,
> we had a lot of things happen when we were in
> school. We lost Billy Mehnert in grade school
> (age 14 – his picture and a memorial poem appear
> in the class yearbook), and so many people had
> parents die (they recite a very long list of classmates
> affected). It was a lot of tragedy. Everyone tried to
> stick together and help each other out…. This is the
> type of thing, and I think everybody became aware of
> everybody's feelings. A lot of heartache. That's why
> I think when we finally got to be state champs we'd
> something to cheer about…. We could just forget
> about everything else for awhile and be happy."

The basketball team brought more to Hurley than a trophy. They were celebrated as heroes and deservedly so, but in reality they were a mirror image of the rest of their classmates, their parents, the school, and the entire Range. Had they or any Hurley Midget team that preceded them chosen to rely on personality only, they would have quit and given up anywhere along this magnificent 26 year journey. Instead they learned from parents, teachers, and coaches to do the hard work of developing character. Personality changes with the realities of life, but character sees you through the tough times. Character causes you to dig deep inside and keep going when life hurts. This team had character that reflected the community. They brought joy to a place and time where their neighbors and families had always found a way to keep going, even when life hurt. It was more than a game. Much more!

EPILOGUE

On Friday, May 27, 1949, The Hurley High School Gymnasium was once again packed to the rafters. The graduating class of 1949 entered the gym, two by two, singing the processional song, "Away, Away." Every spring since 1893 this annual miracle had taken place. Every spring since 1949, it has continued. It is a miracle because in just a single step a high school graduate passes from childhood into adulthood. The last steps of childhood are taken up onto the stage and toward the school official who hands that graduate their diploma. They stop, shake hands, receive the diploma, and with their very next movement, they step into adulthood.

So this isn't the end of the story. It continues because life continues. Of the 98 graduates who walked across the stage that night, 49 were girls and 49 were boys. They believed they were entering a better world than the war torn world of their grade school years. History tells us a different story. On June 25, 1950, the North Korean army swept across the 38th parallel on the Korean peninsula and into South Korea. Americans would once again fight and bleed.

While speaking with members of the class of 1949, many were insistent that I include recognition of five of their classmates in this book. In 1997 I researched and wrote a paper titled, "United They Stand - Hurley's Class of 1949" for at local area history project while I was completing my degree at the University of Wisconsin – Superior. Because of the sincerity of their requests to honor their classmates, and because they remember these five brave men with such respect, love, and compassion, I am including several pages of that paper now, with a few added pieces of information I did not have 22 years ago.

CLASSMATES, FRIENDS, HEROS

Leonard Sullivan, Charles Baron, Jr., Jerome Misuraco, Charles "Ray" Diulio, and John "Buddy" Barton and many of their classmates were drafted or they enlisted in the Army shortly after completing high school. Some remained in the military and retired. Ted Erspamer said it best. "Back then you didn't question your duty. If you got drafted, you went. A lot of guys just enlisted so they could do their part. We really believed in the country."

Leonard Sullivan

In the photograph in the class yearbook he displays a wide grin. He looks good natured, but mischievous. His eyes are sparkling. He is happy, like a kid who just ate the last cookie. Leonard is remembered for his wit, quick quips, a rough edge, and for accepting a tougher challenge. His mother owned the Bluebird Inn on Silver Street. His friends called him "Sully." Doris Thompson Morello was in Leonard's homeroom and other classes. Her memories include:

> The one thing, him being an "S" and me being a "T", he always sat around me. He was always very tired because he had to clean the bar before he came to school in the morning, and he had to go there on lunch hour and empty beer cans, bottles, and stuff, and carry things out…. Miss Frace (literature teacher) especially (took him under her wing), he always took her classes even though he didn't have to. He always took her as an elective. But, she made him work and she made me work. She'd say, 'Now

Doris, you make sure Leonard gets this,' or 'help
him with this paper' or that. He used to chew up
pencils and erasers and spit them down my blouse
(laughing). He was smart. He was too smart for his
own good. He had to grow up fast.

Ellen Kivi Skoveria remembered, "Leonard Sullivan was a mischief
maker (laughing). It seemed like he never took anything seriously,
and well, he just wasn't a serious kid."

George Romanowski recalled, "He was really something. A kid full
of humor. A good sense of humor. He'd sort of take over if there were
any quips to go on, ad-libbing, he would take over a conversation."

Leonard Sullivan. Class cut up and wise guy. Despite the
appearance of not being serious, he sought out the challenge of Miss
Frace's literature classes. Like his classmates who displayed character
in other endeavors, he sought out and accepted the challenges a
caring but tough teacher put before him. He then joined the Army
and did his duty. On September 8, 1950, the reality of the Korean
War hit Hurley.

The Korean War came home to Iron County this
week with the news that Leonard Sullivan, Hurley
youth, is missing in action. The mother, Mrs. Martha
A. Rudolph, 415 Silver Street, received a wire from
the War Department on Wednesday night advising
her that her son is "missing in action in Korea." The
Hurley youth will be 19 years old this next January.
His father is Jerry Sullivan, also of Hurley. The wire
said he was missing since Aug. 11.

Further correspondence confirmed the Leonard died in combat that August day. The cruelty of war has no bounds. His body would not return to Hurley for burial until December 28, 1951, about 16 months after his death. His funeral services were held on New Year's Eve, December 31, 1951 at St. Mary's church.

Charles Baron, Jr.

Charlie Baron was close friends with Jerome Misuraco and George Romanowski. Wayland Baron and he were cousins. He is remembered as being short, but strong. Helen Misuraco Kasper remembered him.

> Charlie used to spend a lot of time at our house. They would visit and hang around the house…. Jerry used to play the accordion and then they would go bumming around…. Who knows what they got into? They never told me all the things they did…. They were very, very close, you know. They would spend every Sunday together. All their free time would be together. Chucky Baron, he was another nice boy, just the sweetest kid.

Most people remember Charlie as being very shy. George Romanowski remembers him as one of his closest friends. They hunted, fished, and hung out together. They joined the army together and stayed together through basic training. "We got down there (Fort Riley, Kansas) and I called my wife during basic training and said, 'come on down, we'll get married.' So we got married there and Charlie was my best man. Unfortunately, after basic I never did see him again. He went to Korea of course, and we got the word he got killed over there."

Charlie became the second casualty from the class of '49 and from Iron County. He was wounded and sent to Osaka hospital in Japan on September 5, 1950. He died on October 25, 1950, ten days before his 19th birthday. He was buried in the Hurley cemetery on November 21, 1950.

Jerome Misuraco

Jerry was quiet, shy, and very polite. He was also determined and meticulous about things. His pals called him "Muz." He loved music and played the accordion at home and was a member of the school band. He was one of 17 children in a very tight knit family. His father died in 1944, he was the youngest boy and his mother's pride and joy. Charlie Baron and George Romanowski used to love going to the Misuraco farm to hunt with him and hopefully get in on one of Mrs. Misuraco's fabulous suppers.

Helen Misuraco Kasper was seven years older than Jerry. She recalled, "When Jerry was a little boy, he stepped on a rusty nail and got a very bad infection. And every day, there was no way to bring him to town. I had to carry him piggy back every day to the doctor's office for treatment. He was maybe 7 years old."

Helen also retold a story given to her by Mary Jean Schomisch Springhetti, Hurley '49.

> When they were at St. Mary's school, Mary Jean
> had something or other on her desk when it wasn't
> supposed to be. Anyway, she knocked it on the floor

and made a mess. The sister wanted to know who had done it, and Mary Jean knew there would be a punishment. Jerry was sitting next to her and looked over at her, put his finger to his lips to ssshh her, and said he did it and took the punishment. To this day she remembers that. She said she prays for him every day.

One of the class of '49's nicest kids, a young man who displayed kindness and courage very early in life died in combat in Korea. In another one of war's cruelties, his mother received the telegram notifying her of her son's death on November 11th, Armistice Day, the day which commemorates the end of World War I, "The War to End All Wars." Two days later she received two letters from Jerry, dated October 29, the day before he was killed. Jerry Misuraco was killed just five days after his best friend, Charlie Baron died in a hospital in Japan. They are buried near each other in the Hurley cemetery. I for one believe they still spend every Sunday together.

Charles Raymond Diulio

He was tall and handsome. Ray DiUlio was a class favorite. They called him "Chocolate." George Romanowski said, "He had a personality all his own. You couldn't help but like the guy. He just fit into everything." From being a member of the school baseball team, to his role in the class play, Ray showed up and participated. Ted Erspamer echoed that thought. "Ray seemed to be involved with everything, If not doing it, then there to support it or watch."

Ellen Kivi Skoveria recalled, "I remember Ray DiUlio was in my dance class and I always thought he was good looking, so I'd count.

The girls lined up on one side and the boys lined up on the other and you'd take a partner, so I'd look and count which number he was going to be, and I made sure I was the girl lined up on the other side of him." As handsome as Ray was, has also quiet and reserved. Anna Kangas Gertz was his prom date. "He was so nice. He had a quiet sense of humor. Kind of a dry humor (laughs). You'd look at him and he had this serious face, and you didn't know if he was serious or joking."

News of Ray's death reached his mother by telegram on March 9, 1951. His last letter to her was dated February 4, while he was at rest camp after 87 days of combat duty. He was killed on February 22, 1951. Ray was 19 years old.

John "Buddy" Barton

What would you expect of a kid nicknamed "Buddy?" True to his name, he was a buddy to his classmates. Friendly and outgoing, Buddy enjoyed life. Doris Thompson Morello recalls him as a fine dancer who loved to "jitterbug." Pete Savant recalled him as an excellent football player. Ted Erspamer recalled, "Buddy's parents were divorced and his dad gave him a car. It was unheard of in those days that a kid would have their own car. I think he was the first one I know of to ever have a car. We really had a good time driving around Hurley and Ironwood."

Anna Kangas Gertz saw a different side to her friend.

> He was really nice. We liked to dance a lot together.
> He liked to dance. He was a lot of fun and a joker.
> He liked practical jokes. At graduation his dad came
> from Chicago. He introduced me to him and gave

him a package. Buddy didn't open it. He said, 'I know what it is. A wallet with a hundred dollar bill in there, that's all I ever get.' I almost cried. He was lonely because he wasn't close with his father.

In August of 1949 Buddy joined the Army. Doris Morello Thompson remembered one of Buddy's letters from Korea. "He had said that he had just seen Leonard Sullivan and then he died, and then Buddy had seen Ray, and then he found out a week later that Ray was dead, and he said that, 'I don't want to run into anyone else I know over here.'" Buddy became the last casualty of the war from the class of '49 and from Iron County. He died on June 30, 1951, 323 days after the first of his classmates, Leonard Sullivan, was killed. The next day, on July 1, peace talks began in Paris.

In the years following his death, Buddy's mother befriended many of his classmates. She helped Anna Kangas Gertz write little notes about and for each class member for their tenth reunion. She found comfort in being with the friends of her only child.

June 30, 1989

Exactly 38 years after Buddy Barton became the last casualty of the Korean War from Iron County, the Class of '49 unveiled a Korean War Memorial. It was the day of their 40th Class Reunion. True to their character, they included the names of the other three men from Iron County who died in the fighting on the memorial. Hurley and Iron County will always be a team. They were, Adolph Snarski of Montreal, Stanley Kountney of Mercer, and Stanley Conhartoski of Gile, Hurley '47.

Standing proudly beneath the flag of the United States, south of the courthouse, across from the cemetery, is a six foot high granite monument with the Great Seal of the United States emblazoned at the top, honoring the eight men who sacrificed their lives during the Korean Conflict.

The Korean Conflict was never a declared war. It also never ended. The agreement signed in Paris provided only for a cease fire. I have heard so many people say that it was all in vain. The facts do not support that opinion. There are nearly 52 million people living in South Korea today. The fruits of liberty were bestowed upon them by the actions of America and the nearly 37,000 soldiers who gave their lives for freedom.

For the record, the South Koreans did not waste that precious gift. Today South Korea is one of the most amazing success stories any nation could ever boast of being. Their people enjoy a high standard of living that grows better each day. The nation is an economic dynamo and their people are well educated and among the most productive on the planet. Check out the satellite photo taken of the Korean peninsula at night and see the difference between North and South Korea. North Korea is among the most backwards of nations on the planet. A brutal regime has terrorized the population for more than seven decades. This gruesome abuse of power is evident in the Kim family's insistence upon developing their military power. In North Korea farming is done by hand as all production goes for weaponry. Most of her citizens are malnourished at best, and starving at worst. This government oversees a country that can barely produce a loaf of bread but spends every dime they can on developing a nuclear bomb. No! Our Korean War dead did not die in vain! There are 52 million reasons to believe in the power of liberty.

2019 – Final Notes And Thoughts

---

70 years have passed since the Hurley basketball team captured the imagination of an entire state. The Midgets were the second smallest school to win a state basketball championship in the one class format. The following year, St. Croix Falls became the third smallest to do it. Of course, Reedsville (not to be confused with Reedsburg) was the smallest. It was a time when people thought big, especially kids. Kids need to dream. Adults need to get out of the way and let them.

Hurley High School has some incredible alumni. I urge the folks from Hurley to check out the Academic and Athletic Hall of Fame. They are on the school website. Many of the people mentioned in this book are there.

The story of Bob Sohl was incredible.

Hurley won the 1964 Wisconsin State Ski Meet in 1964 the second state championship for a Hurley team.

Mickey Brown, one of Hurley's greatest athletes joined the Marine Corps in 1947.

Len Bartolutti played for the University of Wisconsin freshmen team in 1950. The following year he came down with the mumps and missed a large segment of the season. When he returned to the team there was a note in his locker informing him that he was cut from the team. He transferred to Superior State and joined the Air Force

ROTC unit. Len served nearly thirty years in the Air Force and retired as a colonel. His steadfast commitment served the nation well.

John Tocci played briefly against LaCrosse in the second quarter of the championship game. He scored 1 point. That was a pretty big 1 point! John moved to Hoyt Lakes, MN after the mines on the range closed. He moved up from miner to being a manager. He was so well liked by the miners and the mining company management that when he retired they all showed up out of respect for him. It was the only time anyone could remember when both sides ever did that. They normally didn't mix.

Eugene "Smocky" Martino became a teacher and was later the principal in Ashland at Beezer Elementary School. The tough fullback was a soft touch with kids.

Bill "Wyoming" Anich became a teacher and taught in Wakefield.

Bob Rainaldo also became a teacher and taught in Hurley.

Ted Erspamer became the Hurley Chief of Police. Fitting for a guy whose friend, Wayland Baron, called "The Enforcer." As an offensive tackle on the football team he was supposed to protect the quarterback. He did that well and then he protected a town. When I was in high school the Erspamer's moved in next door to us. I behaved.

Wayland Baron served in the Army and then attended Gogebic Junior College and Northland College in Ashland. The kid who scored the last ten points for Hurley in the state championship game became a teacher, coach, and counselor in Pulaski, WI. His drive and never quit attitude was thus passed along to another generation.

Carl Hermanson worked for Evinrude Outboard Motors and became one of their top managers before retiring. Like a tireless rebounder, he was always working to do the job the right way.

Pete "Pupsy" Savant owned Porky's Bar on the corner of Silver Street and 4th Avenue in Hurley for many years. When his wife Darlene became terminally ill they left Hurley to seek care for her in Milwaukee, where she could receive treatment. Wayland Baron recalled how tenderly he cared for her over those years, never complaining and always praying for her recovery. His steadfast devotion and selflessness with Darlene were the same attributes he brought to his basketball team. Pupsy was the consummate team mate.

Clayton Corrigan also became an officer in the Air Force. He was a pilot who flew the KC – 135 tankers. He missed the official team picture taken in Hurley after the tournament. That left many people wondering if he was on the team. He was. There are several team photos that appeared in the papers after the last game in which he appears.

Noel Mattei, the most under rated of the Midget staring five on the '49 team continued to think like a champion. He and his wife Jeanne bought an arcade in the resort town of Wisconsin Dells. Noel parlayed his keen sense of what was going on during a ball game to knowing what was going on in the resort business. They started a resort called "Family Land" which became a favorite destination for thousands of families each year.

Of the 1943 state tournament team, Eino "Lefty" Martino survives. He was also a sophomore on the 1941 football team that ended the two decades old drought against Ironwood.

Of the 1946 football team that stunned Ironwood 7 – 0, Tony Brunello, the team leader and prophet who predicted the win a year earlier, is still alive in living in Maple Grove, MN. The kid from Dago Valley went on to become a successful insurance agent and a leader in the local community.

Of the 1947 state tournament runners up team Carl Kaffine is still with us as is Len Bartolutti.

Dom Gentile '47 went on to become the head trainer for the Green Bay Packers.

Eugene "Cotton" Van Hoof '47, graduated from the United States Naval Academy in 1951. He became one of the early graduates of Admiral Rickover's Navy Nuclear Propulsion School and went on to become the Commanding Officer of the USS Daniel Boone (SSBN-629).

Of the 1948 state tournament consolation champions Len Bartolutti and Wayland Baron are with us.

Of the members of the state champions of 1949 we still have Len Bartolutti, Wayland Baron, Pete Savant, Ted Erspamer and Clayton Corrigan to still tell us of the tale.

In three state tournaments from 1947 – 1949 Hurley defeated the top ranked team in the state. Stevens Point, Wisconsin Rapids and Wauwatosa were the teams that the Mighty Midgets knocked off.

Chief Gianunzio continued to coach the Hurley freshmen team into the 1970's. His life was dedicated to the kids of Hurley as a teacher and coach. In 1954 he coached Hurley to its only undefeated football season. As the varsity basketball coach for the Midgets over six seasons his record was 80 – 33. He helped run summer youth programs and was a driving force in the development of many of Hurley's Hall of Fame athletes and students.

Roy Melvin eventually ended his coaching career in Beloit. He was inducted into the Wisconsin Football Coaches Hall of Fame in 1981. He will always be remembered as the architect of the Hurley athletic program.

Carl Vergamini left Hurley to coach basketball at Superior State in 1954. He is the only coach in Wisconsin high school history to take his teams to the state tournament in each of his first four years as a coach. In those four years his team's record was 85 – 12. His record for Hurley through 1954 was 160 – 39. In football his record was 41 – 20 – 6. Like Chief Gianunzio and Roy Melvin he was loved by his players. All three men formed strong friendships with their former players as they stayed in touch with letters, calls, and visits throughout their lives.

Hurley won 11 M-W Conference Basketball title in 20 years from 1943 – 1962. They won 10 in 16 years from 1947 – 1963.

In closing we say a final farewell to the Hurley Midgets. After 95 years this beloved mascot is retired. Hurley will now be known as the North Stars. Traditions fade and times change. What remains the same is the decency of the people of Hurley. The hot button issue of this mascot change has many people on edge.

I will paraphrase the words of my brother, Jay LaMarche when he compiled our family genealogy. They were written about our family, but these words describe your family and our town as well.

The true strength of our town has always been found in the strength of character of most of her people. We have been miners, farmers, artisans, tradesmen, teachers, doctors, and all manner of workers for over 135 years. Our minds and backs have contributed to the building and flourishing of our nation. We are dignified by our toil as much as any king was ever dignified by a crown.

NOTES

PROLOGUE

1. Phil Vergamini, personal interview, 23 April 2018.
2. Jerome Vergamini, personal interview, 23 April 2018.

CHAPTER ONE

1. Catherine Techtmann, Rooted in Resources Iron County, Wisconsin 1893-1993 (Friendship, WI: New Past Press Inc., 1993) 145.
2. https://www.arboristsite.com/community/threads/largest-white-pine-ever-cut-in-wisconsin.114292/
3. Techtmann 52.
4. Techtmann 23.

CHAPTER TWO

1. Catherine Techtmann, Rooted in Resources Iron County, Wisconsin 1893-1993 (Friendship, WI: New Past Press Inc., 1993) 146.
2. Catherine Techtmann, Rooted in Resources Iron County, Wisconsin 1893-1993 (Friendship, WI: New Past Press Inc., 1993) 77.
3. Jean Nordin, "Hurley Kicks off Anniversary Celebration," The Daily Globe 28 July 2018 Page unknown.

CHAPTER THREE

1. https://en.wikipedia.org/wiki/The_Long_Count_Fight
2. Stuart Melvin, A Coach for All Seasons (Lexington, KY: Trafford Publishing, 2015) 7 – 12.

CHAPTER FOUR

1. Stuart Melvin, A Coach for All Seasons (Lexington, KY: Trafford Publishing, 2015) 21 - 33.
2. Ralph A. Piper, Trends in Athletic Safety (Journal of health and Physical Education, Volume XI, January 1940, Number 1) 467 – 468.
3. Sir Riley, "Comment On Sports" Iron County Miner, 7 November 1947, 7
4. Sir Riley, "Comment On Sports" Iron County Miner, 14 November 1947, 7
5. Hurley High School Football Records compiled by Hurley High School Booster Club.
6. Hurley High School Basketball Records compiled by Hurley High School Booster Club
7. Personal conversation with Tom Hunt, August 1982.
8. Bud Grant, Personal Interview, 25 February 2019.
9. https://www.wiaawi.org/Portals/0/PDF/Results/Basketball_Boys/teamchamps.pdf
10. https://hooptactics.com/Basketball_Basics_History

CHAPTER FIVE

1. Stuart Melvin, A Coach for All Seasons (Lexington, KY: Trafford Publishing, 2015) 33.

2. Personal conversation with Tom Hunt, August 1982.

3. "Melvin's Midgets to Play Wakefield" Ironwood Daily Globe 24 October 1924, 14.

4. "Coach Melvin's Midgets of Hurley Cop Contest by Score of 55 – 6" Ironwood Daily Globe 03 November 1924, 10.

5. "Midgets and Speed Boys Conclude Football Season at Hurley Park" Ironwood Daily Globe 07 November 1924, 8.

6. EJS, "On The Sidelines" Montreal River Miner, 5 March 1944, 7.

7. "'Red Devils' 25 years Old – How Did They Get That Name?" Ironwood Daily Globe, 28 January 1949, 8.

8. "High School Teams Hereafter to be Known as Red Devils" Ironwood Daily Globe, 22 January 1924, 8.

CHAPTER SIX

1. Stuart Melvin, A Coach for All Seasons (Lexington, KY: Trafford Publishing, 2015) 24.

2. Ralph A. Piper, Trends in Athletic Safety (Journal of health and Physical Education, Volume XI, January 1940, Number 1) 467 – 468.

3. Hurley High School Football Records compiled by Hurley High School Booster Club.

4. Hurley High School Basketball Records compiled by Hurley High School Booster Club

CHAPTER SEVEN

1. Stuart Melvin, A Coach for All Seasons (Lexington, KY: Trafford Publishing, 2015) 28.

2. Ralph A. Piper, Trends in Athletic Safety (Journal of Health and Physical Education, Volume XI, January 1940, Number 1) 467 – 468.

3. Hurley High School Football Records compiled by Hurley High School Booster Club.

4. Hurley High School Basketball Records compiled by Hurley High School Booster Club

5. "Midgets Upset Park Falls Five" Ironwood Daily Globe 11 march 1938, 12.

6. "Midgets top Superior, Win first District Crown" Ironwood Daily Globe 14 March 1938, 8.

7. "Hurley Loses 26 – 22" Ironwood Daily Globe 19 March 1938, 10.

8. https://www.wiaawi.org/Portals/0/PDF/Sports/Basketball_Boys/History/1930/1938.pdf

CHAPTER EIGHT

1. Hurley High School Football Records compiled by Hurley High School Booster Club.

2. Hurley High School Basketball Records compiled by Hurley High School Booster Club

CHAPTER NINE

1. Thomas Hine, The Rise and Decline of the Teenager (American Heritage, September 1999, Volume 50, Issue 5) https://www.americanheritage.com/content/september-1999.

2. Thomas Snyder, National Center for Education Statistics, 120 Years of American Education: A Statistical Portrait (Publication # NECS 93442, January 1993) 26.

CHAPTER TEN

1. Stuart Melvin, <u>A Coach for All Seasons</u> (Lexington, KY: Trafford Publishing, 2015) 30.
2. "Newport Wins Over Central" <u>Ironwood Daily Globe</u> 16 March 1936, 7.
3. "Ashland Quint Wins at Cedar" <u>Ironwood Daily Globe</u> 16 March 1936, 7.
4. "Eight Teams To Be In Tourney" <u>Montreal River Miner</u> 20 March 1942, 1.

CHAPTER ELEVEN

1. Stuart Melvin, <u>A Coach for All Seasons</u> (Lexington, KY: Trafford Publishing, 2015) 34, 49 – 54.
2. "Sophomores Valuable to Midgets in Cage Season". <u>Ironwood Daily Globe</u> 3 March 1941, 8.
3. "Red Devils vs. Midgets Friday Night. 'Nuff Said! <u>Ironwood Daily Globe</u> 9 October 1941, 14.
4. "Hurley Trounces Ironwood Red Devils, 20 – 7! <u>Ironwood Daily Globe</u> 11 October 1941, 8.
5. Jim Rasmusen, "Highlights of Hurley's Win" <u>Ironwood Daily Globe</u> 11 October 1941, 8.
6. 'Sports" <u>Montreal River Miner</u> 17 October 1941, 6.
7. Eino Martino, personal interview, 28 August 2018.

CHAPTER TWELVE

1. "Midgets Rally to Defeat Red Devils" <u>Ironwood Daily Globe</u> 4 December 1937, 7.
2. 'Hurley Loses to Superior 5" <u>Ironwood Daily Globe</u> 23 March 1936, 7.
3. 'Hurley Beats Saxon Easily" <u>Ironwood Daily Globe</u> 12 November 1941, 10.
4. 'Dick Leads Midgets to 29 – 16 Victory Over Devils in League Opener" <u>Ironwood Daily Globe</u> 28 November 1941, 10.
5. "Midgets Win 26 – 22 to Take Loop Lead" <u>Ironwood Daily Globe</u> 2 December 1941, 8.
6. "Cards Upset Midgets 20 – 19, Take Lead in Loop" <u>Ironwood Daily Globe</u> 6 December 1941, 8.
7. Armand Cirilli, "Sports" <u>Montreal River Miner</u> 19 December 1941, 3.

CHAPTER FOURTEEN

1. "Midgets Take 52 -23 Victory" <u>Ironwood Daily Globe</u> 13 December 1941, 8.
2. "Hurley Beats Glidden Club" <u>Ironwood Daily Globe</u> 18 December 1941, 14.
3. "Midgets Batter Castle Guards with 55 – 12 Win" <u>Ironwood Daily Globe</u> 10 January 1942, 8.
4. "Midgets beat Cards, Give Speed Boys Loop Lead" <u>Ironwood Daily Globe</u> 17 January 1942, 8.
5. "Midgets Batter Glidden into Submission 55 – 17" <u>Ironwood Daily Globe</u> 24 January 1942, 8.
6. "Hurley and Ironwood Win in League Cage Games" <u>Ironwood Daily Globe</u> 31 January 1942, 8.

CHAPTER FIFTEEN

1. Stuart Melvin, <u>A Coach for All Seasons</u> (Lexington, KY: Trafford Publishing, 2015) 30 - 31.

CHAPTER SIXTEEN

1. "Hurley and Ironwood Win in League Cage Games" <u>Ironwood Daily Globe</u> 31 January 1942, 8.
2. "Midgets beat Alumni in Iron Lung Benefit Game" <u>Ironwood Daily Globe</u> 6 February 1942, 10.

3. "Red Devils Defeat Speed Boys 27 – 26" Ironwood Daily Globe 7 February 1942, 8.

4. "Midgets Defeat Saxon 40 – 15" Ironwood Daily Globe 11 February 1942, 10.

5. "Speed Boys in Defeat 42 – 31" Ironwood Daily Globe 6 December 1941, 8.

6. "Iron River Repeats Win Over Speed Boys 39 – 28" Ironwood Daily Globe 13 December 1942, 8.

7. "Devils beaten By Iron River" Ironwood Daily Globe 21 January 1942, 8.

8. "Wakefield Defeats Iron River 26 – 23" Ironwood Daily Globe 14 February 1942, 8.

9. https://www.mhsaa.com/sports/boys-basketball/yearly-champions

10. "Devils Defeat Falls Quintet" Ironwood Daily Globe 6 December 1941, 8.

11. "Speed Boys Whip Midgets 39 – 28 to Gain Tie for Conference Cage Lead" Ironwood Daily Globe 14 Feb 1942, 8.

12. "Bessemer Leads Conference Race" The Bessemer Herald 20 February 1942, 5.

13. "Hurley Loses Overtime Tilt" Ironwood Daily Globe 19 February 1942, 12.

14. "Speed Boys Nearer to Title. Defeat Cards 32 – 24" Ironwood Daily Globe 21 February 1942,

15. "Butherus Set Pace in His First Year" Ironwood Daily Globe 21 February 1942, 8.

16. "Speed Boys Quintet Takes Conference Cage Title" Ironwood Daily Globe 25 February 1942, 8.

17. "Midgets Trim Kaufman Team" Ironwood Daily Globe 25 February 1942, 8.

18. "Hurley Earns 2ND Spot Tie" Ironwood Daily Globe 28 February 1942, 8.

CHAPTER SEVENTEEN

1. https://www.wiaawi.org/Sports/BoysBasketball/History.aspx

2. "Badger Cage Play Opens Wednesday, Hurley faces Prentice Thursday" Ironwood Daily Globe 3 March 1942, 8.

3. "East, Central Win; Hurley team Plays Tonight" Ironwood Daily Globe 5 March 1942, 12.

4. "Superior Central Upsets East to Enter Finals with Hurley 44 – 20 Winners Over Phillips Ironwood Daily Globe 7 March 1942, 8.

5. https://en.wikipedia.org/wiki/Dom_Moselle

6. https://en.wikipedia.org/wiki/Bud_Grant

7. "Hurley Bows to Central 33 – 29" Ironwood Daily Globe 9 March 1942, 8.

8. https://www.wiaawi.org/Portals/0/PDF/Sports/Basketball_Boys/History/1940/1942.pdf

CHAPTER EIGHTEEN

1. "Bessemer to Start Grid Practice Monday Under New Athletic Coach" Ironwood Daily Globe 15 August 1942, 8.

2. "Melvin Resigns Hurley Post After 19 Years to Take Similar Position at Ashland High School" Ironwood Daily Globe 20 August 1942, 12.

3. Stuart Melvin, A Coach for All Seasons (Lexington, KY: Trafford Publishing, 2015) 63 - 66.

4. "Melvin Sign New Contract" Ironwood Daily Globe 21 August 1942, 8.

5. "Sports Comment" Montreal River Miner 28 August 1942, 11.

6. "Melvin Sings Swan Song" Montreal River Miner 28 August 1942, 7.

7. It's - All - In - The - Slant" Ironwood Daily Globe 22 August 1942, 8.

CHAPTER NINETEEN

1. "Melvin Resigns Hurley Post After 19 Years to Take Similar Position at Ashland High School" Ironwood Daily Globe 20 August 1942, 12.
2. "Appoint Vergamini as Hurley's Coach" Ironwood Daily Globe 29 August 1942, 8.
3. "Sports" Montreal River Miner 4 September 1942, 11.
4. http://grfx.cstv.com/photos/schools/iowa/sports/m-wrestl/auto_pdf/0910guide5.pdf
5. Jerome Vergamini, Personal interview, 18 April 2018.
6. Phil Vergamini, Personal Interview, 23 April 2018.
7. Jerome Vergamini, Personal Interview, 11 June 2018.
8. Jerome Vergamini, Personal Interview, 2 February 2019.
9. https://en.wikipedia.org/wiki/Herbert_Hoover

CHAPTER TWENTY

1. It's - All - In - The - Slant" Ironwood Daily Globe 22 August 1942, 8.
2. "Appoint Vergamini as Hurley's Coach" Ironwood Daily Globe 29 August 1942, 8.
3. "Midgets Iron Out Kinks for Opening Grid Battle" Ironwood Daily Globe 12 September 1942, 8.
4. "Midgets Hurry Practice as Ashland Battle Nears" Ironwood Daily Globe 16 September 1942, 14.
5. Armand Cirilli, "Sports Comment" Montreal River Miner 11 September 1942, 11.
6. Armand Cirilli, "Sports Comment" Montreal River Miner 18 September 1942, 11.
7. "Midgets in 18 – 6 win over Ashland" Montreal River Miner 25 September 1942, 6.
8. "Moselle Star in 18 – 6 Game" Ironwood Daily Globe 22 September 1942, 8.

CHAPTER TWENTY ONE

1. Armand Cirilli, "Sports Comment" Montreal River Miner 25 September 1942, 6.
2. " 'Touchdown Twins' Spark Midgets in 20 – 6 Victory" Ironwood Daily Globe 28 September 1942, 6.
3. "Pertile Beats Devils 7 – 0" Ironwood Daily Globe 28 September 1942, 6.
4. Armand Cirilli, "Sports Comment" Montreal River Miner 2 October 1942, 7.
5. "Moselle Star in 27 – 13 Win" Ironwood Daily Globe 5 October 1942, 8.
6. "Hurley Tops Devils 12 – 7 To Stay Ahead" Ironwood Daily Globe 12 October 1942, 8
7. Steve Mrdjenovich, Jr., Personal Interview, 1 April 2019.

CHAPTER TWENTY TWO

1. "Calumet tops Bessemer 13 – 6" Ironwood Daily Globe 5 October 1942, 8.
2. "Bessemer Topples Hurley 24 – 6 For Conference Lead" Ironwood Daily Globe 19 October 1942, 8.
3. "Washburn Trounced 46 – 0 by Midgets on Saturday" Ironwood Daily Globe 26 October 1942, 8.
4. "Ashland Defeats Superior East Yesterday 12 – 7" Ironwood Daily Globe 24 October 1942, 8.
5. "Ashland Wins 14 -7, Gives Hurley Share in Title" Ironwood Daily Globe 2 November 1942, 8.

6. Stuart Melvin, <u>A Coach for All Seasons</u> (Lexington, KY: Trafford Publishing, 2015) 68 -69.

CHAPTER TWENTY THREE

1. Jerome Vergamini, Personal Interview, 2 February 2019.
2. Carl Vergamini, Personal Interview, 21 October 1997.
3. "Hurley Marshalling Cage Talent For Stiff Season" <u>Ironwood Daily Globe</u> 3 November 1942, 8.
4. "Favorable Report on Hurley High" <u>Iron County News</u> 13 November 1942, 1.
5. "Hurley Girl Teaching Aeronautics at Stout Institute" <u>Iron County Miner</u> 4 December 1942, 9.

CHAPTER TWENTY FOUR

1. June Gimson, "Hurley Hi – Lites" <u>Iron County News</u> 6 November 1942, 4
2. https://www.u-s-history.com/pages/h1674.html
3. "5 Cage Teams to Usher in 1942 – 1943 Cage Season" <u>Ironwood Daily Globe</u> 25 November 1942, 6.
4. "Midgets Open Cage Season in Own Gym Tonight" <u>Ironwood Daily Globe</u> 13 November 1942, 6.
5. "Hurley, Ashland Whip Ironwood, Bessemer Fives" <u>Ironwood Daily Globe</u> 26 November 1942, 8.
6. "Loop Fives Resume Battles This Week" <u>Ironwood Daily Globe</u> 1 December 1942, 8.

CHAPTER TWENTY FIVE

1. "Moselle, Dick Lead Hurley to Top of Cage Loop" <u>Ironwood Daily Globe</u> 5 December 1942, 6.
2. "Ashland Beats Superior East" <u>Ironwood Daily Globe</u> 5 December 1942, 6.
3. "Beat Crystal Falls 37 – 3; Hammerberg Scores 28" <u>Ironwood Daily Globe</u> 5 December 1942, 6.
4. "Speed Boys Crush Midgets, Ashland Takes Lead" <u>Ironwood Daily Globe</u> 12 December 1942, 6.
5. "62 – 30 Battle Sets Records" <u>Ironwood Daily Globe</u> 14 December 1942, 6.
6. "Devils Beaten in 43 – 31 Tilt" <u>Ironwood Daily Globe</u> 14 December 1942, 6.
7. "Ashland Rallies To Beat Hurley And Retain Lead" <u>Ironwood Daily Globe</u> 18 December 1942, 8.

CHAPTER TWENTY SIX

1. "Sports" <u>Montreal River Miner</u> 1 January 1943, 7
2. "Midgets to Meet De Padua Friday" <u>Montreal River Miner</u> 8 January 1943, 7
3. "Hurley Scores 25 – 23 Victory" <u>Ironwood Daily Globe</u> 9 January 1943, 6.
4. "Cards Defeat Ashland Five" <u>Ironwood Daily Globe</u> 9 January 1943, 6.
5. "Speed Boys Defeat Ironwood 40 – 33" <u>Ironwood Daily Globe</u> 9 January 1943, 6.
6. Armand Cirilli, "Sport Comment" <u>Montreal River Miner</u> 15 January 1943, 7.
7. "Ashland and Hurley Win Conference Ball Games" <u>Ironwood Daily Globe</u> 16 January 1943, 6.
8. "Wakefield 5, Midgets Lose" <u>Ironwood Daily Globe</u> 23 January 1943, 8.

CHAPTER TWENTY SEVEN

1. "Hurley Drive in Second Half Beats St Ambrose" <u>Ironwood Daily Globe</u> 3 February 1943, 10.

2. "Hurley Squad in 36 – 33 Victory" <u>Ironwood Daily Globe</u> 6 February 1943, 8.

3. "Sports" <u>Montreal River Miner</u> 12 February 1943, 7.

4. Armand Cirilli, "Sports Comment" <u>Montreal River Miner</u> 12 February 1943, 7.

5. https://www.yourdailyglobe.com/story/2013/05/04/obituaries/william-bill-velin/461.html

6. "Ironwood, Hurley Win; Bessemer Is Still In Lead" <u>Ironwood Daily Globe</u> 13 February 1943, 8.

7. 'Hurley Topples Bessemer From Loop Lead 44 – 17" <u>Ironwood Daily Globe</u> 17 February 1943, 8.

8. "Hurley Beats Ironwood 48 – 35, Takes Loop Lead" <u>Ironwood Daily Globe</u> 20 February 1943, 8.

9. 'Hurley Beats Ashland To Retain Conference Lead" <u>Ironwood Daily Globe</u> 24 February 1943, 8.

10. Armand Cirilli, "Sports Comment" <u>Montreal River Miner</u> 5 March 1943, 7.

CHAPTER TWENTY EIGHT

1. "Hurley Defeats Ashland In WIAA Tourney Play" <u>Ironwood Daily Globe</u> 6 March 1943, 8.

2. "Midgets Cop Tournament In Ashland" <u>Montreal River Miner</u> 12 March 1943, 3.

3. Bud Grant, Personal Interview, 25 February 2019.

4. https://www.wiaawi.org/Portals/0/PDF/Results/Basketball_Boys/teamchamps.pdf

5. https://www.wiaawi.org/Portals/0/PDF/Results/Basketball_Boys/teamparticipation.pdf

6. "Hurley Wins Regional Tourney Championship" <u>Ironwood Daily Globe</u> 8 March 1943, 8.

CHAPTER TWENTY NINE

1. Carlo Kumpala, "<u>When all Roads Led to Spooner</u>" (Eau Claire, WI: EC Press, 2018) 2 – 4.

2. Chippewa High Captures Regional Basketball Title" <u>The Chippewa Herald-Telegram</u>, 8 March 1943, 5.

3. "Chippewa High Cagers Defeat Superior East Squad" <u>The Chippewa Herald-Telegram</u>, 22 January 1943, 5.

4. "Chippewa beats Old Abes" <u>The Chippewa Herald-Telegram</u>, 9 January 1943, 5.

5. "Menomonie Cagers Upset Chippewa 36 – 26" <u>The Chippewa Herald-Telegram</u>, 25 January 1943, 5.

6. "Hurley Defeats Chippewa in Sectional tournament" <u>The Chippewa Herald-Telegram</u>, 10 March 1943, 5.

7. "Midgets Win in Tournament at Spooner" <u>The Montreal River Miner</u>, 12 March 1943, 1.

CHAPTER THIRTY

1. Armand Cirilli, "Sports Comment" <u>Montreal River Miner</u>, 12 March 1943, 3.

2. "Park Hold Five Tournament Foes to Total of 98 Points" <u>Racine Journal Times</u> 10 March 1943, 10.

3. "Hurley Midgets to Enter Wisconsin Cage Finals" <u>Ironwood Daily Globe</u> 10 March 1943, 8.

4. "Hurley Takes Third Place in Wisconsin Tourney" <u>Ironwood Daily Globe</u> 15 March 1943, 8.

5. "Washington Park Cagers Give Racine First State Basketball Title, Total 22 Wins for the Season" <u>Racine Journal Times</u> 15 March 1943, 10.

6. "Sports" <u>Montreal River Miner</u>, 19 March 1943, 3.

7. Armand Cirilli, "Sports Comment" <u>Montreal River Miner</u>, 2 April 1943, 7.

CHAPTER THIRTY ONE
1. https://en.wikipedia.org/wiki/List_of_territories_occupied_by_Imperial_Japan
2. "Number 1 Hero" <u>Montreal River Miner</u> 20 March 1942, 1.
3. https://en.wikipedia.org/wiki/Battle_of_Stalingrad
4. https://en.wikipedia.org/wiki/North_African_Campaign
5. https://en.wikipedia.org/wiki/Allied_invasion_of_Sicily
6. https://en.wikipedia.org/wiki/Allied_invasion_of_Italy

CHAPTER THIRTY TWO
1. Phil Vergamini, personal interview, 23 April 2018.
2. Jerome Vergamini, personal interview, 23 April 2018.
3. Phil Vergamini, personal interview, 21 March 2019.
4. Arne Wicklund, "Hurley High School Notes" <u>Montreal River Miner</u>, 17 September 1943, 6.

CHAPTER THIRTY THREE
1. "Purgolders Get Conference Win; Bessemer Loses" <u>Ironwood Daily Globe</u>, 20 September 1943, 6.
2. "On the Sidelines" <u>Montreal River Miner</u>, 24 September 1943, 6.
3. "Park Falls Wins From Hurley 13 – 12" <u>Ironwood Daily Globe</u>, 27 September 1943, 6.
4. "Ironwood Red Devils Win from Midgets 19 – 0" <u>Ironwood Daily Globe</u>, 2 October 1943, 8.
5. "Iron River Opponent of Ironwood here Tonight" <u>Ironwood Daily Globe</u>, 11 September 1943, 8.
6. Ironwood Red Devils Win From Iron River 33 – 0" <u>Ironwood Daily Globe</u>, 13 September 1943, 6.
7. "Ashland Loses To Park Falls 21 – 19" <u>Ironwood Daily Globe</u>, 1 November 1943, 6.

CHAPTER THIRTY FOUR
1. "Range Season Opens Friday" <u>Ironwood Daily Globe</u>, 1 November 1943, 8.
2. E.J.S. "On The Sidelines" <u>Montreal River Miner</u>, 12 November 1943, 7-8.
3. "Ironwood, Wakefield, Ashland Win Cage Contests" <u>Ironwood Daily Globe</u>, 25 November 1943, 10.

CHAPTER THIRTY FIVE
1. "Hurley 27, Mellen 25" <u>Montreal River Miner</u>, 10 December 1943, 10.
2. "DePadua Noses Out the Midgets 19 - 17" <u>Montreal River Miner</u>, 12 December 1943, 10.
3. "Ironwood Beats Stambaugh; Hurley, Ashland Win" <u>Ironwood Daily Globe</u>, 11 December 1943, 8.
4. "Ironwood Wins On Skud's Goal In Final Seconds" <u>Ironwood Daily Globe</u>, 18 December 1943, 5.
5. "Ironwood, Ashland, Wakefield Win Court Games" <u>Ironwood Daily Globe</u>, 8 January 1944, 8.
6. "Midgets Nosed Out By Ashland" <u>Ironwood Daily Globe</u>, 14 January 1944, 7.

7. "Bessemer Defeats Midgets 23 – 19" <u>Montreal River Miner</u>, 21 January 1944, 7.

8. "Midgets Defeat Saint Ambrose 32 – 23" <u>Montreal River Miner</u>, 28 January 1944, 7.

9. "Ironwood Noses Out the Midgets 25 – 24" <u>Montreal River Miner</u>, 4 February 1944, 7.

10. "Devils Put On Game Ending Spurt To Defeat Hurley" <u>Ironwood Daily Globe</u>, 29 January 1944, 8.

CHAPTER THIRTY SIX

1. "Midgets Take Twin Bill" <u>Montreal River Miner,</u> 11 February 1944, 7.

2. "Midgets 25, Wakefield Cards 21" <u>Montreal River Miner</u>, 11 February 1944, 7.

3. "Hurley Hands Ironwood First Defeat of Season" <u>Ironwood Daily Globe</u>, 19 February 1944, 8.

4. "Midgets Trim Ashland, Cinch Second Place" <u>Montreal River Miner</u>, 3 March 1944, 7.

5. "16 Teams Left In WIAA Games" <u>Ironwood Daily Globe</u>, 6 March 1944, 8.

6. "Sup Central Champs, Hurley Cops 3rd Place" <u>Montreal River Miner</u>, 10 March 1944, 7.

7. EJS "Sports" Montreal River Miner, 17 March 1944, 7.

8. https://www.legacy.com/obituaries/name/gerald-rosendahl-obituary?pid=572373

9. https://wisconsintrackonline.com/features16/hof2016/pdf16hof/Coach_Eino_J._Martino_website.pdf

10. 1944 Lincoln Log

11. Montreal's Bob Sohl Triumphs in One of Breaststroke Heats" <u>Ironwood Daily Globe</u>, 6 August 1948, 10.

12. https://en.wikipedia.org/wiki/Bob_Sohl

CHAPTER THIRTY SEVEN

1. Stephen E. Ambrose, <u>D-DAY June 6th, 1944: The Climactic Battle of World War II</u> (New York, NY: Touchstone of Simon and Schuster, 1995) 577.

CHAPTER THIRTY EIGHT

1. EJS, "On the Sidelines" <u>Montreal River Miner</u>, 15 September 1944, 7.

2. "Sports" <u>Montreal River Miner</u>, 22 September 1944, 7.

3. "Ashland Loses To Ironwood 6 – 0 On a Blocked Punt" <u>Ironwood Daily Globe</u>, 23 September 1944, 8.

4. "Ironwood Beats Hurley 7 – 0 On Blocked Punt" <u>Ironwood Daily Globe</u>, 9 October 1944, 8.

5. "Speed Boys Hold Ironwood 0 – 0" <u>Montreal River Miner</u>, 6 October 1944, 7.

6. EJS "Comment on Sports" <u>Montreal River Miner</u>, 6 October 1944, 7.

7. EJS "Comment on Sports" <u>Montreal River Miner</u>, 13 October 1944, 7.

8. EJS "Comment on Sports" <u>Montreal River Miner</u>, 20 October 1944, 7.

9. EJS "Comment on Sports" <u>Montreal River Miner</u>, 3 November 1944, 5.

10. EJS "Comment on Sports" <u>Montreal River Miner</u>, 10 November 1944, 7.

11. "Sponsor a Movie Projector For LST" <u>Montreal River Miner</u>, 17 November 1944, 1.

12. EJS "On the Sidelines" <u>Montreal River Miner</u>, 17 November 1944, 7.

13. Stuart Melvin, <u>A Coach for All Seasons</u> (Lexington, KY: Trafford Publishing, 2015) 75 - 76.

14. "Ashland Defeats Midgets in Opener" <u>Montreal River Miner</u>, 24 November 1944, 7.

15. "Hurley Victor In 30 – 14 Tilt" <u>Ironwood Daily Globe</u>, 23 November 1944, 9.

16. "Hurley Wins From Wakefield, Bessemer Defeated" <u>Ironwood Daily Globe</u>, 2 December 1944, 8.

17. "Midgets Lose To Park Falls 18 – 14" <u>Montreal River Miner</u>, 15 December 1944, 9.

18. "Ashland 26, Bessemer 24" <u>Montreal River Miner</u>, 15 December 1944, 9.

19. "Hurley Midgets Defeated By St. Ambrose Cagers" <u>Ironwood Daily Globe</u>, 21 December 1944, 10.

20. "Midgets Lose to DePadua, 26 – 24" <u>Montreal River Miner</u>, 12 January 1945, 7.

21. "Ashland Defeats the Midgets 29 – 16" <u>Montreal River Miner</u>, 19 January 1945, 7.

22. "Hurley Takes DePadua In a Thriller by 29 – 28 Score" <u>Montreal River Miner</u>, 19 January 1945, 7.

23. "Midgets Defeat Eagle River 33 – 24" <u>Montreal River Miner</u>, 26 January 1945, 7.

24. "Hurley Loses Tough Contest by 26 – 21 Score" <u>Montreal River Miner</u>, 2 February 1945, 7.

25. "Park Falls Defeats the Midgets, 41 – 32" <u>Montreal River Miner</u>, 9 February 1945, 7.

26. "Bessemer Defeats Hurley by 25 – 14 Score" <u>Montreal River Miner</u>, 16 February 1945, 7.

27. "Ironwood Takes The Midgets 27 – 19" <u>Montreal River Miner</u>, 23 February 1945, 7.

28. "Hurley Defeats Wakefield 28 – 25" <u>Montreal River Miner</u>, 2 March 1945, 7.

29. "Midgets Lose Thriller To Superior Central" <u>Montreal River Miner</u>, 9 March 1945, 7.

30. "Ashland Wins Regional; Hurley Cops Consolation" <u>Montreal River Miner</u>, 9 March 1945, 7.

31. Stuart Melvin, <u>A Coach for All Seasons</u> (Lexington, KY: Trafford Publishing, 2015) 84 - 96.

CHAPTER THIRTY NINE

1. https://www.history.com/topics/world-war-ii/battle-of-okinawa

2. http://www.navsource.org/archives/10/16/160546.htm

3. Phil Vergamini, personal interview, 23 April 2018.

4. Jerome Vergamini, personal interview, 23 April 2018.

5. "Celebrate V-J Day In Hurley" <u>Iron County Miner</u>, 17 August 1945, 1, 4.

6. https://worldwar2.org.uk/how-many-people-died-in-world-war-2

7. https://www.nationalww2museum.org

8. https://www.mckevittpatrickfuneralhome.com/?action=obituaries.obit_view&o_id=1922143

9. "Lloyd B. Barto Returns Home" <u>Ironwood Daily Globe</u>, 5 October 1945, 2.

10. https://en.wikipedia.org/wiki/USS_Indianapolis_(CA-35)

11. "LT D.R. Rautio Awarded the DFC" <u>Montreal River Miner</u>, 1 December 1944, 1.

12. https://youtu.be/dR3ZVOGlbNM

13. https://www.tracesofwar.com/persons/34417/Kero-William-E.htm?c=aw

14. "Saxon War Hero Being Returned" <u>Ironwood Daily Globe</u>, 12 February 1949, 10.

15. https://military.wikia.org/wiki/Emil_Bernard_Stella

16. "Lt. Emil Stella Has Been Awarded the Navy Cross" <u>Iron County News</u>, 7 September 1945, 1.

17. https://www.tracesofwar.com/persons/38319/Geach-James-L.htm

18. Kristin Gilpatrick <u>The Hero Next Door</u> (Oregon, WI: Badger Books Inc., 2000) 14 – 31.

19. https://www.dpaa.mil/Our-Missing/World-War-II/

CHAPTER FORTY

1. https://www.thebalance.com/unemployment-rate-by-year-3305506
2. https://www.cdc.gov/nchs/data/vsus/vsrates1940_60.pdf
3. https://livinghistoryfarm.org/farminginthe40s/life_20.html
4. https://en.wikipedia.org/wiki/Iron_County,_Wisconsin
5. https://en.wikipedia.org/wiki/Ironwood,_Michigan
6. https://en.wikipedia.org/wiki/Bessemer,_Michigan#Demographics
7. https://en.wikipedia.org/wiki/Wakefield,_Michigan#Demographics
8. https://en.wikipedia.org/wiki/Ashland,_Wisconsin#Demographics
9. https://en.wikipedia.org/wiki/St._Louis_County,_Minnesota#Demographics
10. https://en.wikipedia.org/wiki/Taconite
11. https://minerals.usgs.gov/minerals/pubs/commodity/iron_ore/stat/

CHAPTER FORTY ONE

1. EJS "Comment on Sports" Montreal River Miner, 31 August 1945, 7.
2. EJS "Comment on Sports" Montreal River Miner, 7 September 1945, 7.
3. Tony Brunello, Personal Interview, 23 March 2019.
4. "Red Devils Scorch Hurley Midgets 42 – 0" Montreal River Miner, 12 October 1945, 7.
5. EJS "Comment on Sports" Montreal River Miner, 9 November 1945, 7.
6. EJS "Comment on Sports" Montreal River Miner, 16 November 1945, 7.
7. Phil Vergamini, personal interview, 23 April 2018.
8. Jerome Vergamini, personal interview, 23 April 2018.
9. "Hurley Midgets Win Opener 43 – 36" Montreal River Miner, 23 November 1945, 7.
10. "Ashland Upsets Midgets 41 – 39" Montreal River Miner, 23 November 1945, 7.
11. "Hurley Loses to Ashland 5" Ironwood Daily Globe, 21 November 1945, 10.
12. EJS "Comment on Sports" Montreal River Miner, 7 December 1945, 7.
13. "Midgets Defeat DePadua, 23 – 18" Montreal River Miner, 7 December 1945, 7.
14. "Midgets take Bessemer, 32 – 24" Montreal River Miner, 14 December 1945, 7.
15. "Midgets Swamp Wakefield, 50 – 25" Montreal River Miner, 21 December 1945, 5.
16. "Hurley Cagers Easily Defeat St. Ambrose 34 – 19" Ironwood Daily Globe, 22 December 1945, 8.
17. "Red Devils Defeat Hurley 29 – 27 In Rough Game" Ironwood Daily Globe, 5 January 1946, 8.
18. EJS "Comment on Sports" Montreal River Miner, 11 January 1946, 7.
19. "Red Devils Clip Midgets 29 – 27 In Bruising Game" Montreal River Miner, 11 January 1946, 7.
20. "Ashland Leads M-W Conference; Defeats Hurley" Montreal River Miner, 18 January 1946, 7.
21. EJS "Comment on Sports" Montreal River Miner, 18 January 1946, 7.
22. "Hurley Romps 65 – 45 over Eagle River" Montreal River Miner, 25 January 1946,

23. https://www.legacy.com/obituaries/chicagotribune/obituary.aspx?pid=19866230

24. "Hurley Five Smothers Ironwood Red Devils 39 – 21" <u>Ironwood Daily Globe</u>, 26 January 1946, 8.

25. EJS "Comment on Sports" <u>Montreal River Miner</u>, 1 February 1946, 7.

26. "Midgets Cop 2 Past Weekend" <u>Montreal River Miner</u>, 8 February 1946, 7.

27. "Midgets Down Wakefield 41 – 20" <u>Montreal River Miner</u>, 15 February 1946, 7.

28. "Midgets Out Play Speed Boys 36 – 25" <u>Ironwood Daily Globe</u>, 16 February 1946, 10.

29. "Hurley scores 39 – 31 Win Over Park Falls Five" <u>Ironwood Daily Globe</u>, 20 February 1946, 10.

30. "Cage Records Fall As Axness Scores 53 Points" <u>Ironwood Daily Globe</u>, 21 February 1946, 10.

31. "Red Devils Defeat Speed Boys, Share In Crown" <u>Ironwood Daily Globe</u>, 23 February 1946, 10.

CHAPTER FORTY TWO

1. Carlo Kumpala, "<u>When all Roads Led to Spooner</u>" (Eau Claire, WI: EC Press, 2018) 9.

2. "Regional Tournament Opens Here Feb. 28" <u>Montreal River Miner</u>, 22 February 1946, 1, 8.

3. "Superior Central, Ashland Win In Opening Round" <u>Ironwood Daily Globe</u>, 1 March 1946, 10.

4. "Ashland Meets Park Falls for Regional Title" <u>Ironwood Daily Globe</u>, 2 March 1946, 10.

5. "Ashland Purgolders Win Regional Tournament Here" <u>Montreal River Miner</u>, 8 March 7, 1.

6. EJS "Comment on Sports" <u>Montreal River Miner</u>, 8 March 7, 7-8.

7. "Drummond Again District Champ" <u>Ironwood Daily Globe</u>, 25 February 1946, 8.

8. Kumpala 13- 15.

9. https://www.wiaawi.org/Portals/0/PDF/Sports/Basketball_Boys/History/1940/1946.pdf

10. Stuart Melvin, <u>A Coach for All Seasons</u> (Lexington, KY: Trafford Publishing, 2015) 103.

CHAPTER FORTY THREE

1. EJS "Comment On Sports" <u>Montreal River Miner</u>, 23 August 1946, 7.

2. "Hurley Outlucked by Purgolders in Grid Opener" <u>Ironwood Daily Globe</u>, 16 September 1946, 10.

3. "Hurley Midgets Rout DePadua Bruins 33 – 2" <u>Ironwood Daily Globe</u>, 23 September 1946, 8.

4. "Midgets Trounce Park Falls 31 – 7" <u>Ironwood Daily Globe</u>, 30 September 1946, 8.

5. Stuart Melvin, <u>A Coach for All Seasons</u> (Lexington, KY: Trafford Publishing, 2015) 130 - 135.

6. Tony Brunello, Personal Interview, 28 July 2018.

7. Bill Cattoi, Personal Interview, 28 July 2018.

8. "Midgets Deal Red Devils 7 – 0 Conference Setback" <u>Ironwood Daily Globe</u>, 7 October 1946, 8.

9. "Midgets Outclass Ironwood 7 – 0" <u>Montreal River Miner</u>, 11 October 1946, 8.

10. "Bessemer Upsets Midgets, 7 – 6" <u>Montreal River Miner</u>, 25 October 1946, 8.

11. "Vikings of Superior Central Defeat Hurley Midgets 21 – 6" <u>Ironwood Daily Globe</u>, 2 November 1946, 10.

12. EJS "Comment On Sports" <u>Montreal River Miner</u>, 8 November 1946, 7.

13. EJS "Comment On Sports" <u>Montreal River Miner</u>, 15 November 1946, 7.

14. Carl Kaffine, Personal Interview, 13 April 2019.

15. "Midgets Down DePadua In Opener, 23 – 19" <u>Montreal River Miner</u>, 22 November 1946, 8.

16. EJS "Comment On Sports" <u>Montreal River Miner</u>, 22 November 1946, 7.

17. "Midgets Edge Ashland In Thriller 29 – 28" <u>Montreal River Miner</u>, 29 November 1946, 10.

18. "Midgets holding Michigan-Wisconsin Cage Lead" <u>Ironwood Daily Globe</u>, 7 December 1946, 10.

19. "Park Falls Downs Hurley" <u>Montreal River Miner</u>, 13 December 1946, 8.

20. EJS "Comment On Sports" <u>Montreal River Miner</u>, 13 December 1946, 7.

21. "Midgets Trip Cards To Strengthen League Lead" <u>Ironwood Daily Globe</u>, 14 December 1946, 10.

22. "Midgets Defeat Phillips, 48 – 42" <u>Montreal River Miner</u>, 27 December 1946, 7.

23. "Midgets Wind up Pre-Holiday Slate With Victory" <u>Ironwood Daily Globe</u>, 21 December 1946, 10.

24. "Sport Slants" <u>Ironwood Daily Globe</u>, 14 December 1946, 10.

25. EJS "Comment On Sports" <u>Montreal River Miner</u>, 3 January 1947, 7.

26. "Midgets Nose Out Red Devils 23 – 21" <u>Ironwood Daily Globe</u>, 4 January 1947, 8.

27. "Midgets Nose Out Red Devils 23 – 21" <u>Montreal River Miner</u>, 10 January 1947, 8.

28. EJS "Comment On Sports" <u>Montreal River Miner</u>, 10 January 1947, 7.

29. "Midgets Trounce Ashland 37 – 20" <u>Montreal River Miner</u>, 17 January 1947, 8.

30. EJS "Comment On Sports" <u>Montreal River Miner</u>, 17 January 1947, 7.

31. "Hurley Takes Second From Phillips Quint" <u>Ironwood Daily Globe</u>, 18 January 1947, 8.

32. "Games Last Week" <u>Montreal River Miner</u>, 24 January 1947, 7.

33. "Ramblers Beaten 33 – 32 by Hurley" <u>Ironwood Daily Globe</u>, 22 January 1947, 10.

34. "Midgets Clinch Conference Crown, 2 Games Today" <u>Ironwood Daily Globe</u>, 25 January 1947, 8.

35. "Midgets Easily Down Wakefield 41 – 32" <u>Montreal River Miner</u>, 14 February 1947, 8.

36. "Midgets Defeat Park Falls 53 – 42" <u>Montreal River Miner</u>, 14 February 1947, 8.

37. "Midgets Defeat Bessemer 43 – 34" <u>Ironwood Daily Globe</u>, 15 February 1947, 8.

38. "Hurley Bumps Superior East" <u>Ironwood Daily Globe</u>, 19 February 1947, 8.

39. "Red Devils, Midgets and Saints Score Victories" <u>Ironwood Daily Globe</u>, 22 February 1947, 8.

CHAPTER FORTY FOUR

1. "Hurley Bumps East 32 -28" <u>Ironwood Daily Globe</u>, 28 February 1947, 8.

2. "Midgets gain Finals" <u>Ironwood Daily Globe</u>, 1 March 1947, 8.

3. "Midgets Cop Honors in Superior regional Event" <u>Ironwood Daily Globe</u>, 3 March 1947, 8.

4. "Midgets Cop regional Meet; Play in Sectional Tonight" <u>Montreal River Miner</u>, 7 march 1947, 1.

5. EJS "Comment On Sports" <u>Montreal River Miner</u>, 7 March 1947, 7.

6. Carlo Kumpala, "<u>When all Roads Led to Spooner</u>" (Eau Claire, WI: EC Press, 2018) 16 – 18.

7. "Midgets Depart For Spooner After Rally At Lincoln School" <u>Ironwood Daily Globe</u>, 7 March 1947, 8.

8. "Midgets Gain Finals In Sectional Tourney" <u>Ironwood Daily Globe</u>, 8 March 1947, 8.

9. "Hurley Wins Sectional Meet; Now At State Tournament" <u>Montreal River Miner</u>, 14 March 1947, 1.

10. "Midgets, Spooner Titlists, Enter State Tourney" <u>Ironwood Daily Globe</u>, 10 March 1947, 10.

11. Bud Grant, Personal Interview, 25 February 2019.

12. Carl Kaffine, Personal Interview, 13 April 2019.

13. "Drive Opens For State Prep Title" <u>Wisconsin State Journal</u>, 13 March 1947, 26.

14. "State Basketball Tournament Begins Today" <u>The Capitol Times</u>, 13 March 1947, 26.

15. Joe Dommershausen, "What Do You Want to Know About Preps?" <u>Wisconsin State Journal</u>, 13 March 1947, 27.

16. Lew Cornelius, "Hurley Midgets Trip Tomah 35 – 33" <u>The Capitol Times</u>, 14 March 1947, 18.

17. Henry J. McCormick, "Beloit, Hurley Decide State Prep Title Tonight" <u>Wisconsin State Journal</u>, 15 March 1947, 15.

18. Joanne Kopacz Sullivan, Personal Interview, 31 October 1997.

19. EJS "Comment On Sports" <u>Montreal River Miner</u>, 21 March 1947, 13.

20. "Beloit Wins Fifth State Crown, Beats Hurley 56 – 37" <u>The Capitol Times</u>, 15 March 1947, 61.

CHAPTER FORTY FIVE

1. "Comment on Sports" <u>Montreal River Miner</u>, 12 September 1947, 7.

2. "Midgets Beaten By Calumet 6 – 0" <u>Ironwood Daily Globe</u>, 8 September 1947, 8.

3. "Midgets Lose to Park Falls" <u>Ironwood Daily Globe</u>, 15 September 1947, 8.

4. "Park Falls Downs Hurley, 26 – 0" <u>Montreal River Miner</u>, 19 September 1947, 10.

5. "Midgets Beat Phillips 25 – 0" <u>Ironwood Daily Globe</u>, 22 September 1947, 8.

6. Sir Riley, "Comment On Sports" <u>Montreal River Miner</u>, 26 September 1947, 9.

7. Sir Riley, "Comment On Sports" <u>Montreal River Miner</u>, 3 October 1947, 9.

8. "Hurley Smashes Ashland, 21 – 0" <u>Montreal River Miner</u>, 3 October 1947, 9.

9. "Red Devils Best Midgets For First M-W Triumph" <u>Ironwood Daily Globe</u>, 4 October 1947, 10.

10. "Midgets Swamp De Padua 40 – 13" <u>Montreal River Miner</u>, 17 October 1947,7.

11. "Rally By Speed Boys Tops Midget Uprising 13 – 12" <u>Ironwood Daily Globe</u>, 20 October 1947, 8.

12. Speed Boys Squeeze by Hurley 13 – 12" <u>Montreal River Miner</u>, 24 October 1947, 9.

13. "Midgets lose to Vikings 13 – 6" <u>Ironwood Daily Globe</u>, 27 October 1947, 8.

14. Sir Riley, "Comment On Sports" <u>Montreal River Miner</u>, 14 November 1947, 7.

15. "Midgets Defeat Rhinelander Hodags" <u>Montreal River Miner</u>, 21 November 1947, 8.

16. "Defeat Ashland In Fourth Period Rally" <u>Montreal River Miner</u>, 28 November 1947, 9.

17. "Midgets "Race Horse" Over hapless Phillips Quint By 68 – 27, Here" <u>Montreal River Miner</u>, 28 November 1947, 9.

18. "Speed Boys, Devils In Upsets" <u>Ironwood Daily Globe</u>, 1 March 1947, 8.

19. "Speed Boys Trim Iron River 44 – 33" <u>Ironwood Daily Globe</u>, 5 March 1947, 12.

20. "Bessemer Captures First U.P. Basketball Title" <u>Ironwood Daily Globe</u>, 24 March 1947, 8.

21. Sir Riley, "Comment On Sports" <u>Montreal River Miner</u>, 28 November 1947, 7.

22. "Midgets Lose To Bessemer, 39 – 35" <u>Montreal River Miner</u>, 12 December 1947, 8.

23. "Midgets Hope to Get Back Into Win Column Tonight" <u>Montreal River Miner</u>, 12 December 1947, 1.

24. "Midgets Down Wakefield Cardinals" <u>Montreal River Miner</u>, 19 December 1947, 10.

25. "Midgets Spank Ironwood 45 – 36" <u>Ironwood Daily Globe</u>, 3 January 1948, 8.

26. "Midgets Down Red Devils 45 – 36" <u>Montreal River Miner</u>, 9 January 1948, 7.

27. Jim Goeltz, "Ashland Defeats Hurley 40 – 32" From the Ashland Press, reprinted in the Montreal River Miner, 16 January 1948, 4.

28. "Hurley Downs Phillips 49 – 34" Montreal River Miner, 23 January 1948, 7.

29. "Midgets Clinch Second Place in Mich – Wis Conference" Montreal River Miner, 30 January 1948, 7.

30. "Hurley defeats St. Ambrose 58 – 38" Montreal River Miner, 6 February 1948, 7.

31. "Hurley Tops East 38 – 34" Ironwood Daily Globe, 5 February 1948, 14.

32. "Hurley Wins M-W Tilt" Ironwood Daily Globe, 7 February 1948, 8.

33. "Bessemer Loses In Overtime Play" Ironwood Daily Globe, 14 February 1948, 8.

34. "Midgets Defeat Bessemer, 43 – 39" Montreal River Miner, 20 February 1948, 7.

35. "Speed Boys Cop Mich – Wis Title" Ironwood Daily Globe, 21 February 1948, 8.

36. "DePadua Beaten At Hurley 57 – 33" Ironwood Daily Globe, 21 February 1948, 8.

CHAPTER FORTY SIX

1. ' Hurley Midgets hurdle First Obstacle; Reach Tourney Finals" Montreal River Miner, 27 February 1948, 8.

2. "Vikings beaten By Hurley 32 – 26" Ironwood Daily Globe, 26 February 1948, 14.

3. "Hurley Shades Ashland In Sub-regional Thriller" Ironwood Daily Globe, 28 February 1948, 8.

4. Jim Goeltz, "Hurley Downs Ashland 30 – 29" From the Ashland Press, reprinted in the Montreal River Miner, 5 March 1948, 7.

5. Sir Riley, "Comment On Sports" Montreal River Miner, 5 March 1948, 7.

6. "Hurley Easily Wins Over Park Falls" Montreal River Miner, 5 March 1948, 8.

7. "Midgets Spooner Bound With Sights Set On State Tourney" Montreal River Miner, 5 March 1948, 1.

8. "Midgets Listed as No. 10 In Roll" Montreal River Miner, 27 February 1948, 1.

9. Len Bartolutti, Personal Interview, 17 April 2018.

10. Wayland Baron, Personal Interview, 27 May 2019.

11. "Hurley Defeats St. Croix In Sectional Opener" Montreal River Miner, 12 March 1948, 11.

12. "Midgets Come From Behind To Win From Bloomer" Montreal River Miner, 12 March 1948, 12.

13. Carlo Kumpala, "When all Roads Led to Spooner" (Eau Claire, WI: EC Press, 2018) 19 – 21.

14. "Midgets Go To Madison" Montreal River Miner, 12 March 1948, 1.

15. "Bessemer Speed Boys Capture Class B District Cage Crown" The Bessemer Herald, 11 March 1948, 1.

16. "These 8 Prep Quintets Battle For State Title" The Capitol Times, 11 March 1948, 26.

17. "State Meet Field Will Be Pared" The Wisconsin State Journal, 11 March 1948, 26

18. "Eau Claire 39, Hurley 31" The Wisconsin State Journal, 12 March 1948, 20.

19. "Wauwatosa, Janesville, Menasha, and Eau Claire In Opening Tourney Wins" The Capitol Times, 12 March 1948, 17.

20. "Hurley and Wisconsin Rapids Fives Qualify For Consolation Final" The Capitol Times, 13 March 1948, 6.

21. "Wauwatosa Battles Eau Claire For State Crown" The Capitol Times, 13 March 1948, 5.

22. "Hurley Wins 39 – 35 For Consolation Title" The Wisconsin State Journal, 14 March 1948, 37.

23. "Wauwatosa Wins State Title" <u>The Wisconsin State Journal</u>, 14 March 1948, 37.

24. "Bessemer Enters Semi Finals At Lansing Friday Night" <u>The Bessemer Herald</u>, 18 March 1948, 1.

25. "Speed Boys Bid For State Title Dashed by St. Joseph High 60 – 49" <u>The Bessemer Herald</u>, 25 March 1948, 4.

26. "Bessemer Fans Give Speed Boys Hero's Welcome" <u>The Bessemer Herald</u>, 25 March 1948, 1.

CHAPTER FORTY SEVEN

1. Sir Riley, "Comment On Sports" <u>Montreal River Miner</u>, 20 August 1948, 7.

2. Phil Vergamini, Personal Interview, 23 April 2018.

3. Jerome Vergamini, Personal Interview, 23 April 2018.

4. Ted Erspamer, Personal Interview, 14 April 2018.

5. Carl Vergamini, Personal Interview, 21 October 1997.

6. "Midgets Whip Calumet" <u>Ironwood Daily Globe</u>, 7 September 1948, 10.

7. "Hurley, Wakefield Win" <u>Ironwood Daily Globe</u>, 13 September 1948, 10.

8. "Midgets Top Ashland 7 – 0 in M – W Game" <u>Ironwood Daily Globe</u>, 18 September 1948, 10.

9. "Hurley Wins Thriller 7 – 0" <u>Montreal River Miner</u>, 8 October 1948, 8.

10. "Pass In Fourth Quarter Gives Hurley Victory" <u>Ironwood Daily Globe</u>, 4 October 1948, 8.

11. "Hurley defeats Phillips 27 – 13 For Fifth Win" <u>Ironwood Daily Globe</u>, 10 October 1948, 10.

12. "Hurley Whips Bessemer For M – W Loop Grid Title" <u>Ironwood Daily Globe,</u> 18 October 1948, 8.

13. "Hurley Midgets Cop M – W Crown" <u>Montreal River Miner</u>, 22 October 1948, 10.

14. "Hurley Loses Last Game" <u>Montreal River Miner</u>, 22 October 1948, 9.

15. Len Bartolutti, Personal Interview, 17 April 2018

16. Wayland Baron, Personal Interview, 27 May 2019.

17. Pete Savant, Personal Interview with Carter Kuehn, July 2014.

18. "Midgets Top Hodags 30 – 24 In Opener" <u>Ironwood Daily Globe</u>, 13 November 1948, 10.

19. "Hurley Seniors Present Three One Act Plays" <u>Ironwood Daily Globe</u>, 12 November 1948, 7.

20. "Hurley Defeats Ashland. 29 – 24, In M – W Contest" <u>Ironwood Daily Globe</u>, 20 November 1948, 8.

21. "Hurley Wallops Phillips 62 – 30 For Third Win" <u>Ironwood Daily Globe</u>, 24 November 1948, 10.

21. "Hurley Defeats Bessemer 47 – 27" <u>Montreal River Miner</u>, 10 December 1948, 6.

22. "Midgets Swamp Park Falls, 64 – 33" <u>Montreal River Miner</u>, 10 December 1948, 8.

23. "Hurley 'B' s' Win 45 – 28" <u>Ironwood Daily Globe</u>, 6 December 1948, 12.

24. "Wakefield Cards Upset Hurley Midgets By 38 – 33" <u>Ironwood Daily Globe</u>, 11 December 1948, 7.

25. "Hurley Whips St. Ambrose" <u>Ironwood Daily Globe</u>, 18 December 1948, 10.

26. "Hurley, Ashland Win At Antigo; Play On Merrill Court Tonight" <u>Ironwood Daily Globe</u>, 30 December 1948, 10.

27. "Hurley, Ashland Make Sweep of Doubleheaders" <u>Ironwood Daily Globe,</u> 31 December 1948, 14.

28. "St. Ambrose Wins U.P. Catholic Prep Cage Meet" <u>Ironwood Daily Globe</u>, 30 December 1948, 10.

29. "Hurley Trounces Ashland To Take M – W Loop Lead" <u>Ironwood Daily Globe</u>, 8 January 1949, 8.

30. Len Bartolutti, Personal Interview, 6 June 2019.

31. Wayland Baron, Personal Interview, 6 June 2019.

32. "Hurley Downs Superior For Tenth Victory" <u>Ironwood Daily Globe</u>, 15 January 1949, 8.

33. Sir Riley, "Comment On Sports" <u>Montreal River Miner</u>, 21 January 1949, 7.

34. "Hurley ranked 7th in 'Big Sixteen' As WIAA Renews Cage Ratings" <u>Ironwood Daily Globe</u>, 18 January 1949, 12.

35. "Ironwood Gets Decisive 47 – 37 Win Over Hurley" <u>Ironwood Daily Globe</u>, 22 January 1949, 10.

CHAPTER FORTY EIGHT

1. Wayland Baron, Personal Interview, 9 June 2019.

2. "Midgets Swamp Phillips 61 – 31" <u>Montreal River Miner</u>, 4 February 1949, 7.

3. "St. Ambrose Cuts Mass Win String At 59 games" <u>Ironwood Daily Globe</u>, 29 January 1949, 7.

4. "Ashland leads M – W After Stopping Red Devils" <u>Ironwood Daily Globe,</u> 29 January 1949, 7.

5. "Hurley Trounces Wakefield; Martino, Tocci Star" <u>Montreal River Miner</u>, 4 February 1949, 8.

6. "Red Devils Bow To Midgets" <u>Montreal River Miner</u>, 11 February 1949, 7.

7. "Wakefield Cards Beat St. Ambrose" <u>Ironwood Daily Globe</u>, 5 February 1949, 8.

8. Sy Castagna, Personal Interview, 26 July 2018.

9. Sir Riley, "Comment On Sports" <u>Montreal River Miner</u>, 28 January 1949, 7.

10. "Midgets Trounce Park Falls 48 – 30; Play Bessemer Friday" <u>Ironwood Daily Globe</u>, 9 February 1949, 14.

11. "Cards Whip Red Devils 50 – 42" <u>Ironwood Daily Globe</u>, 9 February 1949, 14.

12. "Hurley Downs Bessemer 64 – 41" <u>Montreal River Miner</u>, 18 February 1949, 7.

13. "Cards Top Ashland; Hand Hurley M – W Cage Title" <u>Ironwood Daily Globe</u>, 16 February 1949, 10.

14. "Ramblers Crush State D Champion Mass By 60 – 30" <u>Ironwood Daily Globe</u>, 18 February 1949, 10.

15. "Knights of Saxon Grab Cage Glory" <u>Ironwood Daily Globe</u>, 21 February 1949, 10.

16. "Knights of Saxon In Three Big Victories" <u>Iron County News</u>, 25 February 1949, 6.

17. "Hurley Wins Thriller Against Superior East In Overtime; Central Wins Over Ashland" <u>Montreal River Miner</u>, 25 February 1949, 1

18. "Hurley defeats East in Overtime" <u>Iron County News</u>, 25 February 1949, 1.

19. Len Bartolutti, Personal Interview, 17 April 2018.

20. "Midgets Down Vikings In Sub-regional Finals" <u>Iron County News</u>, 25 February 1949, 1, 4.

21. "Hurley Retains Regional Title, Play Saxon Next" <u>Ironwood Daily Globe</u>, 28 February 1949, 8.

23 "Saxon Defeats Prentice 50 – 48" <u>Montreal River Miner</u>, 4 March 1949, 7.

24. 13. Carlo Kumpala, "<u>When all Roads Led to Spooner</u>" (Eau Claire, WI: EC Press, 2018) 22 – 25.

25. "Midgets Swamp Saxon's Knights by 61 – 34" <u>Ironwood Daily Globe</u>, 5 March 1949, 8.

26. "Hurley Outlasts Bloomer in Spooner Sectional" <u>The Chippewa Herald – Telegram</u>, 7 March 1949, 5.

27. "Hurley Wins Sectional Meet" <u>Montreal River Miner</u>, 11 March 1949, 9.

CHAPTER FORTY NINE

1. Len Bartolutti, Personal Interview, 17 April 2018.

2. Peter Savant, Personal Interview, 17 October 1997.

3. Wayland Baron, Personal Interview, 6 June 2019.

4. Mark Gianunzio, Personal Interview, 12 June 2018.

5. "Eight Prep Quintets Ready For Title Bid" The Capitol Times, 10 March 1949, 29.

6. "Season Records Of Prep Fives" The Capitol Times, 10 March 1949, 30.

7. "Eau Claire, Logan Win" The Wisconsin State Journal, 11 March 1949, 25.

8. "Rapids is 39th Tosa Victim; Hurley Tips Reedsburg 48 – 44" The Wisconsin State Journal, 11 March 1949, 25-26.

9. "Roundy says" The Wisconsin State Journal, 12 March 1949, 15.

10. Roy Wolff, Personal Interview, 20 June 2018.

11. "Reedsburg Nips Wisconsin Rapids, 41 – 39" The Wisconsin State Journal, 12 March 1949, 13.

12. "Kimberley Edges Out Cuba City" The Wisconsin State Journal, 12 March 1949, 13.

13. "Hurley Upsets Wauwatosa; Logan Wins" The Wisconsin State Journal, 12 March 1949, 13-14.

14. "Hurley, LaCrosse Logan Battle For Crown Tonight; 'Midgets' Wallop Mighty Tosa, 62 – 50" The Capitol Times, 12 March 1949, 7.

15. Lew Cornelius, "Notes On The Score Book Margin" The Capitol Times, 12 March 1949, 8.

16. "High School Coaches' Association to Select All Tourney Squad" The Wisconsin State Journal, 12 March 1949, 13.

17. Sir Riley, "Comment On Sports" Montreal River Miner, 18 March 1949, 9.

18. Gloria Stremski Fillion, Personal Interview, 27 January 2019.

19. Harry J. McCormick, "Hurley Cops State Prep Crown" The Wisconsin State Journal, 13 March 1949, 23.

20. Doris Thompson Morello, Personal Interview, 24 October 1997.

21. John R. Tunis, Yea! Wildcats! (New York: Harcourt, Brace and World, Inc., 1944) 222.

22. Wayland Baron, Personal Interview, 11 June 2019.

23. "Championship Sidelights" Iron County News, 18 March 1949, 1.

24. Carl Vergamini, Personal Interview, 21 October 1949.

25. Anna Kangas Gertz, Personal Interview, 24 October 1997.